DOING POLITICS
DIFFERENTLY?

DOING POLITICS DIFFERENTLY?

WOMEN PREMIERS IN CANADA'S PROVINCES AND TERRITORIES

Edited by Sylvia Bashevkin

UBCPress · Vancouver · Toronto

27 26 25 24 23 22 21 20 19   5 4 3 2 1

Printed in Canada on FSC-certified ancient-forest-free paper
(100% post-consumer recycled) that is processed chlorine- and acid-free.

Cataloguing data is available from Library and Archives Canada.

ISBN 978-0-7748-6080-2 (hardcover)
ISBN 978-0-7748-6081-9 (softcover)
ISBN 978-0-7748-6082-6 (pdf)
ISBN 978-0-7748-6083-3 (epub)
ISBN 978-0-7748-6084-0 (Kindle)

Canadä

UBC Press gratefully acknowledges the financial support for our publishing program of the Government of Canada (through the Canada Book Fund), the Canada Council for the Arts, and the British Columbia Arts Council.

This book has been published with the help of a grant from the Canadian Federation for the Humanities and Social Sciences, through the Awards to Scholarly Publications Program, using funds provided by the Social Sciences and Humanities Research Council of Canada.

Printed and bound in Canada by Friesens
Set in Segoe and Warnock by Artegraphica Design Co. Ltd.
Copy editor: Joanne Richardson
Proofreader: Sara Hall
Indexer: Judy Dunlop

UBC Press
The University of British Columbia
2029 West Mall
Vancouver, BC V6T 1Z2
www.ubcpress.ca

Contents

Figures and Tables

Tables

DOING POLITICS
DIFFERENTLY?

1

Exploring Women's Leadership

SYLVIA BASHEVKIN

What difference, if any, does it make that women have reached the highest levels of political responsibility in Canada's provinces and territories? In response to considerable public as well as academic interest in this question, this volume offers the first systematic assessment of the track records of women premiers – defined as leaders of constitutionally recognized, subnational jurisdictions in the Canadian federal system.

The significance of the country's ten provincial and three territorial governments is hard to exaggerate. Responsibility for the design and delivery of health care services, a crucial and long-standing priority of Canadians according to public opinion surveys, rests with subnational decision makers, as does core control over other important policy areas, including education, social welfare and local government (see Research Canada 2015; Soroka 2007, 24). The fact that more than 31.1 million Canadians among a population of 35.5 million (or roughly 88 percent) were governed by a female premier at the beginning of 2014 underlines the importance of who holds power in provinces and territories (Statistics Canada 2017). Stated simply, this book asks how the arrival in power of a wave of female political executives shaped the decisions, personnel, and processes of subnational government.

As the first comprehensive look at women premiers, our account reflects a conscious effort to widen the scope of gender and politics research beyond its long-standing preoccupation with lawmakers in parliaments. The project builds directly on Trimble et al.'s (2013b, 302) observation that "the true locus of power in the Canadian system is the political executive." A similarly strong rationale for this line of inquiry can be found in comparative research in the field, notably Atchison and Down's (2009, 4–6, 17) analysis of eighteen industrialized countries. Their article concludes that the presence of women in political executive roles is more significant for policy outcomes than numbers in legislatures – particularly in parliamentary systems.

For readers with a primary interest in Canada, this volume widens our understanding of the consequences for subnational politics of demographic and, especially, gender diversity among decision makers (see Andrew and Biles 2009). For readers with a cross-national focus, Canada offers an unparalleled opportunity to examine women's impact as leaders. As demonstrated in the next section of this chapter, no other federal jurisdiction in the world has seen either the proportion or variety of female elites as has Canada since the early 1990s – when Rita Johnston in British Columbia (BC), Catherine Callbeck in Prince Edward Island (PEI), and Nellie Cournoyea in the Northwest Territories (NWT) took the oath of office as political executives. Significant growth in numbers of women leaders in Canada is reflected in the fact that, within twenty years of the arrival in power of these trailblazers, half of Canada's provinces and nearly 90 percent of the country's population were governed by female premiers.

Materials presented in Chapters 2 through 11 of this volume show the varied political origins of female premiers. They extend across the left/right ideological spectrum in seven party-based systems and encompass non-partisan backgrounds in the two northern territories, the NWT and Nunavut, which operate on the basis of consensus government. As detailed in Chapters 2 and 4, Nellie Cournoyea in the NWT and Eva Aariak in Nunavut were elected as government leaders in legislatures that do not have formal party organizations or party discipline; instead, these parliaments choose premiers via a secret ballot of all territorial lawmakers. In jurisdictions with party systems, four women premiers led Liberal governments, three were conservatives, one was from the New Democratic Party (NDP), and one led the independentist Parti Québécois (PQ) in Quebec.

Later in this chapter we discuss how the political circumstances under which women became Canadian premiers also diverged markedly. Outside the NWT and Nunavut, five of the nine premiers we consider attained top executive office after their predecessors as party leader fell to dangerously low levels of public support – a circumstance we term *imperiled leadership*, given the endangered status of the party formation. Two of nine inherited the mantle of office from a strong party leader who resigned his position at a peak of personal popularity – a scenario we call *empowered leadership*, given the buoyant status of the political organization. Two others governed under a combination of imperiled and empowered circumstances: these were *pioneering leaders*, the first political executives in a jurisdiction to reach top office from what had been a weak opposition party. A number who served as the first female premiers of their respective provinces, including Catherine Callbeck in PEI, Kathy Dunderdale in Newfoundland and Labrador (NL), Alison Redford in Alberta, and Kathleen Wynne in Ontario, held the additional distinction of facing women leaders of opposition parties across the legislative aisle.

Beginning with a workshop held at the University of Toronto in May 2017, researchers with specialized knowledge of Canadian provincial and territorial politics came together to document and assess the contributions of women elites. The primary subjects of analysis for the workshop and this volume were provincial political executives from Alberta, BC, NL, Ontario, PEI, and Quebec; and territorial government leaders from the NWT, Nunavut, and Yukon. It is important to clarify that at the time Cournoyea served as premier of the NWT, that jurisdiction comprised what is now both Nunavut and the NWT.

Guided by a larger international literature about gender and politics, the contributors to this volume analyze the impact of female political leaders across provinces and territories. They address executive influence by focusing on the following core question: How has women's leadership shaped the climate of political debate, the content of public policy, and the numbers of women in party, cabinet, and civil service positions? In turn, each chapter breaks down that primary focus into a set of subquestions that I examine later in this introduction.

In considering these points, chapters evaluate women premiers in the context of the specific challenges they faced. For example, how did strong majority mandates for parties led by women unravel in a single term or less, notably for Pat Duncan in Yukon, Catherine Callbeck in PEI, Kathy Dunderdale in NL, and Alison Redford in Alberta? What factors explain the sharp contrast between Pauline Marois's policy directions as a Quebec cabinet minister as opposed to as a premier? How did one imperiled premier in BC, Christy Clark, secure re-election for her party after another,

Rita Johnston, failed? Close attention to biographical detail ensures that each chapter offers a compelling narrative grounded in a particular time and place, which is, in turn, closely linked to the larger concerns of the volume.

Comparative and Historical Perspectives

The remarkable gains made by women as premiers in Canada stand out in bold terms once they are placed in the context of data pertaining to other federal political systems. At the state level in the United States, the most common comparator to Canadian provinces and territories, 6 of 50 states (12 percent) had female governors at the time of writing. Peak numbers for American state leaders were reached in 2004 and 2007, when 9 of 50 governors, or 18 percent, were women. This figure ranks well below the Canadian parity level for premiers reached in 2014. Moreover, all American governors held a party affiliation with about 60 percent Democrats and 40 percent Republicans (Center for American Women and Politics 2017). This background shows how the numerical density and political diversity of premiers in Canada are both absent in the US.

In Germany, a total of five women have at some point headed a state within the federation such that three of the sixteen länder executives, or 19 percent who held office at the time of writing, were women (see Delcker 2016; Dowling 2011). Since 1989, eleven women have at one time or another headed five of Australia's six states and both of its self-governing territories. The highest number of Australian women premiers at a single moment was three, a peak reached between 1991 and 1992, and again in 2011 (Parliament of Australia 2014; Bramston 2017). Information on subnational government leaders in systems including India, Mexico, and Nigeria reveals a similar pattern whereby men continue to far outnumber women as political executives. As a result, scholars of gender and politics have few subnational leaders to study in other federal states.

It remains clear, however, that the presence of female premiers in half of Canada's provinces in 2014 came after a long period during which women were far from seats of power. To wit, most women in Quebec were only able to vote in provincial elections beginning in 1944. Indigenous peoples in Canada, including Inuit in the Far North, faced restricted access to voting in general elections until the 1960s.

Moreover, removing formal restrictions on rights did not end informal practices that kept women far from premiers' offices. Thérèse Casgrain (1972), the first woman in Canada to lead a political party, chose the following title for her memoir: *A Woman in a Man's World*. Casgrain headed the Quebec wing of the NDP during an era of conservative nationalism in the 1950s, when the prospects were extremely dim for any social democratic party leader. Although Casgrain's circumstances were rendered even more challenging by the fact that she was known as a feminist and peace activist, her important contributions to public life were later recognized in an appointment to the Canadian Senate.

In general terms, women who have led provincial parties in Canada tend to more closely resemble Casgrain than the politicians chronicled in this book. Female leaders at the provincial level have typically not held executive office because, like Casgrain, the organizations they headed were weak opposition formations with few (if any) elected legislators and, as a result, little chance of winning power. For the most part, provincial parties that have had more than one woman leader were in a weak, relatively uncompetitive position when those women assumed the top job: the parties were not expected to form the government in the next election and their women leaders were unlikely to become premier. Examples of women who led their parties during uncompetitive periods include Joy MacPhail and Carole James in the BC NDP, Sharon Carstairs and Ginny Hasselfield in the Manitoba Liberals, Elizabeth Weir and Allison Brewer in the New Brunswick NDP, and Alexa McDonough and Helen MacDonald in the Nova Scotia NDP.

What remains significant about these leaders is that many of them vastly improved the standing of their parties. James, for instance, revived the BC NDP such that the party rose from two to thirty-three legislative seats. In 1988, Carstairs brought the Manitoba Liberal caucus from a sole parliamentarian (herself) to twenty members, thus becoming the first woman in Canada to lead the official opposition in a legislature. By winning her constituency in St. John in 1991, Weir erased a pattern whereby the provincial NDP held no parliamentary seats in New Brunswick. McDonough's election in a Halifax constituency in 1981 marked the first time the Nova Scotia NDP secured a seat outside Cape Breton Island.

Consistent with this historical background, research indicates party competitiveness is a key correlate of female party leadership in Canada. According to Bashevkin (2010), Canadian women have tended to secure the top position in minor parties that have lower competitive stakes and hence fewer barriers to entry than major parties – defined as those that either hold or seem close to holding power (see also Thomas 2018). The costs of winning a party leadership race, whether measured by dollars invested, numbers of high-profile endorsements, or campaign team size, remain far less in weak opposition than strong governing or likely-to-win organizations (Bashevkin 2010).

Other studies point to left/right explanations of women's leadership. O'Neill and Stewart's (2009) analysis of federal and provincial leadership races in Canada between 1980 and 2005 finds that left parties were more likely to select a woman head than were centre or right formations. Given that, as of 2005, the NDP had held power neither at the federal level nor in the provinces of Alberta, New Brunswick, NL, Nova Scotia, PEI, or Quebec, the overlap between women's leadership of left parties and uncompetitive parties is striking.

Consistent with Margaret Thatcher's breakthrough as the first woman prime minister of the UK and Kim Campbell's as the first in Canada, this study finds left/right party ideology is not a meaningful predictor of women's leadership at the subnational level. Just as Thatcher and Campbell both came from parties of the right, this volume shows that seven of the nine female premiers who led party-based governments in Canada came from centrist or right-of-centre parties. In chronological order, the Liberals included Catherine Callbeck in PEI, Pat Duncan in Yukon, Christy Clark in BC, and Kathleen Wynne in Ontario. The conservatives were Rita Johnston in BC, Kathy Dunderdale in NL, and Alison Redford in Alberta. As discussed in Chapter 11, one NDP woman has thus far held office – Rachel Notley in Alberta. Quebec has had one female premier, Pauline Marois, whose government was criticized for abandoning progressive PQ policies (see Chapter 7). Although party ideology seems to shed little light on who becomes a premier, left/right distinctions are often relevant to the substance of what women do in top office. I develop this argument further in the section below on substantive impact, where I introduce the concept of critical actors.

One crucial dimension of left/right markers in Canadian politics involves variation among parties with the same name, not only across jurisdictions but also longitudinally within them. For example, the Ontario Liberals under Kathleen Wynne were arguably more progressive than the same party under Dalton McGuinty, the BC Liberals under Christy Clark, and the federal Liberals under Justin Trudeau. The federal Conservative Party established in 2003 was not constitutionally linked to Progressive Conservative organizations in any province and was generally more right-wing than the older federal PCs. New Democrats in Alberta under Rachel Notley tended to be far more supportive of energy pipelines than NDP activists in other provinces and at the federal level.

The fact that women from across Canada's political spectrum gained power under varied competitive circumstances encourages us to probe how circumstances at the point at which they became premiers may have shaped their careers. In the next section, I present a threefold typology for understanding how females reached top office in subnational systems with party organizations.

When Do Women Lead?

Kim Campbell's experiences as the first and, thus far, only female prime minister of Canada illustrate the pathway by which many other women have become government leaders. Campbell succeeded Brian Mulroney as leader of the federal Progressive Conservatives. At the point at which his replacement was selected at the PC leadership convention in spring 1993, Mulroney had headed two consecutive majority governments during roughly nine years in power. His public approval ratings were extremely low. The fact that the PCs spent roughly $18 million to win two seats in the federal election that was held a few months later reflects the extremely tenuous status of the governing party that Campbell inherited.

Popular accounts of women's leadership often point to an idea known as the "glass cliff." Instead of a "glass ceiling," which prevents women from rising to elite levels, the notion of a glass cliff suggests that those who reach the top may be set up to fail because their ascent is often precarious, crisis-fuelled, and riddled with hidden risks (see Ryan and Haslam 2005). This volume refines the glass cliff concept by documenting both (1) institutional challenges associated with women's political leadership based on the competitive status of their parties and (2) assets or supports that accrued or failed to accrue to women leaders. We view competitive circumstances as closely associated with political resources since leaders of weak parties by definition control fewer tangible and intangible resources than do those in charge of strong parties. In a number of chapters, we probe how female politicians were pushed off the stage, whether because they failed to command public confidence, lost the support of key observers and party insiders, or otherwise.

Like Kim Campbell, most female premiers considered in this study headed parties that faced a precarious future. For each woman, the challenging circumstances she confronted can be summarized as follows: a once-powerful political organization was operating in a measurably weakened competitive position. This scenario of *imperiled leadership* describes the status of five out of nine women premiers (or roughly 55 percent) who held office in partisan systems.

As detailed in Chapter 9, Rita Johnston succeeded the discredited Bill Vander Zalm in 1991 as leader of the BC Social Credit Party and head of a provincial government that (like the Mulroney regime at the federal level) was close to the end of its time in office. Chapter 10 explains how Alison Redford took over in 2011 from the enfeebled PC premier of Alberta, Ed Stelmach. Among Liberals, Christy Clark became BC premier in 2011 following the precipitous decline of Gordon Campbell (see Chapter 9), while Kathleen Wynne took the reins in Ontario in 2013 as public support for Dalton McGuinty went into steep decline (see Chapter 8). Pauline Marois's ascent echoes this same pattern: she became PQ head in 2007 on her third try, at a point when the once-governing party had been reduced under André Boisclair to third place status in the Quebec National Assembly (see Chapter 7).

In short, most women who headed party governments in Canada's provinces became leaders under imperiled circumstances. Their political formations faced significant crises that were reflected in weak incumbent leaders, modest support in public opinion polls, and diminished electoral prospects. Although every party these women led had once been a highly successful organization, each of them faced an ominous future at the point at which she took the helm.

This situation stands in stark contrast to the scenario of *empowered leadership*. Under the latter circumstances, a party faces promising prospects because it is (1) experienced in power under an incumbent leader who retains public legitimacy and support within the organization, and (2) selects a new leader who can reasonably expect to maximize those advantages in order to win the premier's office on her own. Few women have reached top positions in Canada in an empowered situation, following the resignation of a popular and politically credible premier from the same party. They include Catherine Callbeck, who succeeded Joe Ghiz as provincial Liberal leader and PEI premier (see Chapter 5), and Kathy Dunderdale, who followed Danny Williams as provincial PC head and NL premier (see Chapter 6).

A third category combines elements of imperiled and empowered conditions. Circumstances of *pioneering leadership* occur when the head of a long-term opposition party brings her organization to power for the first time, as occurred with Pat Duncan in Yukon (see Chapter 3) and Rachel Notley in Alberta (see Chapter 11). Pioneers lead parties that were historically in opposition rather than in government, meaning that their formations have been politically imperiled because they were for many years only marginally competitive compared to major players in a given jurisdiction. At the same time, pioneers operate under empowered circumstances in that they carry the positive halo that comes from turning the tables on an established governing elite and installing a new regime. In Yukon and Alberta, conservative parties had long dominated subnational politics, with the result that both Duncan and Notley were seen as breakthrough leaders for their respective organizations.

Clearly, each set of conditions carries both advantages and disadvantages. In terms of positives, imperiled leaders take on the top job in a party with experience in government and usually have an individual record of cabinet service. This was the case not just for Kim Campbell but also for all five imperiled provincial leaders discussed in this book. In addition, imperiled premiers face the possibility, however slim, that they will manage to hang on to power in a general election after taking over from an embattled party leader. Imperiled leaders who beat the odds include Clark after Gordon Campbell, Redford after Stelmach, Marois after Boisclair, and Wynne after McGuinty. These women rank as political heroes since they rescued their organizations from what seemed like certain political oblivion.

On the negative side, electoral victory under imperiled circumstances raises expectations that women leaders will consistently perform miracles by injecting life into what looks like a moribund or even defunct party. The fact that one of the five provincial leaders who faced imperiled circumstances, Rita Johnston, was unable to save her party provides a helpful cautionary note regarding the limits of political resuscitation (see Chapter 9). Redford's difficulty in steering her PC government in Alberta led to harsh criticism and her early departure from office, even though the longer-term decline of the dominant party likely posed a more serious problem (see Chapter 10).

Among empowered leaders who follow popular male premiers, the advantages are obvious. The party holds power, the departing premier is held in high public esteem, and the incoming premier likely commands her own background of cabinet service. Yet the dangers are also apparent. Expectations not only that the party will remain in government but also that the new leader will dominate the political scene like her charismatic male predecessor might prove impossible to meet. Callbeck and Dunderdale led their parties to victory in general elections, but neither was seen as meeting the high standards set by her predecessor. Above all, as discussed later in this chapter, perceptions of male and female leaders typically build on gender stereotypes that make it hard for women to be seen as effective decision makers. Any woman leader has trouble making the grade, but this is especially true when she arrives in office following the resignation of a high-profile man who has skilfully and unabashedly wielded the levers of power.

For pioneers, a key advantage is not being compared with party predecessors – since none of the previous leaders of the same formation won the premier's job. Pioneers not only avoid the dark shadow cast by a weakened leader from the same party (as in imperiled circumstances) but also avoid inheriting an oversized halo from the former party leader (as in empowered circumstances). At the same time, pioneers such as Duncan and Notley lack cabinet experience and are unable to call on a loyal cadre of party supporters with experience in governing their jurisdiction. No pool of veteran cabinet ministers, deputy ministers, or ministerial assistants waits in the wings at the point at which they win election. This reality helps to explain Notley's decision in 2015 to recruit many bureaucratic and political staffers to her government from outside Alberta.

This section has focused exclusively on premiers in partisan as opposed to consensus-based systems. If Cournoyea in the NWT and Aariak in Nunavut – who were selected as political executives by a secret vote of all legislators – were to be evaluated in light of this typology, then they would seem to share similarities with all three categories. Like imperiled and empowered leaders, both women had government experience prior to becoming premier. Cournoyea had served in the NWT cabinet and Aariak in the territorial bureaucracy (see Chapters 2 and 4). Like pioneers in an environment with party discipline, they were both trailblazers who came into office on their own – in the case of the NWT and Nunavut, without the benefit of a formal political organization. Similar to other pioneers, neither Cournoyea nor Aariak had to contend with either a dark shadow or a bright halo cast by any predecessor since they were voted in as individual leaders without party affiliations.

We return to the varied political circumstances facing women premiers in Chapter 12.

Making a Difference
This book is organized around three main empirical questions. The first probes *how women lead,* asking whether the tone and style of subnational politics were more constructive and less conflictual during periods when women political executives held office. Is the concept of leadership itself masculine? What constraints do gender stereotypes impose on female

elites? Was the tenor of legislative discussion affected by the presence of multiple women as party leaders? Empirical data that help to inform these discussions include patterns of ejection from the legislature, use of time allocation measures, and commentary offered by legislators, political advisors, and journalists about women leaders.

Second, we examine the *policy records* of elites, asking how pro-equality social movements shape the actions of elected decision makers. In particular, we consider whether substantive issues that feminist interests historically placed on the public agenda that pertain to child care services, equal pay, and violence against women were more likely to figure in the parliamentary record when female premiers held office. How did women's issue policy debates and outcomes feature under female leaders as compared with their male predecessors and successors?

Given that organized campaigns for gender equality often emerged on the political left, policy impact tends to be closely related to ideology. Using the language of comparative gender and politics research, we ask whether any female premier championed feminist movement claims to the extent that she was a transformative "critical actor" who carried forward a vigorous pro-equality agenda (see Celis and Childs 2008, 420–21; Celis et al. 2008, 104; Childs and Krook 2008, 734; Childs and Krook 2009, 138). The types of data that authors consider in responding to this set of concerns include left/right ideology, patterns of legislative action while a given premier held office, and the use versus the absence of gendered language in official statements of government intentions (such as throne speeches) and legislative debate.

Third, what are the main patterns of *women's recruitment* as party candidates, cabinet ministers, and senior civil servants under female premiers as compared with their male predecessors and successors? Did leaders actively seek out and promote women to senior positions? Did they advance an approach to equality that can be considered intersectional in that it emphasized the recognition of differences among women along such lines as Indigeneity, sexual orientation, social class, and ethno-cultural background (see Crenshaw 1991)? To what extent were the careers of leaders such as Wynne, the first declared lesbian premier in Canada, as well as Cournoyea and Aariak, both from Indigenous communities, shaped by intersectional identities? Did some premiers believe that the specific merits and qualities of individuals, and not considerations related to demographic groups, formed the proper basis of recruitment to positions of responsibility? In what ways have the appointment records of women leaders varied, especially with respect to geographic region, ideological positioning, feminist movement background, and the time they arrived in senior office?

How Do Women Lead?

A primary concern of this book is the climate of political discussion during the terms of female leaders. The tenor of public debate and the treatment of women elites have, unfortunately, received far less attention than matters of policy action and descriptive representation.

How do women operate as public leaders? This question rests at the core of a long-standing discomfort with the juxtaposition of women and power, which can be traced at least as far back as classical Greek philosophy. The association of strong, articulate men with the public domain of the *polis*, on one side, and weaker, quieter women with a lesser private sphere of home and family, on the other, underpins traditional views of women as partial or impaired citizens. It also helps to explain portrayals of males as excellent debaters and warriors, and females as virtuous, caring nurturers with more skills in securing collaboration than in winning conflicts (see Bashevkin 2009, ch. 2).

What do the noun "leadership" and the verb "to lead" actually mean? According to Genovese and Thompson (1993, 1, emphasis in original), "Leadership is a complex phenomenon revolving around *influence* – the ability to move others in desired directions. Successful leaders are those who can take full advantage of their opportunities and their skills." This conceptualization of leading as the ability to "move others" fits better with conventional dichotomies between masculine and feminine than do dictionary definitions of power, which usually cite command-based scenarios whereby a dominant actor controls multiple subordinates.

Following from ancient political theory, women might be seen as able to convince others to follow a particular course of action because they are perceived to hold talents as consensus-builders. By contrast, the capacity to operate as a unilateral, autonomous commander who orders other players around would be seen as a masculine rather than as a feminine leadership style. In her account of contemporary organizations, Keohane (2010, 26–27) combines group- or team-based with hierarchical views in arguing that "a leader directs the activities of others and coordinates their energies, which is a basic form of power."

If power is seen as the capacity to act upon, shape, or accomplish meaningful objectives in the public domain – likely through some combination of collective and individual action – then why do more men than women reach leadership positions? Social scientists posit that leadership in many cultures remains a stereotypically masculine concept. American psychologist Virginia Valian (1998, 136), for instance, finds that "the more a woman is perceived as a woman the less likely it is that she will be perceived as professionally competent. The qualities required of leaders and those required for femininity are at odds with each other" (see also Jamieson 1995). Similarly, Eagly and Karau (2002) conclude that perceptions of ambition and readiness to lead are gender-based. Not only are women presumed to hold strengths in team-based as opposed to autonomous leadership skills, but men remain more likely than women to be viewed as effective decision makers.

Women politicians face particular constraints in projecting typically masculine leadership characteristics such as self-reliance and authoritativeness. According to Schneider et al. (2010, 363, emphasis in original), they "seem to face a choice of being seen as likeable or as competent, but not as both." Dunaway et al.'s (2013) study of media coverage shows a particularly strong focus on personality traits rather than on public issues in accounts of American women running for the office of state governor. The political styles of women versus men thus figure in efforts to study not just how politicians lead but also how commentators and members of the public view that leadership.

These results help to explain the timing of female enfranchisement and the ascension of women to elite positions. Both occurred earlier in unsettled or sparsely settled frontier communities than in established urban areas. Just as Wyoming and Utah were the first territories to grant women the right to vote in the US, so were Manitoba, Saskatchewan, and Alberta the first in Canada to act on both the franchise and eligibility to hold public office. Consistent with this trend, the first woman to win a legislative seat in the entire British Commonwealth was Louise McKinney, a candidate for the Alberta Non-Partisan League who won her provincial seat in 1917. The first female cabinet minister in the Commonwealth was Mary Ellen Smith, a Liberal member of the BC legislature. Audrey McLaughlin, the first woman to head a major Canadian federal party as leader of the NDP beginning in 1989, was the MP for Yukon (see Bashevkin 1993, ch. 1).

Frontier areas are relatively open to outsiders given their fluidity and lack of established political traditions. As well, they are typically places where challenging conditions make it essential for people to know their neighbours and find ways to cooperate and share with each other – since harsh circumstances place everyone's life at risk. The high valuation that frontier societies place on the ability to work constructively in groups sheds light on the ascent of not just McKinney, Smith, and McLaughlin but also on the breakthroughs made in 1991 by Rita Johnston as BC premier and Nellie Cournoyea as leader of the NWT. The histories of both BC and the NWT are steeped in tales of survival in the wilderness – such that the contributions of every individual mattered to the well-being of the community (see Cournoyea's reflections in Chapter 2). This same argument is helpful in interpreting the fact that all three of Canada's northern territories had at least one woman premier by 2017, compared with only 60 percent of its provinces (six of ten).

In frontier jurisdictions as well as in long-settled regions, research shows female politicians project a stronger community orientation than do the men with whom they work. Studies beginning with Jeane Kirkpatrick's (1974) account of US state lawmakers reveal that women are more likely than their male counterparts to cite service to local constituents (known as expressive motives) rather than ambition and career mobility (or instrumental) reasons for getting involved in politics (see Bashevkin 1993, 156). Given that traditional norms present women as collaborative, selfless carers and construct ambitious, confident women as deviant, it makes sense that female legislators would – when interacting with voters, researchers, or journalists – highlight their commitment to serving local community needs. This orientation is also consistent with divergent professional backgrounds: women in politics have often come from fields (such as social work, education, and communications) that were more open to them than occupations traditionally pursued by male politicians – namely, law and business (see Kirkpatrick 1974, 43, 60–61).

What happens when women arrive as legislators in disciplined parliamentary environments? Does their presence serve to moderate the often polarized tone of debate? Among the only contexts in Canada that have been studied with respect to this factor is the Alberta House, where Arscott and Trimble (1997a, 14) report that government as well as opposition women members "embraced a noticeably different legislative style. They avoided partisan grandstanding and name-calling in favour of focusing on the issue at hand and seeking or offering information." Reinforcing this trend, Trimble (1997, 145) concludes that male MLAs in Alberta typically projected more "adversarial" debating styles and females more "co-operative" ones.

In the comparative literature, analyses of interventions by New Labour women first elected to the British House of Commons in 1997 show that many preferred and tried to practice a "less combative and aggressive style" than men MPs (Childs et al. 2005, 68). Yet these same parliamentarians expressed concern that "women's different approach is not considered equal to the masculinised style of male politicians" (Childs et al. 2005, 70). More recent research indicates that female MPs in the UK use a more women-focused vocabulary in their parliamentary interventions than do men, although this practice has not altered the overall tenor of legislative discussion (Blaxill and Beelen 2016, 431, 442; see also Mendelberg et al. 2014).

Provincial and territorial patterns reported in this volume coincide with British findings that women MPs did not transform the parliamentary environment. Consistent with a larger literature on feminist institutionalism, it appears that, in deliberative bodies with overwhelmingly male members, female legislators cannot easily alter either the "rules of the game," including hours of work, seniority practices, styles of debate, and norms of socializing that men create over successive legislative generations, or the policy priorities of parliaments (see Krook and Mackay 2011; Mackay 2008; Poggione 2011). As Kathlene (1998, 197) observes with respect to US state politics, "gender affects more than just the individuals who occupy the legislature. The institution itself is gendered through the rules, norms, and expectations of how business should proceed. In our society, this gendering is also inextricably linked to power," with the result that those voicing disparate perspectives inside gendered institutions are frequently silenced or excluded. One obvious possibility, as Lovenduski (1993) notes in an early discussion of party organizations, is that institutions may alter or co-opt the women inside them long before those women have a chance to change institutions from within.

The following chapters probe the tone and style of politics during periods when women political executives held office at the subnational level in Canada. In Chapters 2 and 4, authors consider whether consensus-based systems in the NWT and Nunavut, where formal parties and party discipline were absent, assisted female leaders. To assess patterns of cooperation and polarization, we consider whether legislators were expelled more often under male than female premiers. How frequently did leaders close off parliamentary debate? Was the tenor of legislative discussion altered by the presence of multiple women party leaders? How did political observers describe the actions of women premiers, particularly when those leaders faced serious crises?

Policy Impact

On questions of feminist influence in politics, the primary starting point for both Canadian and comparative work is Pitkin's (1967) concept of substantive versus numerical or descriptive representation. Substantive representation involves how female politicians carry forward the issue priorities of feminist movements or, in Pitkin's (1967, 111) words, "act for" those interests. In a classic study, Thomas (1994, 57) identifies "the chief area of interest of researchers concerned with the impact of women on politics" as substantive representation – meaning "whether women among the political elite contribute to a political product that differs in any way from men's."

Scholars pay close attention to legislators' rhetoric and behaviour in what have been termed women's policy fields. According to Swers (2002, 261), this domain encompasses "issues that are particularly salient to women because they seek to achieve equality for women; they address women's special needs, such as women's health concerns or child care; or they confront issues with which women have traditionally been concerned in their role as caregivers, such as education or the protection of children." While researchers since the 1980s have focused intensely on lawmakers in the US and elsewhere, they have directed considerably less attention towards political executives.

What is known about the ripple effects of women's participation? Arscott and Trimble's (1997b) volume on Canadian politics reports that the conversion from numbers to outcomes is far from simple. According to studies of British Columbia (Erickson 1997), Saskatchewan (Carbert 1997), and Ontario (Burt and Lorenzin 1997), the ideology of the governing party matters more to policy outcomes than does the percentage of female parliamentarians. In particular, scholars report, the presence of a New Democratic provincial government in each jurisdiction is a better predictor of feminist policies than is the proportion of women holding legislative seats.

The finding that "party ideology can easily trump gender" parallels subsequent conclusions in the Canadian literature (Arscott and Trimble 1997a, 13), including Trimble's (1998) study of Alberta when PC premier Ralph Klein held power. Trimble (1998, 285) reports that relatively high numbers of women legislators could not override a right-wing, "universalizing discourse" that rejected feminist claims. Writing about the other end of the ideological spectrum, Burt and Lorenzin (1997) as well as Byrne (2009) link women's strong numerical representation in the NDP cabinet of Ontario premier Bob Rae to that government's significant pro-equality policy advances.

Comparative scholarship also pays close attention to the correlates of women's substantive representation. It shows significant variation over time and across systems, especially, since the 1970s, with the growth in the United States of organized anti-feminism and a broader "new right" resistance to equality claims (see Klatch 1987; Schreiber 2008). While early US studies report a positive association between female numerical presence in state houses, on one side, and attention to women's issues and pro-feminist policy outcomes, on the other, subsequent inquiry finds a far less automatic translation from descriptive to substantive representation (see Berkman and O'Connor 1993; Osborn 2012; Saint-Germain 1989; Thomas 1994). Swers (2002, 263) echoes the conclusions of Canadian scholars in writing that, in the US Congress, "party affiliation is one of the most reliable predictors of legislative behavior." Similarly, Beckwith and Cowell-Meyers (2007) cite the presence of a left governing party plus high numbers of females in a governing party caucus as crucial predictors of women-friendly policies.

Given the institutional constraints noted earlier, can individuals alter legislative environments (see Childs and Krook 2009, Figure 1; Childs and Withey 2005, 11)? To invoke the language of comparative gender and politics research, parliaments might in some instances reach a "critical mass" threshold of roughly one-third female members but – in the absence of "critical actors" within that mass – fail to enact pro-equality policies. Conversely, legislatures with relatively few women or with only a handful of progressive men could take major steps forward on those same issues. Analyses of substantive representation thus concentrate on critical acts, defined as initiatives that alter the status of women in political institutions (such as legislatures and political parties) and society more generally, performed by critical actors "who initiate policy proposals on their own and/or embolden others to take steps to promote policies for women, regardless of the numbers of female representatives" (Childs and Krook 2009, 138; see also Celis and Childs 2008, 420–21; Celis et al. 2008, 104; Childs and Krook 2008, 734; Dahlerup 1988).

What factors explain the likelihood that an elected politician will be a critical actor? Gender consciousness ranks as an important predictor. As Childs and Krook (2008, 728) note, overall numbers of women parliamentarians tend to matter less than the feminist identity of key change agents. In particular, comparative scholarship maintains that critical actors are usually women and, in some cases, men who have built and remained engaged with feminist reference groups since early in their careers (see Childs and Krook

2009, 137; Curtin 2008). This stream of inquiry predicts that the most promising opportunities for pro-equality policy change rest in the confluence of
critical actors, mobilized women's movements, and ideologically congenial
political environments (Celis and Childs 2008, 421).

The chapters that follow assess the content and outcomes of women's
issue policy debates when female leaders held top provincial and territorial
office. Authors consider the track records of these women's predecessors
and successors in order to understand the degree to which the presence of
a female executive mattered. In some cases, premiers were conservative individualists who were averse to highlighting their gender. These individuals
tended not to intervene in ways that made a measurable difference to substantive outcomes for women in the general population (see Chapters 2,
6, and 9). In other cases, such as NDP premier Rachel Notley, a woman
leader consistently advanced feminist policy claims (see Chapter 11). Still
others defended strong pro-equality positions in the course of their careers,
notably Marois in Quebec and Wynne in Ontario (see Chapters 7 and 8,
respectively).

Recruitment Patterns

During recent decades, scholars have explored the numerical representation of women in Canadian parliaments as well as its correlates. In the absence of constitutional or legislated quotas in any jurisdiction in the country,
much of this research asks whether strategies adopted by individual political parties to increase numbers of women legislative candidates make much
difference.

From a comparative perspective, this question is especially significant
because Canadian parties tend to function as highly decentralized operations. For the most part, they expect local constituency organizations to
select their own parliamentary candidates. Among the only deviations from
this pattern are decisions made from time to time by federal Liberal leaders
to appoint women nominees, and by federal and some provincial NDP organizations to apply quotas for female candidates. Apart from these instances, legislative recruitment in Canada has been more influenced by informal
efforts to attract women candidates – whether by parties themselves or by
external organizations such as Equal Voice – than by formal rules and regulations (see Bashevkin 1993, ch. 4).

What factors are associated with higher numbers of women parliamentarians? Arscott and Trimble (1997a, 7) find a close association between the
electoral strength of formations such as the NDP that actively seek to recruit

more women to public life, on one side, and higher numbers of female legislators, on the other. Arscott and Trimble (1997a, 7–9) also report that women's proportions in parliaments rise markedly following elections that remove the incumbent party with the result that large numbers of male legislators lose their seats (see also Praud 1998; Moncrief and Thompson 1991).

More recently, Trimble et al. (2013a) document how left parties like the NDP are generally more likely to nominate female legislative candidates than are their counterparts on the right and centre. This result resonates with findings in the comparative literature. Krook's (2009) cross-national analysis of internal party rules as well as constitutional quotas that promote women's election to public office, alongside Kantola's (2009) study of the extent to which European Union countries have pursued informal, or "soft," versus mandated, or "hard," approaches to this objective, suggest that left parties often nominate and elect more women than do centre and conservative formations.

Yet the partisan pathways women follow to legislative office are not necessarily relevant at the level of political executives. While two of Canada's three northern territories operate without formal party formations, most female premiers who held power elsewhere in the country came from centre and right-of-centre organizations. Contrary to patterns reported in the legislative literature, material presented in this volume shows that only one (Rachel Notley of the Alberta NDP) of the nine women premiers to hold office in a partisan parliament came from a left organization. Aside from Notley, all party-based leaders had roots either in conservative or centrist political formations or, in the case of Marois, in the moderate stream of the sovereignist PQ. In short, their political ascents occurred mainly in organizations that lacked the formal practices for recruiting women that have typified the NDP and parties of the left outside Canada since the late 1970s.

In explaining peaks and valleys in legislative representation, some scholars point towards the willingness of women in positions of political responsibility to recruit other women. Using Canadian federal data, Cheng and Tavits (2011) conclude that numbers of female constituency association presidents as well as the presence of internal party affirmative action policies are positively correlated with the proportions of female candidates (see also Brodie 1994; Carbert 2002; Tremblay and Pelletier 2001). Whitford et al.'s (2007, 574) account of OECD systems demonstrates that a key precondition for women's advancement into political executive roles is their achieving sustained numerical representation in legislatures. According to Windett (2011), successful female candidacy for state-level office in the US is associated with gender equality, with the result that progressive jurisdictions with more feminist policies and histories of elected women stand out from more traditional states, notably in the US South.

By contrast, O'Brien et al.'s (2015) study of the impact of prime ministers concludes that women in top posts appoint fewer women to cabinet than do their male comparators. This finding resonates closely with Thatcher's record in British politics. While campaigning for a seat in the House of Commons in the early 1950s, Thatcher argued that the UK would be better off with more women MPs and cabinet ministers. During her time as prime minister between 1979 and 1990, however, Thatcher appointed a total of one other woman to cabinet. Moreover, within two years she demoted Janet Young from the post of government leader in the House of Lords on the basis that Young lacked "presence" (Thatcher 1993, 307; see Bashevkin 1998, 24–25, 173).

Given that scholars have devoted far less scrutiny to the study of female political executives than to legislators, this volume pays close attention to the political recruitment trajectories of women premiers in Canada. What backgrounds and experiences did they bring to public life? To what extent were close ties with political parties or, alternatively, community groups crucial to their upward mobility? Did women leaders champion the recruitment of other women, whether in their rhetoric or actions? In particular, were they more willing than men to name women to cabinet posts outside lower-prestige social and cultural portfolios where females tend to be clustered (see Krook and O'Brien 2012, 842; Tremblay and Stockemer 2013)?

The chapters in this volume trace female premiers' candidate recruitment as well as public appointment records. If the presence of women as constituency association presidents enhances the recruitment of female candidates, then does the same hold for political executives and their nominees for public office, cabinet, and bureaucratic leadership? Are higher percentages of female candidates fielded during election campaigns when women head parties? Do women leaders demonstrate a willingness to recruit more diverse nominees on bases other than gender, notably with respect to ethno-cultural, sexual orientation, or occupational characteristics? In chronological terms, did the presence of more women premiers as time passed lead to greater willingness to promote other women?

Organization of the Book

This volume is organized by geographic region and, within regions, by chronology. We begin with the three northern territories and then consider the

Atlantic region where two provinces, PEI and NL, were governed by female premiers who succeeded popular male predecessors from the same political party under what we term empowered circumstances. Subsequent sections then move across the country in a westward direction.

The next ten chapters conclude with a female political executive elected in 2015: Rachel Notley, a pioneer in that she was the first NDP leader to serve as premier of Alberta. This way of organizing the book means that we initially consider three frontier jurisdictions in the North (two of them operating as consensus rather than as party systems) with women leaders beginning in 1991, and then turn to an established province that featured the first female political executive to win an electoral mandate of her own – PEI's Catherine Callbeck in 1993. As noted earlier in this chapter, the five leaders we consider in Parts 3 and 4, from Quebec, Ontario, Alberta, and British Columbia, headed imperiled parties whose political fortunes were decidedly weak at the point at which they took the helm.

Part 1 opens with Graham White's account of NWT premier Nellie Cournoyea. Selected via a secret ballot of all territorial legislators, Cournoyea led a cabinet whose members were also chosen by their fellow lawmakers. Cournoyea welcomed the contributions of everyone in the NWT and did not actively intervene in order to recruit more women to public life. Widely lauded as a hard-working politician, Cournoyea was seen as both tough and demanding yet also as weak in so far as she permitted underperforming ministers to remain in cabinet. White argues that Cournoyea's willingness to support ministers who were under attack demonstrates her decisiveness in that she placed a long-term commitment to the public good above short-term demands to shuffle her cabinet.

In Chapter 3, Maura Forrest examines Pat Duncan's career as the first female as well as the first Liberal premier in Yukon. Forrest shows how Duncan had to navigate challenging economic circumstances as a pioneer whose party had no experience holding the levers of power in the territory and who had not served as a cabinet minister prior to becoming premier. Despite Yukon's frontier history, Duncan found it hard to get a fair hearing as a woman leading the territorial government. She stands out for having appointed the first cabinet in Canadian history with half men and half women, although doing so did not hold significant implications for the content of public policy or the tenor of debate.

In Chapter 4, Sheena Kennedy Dalseg assesses the record of Eva Aariak as Nunavut premier. Aariak brought an extensive record of Indigenous activism to her career in public office, and she sought to engage local citizens in cooperative relations with the territorial government. Kennedy Dalseg traces the difficulties Aariak and her government faced in trying to evaluate and improve the new territory's operations through the use of a "report card." She shows how Aariak was criticized as weak and indecisive even though she reached the premier's position in part because of views that her predecessor had been abrasive and doctrinaire. Like Forrest's account of public frustration over the absence of an economic turnaround in Yukon (Chapter 3), Dalseg's discussion reveals how, in Nunavut, impatience with Aariak's report card weakened her standing.

Part 2 of the volume considers Atlantic Canada. In Chapter 5, Don Desserud and Robin Sutherland discuss Catherine Callbeck's contributions as the first woman in Canada to win her own popular mandate. In PEI, Callbeck took over an experienced governing party in which she had spent time as a legislator and cabinet minister prior to becoming leader. Desserud and Sutherland evaluate Callbeck using a metric she herself proposed: the ability to strike a balance among conflicting interests – which was not easy during a period of fiscal restraint. They show how Callbeck's extensive experience was not able to insulate her from the realities that face many other women at the apex of power. These include harsh media criticism and the unwillingness of top party insiders to demonstrate the same degree of personal loyalty towards her as they might have offered a male leader.

In Chapter 6, in their analysis of NL politics, Drew Brown, Elizabeth Goodyear-Grant, and Amanda Bittner explore how, in 2010, Kathy Dunderdale won a majority mandate for a party that had already held power for some time. Yet, following that election, her predecessor Danny Williams's "large shoes" proved difficult to fill. Chapter 6 reports that Dunderdale named significantly more women than did Williams to top civil service posts. Yet lower numbers of female PC candidates and legislators made it hard for her to appoint women to the provincial cabinet. On the policy front, Chapter 6 explains how Dunderdale's focus on a major dam construction project as well as a series of political crises diverted attention away from social policy in general and women's rights in particular.

Part 3 considers leaders in central Canada. In Chapter 7, Philippe Bernier Arcand probes the paradoxical record of PQ premier Pauline Marois. A political veteran who held more than a dozen cabinet portfolios under other PQ premiers, Marois's priorities as a minister versus as a premier clearly diverged. Unlike the strong social policy focus of her formative years in cabinet, when she championed an innovative and popular five-dollar-per-day child care program, Marois's time as provincial leader was largely devoted to debates over the "reasonable accommodation" of ethno-cultural minorities in Quebec. Her government's proposal for a charter of secular social values drew widespread criticism, including from many feminists. The chapter shows how controversies over the charter, alongside the growth of competing nationalist parties, combined to defeat Marois's government less than thirty months into its minority mandate.

In Chapter 8, Sylvia Bashevkin considers Kathleen Wynne's record as Ontario premier. Wynne was the first woman and first declared member of a sexual orientation minority to hold this position. She also stood out from her predecessors because her political origins were in progressive social movement activism. Particularly towards the end of a majority mandate in 2018, Wynne's government moved policy markers forward in the areas of pay transparency and child care. This same period saw the appointment of a provincial cabinet that approached numerical parity, thus surpassing a high-water mark of 42 percent female ministers that dated from the early 1990s. Data on the climate of parliamentary debate suggest the legislative atmosphere was more rather than less conflictual under Wynne's leadership. Overall, Wynne's background as a left-of-centre activist helps to explain her willingness, towards the end of her mandate, to operate as a critical actor on matters of gender equality.

Part 4 of the volume opens with Tracy Summerville's account in Chapter 9 of two BC premiers: Rita Johnston and Christy Clark. Summerville details how Johnston faced not only the need to call an election right away but also a Social Credit Party that was internally divided and an electorate that saw her as too close to her embattled predecessor. By contrast, Clark had resigned years earlier from cabinet, thus creating distance between herself and her unpopular predecessor. Clark also benefited from more time before her party's electoral mandate was exhausted in order to frame a distinctive political profile. Summerville contrasts improvements over time in the numerical representation of women in BC politics with the unwillingness of both Johnston and Clark to address structural sources of inequality.

In Chapter 10, Clark Banack considers the brief term in office of Alberta PC premier Alison Redford. He shows how Redford won a majority mandate by convincing moderate and progressive voters that the Wildrose Party threatened to take Alberta far to the right. She reversed some widely criticized actions of the preceding PC government, including cuts to social spending, and made incremental improvements to equality policies, including violence against women and gender-based budgeting. Yet Redford believed women's presence in top positions made little difference to political outcomes and was unwilling to introduce the types of programs later implemented by the NDP. A series of scandals engulfed Premier Redford with the result that, parallel with the record of Pauline Marois in Quebec, she stands as the elected Alberta premier with the shortest term in office.

In Chapter 11, Melanee Thomas examines Rachel Notley, Alberta's first NDP premier. A pioneer who led her party to a majority government, Notley was a critical actor who created a status of women department, appointed the first parity cabinet in Alberta's history, and pressed for more women to contest elective office. On the policy front, Notley's government faced budgetary problems, which meant the province undertook a pilot study of twenty-five-dollar-per-day child care but did not immediately implement either a wider child care program or full-day kindergarten. Thomas shows how the ideologically polarized environment of Alberta politics meant that the arrival of progressive women leaders, beginning in 2015, sharpened rather than reduced the corrosive tenor of public as well as legislative debate.

Chapter 12 concludes the volume with a systematic look at findings from the ten substantive chapters. Following from this introductory chapter, we organize, analyze, and interpret the empirical data on individual leaders in order to respond to larger themes concerning women and public leadership.

References

Andrew, Caroline, and John Biles, eds. 2009. *Electing a Diverse Canada: The Representation of Immigrants, Minorities and Women.* Vancouver: UBC Press.

Arscott, Jane, and Linda Trimble. 1997a. "In the Presence of Women: Representation and Political Power." In *In the Presence of Women: Representation in Canadian Governments*, ed. Jane Arscott and Linda Trimble, 1–17. Toronto: Harcourt Brace.

–, eds. 1997b. *In the Presence of Women: Representation in Canadian Governments.* Toronto: Harcourt Brace.

Atchison, Amy, and Ian Down. 2009. "Women Cabinet Ministers and Female-Friendly Social Policy." *Poverty and Public Policy* 1, 2, article 3. http://www.psocommons.org/ppp/vol1/iss2/art3.

Bashevkin, Sylvia B. 1993. *Toeing the Lines: Women and Party Politics in English Canada.* 2nd ed. Toronto: Oxford University Press.

–. 1998. *Women on the Defensive: Living through Conservative Times.* Toronto: University of Toronto Press.

–. 2009. *Women, Power, Politics: The Hidden Story of Canada's Unfinished Democracy.* Don Mills: Oxford University Press.

–. 2010. "When Do Outsiders Break In? Institutional Circumstances of Party Leadership Victories by Women in Canada." *Commonwealth and Comparative Politics* 48, 1 (February): 72–90.

Beckwith, Karen, and Kimberly Cowell-Meyers. 2007. "Sheer Numbers: Critical Representation Thresholds and Women's Political Representation." *Perspectives on Politics* 5, 3: 553–65.

Berkman, Michael B., and Robert E. O'Connor. 1993. "Do Women Legislators Matter? Female Legislators and State Abortion Policy." *American Politics Quarterly* 21, 1: 102–24.

Blaxill, Luke, and Kaspar Beelen. 2016. "A Feminized Language of Democracy? The Representation of Women at Westminster since 1945." *Twentieth Century British History* 27, 3: 412–49.

Bramston, Troy. 2017. "Gladys Berejiklian Is Liberals' First Premier." *The Australian*, 24 January.

Brodie, Janine. 1994. "Women and Political Leadership: The Case for Affirmative Action." In *Leaders and Leadership in Canada*, ed. Maureen Mancuso, Richard G. Price, and Ronald Wagenberg, 75–96. Toronto: Oxford University Press.

Burt, Sandra, and Elizabeth Lorenzin. 1997. "Taking the Women's Movement to Queen's Park: Women's Interests and the New Democratic Government of Ontario." In *In the Presence of Women: Representation in Canadian Governments*, ed. Jane Arscott and Linda Trimble, 202–27. Toronto: Harcourt Brace.

Byrne, Lesley. 2009. "Making a Difference When the Doors Are Open: Women in the Ontario NDP Cabinet, 1990–95." In *Opening Doors Wider: Women's Political Engagement in Canada*, ed. Sylvia Bashevkin, 93–107. Vancouver: UBC Press.

Carbert, Louise. 1997. "Governing on 'the Correct, the Compassionate, the Saskatchewan Side of the Border.'" In *In the Presence of Women: Representation in Canadian Governments*, ed. Jane Arscott and Linda Trimble, 154–79. Toronto: Harcourt Brace.

–. 2002. "Historical Influences on Regional Patterns of Election of Women to Provincial Legislatures." In *Political Parties, Representation and Electoral Democracy in Canada*, ed. William Cross, 201–22. Toronto: Oxford University Press.

Casgrain, Thérèse. 1972. *A Woman in a Man's World*. Toronto: McClelland and Stewart.

Celis, Karen, and Sarah Childs. 2008. "Introduction: The Descriptive and Substantive Representation of Women: New Directions." *Parliamentary Affairs* 61, 3: 419–25.

Celis, Karen, Sarah Childs, Johanna Kantola, and Mona Lena Krook. 2008. "Rethinking Women's Substantive Representation." *Representation* 44, 2: 99–110.

Center for American Women and Politics. 2017. "History of Women Governors." http://cawp.rutgers.edu/history-women-governors.

Cheng, Christine, and Margit Tavits. 2011. "Informal Influences in Selecting Female Candidates." *Political Research Quarterly* 64, 2: 460–71.

Childs, Sarah, and Julie Withey. 2005. "The Substantive Representation of Women: The Case of the Reduction of VAT on Sanitary Products." *Parliamentary Affairs* 59, 1: 10–23.

Childs, Sarah, and Mona Lena Krook. 2008. "Critical Mass Theory and Women's Political Representation." *Political Studies* 56, 3: 725–36.

–. 2009. "Analysing Women's Substantive Representation: From Critical Mass to Critical Actors." *Government and Opposition* 44, 2: 125–45.

Childs, Sarah, Joni Lovenduski, and Rosie Campbell. 2005. *Women at the Top 2005: Changing Numbers, Changing Politics?* London: Hansard Society.

Crenshaw, Kimberlé. 1991. "Mapping the Margins: Intersectionality, Identity Politics, and Violence against Women of Color." *Stanford Law Review* 43: 1241–99.

Curtin, Jennifer. 2008. "Women, Political Leadership and Substantive Representation: The Case of New Zealand." *Parliamentary Affairs* 61, 3: 490–504.

Dahlerup, Drude. 1988. "From a Small to a Large Minority: Women in Scandinavian Politics." *Scandinavian Political Studies* 11: 275–97.

Delcker, Janosch. 2016. "Merkel's 'Crown Princess' Tries to Win Back Rhineland." *Politico*, 11 March. http://www.politico.eu/article/merkels-crown-princess-tries -to-win-back-rhineland-julia-kloeckner-malu-dreyer/.

Dowling, Siobhán. 2011. "Germany's New Generation of Female Political Leaders." *Der Spiegel*, 25 January. http://www.spiegel.de/international/germany/letter-from -berlin-germany-s-new-generation-of-female-political-leaders-a-741348.html.

Dunaway, Johanna, Regina G. Lawrence, Melody Rose, and Christopher R. Weber. 2013. "Traits versus Issues: How Female Candidates Shape Coverage of Senate and Gubernatorial Races." *Political Research Quarterly* 66, 3 (September): 715–26.

Eagly, Alice H., and Steven J. Karau. 2002. "Role Incongruity Theory of Prejudice toward Female Leaders." *Psychological Review* 109, 3: 573–98.

Erickson, Lynda. 1997. "Parties, Ideology, and Feminist Action: Women and Political Representation in British Columbia Politics." In *In the Presence of Women: Representation in Canadian Governments*, ed. Jane Arscott and Linda Trimble, 106–27. Toronto: Harcourt Brace.

Genovese, Michael A., and Seth Thompson. 1993. "Women as Chief Executives: Does Gender Matter?" In *Women as National Leaders*, ed. Michael A. Genovese, 1–12. Newbury Park, CA: Sage.

Jamieson, Kathleen Hall. 1995. *Beyond the Double Bind: Women and Leadership.* New York: Oxford University Press.

Kantola, Johanna. 2009. "Women's Political Representation in the European Union." *Journal of Legislative Studies* 15, 4: 379–400.

Kathlene, Lyn. 1998. "In a Different Voice: Women and the Policy Process." In *Women and Elective Office*, ed. Sue Thomas and Clyde Wilcox, 188–202. New York: Oxford University Press.

Keohane, Nannerl O. 2010. *Thinking about Leadership.* Princeton: Princeton University Press.

Kirkpatrick, Jeane J. 1974. *Political Woman.* New York: Basic.

Klatch, Rebecca. 1987. *Women of the New Right.* Philadelphia: Temple University Press.

Krook, Mona Lena. 2009. *Quotas for Women in Politics: Gender and Candidate Selection Reform Worldwide.* New York: Oxford University Press.

Krook, Mona Lena, and Fiona Mackay, eds. 2011. *Gender, Politics and Institutions: Towards a Feminist Institutionalism.* Basingstoke: Palgrave Macmillan.

Krook, Mona Lena, and Diana Z. O'Brien. 2012. "All the President's Men? The Appointment of Female Cabinet Ministers Worldwide." *Journal of Politics* 74, 3 (July): 840–55.

Lovenduski, Joni. 1993. "Introduction: The Dynamics of Gender and Party." In *Gender and Party Politics*, ed. Joni Lovenduski and Pippa Norris, 1–15. Newbury Park, CA: Sage.

Mackay, Fiona. 2008. "'Thick' Conceptions of Substantive Representation: Women, Gender and Political Institutions." *Representation* 44, 2: 125–39.

Mendelberg, Tali, Christopher F. Karpowitz, and J. Baxter Oliphant. 2014. "Gender Equality in Deliberation: Unpacking the Black Box of Interaction." *Perspectives on Politics* 12, 1: 18–44.

Moncrief, Gary F., and Joel A. Thompson. 1991. "Urban and Rural Ridings and Women in Provincial Politics in Canada: A Research Note on Female MLAs." *Canadian Journal of Political Science* 24, 4: 831-40.

O'Brien, Diana Z., Matthew Mendez, Jordan Carr Peterson, and Jihyun Shin. 2015. "Letting Down the Ladder or Shutting the Door: Female Prime Ministers, Party Leaders, and Cabinet Ministers." *Politics and Gender* 11, 4: 689–717.

O'Neill, Brenda, and David Stewart. 2009. "Gender and Political Party Leadership in Canada." *Party Politics* 15, 6 (November): 737–57.

Osborn, Tracy L. 2012. *How Women Represent Women: Political Parties, Gender, and Representation in the State Legislatures*. New York: Oxford University Press.

Parliament of Australia. 2014. "Australia's Female Political Leaders: A Quick Guide." http://www.aph.gov.au/About_Parliament/Parliamentary_Departments/Parliamentary_Library/pubs/rp/rp1314/QG/FemalePolLeaders.

Pitkin, Hanna F. 1967. *The Concept of Representation*. Berkeley: University of California Press.

Poggione, Sarah. 2011. "Gender and Representation in State Legislatures." In *Women in Politics: Outsiders or Insiders?* 5th ed., ed. Lois Duke Whitaker, 169–84. Boston: Longman.

Praud, Jocelyne. 1998. "Affirmative Action and Women's Representation in the Ontario New Democratic Party." In *Women and Political Representation in Canada*, ed. Manon Tremblay and Caroline Andrew, 171–93. Ottawa: University of Ottawa Press.

Research Canada. 2015. "Canada Speaks 2015: A National Public Opinion Poll on Health and Medical Research." https://rc-rc.ca/6206-2/.

Ryan, Michelle K. and S. Alexander Haslam. 2005. "The Glass Cliff: Evidence That Women Are Over-Represented in Precarious Leadership Positions." *British Journal of Management* 16, 2: 81–90.

Saint-German, Michelle A. 1989. "Does Their Difference Make a Difference? The Impact of Elected Women on Public Policy in Arizona." *Social Science Quarterly* 70, 4: 956–68.

Schneider, Andrea Kupfer, Catherine H. Tinsley, Sandra Cheldelin, and Emily T. Amanatullah. 2010. "Likeability v. Competence: The Impossible Choice Faced by Female Politicians, Attenuated by Lawyers." *Duke Journal of Gender Law and Policy* 17, 2: 363–84.

Schreiber, Ronnee. 2008. *Righting Feminism: Conservative Women and American Politics*. New York: Oxford University Press.

Soroka, Stuart N. 2007. "A Report to the Health Council of Canada: Canadian Perceptions of the Health Care System." Health Council of Canada. http://www.queensu.ca/cora/_files/PublicPerceptions.pdf.

Statistics Canada. 2017. "Population by Year, by Province and Territory." http://www.statcan.gc.ca/tables-tableaux/sum-som/l01/cst01/demo02a-eng.htm.

Swers, Michele L. 2002. "Transforming the Agenda: Analyzing Gender Differences in Women's Issue Bill Sponsorship." In *Women Transforming Congress*, ed. Cindy Simon Rosenthal, 260–83. Norman: University of Oklahoma Press.

Thatcher, Margaret. 1993. *The Downing Street Years*. New York: HarperCollins.

Thomas, Melanee. 2018. "In Crisis or Decline? Selecting Women to Lead Provincial Parties in Government." *Canadian Journal of Political Science* 51, 2: 379–403.

Thomas, Sue. 1994. *How Women Legislate*. New York: Oxford University Press.

Tremblay, Manon, and Réjean Pelletier. 2001. "More Women Constituency Party Presidents: A Strategy for Increasing the Number of Women Candidates in Canada?" *Party Politics* 7, 2: 157–90.

Tremblay, Manon, and Daniel Stockemer. 2013. "Women's Ministerial Careers in Cabinet, 1921–2010: A Look at Socio-Demographic Traits and Career Experiences." *Canadian Public Administration* 56, 4 (December): 523–41.

Trimble, Linda. 1997. "Feminist Politics in the Alberta Legislature, 1972–1994." In *In the Presence of Women: Representation in Canadian Governments*, ed. Jane Arscott and Linda Trimble, 128–53. Toronto: Harcourt Brace.

–. 1998. "Who's Represented: Gender and Diversity in the Alberta Legislature." In *Women and Political Representation in Canada*, ed. Manon Tremblay and Caroline Andrew, 25–89. Ottawa: University of Ottawa Press.

Trimble, Linda, Jane Arscott, and Manon Tremblay, eds. 2013a. *Stalled: The Representation of Women in Canadian Governments*. Vancouver: UBC Press.

Trimble, Linda, Manon Tremblay, and Jane Arscott. 2013b. "Conclusion: A Few More Women." In *Stalled: The Representation of Women in Canadian Governments*, ed. Linda Trimble, Jane Arscott, and Manon Tremblay, 290–314. Vancouver: UBC Press.

Valian, Virginia. 1998. *Why So Slow? The Advancement of Women*. Cambridge: MIT Press.

Whitford, Andrew B., Vicky M. Wilkins, and Mercedes G. Ball. 2007. "Descriptive Representation and Policymaking Authority: Evidence from Women in Cabinets and Bureaucracies." *Governance* 20, 4: 559–80.

Windett, Jason Harold. 2011. "State Effects and the Emergence and Success of Female Gubernatorial Candidates." *State Politics and Policy Quarterly* 11, 4 (December): 460–82.

PART 1

THE TERRITORIES

2

"Never in My Life Did I Do Anything Alone"

Nellie Cournoyea as Premier of the Northwest Territories

GRAHAM WHITE

When Nellie Cournoyea became government leader (premier) of the Northwest Territories in November 1991, commentators elsewhere in Canada focused on her as the first Aboriginal woman to become a Canadian first minister – indeed, she was only the second woman of any background to reach that status. In the NWT, however, these milestones drew little attention. Instead, the common view was that a hardworking, experienced, and effective leader – empathetic to the human problems of the North – had taken the helm of the Government of the Northwest Territories.

Serving as premier from 1991 until 1995 of what now comprises both the NWT and Nunavut may have been the highest profile position in her long public career. Yet for "Nellie," as she has long been referred to in the North, it was simply another way to advance the goals she had pursued throughout her political life. Her key priorities were protecting and promoting the interests and rights of Northern Aboriginal people; empowering local communities to control their own affairs; improving the social and economic well-being of Northerners, especially those in small communities; and drawing the attention of the rest of Canada, especially that of the federal government, to the perspectives, challenges, and opportunities of the modern North.

This chapter argues that Cournoyea's ability to realize many of her priorities followed from the community-based vision she brought to public life coupled with personal qualities that permitted her to operate in a consensus government environment. Since Cournoyea's political career unfolded in a nonpartisan environment, she cannot be described as a "pioneer" premier, as defined in Chapter 1, because the concept is largely framed in terms of political party experiences. She most certainly, however, can be described as a trailblazer. As discussed below, Cournoyea sought elective office initially in order to serve the Northern Aboriginal communities in which she grew up. She thus resembled female US state legislators who, unlike many of their male counterparts, explain their decisions to enter politics in terms of giving voice to the concerns of their local constituents rather than fulfilling their own personal ambitions (see Kirkpatrick 1974). Consistent with the literature cited in Chapter 1, Cournoyea also stands at the confluence of arguments about how gender and Aboriginality can assist leaders in finding common ground in a political system that lacks Westminster-style party organizations and party discipline.

Outside the NWT, men who are no longer premiers often remain in the public spotlight by joining prominent law firms and corporate boards or taking on ambassadorships, Senate appointments, or other high-profile public-sector positions. With so few former women premiers in Canada, it is hard to generalize about their careers after politics – in part because such individuals as Pat Duncan in Yukon, Kathy Dunderdale in Newfoundland and Labrador, and Alison Redford in Alberta largely dropped from the public spotlight once they left elective office. By contrast, among the distinctive features of Cournoyea's political career is the fact that, for nearly two decades after leaving the premiership and the legislature, she remained one of the most well-known and influential politicians in the NWT. Even before her first election to the NWT Legislative Assembly, she was a significant player in territorial politics. Accordingly, this chapter focuses on Cournoyea's time as government leader while placing her premiership in the context of activities both before and after. It shows how Cournoyea's extensive political career reflects not only a long-term commitment to public service but also strong attachment to her base in the Inuvialuit region.

The discussion begins with a brief account of Cournoyea's youth and the influence of Inuvialuit culture on her time in politics. The following sections outline her political activities prior to becoming premier; key elements of her premiership, including her governing style; and her views and actions with respect to women's involvement in politics. The final sections look briefly at her political career after leaving the premiership and offer some concluding comments.

Early Influences

While the actions of all politicians in office are to some degree shaped by their formative years, Cournoyea's political philosophy, goals, and governing style were influenced in an unusually direct way by the circumstances of her youth. Her childhood was suffused with the attitudes and values of Northern Aboriginal people, and these powerfully shaped the woman who has been characterized as having "a human touch [and] backbone of steel" (Tom Jackson as narrator in Bartlett and Lerose 2004).

Cournoyea was born in 1940 into a large family on a trapline near the small community of Aklavik in the Mackenzie Delta, just north of the Arctic Circle. Her mother was an Inuvialuk, meaning she was from the Inuit people of the northwestern NWT (see Alunik et al. 2003). Her Norwegian father was a trapper. Cournoyea largely grew up on the land; since she spent little time in school, most of her formal education was completed by correspondence.

In a 2012 address to an international Inuit Studies conference, Cournoyea quoted an Inuvialuit publication that described key features of the local culture:

We have a high regard for certain characteristics and for certain types of individuals. We value curiosity, resourcefulness, patience, kindness, and ability. We appreciate individuals who are successful at whatever they do, who are responsible, who keep their word, and who are modest. These are attitudes which have not changed despite changes in all else around us. (Cournoyea 2014, 18)

In citing this account of Inuvialuit culture, Cournoyea might well have been describing herself. In addition, Cournoyea was known for being resilient and self-reliant – characteristics that reflected her early and continuing experiences on the land. If you needed something done, you did it yourself and, at the same time, you also worked closely with others to accomplish important tasks. It was not an easy life: constant hard work was required just to maintain the basics of survival, which created an ethos – evident during Cournoyea's term as premier – that you made do with what you had.

When her mother was hospitalized for a year following a serious fire, Cournoyea, at age fifteen, took charge of running the large family. She summarized her experiences in taking on the same tasks as her brothers as follows:

I don't think of my background in terms of hardships or obstacles because it really made me who I am today. It gave me a lot of confidence because I can do a lot of other things besides what I am doing here [as premier] and have enough skills to survive no matter what I do. It gives you a certain amount of strength. It makes you pretty practical about life and how you get things done ... there were a lot of women like me; all the women I grew up with can pack a gun and hunt and can do men's work as well as the men can. (Cournoyea as quoted in Moore 1993)

In Cournoyea's view, the chance to prove herself as a teenager thus had positive effects.

Ethel Blondin-Andrew, who served as an assistant deputy minister under Cournoyea, comments with reference to the former territorial leader: "In the corporate business world she is just as comfortable as she would be on a whale hunt" (Thurton 2012). Cournoyea believes her upbringing and Aboriginal heritage helped her to operate in environments that seem as diverse as the cabinet table, corporate boardroom, and the land: "They're definitely connected. It's the confidence that takes away the intimidation of the boardrooms and we learn that as we go. It's how we were brought up ... anybody who grew up in that period of time, you've had a good grounding and it goes back to having pride in what you're doing, knowledge of what you're doing and control over what you're doing" (Anselmi 2016, 14, 17).

Cournoyea is by no means the only Aboriginal leader whose self-confidence guides her in what might seem like intimidating situations. Frances Abele, a political scientist who knows Northern politics well, suggests that "many Indigenous northerners are used to being self-reliant and learning as they go. They have had the experience of providing for themselves in a society that was still fairly autarkic. So they enter new situations with the cast of mind that they can figure out how it works to get what they want or need – how the others see them is not a major concern" (personal communication, 15 June 2017).

When asked whether she had mentors during her time in politics, Cournoyea notes that, "in Inuvialuit society, you learn by watching and listening to those who know more." In that sense she had many mentors, particularly those she describes as "the great people who kept our world going." Throughout her time in politics, she tried to be around people who knew more than she. At the same time, those who worked for Cournoyea emphasize her prodigious work ethic, which means she sometimes knew key files better than the ministers and bureaucrats who reported to her and were responsible for those dossiers.

Perhaps the clearest indication of the influence of Inuvialuit culture on Cournoyea's political outlook is her insistence that, in a long record of remarkable accomplishments, "never in my life did I do anything alone."

Pathway to the Premier's Office

Cournoyea married an air force officer, moved to Halifax and Ottawa, and had two children. After the marriage ended, she returned to the North and worked as an announcer at the CBC radio station in Inuvik. She rose to the position of station manager and then became a land claim fieldworker for the national Inuit organization, at the time called Inuit Tapirisat of Canada (ITC) and currently known as Inuit Tapariit Kanatami, and subsequently for the Committee of Original Peoples' Entitlement (COPE). Cournoyea's media experience doubtless served her well in her subsequent campaigns for elected office, but her local community work for ITC and COPE proved decisive in that it brought her into close contact with many people in the region.

In 1970, Cournoyea helped to found COPE in response to the pervasive development of Inuvialuit lands and waters by oil and gas companies – which proceeded without the involvement of local Inuit communities. COPE aimed at restoring Inuvialuit control over their lands and waters with the power to shape and, if necessary, reject development. COPE initially attempted to represent all Aboriginal peoples of the NWT, but the unrelenting pace of development in the Mackenzie Delta and Beaufort Sea led the organization to concentrate on issues directly affecting Inuvialuit.

ITC submitted a land claim to the federal government in 1974 that covered what is now Nunavut as well as the Inuvialuit region. When ITC withdrew the claim in 1976 for further study, COPE launched its own land claim in the belief that Inuvialuit interests could not afford to wait. Cournoyea became a COPE claim negotiator because she viewed the goal not just as protecting the environment but also as ensuring cultural survival:

> There was a substantial gap for people, between their traditional roots and the modern society. It was not just about the alienation of land for exploration, but our culture, our traditional games, our language, and our drum dancing were disappearing. So the claim was not only about the economics but the social well-being of the Inuvialuit. (Cournoyea as quoted in Inuvialuit Regional Corporation 2009, 9)

Although COPE reached an agreement in principle with the federal government in 1978, progress towards finalizing the land claim was slow and difficult.

As part of their strategy for moving ahead, COPE leaders decided to focus on electing a member to the territorial legislature (Inuvialuit Regional Corporation 2009, 24). Cournoyea (as quoted in Inuvialuit Regional Corporation, 2009, 33) describes the situation as follows: "It was decided that I should go into politics because we were not getting any support from the territorial government ... The main purpose was to try to diminish some of the barriers that were thrown in front of us. It was not a full time job; I could still devote fifty percent of my time to the claim. I tried to build an understanding of the claims with everybody in government."

In the 1979 territorial election, Cournoyea won the predominantly Inuvialuit constituency of Western Arctic with nearly 60 percent of the votes in a three-way race. Her initial intention was to stay for one or two terms in order to advocate for her community. In her words, however, "there was always something that had to be dealt with" so she served a total of four terms (sixteen years) as an MLA. Even after several decades in politics, she speaks of her "political pathway" or "involvement in politics" rather than using the term "political career" to refer to her public service.

By the time the COPE land claim (known formally as the Inuvialuit Final Agreement) was settled in 1984, Cournoyea had been re-elected by acclamation in the renamed Nunakput riding and held the positions of minister of information as well as minister of renewable resources in the NWT government. At the signing ceremony for the final agreement, Cournoyea famously wore a dress in recognition of all those who had worked on the claim, a remarkable departure from her usual practice of wearing trousers. She assured the crowd that the dress was borrowed – it was not a traditional Inuvialuit garment – and said that she would soon return it, noting, "you can't boss people around unless you are in pants and a little bit sweaty" (Cournoyea as quoted in Inuvialuit Regional Corporation 2009, 39). This irreverent quip and the sartorial statement behind it confirm Cournoyea's commitment to the values of her community: she worked hard and got on with the job in front of her, paying little attention to what was not essential. As premier and afterwards, she rarely if ever wore a dress.

In late 1985, Cournoyea lost her ministerial portfolios in a cabinet shuffle in the non-partisan legislature of the NWT. Richard Nerysoo was removed as government leader at the same time. Lewis (1998, 15) maintains that MLAs saw Cournoyea as openly critical of Nerysoo and as more interested in finalizing the COPE claim than in her cabinet roles. Re-elected with 70 percent of the vote in the 1987 territorial election, Cournoyea was chosen by her fellow MLAs to serve in cabinet. Under the terms of consensus government in the NWT, the speaker, premier, and all ministers are selected via a secret ballot of all MLAs. The premier assigns or reassigns portfolios to ministers but can neither dismiss members of the cabinet nor select ministers who fail to win the secret ballot process.[1] During the Eleventh Assembly (1987–91), when Dennis Patterson served as territorial leader, Cournoyea was the workhorse of the government. She simultaneously held three major portfolios: (1) health, (2) public works and highways, and (3) energy, mines and petroleum resources – plus a number of minor responsibilities.

Premier Nellie

After winning her seat by acclamation in the 1991 territorial election, Cournoyea put her name forward as a candidate for premier. Her opponent was Stephen Kakfwi, a Dene from Fort Good Hope who had been a cabinet minister and, before that, president of the Dene Nation. For the first time, the secret ballot vote by MLAs followed the live broadcast of a public session of the NWT Assembly. Cournoyea and Kakfwi gave short speeches and responded to numerous questions from MLAs. Both candidates were well known for their emphasis on empowering local Aboriginal communities, and few substantial differences emerged between them in their responses to questions posed by MLAs (NWT TLC 1991, 22–46).

Cournoyea won the race but the vote totals were never released. Kakfwi pledged to support Cournoyea, commenting as follows: "I would have been happy to win, but I am just as happy to lose" (NWT TLC 1991, 46). Kakfwi, who subsequently became premier of the NWT, said in a recent interview with the author that he developed considerable respect for Cournoyea while serving with her in cabinet between 1987 and 1991.

No recent period of NWT politics has been quiescent or routine, but Cournoyea's term as premier from 1991 until 1995 was especially turbulent. An unusual range of major, contentious issues had to be addressed, including:

- finalization of the Inuit land claim in the Eastern Arctic and initial steps to divide the NWT in order to create Nunavut (see Hicks and White 2015)
- finalization and implementation of two regional land claims in the NWT covering the Gwich'in and the Sahtu Dene and Métis

- negotiations on self-government and land claims in other regions
- constitutional development of the Western NWT, including a wide-ranging constitutional commission and constituent assembly
- protracted and ultimately unsuccessful negotiation of a Northern accord to shift control of non-renewable natural resources from federal to territorial jurisdiction
- reorganization of the territorial bureaucracy, including introduction of a community transfer initiative to devolve territorial policy making and administration to local communities (see White 1998)
- fiscal pressures leading to unprecedented staff and service cutbacks.

These challenges unfolded at the same time as Cournoyea's government faced a lengthy strike at Giant Mine in Yellowknife, which was marked by the murder of nine miners who crossed the picket lines (see Selleck and Thompson 1997). On the national scene, intense constitutional activity unfolded that held potentially far-reaching implications for the NWT – notably, the Mulroney government's proposed Charlottetown Accord, which failed in a country-wide referendum in 1992.

Pierre Alvarez, Cournoyea's cabinet secretary, describes as remarkable the ability of the NWT government not only to manage "the deluge of problems that cascaded onto that small government in its first 12 months" but also to move forward on other fronts. Cournoyea recalls a "packed agenda," noting that the Giant strike "dominated the business of government for a year and a half." The strike not only created bitter social divisions but also cost the NWT millions of dollars. Yet the territorial government's capacity to act was limited because key elements of labour law and policy rested in federal jurisdiction.

In light of this background, Cournoyea considers one of her major successes as premier to have been "just keeping the ball rolling." By making progress on a series of difficult files, she put into practice a key tenet of the Inuvialuit value system. People were judged not by talk but, rather, by action; as Cournoyea reflects, leaders were assessed according to "what you did rather than what you said."

Managing Consensus Government
The consensus government system within which Cournoyea operated as a minister and later as premier creates both constraints and opportunities for all involved – and especially for the first minister. The most notable limit

for the premier is her lack of control over the composition of cabinet. Unlike other Westminster parliamentary systems, the entire NWT Assembly, rather than just the premier, chooses both who is to serve in cabinet and who is to be removed from it.[2] Cabinet cohesion can be problematic in a consensus arrangement since ministers have stronger incentives to operate independently than they do in party-based systems. Premiers are forced to navigate what amounts to a permanent minority government as MLAs without cabinet status always outnumber cabinet ministers. Moreover, since regular MLAs are not organized into stable political parties, the political calculus for premiers and cabinets is more complex and more personalized than is the case in Westminster-style minority governments. As a result, reaching and implementing controversial decisions – especially those that impose losses through budget cuts – can be far more problematic than in situations in which premiers choose their cabinets and in which firm party discipline is the norm.

At the same time, consensus government is advantageous for the cabinet because it does not usually face a cohesive, well-organized legislative opposition. Moreover, cabinets need to convince only a handful of MLAs to support a measure in order to pass legislation.

Leaders who employ effective interpersonal skills to implement a well-formulated vision benefit in consensus-based systems because they hold the tools necessary to realize a broad political agenda. As noted in Chapter 1, organizational research suggests women and Aboriginal people can thrive in environments that place an emphasis on diverse people coming together to reach shared positions, as contrasted with contexts that stress the ability of a single player to emerge victorious in a winner-take-all conflict. Like Northern Aboriginal culture, the NWT Assembly is far less adversarial and confrontational than are southern, party-based legislatures. So, too, it is less subject to the political and organizational rigidities that characterize party-based systems. Thus women, especially Aboriginal women like Cournoyea, may not face the same expectation that they will employ "masculine" leadership styles as do their counterparts elsewhere.

How did Cournoyea develop a leadership style appropriate to success in the NWT? She possessed a clear set of objectives as well as considerable skills as a consensus builder. Simply put, Cournoyea was an astute politician who knew when firm leadership was needed and when it was necessary to reach compromise on difficult issues – and was well suited to the peculiarities of the consensus system.

As premier, Cournoyea's governing style combined team effort with strong leadership. She saw her role as "getting the team [cabinet] to succeed" and supporting ministers as needed. Instead of limiting the ability of ministers to pursue their own ideas, she developed a cabinet culture in which "we all relied on each other." Yet, despite her emphasis on group dynamics, Cournoyea is universally described as tough and demanding. John Todd, an MLA who eventually joined the NWT cabinet, once commented that Cournoyea's "style may be autocratic but at this particular time, that is exactly what's needed" (as quoted in Dickie 1992, 26).

Stephen Kakfwi, one of her most able and powerful ministers, speaks favourably of her dealings with him: "I worked very well with her; she gave me good portfolios and as much leeway as I wanted; she never shut me down; her door was always open to me ... I always felt that she was in total support of me; there were no political games." In her approach to cabinet, Kakfwi comments that, even though Cournoyea had her own ideas, she remained receptive to those of others. He describes her as "a very good leader; she understood consensus in a traditional [Aboriginal] style."

Like many others, Kakfwi emphasizes how hard Cournoyea worked. He notes that she was always available when he called, stayed close to her home base, and – even as premier – rarely left the NWT. By contrast, she travelled extensively throughout the NWT in order to visit communities and meet local people. One summer she visited twenty-three of the twenty-four territorial constituencies, an impressive feat considering that more than two-thirds of the communities in the pre-division NWT were inaccessible by road and could only be reached by air or water.

Cournoyea did leave the NWT to attend constitutional conferences and other intergovernmental meetings. These venues provided opportunities to bring the North and its special conditions and needs to national attention – especially that of the federal government. She became known during the Charlottetown constitutional process as one of the "Mothers of Confederation" together with fellow Inuit Mary Simon and Rosemary Kuptana. Cournoyea's experience with COPE stood her in good stead for dealing with Ottawa on the Constitution and other files: she understood the importance of deploying a clear strategy and effective tactics in the face of an enormously better-resourced and more powerful federal government.

According to her former executive assistant, Bernie Hughes, Cournoyea managed cabinet well. This was no easy task in a consensus system in which the premier can easily lose support. According to Hughes, "She gave ministers a lot of room and they took it," but she could also be firm with them.

Hughes recalls that she met regularly with individual members of cabinet and recognized the need to maintain solid communication with Inuit ministers who were not familiar with the ways of government and bureaucracy in Yellowknife. Cournoyea thus "commanded the respect of her ministers, in part because she was so hard-working; she read everything, often more than ministers." Alvarez concurs: "I've never seen anyone with a work ethic like she had."

Cournoyea's commitment was evident not only in her activities as first minister but also in the other responsibilities she assumed. Progress on the devolution file required difficult negotiations with the federal government over transferring control of non-renewable resources to the NWT. Recognizing the significance of this process, Cournoyea, as government leader, retained the critical energy, mines and petroleum resources portfolio for two years. As well, she held responsibility for the politically demanding Northwest Territories Power Corporation for her entire term as premier. For nearly three years she was minister responsible for the small Women's Directorate, though, given her preference for advancing women's interests through community-level organizations, her involvement with this agency was limited. She also stepped in to take charge of various departments, including personnel, social services, and health, when their respective ministers resigned.

Cournoyea's team approach to governing extended beyond cabinet. She had no reservations about delegating important tasks to bureaucrats. Above all, she was prepared to reach out to anyone – in government, community groups, Aboriginal organizations, and the private sector – whom she thought could help. "She was," says Alvarez, "very confident in reaching out to people she thought could do the job ... the tasks were provincial in size but there were few people available to manage them." Her basic principle was to assemble a good team that could serve the people of the NWT. Hughes comments that, while Cournoyea was hands-on with major policy issues, sometimes knowing the files better than her line officials, she didn't micromanage those she appointed. She believed people were recruited to do a job and should be allowed to get on with it. She was, he adds, very good at taking advice.

Governing Style
Parallel with the discussion in Chapter 1 of the sometimes contradictory criticisms of women leaders, Cournoyea has been portrayed as tough; however, she was also viewed in some quarters, especially among MLAs, as

having failed to deal effectively with underperforming ministers. Cournoyea lost an extraordinary number of cabinet members during her time as
premier, but not because she forced them out. Four of the seven ministers
elected by MLAs in November 1991 resigned, as did two of the five ministers who joined cabinet later in Cournoyea's premiership.[3] Of the original
contingent only Finance Minister John Pollard, Intergovernmental and Aboriginal Affairs Minister Stephen Kakfwi, and Public Works Minister Don
Morin remained in cabinet throughout Cournoyea's four-year term.

Less than a year into her mandate, a special debate took place in the
legislature on a motion brought forward by disgruntled MLAs. It expressed
concern over the weak performance of certain ministers and called on the
premier to "exercise the responsibilities given her regarding her reassigning,
disciplining or acceptance of resignations of Ministers" (NWT *Hansard*, 18
June 1992, 666). The motion passed eleven to one, with cabinet abstaining.
The motion directed Cournoyea to report to the House within a week as
to how she intended to respond to "the expressed concerns and discontent-
ment toward her Ministers by Members of the Legislative Assembly" (NWT
Hansard, 18 June 1992, 666). In her response, Cournoyea said she did "not
believe there [was] good reason to act on the premise of lack of confidence
[in ministers]" but that she would reassign portfolios to create more equal
ministerial workloads and shuffle deputy ministers to provide better support for ministers (NWT *Hansard*, 24 June 1992, 745–46).

At first blush, Cournoyea's willingness to defend ineffective ministers
seems to belie accounts of her as a demanding leader in that they suggest
she was unable to make difficult but necessary choices. On closer inspection,
however, her response to the Legislative Assembly can be seen as demonstrating toughness: she refused to bow to pressures to dismiss weak ministers in a setting in which she and her government did not control a legislative
majority.[4] If decisiveness means following principles rather than taking the
path of least resistance, then Cournoyea can be said to have embodied that
quality.

According to Alvarez, Cournoyea's support for ministers who were not
performing well and who found themselves under attack follows from the
fact that "she had an enormous respect and admiration for people willing
to put themselves forward for elected positions of public service, whether
at the community or territorial level." In his view, she understood the pressures placed on individuals and their families by a rough-and-tumble political system. Concerned that people who offered public service risked being
"eaten up by the system," she tried to be supportive.

Choosing to help rather than to undermine weak ministers illustrates a central dimension of Cournoyea as a politician and as a person. While she cannot be described as a populist, her political career was suffused with commitment and connection to common people. Hughes's comment that "she had time for people ... not just the politicians and important people but also the people on the street" is widely echoed across the NWT. Nor were her dealings with ordinary people politically motivated; instead, most of her contacts with community members occurred outside the public spotlight. These links reflected Aboriginal values she acquired growing up on the land where, in her words, "everyone had a value and everyone had to contribute" (Cournoyea speaking in Bartlett and Lerose 2004).

In a telling scene from the documentary film entitled *Better Ask Nellie*, Cournoyea works at her desk in the regional land claims corporation when an Inuvialuit elder comes in looking to buy beaver pelts for a sewing project. Cournoyea stops what she's doing to show the pelts on her desk and sells one to the woman on behalf of a local trapper. Afterwards she explains why it is important to assist both the trapper and the seamstress: "they may be small things but if they're important to the people I represent, they're just as important as meeting the premier of Alberta" (Cournoyea speaking in Bartlett and Lerose 2004). The scene in the film was no feigned set-up: Cournoyea told this author that she usually travelled, including when she was premier, with crafts and other goods for sale made by people in the NWT.

Hughes recalls that, when Cournoyea was government leader, community visits she made for any purpose included one-on-one meetings with people who needed help. These interactions typically generated a sheaf of notes about problems that staff in Yellowknife were expected to sort out. Moreover, Cournoyea's proclivity for helping people extended to a level of warm personal generosity. Her houses in Tuktoyaktuk and Yellowknife were constantly filled with people needing somewhere to stay. A friend put it this way: "if you need someone with a sympathetic ear, just call Nellie" (Peggy Jay speaking in Bartlett and Lerose 2004).

Modernizing Consensus Government

The 1980s and 1990s were marked by important changes in how consensus government operated in the NWT. Several significant innovations occurred during Cournoyea's term as premier. Not all were directly attributable to her, but she was a key figure in putting them in place. It is notable that Westminster-style responsible government in the NWT only dates from the 1980s. Prior to that time, the commissioner, the equivalent of the lieutenant-governor in Canada's provinces, chaired cabinet meetings and served as head of at least one government department. By the time Cournoyea became premier, a regime was in place whereby ministers individually and collectively held power by dint of retaining the confidence of the House, albeit a House without political parties.

Changes introduced during Cournoyea's time as premier brought greater accountability to the process of choosing political executives. In 1993, the legislature began an open "mid-term review" of the government, whereby the premier and her ministers were subject to extensive public questioning. The idea of a mid-term review was not new, but previously it had been conducted behind closed doors. The new event, broadcast live across the territory, covered not just specific issues but also the general record of ministers and the premier during their entire time in office. The purpose of the review, although rarely stated in explicit terms, was to establish which ministers should remain in office and which removed.

Although these reforms followed from decisions by the NWT Assembly as a whole, Cournoyea pursued specific efforts to make government more transparent. First, she asked her ministers to sign undated letters of resignation. The possibility that the government leader could choose and fire ministers had been under discussion for some time but was explicitly rejected by an Assembly vote in 1991 (see NWT TLC 1991, 16–22). The government leader could allocate portfolios and strip a minister of all cabinet responsibilities but lacked the power to dismiss ministers for poor performance or malfeasance.

As suggested by her minister of finance, Cournoyea collected undated resignation letters from ministers. She viewed this as a way to enhance ministerial accountability in the consensus system and received little pushback from ministers, except for one who complained after leaving cabinet about "having been pressured to sign my undated letter by the other side of the House" (NWT *Hansard*, 22 June 1992, 692). At least one minister declined to sign a letter. It remains unclear whether undated letters of resignation made much difference in terms of either ministerial accountability or cabinet discipline since Cournoyea never used a letter to force a minister's resignation nor did she threaten to do so. No subsequent NWT premier has adopted the practice of holding undated resignation letters.

Second, Cournoyea used the title "premier" rather than "government leader." The latter phrase had been used since the early 1980s with the creation of responsible government. Cournoyea initially told a journalist, only half in jest: "When my [government leader] letterhead runs out, I'll start calling myself premier. So it really depends on how much letterhead Dennis [Patterson, her predecessor as leader] left" (Cournoyea as quoted in Sarkadi 1991). The Assembly subsequently voted to authorize the use of "premier" (NWT *Hansard*, 18 January 1994, 229–31). Cournoyea stated: "Changing the name from Government Leader to Premier did not extend any further powers to my position; it was merely a name change" (NWT *Hansard*, 7 April 1994, 56). Although this may have been true inside the NWT, the change was significant in Canadian politics more broadly. Cournoyea's term in office was marked by notable advances in the status of the territories in national politics. Being referred to as premier and calling herself premier doubtless contributed to these developments.

A far more substantial change that was discussed during Cournoyea's term would have created a presidential-style system of selecting the NWT premier. It did not materialize. Even though the consensus system was in some respects superior to the party-based legislatures of southern Canada and Yukon, the approach had its critics both among MLAs and the general public. Critics argued that the NWT government was accountable to the MLAs but not to the people. At election time, no government defended its record in a bid for re-election since only independent candidates, some of whom had been ministers, were candidates. Concern was also expressed that the NWT cabinet lacked cohesion, direction, and the capacity to make difficult decisions. One way to overcome these and related problems, according to proponents of a presidential-style system, was the direct election of the premier by a territory-wide vote. It is notable that the term "presidential" was not used in debates about this proposal.

MLAs were divided on the idea, which represented a fundamental change to Westminster-style responsible government if not a complete repudiation of it. Some argued that improving accountability and cabinet cohesion was so necessary that it warranted the introduction of a territory-wide vote for the premier. Others were leery not just of concentrating power in the hands of the premier but also of reducing the power of MLAs and risking the arrival of party politics through the direct election of the premier (see Lewis 1994).

Cournoyea understood the objections but favoured the proposal. In her words, "the benefits, such as accountability and stability, would outweigh the objections if the Premier receives a clear mandate from the people in a general election. With some creative thinking, I am sure a process can be found to soften people's concern about a weakened capacity of the Assembly to remove the First Minister or Cabinet" (as quoted in Lewis 1994, C18). The Assembly commissioned a paper on moving to direct election of the premier

(White 1993). This highly contentious proposal lacked sufficient support and proceeded no further.

The issue of the powers of the premier resurfaced towards the end of Cournoyea's term. Prompted by a legislative committee report, the government proposed Bill 28, An Act to Amend the Legislative Assembly and Executive Council Act. It would have given the premier power to revoke a minister's appointment, in the words of the Government House Leader, "should it become necessary to do so for disciplinary purposes" (NWT *Hansard*, 27 April 1995, 1092). Since the committee reviewing the bill concluded that the proposed legislation did not go far enough, the committee chair proposed that the government immediately draft an amendment that would enable the premier to appoint ministers without relying on a secret ballot vote of all MLAs. Although the motion passed, some MLAs expressed serious reservations about the substance of the bill and the process used to enact it. The government House leader offered to delay third reading of the bill but the legislation was not reintroduced (NWT *Hansard*, 27 April 1995, 1092–23).

These various attempts to enhance the premier's powers could be viewed as moving towards a less consensual – and thus less suitable for women – style of politics. Accordingly, Cournoyea's support for them can be interpreted as demonstrating her disinclination to apply a gender lens to the governing process. The possibility of enhancing the premier's powers has since resurfaced in NWT politics but has never come as close to realization as it did in 1995.

A Woman Premier

Cournoyea's actions as a woman premier are best considered in light of the fact that relatively few women have played major roles in territorial politics. Individuals such as Cournoyea, former Nunavut premier Eva Aariak, and former federal MPs and cabinet ministers Ethel Blondin-Andrew and Leona Aglukkaq have held high elected office. Yet the overall numbers of women who became members of territorial assemblies and cabinets remain dismal. When Cournoyea was first elected in 1979, she was the sole female among twenty-two MLAs. For the balance of her time in the NWT Assembly, no more than three of the twenty-four MLAs were women (see White 2013).

Although Cournoyea is reluctant to call herself a feminist because of some negative connotations associated with the term, she has said that she counts herself as a feminist "if it means a woman who is trying to get ahead with all those obstacles" (as quoted in Moore 1993). Given the extensive changes that have transformed the North in her lifetime, she sees women as having different priorities, including in politics, than men. She also views male leaders as often framing important issues differently than women.

Cournoyea held the Status of Women portfolio for most of her time as premier and hired a status of women advisor to oversee policy development. In 1990, when she was in cabinet but not yet premier, she opposed the creation of the NWT Status of Women Council in the belief that the grassroots Native Women's Association of the NWT delivered training for women (through a life skills program) that was more effective – and far less expensive – than what a government bureaucracy could provide. In Cournoyea's words:

> Women particularly found this [program] very fundamental in dealing with the pressures of change. Participants, most with a very limited academic level, found this very important. It dealt with fundamentals of how to move into the work force, alcohol abuse, time and budget issues, which was very important to survive and take advantage of the positive things – like how do grandmothers not get burnt out in dealing with their family members having problems. (personal communication, 6 June 2017)

Consistent with her community-oriented outlook, Cournoyea was concerned that a women's council appointed by the government would undercut local initiative. She worried that a new agency might draw funding away from the successful, grassroots efforts of the Native Women's Association. In political terms, however, Cournoyea was unable to oppose creating the council.[5]

As minister and premier, Cournoyea's approach was not to create specific programs for women, such as initiatives to recruit or promote female civil servants. She saw Northern society as changing so dramatically and so quickly that what was needed, and what she sought, were the best, brightest, and most motivated people for whatever positions were in play. In her words, "we needed everyone." This was in keeping with one of her key principles, which she stated in an interview: "I don't differentiate between people, whether that's men and women or Aboriginal and non-Aboriginal."

Cournoyea was keenly aware that, following the Second World War, traditional men's roles had been vastly transformed in Northern Aboriginal communities. A report entitled *What about the Men?* describes distinctive problems facing Northern Aboriginal men as follows:

Women, too, experience multiple and conflicting roles. However, rites of passage and a key aspect of womanhood in pre-contact times – bearing children – continues to be accessible to most northern Indigenous women whereas the traditional role of hunter and provider is decreasingly access-ible to men due to limited access to and depletion of natural resources ... Also, during the period of most intensive contact and cultural and eco-nomic change in the North (post-Second World War), women across Can-ada were redefining gender roles and this may have created a wider space within which Indigenous women could self-define goals and roles. In con-trast, the primordiality of the hunter-male in northern Indigenous societies and of the working-male in Euro-Canadian society may have left men with less breadth in possible roles, and feeling more trapped between conflicting goals, neither of which they have satisfactory resources to attain ... Men across the North commented on the number of organizations, policies and programs specifically aimed at supporting women. Poignantly, men com-mented, "Women have all these programs. Men have jail." The value on humility and putting others first may have made it harder for men in this context to bring their specific needs to the forefront, resulting in a sense, across Canada's North, that Indigenous men and their needs are invisible. (Tulloch 2015, 13–14)

According to one interviewee, Cournoyea did not emphasize helping women in particular because she saw a pervasive need to respond to every-one's needs and to elevate all people. An important manifestation of this approach was her focus as premier on economic development and job cre-ation. Leaders of women's groups were critical of Cournoyea, however, because they viewed her economic development priorities as advantageous to business interests and as neglecting significant social issues such as alco-holism and spousal assault (Sarkadi 1991).

Cournoyea strongly supported the idea of women becoming involved in politics or any field that appealed to them: "I want them [young women] to be well educated to the point where they can make any choice they want to make" (speaking in Bartlett and Lerose 2004). Women, she believed, needed to prove themselves on the same basis as men so there would be no concerns that they had received positions or promotions just because they were women. Given her emphasis on self-reliance, she maintained that women would succeed in the political arena – as she had – through their own abilities and skills. Still, Cournoyea recognizes that she stands as a role model for women. As she commented towards the end of her political career: "I believe a lot of women look at me and say I have done a lot of things and then translate that for them making it possible to do a lot of things. And I think that's a good thing" (quoted in Thurton 2012).

Although a female first minister's career is not solely assessed in terms of her gender, rarely is gender entirely absent – as it typically is for male premiers. Given that Cournoyea made few specific efforts to promote women in government or to champion "women's issues," gender is infrequently mentioned in assessments of her time in office. Interviewees who were asked to evaluate her actions in office as well as her strengths and weaknesses rarely referred to the fact that she was a woman.[6] Whatever people thought of Cournoyea, they rarely resorted to the stereotypes that so often emerge in discussions of women leaders. This likely reflected Cournoyea's personal characteristics – especially her long-standing reputation as a leader – as well as Dene and Métis social norms, which view women as capable of anything that men are capable of.

Departure from Elected Office

Cournoyea served as premier for four years, the standard period between NWT elections. She describes herself as prepared to step down as premier: "I wasn't that tied to the position; other people could do the job." She says she would have happily stayed on as a minister or an ordinary Assembly member under a different territorial leader.

However, in her words, "I was needed at home." Cournoyea came under considerable pressure to return to the Inuvialuit region to deal with serious problems at the Inuvialuit Regional Corporation, the land claim organization she had helped to establish. She said at the time, "I've been under a great deal of pressure to rebuild the organization and build trust again" (as quoted in Sardi 1995). Given widespread concerns about mismanagement and malfeasance, Cournoyea saw it as her responsibility to step in and revive the IRC. As she reflected, "you can't let something that people worked so hard to build just deteriorate" (speaking in Bartlett and Lerose 2004).

In January 1996, Cournoyea was elected as chair of the IRC. She held that position until 2016, having been re-elected time and again. This was no symbolic sinecure: the IRC is a major player in NWT politics and, through its economic development arms, in the territorial economy. The organization's chair ranks as among the most influential leaders in the region. While Cournoyea's time at the IRC is beyond the scope of this chapter, suffice it to say that she was an active and effective leader both at the local community level and in larger territorial issues such as the Mackenzie Gas Project.

Concluding Thoughts

This chapter presents Nellie Cournoyea as a hard-working premier who accomplished significant successes in leading a consensus-based Northern government through difficult times. The discussion notes that, at a personal level, Nellie Cournoyea remains known for her warm generosity and empathy. As well, it should be pointed out that she has a reputation in communities across the NWT for a well-developed sense of humour and for enjoying a good time – whether a dance, a local feast, or an after-hours party.

Although this chapter offers a positive account of Cournoyea and her time at the helm of the NWT, it acknowledges that she has her critics. If no one disputes her work ethic, integrity, or her capacity to get the job done, not everyone is enamoured of her style. According to one former associate, Cournoyea could deploy a range of tactics: "she can threaten; she can cajole; she can lecture" (Gerry Roy speaking in Bartlett and Lerose 2004).

Former MLA John Todd was quoted earlier as saying that, while Cournoyea could be autocratic, this style was needed at the time. Some observers would agree with the first but not the second part of his assessment. One person interviewed for this project, who asked not to be identified, has known and dealt with Cournoyea since before her time as premier. While respecting her and her record, this individual maintains that "she is a force of nature ... [who] likes to have things her way" and is not keen on listening to opposing viewpoints that she sees as misguided. According to this informant, "arguing with Nellie is not too productive." Other observers say that being on the opposite side of a political issue from Cournoyea can be disconcerting. Although such comments are worth noting, it is fair to ask whether any effective first minister can avoid criticism of this type.

Understanding Nellie Cournoyea's premiership entails recognizing three crucial factors. First, she stands out among Canadian first ministers – male or female – in the extent to which the character traits, abilities, and priorities evidenced by her time in power were determined by her distinct background and upbringing, with its strong Aboriginal cultural underpinning. Indeed, an implicit theme of this chapter is that, in terms of her approaches and accomplishments, Nellie Cournoyea must be considered first and foremost an Aboriginal premier and only secondarily a woman premier.

Second, while Cournoyea's time in public service was devoted to promoting and improving the culture, lifestyle, and economic position of Aboriginal people, she resolutely avoided narratives of "Aboriginals as victims." She remains well aware of the horrors of residential schools, the appropriation of Aboriginal lands, and patterns of discrimination both governmental and societal against Aboriginal people. However, she has consistently operated from the premise that Aboriginal people are strong, resilient, and capable and that public policy must treat them as such.

Finally, the unusual opportunities and constraints of NWT politics – especially but not exclusively those of a consensus government system – shape how she ran her government and contributed to public life. As an Aboriginal woman who remained in close contact with the concerns of local communities across the NWT, Cournoyea saw herself as serving the many diverse constituencies that brought her to elective office. For that reason, she was particularly well suited to finding common ground in a political system that operated according to different norms from those in most other parts of Canada.

Nellie Cournoyea's term as premier of the Northwest Territories was not marked by extensive gains for women in the public sphere, whether measured by major gender-based policy initiatives, recruitment and promotion of women in the senior civil service, or spikes in the number of women holding cabinet posts or running for election to the Legislative Assembly. In fact, the 1995 territorial election at the end of her term saw proportionately fewer women – 13 percent – come forward as candidates than had been the case in the previous election, when women formed 18 percent of territorial nominees (White 2013, 236). The absence of parties under consensus government meant that Cournoyea had little influence over the number of women ministers or candidates.

As premier, however, she could have pushed a political agenda with policies favourable to women, including in the composition of the senior bureaucracy. That she did not do so reflected her views that (1) women did not need special treatment in order to succeed in the public sector or elsewhere and that (2) her responsibility as premier was to work towards a society in which all citizens – men and women, Aboriginal and non-Aboriginal – could realize their potential. Although Aboriginal issues were of great importance to her, Cournoyea's approach to politics and policy did not assign higher priority to them than to gender issues; rather, she saw them as inextricably bound together. That said, Cournoyea unquestionably had a positive influence on women, especially Aboriginal women in the NWT and elsewhere. She demonstrated that women could dominate the normally male preserve of politics and contribute to the public good. Moreover, her career was notable for confirming that it was entirely possible for women to be tough, forceful leaders while engaging in the sort of consensual, low-ego politics more commonly practised by women than by men.

Acknowledgments

I wish to thank those who helped with this project, most notably Nellie Cournoyea. All quotations and paraphrases from her in this chapter that are not otherwise referenced are taken from telephone interviews conducted on 11 April 2017 and 15 May 2017. Thanks also to Stephen Kakfwi, Pierre Alvarez, and Bernie Hughes, who agreed to on-the-record interviews. Quotations and paraphrases from them not otherwise referenced are taken from telephone interviews (Kakfwi – 21 April 2017; Alvarez – 23 March 2017; Hughes – 28 March 2017). Thanks also to interviewees who offered their comments anonymously. Finally, I thank the ever-sage Frances Abele for her comments on an earlier draft and Sylvia Bashevkin for conceiving and realizing this project and for her stimulating comments on an earlier draft.

Notes

1 For an official but unvarnished account of consensus government, see http://www. assembly.gov.nt.ca/visitors/what-consensus. For an analysis of consensus government when Cournoyea was an MLA, see White (1991).

2 Although consensus government may be unconventional in that it operates without political parties, the practices followed in Canada's Northern territories do follow the tenets of British responsible government, whereby the government – that is, the cabinet – gains and retains the authority to govern by maintaining the confidence of the House through winning important votes. Familiar Westminster principles, such as collective and individual ministerial responsibility, cabinet solidarity, and prohibitions against non-cabinet MLAs introducing budget bills, are every bit in evidence in the NWT Assembly as they are in the House of Commons.

3 One minister resigned after sending an inappropriate note, which could have been read as a threat, to another MLA; one resigned because of the pressures of ministerial life; one resigned when it seemed likely that he would be removed by vote of the Assembly; and one resigned when it came to light that he had lied to Cournoyea and to the Assembly about his ministerial activities. Of the five ministers chosen to fill cabinet vacancies during Cournoyea's term, one resigned after being charged with sexual assault and one, who had not signed an undated letter of resignation, resigned after it came to light that she had attended a party in her legally "dry" home community at which people were consuming alcohol. Cournoyea did not force any minister to leave cabinet, but, in one case, she found it necessary to convince a minister in an untenable position that resignation was the only option.

4 Cournoyea had obtained undated letters of resignation from her ministers and thus, unusually for a NWT premier, was in a position to dismiss ministers had she wished.

5 Another potential explanation not cited by Cournoyea involves the likelihood that non-Native bureaucrats would fail to understand social problems – and solutions – that faced Aboriginal women in Northern communities.

6 This is, to be sure, a highly impressionistic statement. It is primarily based on the author's close observation of NWT politics during Cournoyea's term as premier, much of it in person, buttressed by the views of informants who were deeply involved with NWT politics in those years.

References

Alunik, Iashmael, Eddie D. Kolausok, and David Morrison. 2003. *Across Time and Tundra: The Inuvialuit of the Western Arctic.* Vancouver: Raincoast Books.

Anselmi, Elaine. 2016. "The Leader." *Up Here* (magazine), December. https://uphere. ca/articles/leader.

Bartlett, Sharon, and Maria Lerose. 2004. *Better Ask Nellie: The Life and Times of Nellie Cournoyea* (film). Vancouver: Force Four Entertainment.

Cournoyea, Nellie Cournoyea. 2014. "Adaptation and Resilience: The Inuvialuit Story." *Northern Public Affairs.* Special Issue. http://www.northernpublicaffairs. ca/index/volume-2-special-issue-revitalizing-education-in-inuit-nunangat/ adaptation-resilience-the-inuvialuit-story/.

Dickie, Bonnie. 1992. "Just Call Her Nellie: Our Top Politician's Down to Earth Style Goes Clear through to Bedrock." *Up Here* (magazine), June/July, 26–40.

Hicks, Jack, and Graham White. 2015. *Made in Nunavut: An Experiment in Decentralized Government.* Vancouver: UBC Press.

Inuvialuit Regional Corporation. 2009. *COPE: An Original Voice for Inuvialuit Rights.* Inuvik.

Kirkpatrick, Jeane J. 1974. *Political Woman.* New York: Basic.

Lewis, Brian, MLA. 1994. "Choosing a Premier Responsible to the Northwest Territories House or its people?" *The Parliamentarian* 75, 3: C16–18.

–. 1998. "The Development of Responsible Government in the Northwest Territories 1976–1998." *Canadian Parliamentary Review* 21, 2: 12–17.

Moore, Micki. 1993. "Nellie of the North." *Sunday Sun,* 10 January.

Northwest Territories, Legislative Assembly, Territorial Leadership Committee. 1991. Transcript, 12 November.

Sardi, Liza. 1995. "Nellie Bows Out." *Yellowknifer,* 30 August.

Sarkadi, Laurie. 1991. "Meet Canada's Newest 'Premier.'" *Edmonton Journal,* 14 December.

Selleck, Lee, and Francis Thompson. 1997. *Dying for Gold: The True Story of the Giant Mine Murders.* Toronto: HarperCollins.

Thurton, David. 2012. "End of an Era for Nellie Cournoyea, the 'Iron Lady' of the North." *CBC News,* 16 January. http://www.cbc.ca/news/canada/north/iron-lady -of-north-nellie-cournoyea-1.3407161.

Tulloch, Shelley. 2015. *What About the Men? Northern Men's Research Project.* Cambridge Bay, Nunavut: Ilitaqsiniq – Nunavut Literacy Council.

White, Graham. 1991. "Westminster in the Arctic: The Adaptation of British Par-
    liamentarism in the Legislative Assembly of the Northwest Territories." *Canadian
    Journal of Political Science* 24: 499–523.

–. 1993. "Consequences of Electing the Government Leader of the Northwest
    Territories," paper prepared for the Strategic Planning Session of the Legislative
    Assembly of the Northwest Territories, Cambridge Bay, NWT, October.

–. 1998. *Breaking the Trail to Northern Community Empowerment: The Community
    Transfer Initiative in Cape Dorset.* Toronto: Centre for Urban and Community
    Studies.

–. 2013. "In the Presence of Northern Aboriginal Women? Women in Territorial
    Politics." In *Stalled: The Representation of Women in Canadian Governments*, ed.
    Linda Trimble, Jane Arscott, and Manon Tremblay, 233–52. Vancouver: UBC
    Press.

3

Pat Duncan, Yukon's Accidental Premier

MAURA FORREST

For her thirtieth birthday, Pat Duncan received a gift from former Yukon territorial politician and Whitehorse mayor Flo Whyard. It was a T-shirt printed with the following phrase that is widely, though erroneously, thought to have appeared in Canadian legislation around the turn of the twentieth century: "no woman, idiot, lunatic or criminal shall vote." In fact, the quote likely originated with prominent Canadian suffragist Nellie McClung, who declared in a speech in 1915 that it was the law of the land. Though those exact words may never have appeared in any Canadian statute, Duncan has kept the shirt as a reminder of how things have changed for women in politics over the last century.

Pat Duncan was Yukon's lone female premier, leading the territory for about twenty-nine months between spring 2000 and fall 2002. Hers was the only Liberal government the territory had seen until the party returned to office many years later – in November 2016 under a different leader, Sandy Silver. Trimble and Arscott (2003, 90, 75) refer to Duncan as a rare female leader who "staged a come-from-behind victory" and note that Duncan was the first Canadian woman to "win an election in which competing parties were led by men."

Duncan's Liberals won an unexpected majority at a turbulent time: the territory's economy was in a serious downturn, the government proved unable to change the fiscal tide, and Duncan faced accusations of incompetence and heavy-handedness. Once three Liberal MLAs defected to sit as independents, Duncan called an early election. Her party suffered a devastating defeat, and Duncan became the only Liberal to retain a seat in the legislature. Despite her early success, Duncan did not escape what Trimble and Arscott (2003, 71) refer to as a "revolving door" for female political leaders in Canada.

In analyzing Pat Duncan and the fate of her government, it is important to note that many major political positions in the territory were filled by women in 2000. Not only was Duncan the premier but Ione Christensen was Yukon's lone federal senator. Louise Hardy was the territory's federal member of Parliament. Judy Gingell served as commissioner, the territorial equivalent of lieutenant-governor. Kathy Watson held office as mayor of Whitehorse, the territory's capital. Many of Yukon's First Nations chiefs were also women.

Consistent with Chapter 1's discussion of frontier societies, long-time Yukoners view this pattern as no coincidence. Christensen believes the territory's frontier culture was such that people were judged more for their abilities than their gender. "When somebody was willing to do something, it didn't matter whether they were male or female," she said. "I guess people look at you and see what you've done and see how people feel about what you've done" (Ione Christensen, telephone interview with author, 1 August 2017). Shortly after Duncan's election, former Yukon MLA Joyce Hayden made a similar point in an interview with the *Globe and Mail*: "There's not as much sexism in the north as there is in some of the older provinces down south. That old image of the macho male who rules the roost has fallen by the wayside" (Mickleburgh 2000). Duncan herself says the same thing: "I think there's always been the view, certainly when I was growing up, and throughout my time in Yukon, that it's not about your gender, it's not about where you're from, it's not about your race, it's about can you do the job?" (Pat Duncan, telephone interview with author, 12 May 2017 [hereafter Duncan interview 2017]).

Yet Duncan and many of those around her also believe her government was significantly hampered by sexist attitudes. Parallel with Chapter 1's discussion of how women in powerful roles are viewed, some observers believe Duncan might not have suffered the same political fate had she been a man. Evidence presented in this chapter supports this view, showing how women politicians in Yukon were treated differently than men, notably when inappropriate, gendered comments were made in the legislature during Duncan's time in office.

As premier, Duncan appointed the first gender-balanced cabinet in Canadian history. She claims this action was not intentional but, rather, was the result of including the most experienced Liberal MLAs in cabinet – many of them women. In fact, she denies ever having deliberately sought female candidates for the political executive or for legislative office (Duncan interview 2017).

At the same time, Duncan was very aware of the obstacles facing women in politics. She chose to run for the Liberals instead of the right-wing Yukon Party even though her own background was in the Progressive Conservative organization. She felt the Yukon Party was not welcoming towards women like herself (Duncan interview 2017). In short, while Duncan and other female leaders tend to dismiss gender as a factor in Yukon politics, they also recognize that being a woman has a major impact on the fortunes of female politicians.

This chapter first reviews the political context in which Pat Duncan came to power. It then summarizes Duncan's background and entry into politics, her policy priorities, the tenor of debate in the Legislative Assembly during her tenure, and her appointments to cabinet and the senior bureaucracy. The main conclusions are as follows: while Duncan's time in office was undoubtedly influenced by her gender, there is little evidence to suggest that her policy priorities were guided by feminist social movements. Moreover, her leadership of Canada's first gender-balanced cabinet did not appear to make the tone in the legislature any more collaborative or less aggressive.

Context

The fate of Duncan's government cannot be solely attributed to her gender. The Liberals were a largely unknown quantity in Yukon before 2000, when they generally held third-party status in the legislature. Power typically moved back and forth between the Progressive Conservatives (later the Yukon Party) and the NDP. Duncan's victory was widely seen as a repudiation of those major parties and not necessarily as an indication of any newfound faith in the Liberals. As political scientist Linda Trimble (2004) commented in the *Edmonton Journal*, "The parties women lead are typically in such dire shape their political resuscitation necessitates electoral miracles." As a pioneering party leader without cabinet service let alone political executive leadership of her own, it is not surprising that Duncan confronted serious challenges as premier. With a deteriorating economic situation in 2000 and following, her Liberals faced waning public support and no obvious reservoir of experience on which to draw in order to address the territory's woes.

One reason the Liberals have often been marginalized in Yukon politics follows from there being similarities among all the territory's parties. As an editorial in the *Yukon News* once put it: "Right, left and centre has been churned together into three Neapolitan confections. You can't tell one party from the other from a distance" (Mostyn 2002a). White (2016, 201) contends that Yukon MLAs frequently defect or move between parties because of their "strong personalities and independence of spirit." Before running for the Liberals, Duncan had been a staunch Progressive Conservative. Her successor as premier, Dennis Fentie, defected from the NDP to become leader of the Yukon Party. With so little distance between left and right, the Liberals seemed to occupy an invisible space in the middle.

Party boundaries in Yukon are fluid because most campaigning takes place door-to-door. Many candidates are elected simply because they are recognized in their communities rather than because they or their parties hold a particular political ideology. In addition, the vast majority of Yukon's budget comes from an annual transfer payment from the federal government, meaning the options for diversifying the territorial economy are relatively limited. It is also worth noting that, in 2000, the territory had only had a partisan political system for twenty-two years.

Yukon is unique among Canada's territories for its party-based political system. While the Northwest Territories and Nunavut continue to govern by consensus, Yukon adopted partisan politics in 1978. Yukon also has the largest non-Indigenous population of the three territories. Indigenous people account for about a quarter of Yukon's population, compared with about 50 percent in the Northwest Territories and 86 percent in Nunavut.

Regardless of the fact that many Yukon politicians shift party affiliations during the course of their careers, the tone of legislative debate cannot be described as compromising or consensual. Before, during, and after Pat Duncan served as premier, the tenor of debate in the Yukon Legislative Assembly was often highly aggressive. Several years after her party lost power in 2002, Duncan (as quoted in Skikavich 2005) described the climate of discussion as "nasty and divisive."

The percentage of Yukon MLAs who are female has grown slowly since 1978. Before 2011, women rarely accounted for more than 20 percent of elected representatives. During Duncan's time as premier, the five women

MLAs constituted a record 29 percent of the legislature. In 2011, six out of nineteen MLAs were women, or about 32 percent. The results of the 2016 election set a new record such that 37 percent of Yukon MLAs (seven out of nineteen) were women (see Figures 3.1 to 3.4 at end of chapter for numbers and percentages of female MLAs and candidates in the Yukon legislature from 1978 to 2016).

Yukon's strong tradition of female political leaders has not translated into gender parity in politics more broadly. White (2013) explains the prominence of women leaders in Yukon as compared to in Canada generally: while, as of 2013, only six women had led Canadian parties to electoral victory, one-third (two) of them were from Yukon. They were Hilda Watson, who led the territorial PCs to victory in 1978 but lost her own seat, and Pat Duncan in 2000. Moreover, of the ten women who had been first ministers in Canada by 2013, roughly a third of them led territories: Duncan in Yukon, Nellie Cournoyea in the NWT, and Eva Aariak in Nunavut. But in what White (2013, 243) describes as a paradox, "these notable successes at the highest level of territorial politics stand in sharp contrast to the low overall rate of women holding elected office in the territories."

Background

Patricia Jane Duncan was born in 1960 in Edmonton, the youngest of five siblings. She moved to Yukon with her family when she was four years old. Duncan was raised in Whitehorse and spent most of her life in the territory. This strong local background is an important consideration for many voters in a Northern jurisdiction, where credibility as a politician often has more to do with one's presence in the local community than it does with political experience.

Duncan's father was a public servant in the territorial government, where he worked on the Yukon Hospital Insurance Services program and was eventually promoted to the position of deputy minister of health. Duncan credits him with cultivating her sense of fiscal responsibility. He taught her, she says, that "you spend the taxpayers' last nickel as if it was your own ... You don't spend money foolishly, you don't waste money, and you really have to have value for what you're spending of the taxpayers' money. It has to contribute to the community. It has to build the community" (Duncan interview 2017).

Duncan earned an undergraduate political science degree in 1983 from Carleton University. She returned to Yukon and began working as a researcher for the territory's Department of Education, but soon got involved in politics. The federal Progressive Conservatives governed at the time. Her initial role was in the 1984 campaign organization of Yukon's long-time Progressive Conservative MP Erik Nielsen. Duncan did advance work, making arrangements for Nielsen's visits around the territory and sometimes travelling with him. Nielsen, Duncan reports, was "very aware of the role of women in politics and how important they were." When she referred to herself as an "advance man," he would correct her, calling her an "advance person" (Duncan interview 2017).

Once Brian Mulroney's Progressive Conservatives formed a majority government in Ottawa, Nielsen became deputy prime minister. He asked Duncan to move to Ottawa to work as his special assistant for constituency affairs. She accepted and moved to the federal capital for two years. This was the last significant period of time that Duncan would spend outside the territory.[1]

When she returned to Whitehorse, Duncan was unable to find work. As in any small jurisdiction when there is a change of government, people who are tied too closely to the former governing party find themselves out of favour. The territorial NDP had unseated the Progressive Conservatives in 1985. Duncan recalls that, on her return from Ottawa, she had no chance of a job with the Yukon government: "There was no way. And not because I didn't want to" find public-sector work (Duncan interview 2017).

Instead, she worked briefly on the 1989 territorial election campaign of Peter Jenkins, the Progressive Conservative candidate for Dawson City. Jenkins, who later became one of Duncan's most vocal opponents, failed to win his seat. In 1990, Duncan was hired as manager of the Whitehorse Chamber of Commerce. She remained in that position until 1994, and she used it to build her credibility among local businesspeople.

Duncan says that during her time at the Chamber of Commerce, she was approached to contest the Whitehorse mayoralty but decided against it. As the 1992 election approached, John Ostashek, the leader of what had been the PC organization, asked her to run at the territorial level. As head of what was now the Yukon Party, Ostashek claimed Duncan refused because of a disagreement over which constituency she would contest (Small 2001f). Duncan recalls the situation differently: "I didn't want to run for John Ostashek's government or the Yukon Party because I felt and still feel that there was no room for women's voices at their table ... And I just felt very strongly that you need balance at the cabinet table. You need to have people who know what it costs for a box of formula or a bag of diapers or a grocery bill" (Duncan interview 2017).

Before the next election in 1996, Ken Taylor approached her as leader of the territorial Liberals. The party at that point had never won power in Yukon and held only one seat in the legislature. Still, Duncan was impressed by his pitch. In her words, "It was an inclusive picture, and ... he heard what I had to say. He thought that there was a role for [all] people, and a future for Yukon. And just having had a daughter, it was really important to me" (Duncan interview 2017). Duncan agreed to run for the Liberals and, soon afterwards, learned she was pregnant with her second child. As events turned out, the writ for the territorial election was dropped three days after her son was born. So began the decade Duncan spent as a Yukon politician.

First Election

Duncan ran as a Liberal candidate in Porter Creek South, a suburban riding in Whitehorse near where she lived with her husband and two children. During the campaign she left her baby with her mother-in-law in the evenings. This meant she could chat with voters on their doorsteps, where Yukon elections are won and lost. As one *National Post* columnist noted, there was "only one polling firm in the Yukon and ... no televised ads for politicians. Campaigning is traditionally conducted door to door" (Vincent 2001).

The fact that Duncan had just given birth was not lost on voters, and it presented an opportunity her opponents could exploit. Jason Cunning, who later became Duncan's principal secretary, remembers Yukon Party canvassers in Porter Creek telling voters, "Isn't it great that she's out here while her small kid's at home?" For Cunning, the comment implied that opponents believed Duncan should be at home with her child. "It was subtle, but it was there," he recalls (Jason Cunning, telephone interview with author, 17 May 2017 [hereafter Cunning interview 2017]).

Duncan was aware of the same messages. She remembers an exchange on a doorstep with one woman voter who asked about Duncan's child. Duncan reminded her that former Yukon premier Tony Penikett had been out campaigning within days of the birth of his own twins. According to Duncan, "that woman stepped back ... and she said, 'You know what? I'm so sorry. I have been a lifelong feminist'" (Duncan interview 2017).

In the territorial election of September 1996, Duncan won her seat. While the father-daughter team of Jack Cable and Sue Edelman was also successful, leader Ken Taylor failed to win his riding. Having secured three seats out of seventeen, the Liberals could claim their best showing ever – although some observers had expected a closer race (Canadian Press 1996a).

The same election saw the defeat of the Yukon Party and brought to power the territorial NDP under Piers McDonald. The NDP initially won ten seats to form a majority government, and it quickly gained an eleventh when an election official broke a tie between NDP and Yukon Party candidates in Vuntut Gwitchin in northern Yukon by drawing a name from a hat (Canadian Press 1996b). Since the draw reduced the Yukon Party to three seats, a debate ensued as to whether that party or the Liberals would form the official opposition. While the Liberals suggested the two parties share that status, the Yukon Party rejected the idea (Canadian Press Newswire 1996a). The speaker in the legislature named the Yukon Party as the official opposition on the basis that it had formed the government prior to the election (Canadian Press Newswire 1996b).

On election night, Taylor announced that he planned to resign as Liberal leader. Yet supporters encouraged him to reconsider and, by December 1996, he said he intended to lead the party in the next election. Within nine months, Taylor had changed his mind again and announced his resignation (Canadian Press Newswire 1997a).

Taylor asked Duncan to succeed him as leader. As Duncan recalls, "I didn't have the ambition. I didn't set out to do this," but she remembered a saying Erik Nielsen had once told her: "Opportunity only knocks once" (Duncan interview 2017). Given that no other candidate stepped forward, Duncan was acclaimed as leader of the Yukon Liberals on 17 November 1997 (Canadian Press Newswire 1997b). She thus became the second woman to lead a political party in the territory, following former PC leader Hilda Watson.

Duncan's major challenges as leader were renewing the party, recruiting candidates for the next election, and garnering public attention. As she explains: "You can't just show up at the legislature and expect that the media will come to you and ask for opinions. You've got to be asserting yourself, putting yourself out there and building the party" (Duncan interview 2017). The Liberals leapt forward in October 1999, when Pam Buckway won a by-election in the rural constituency of Lake Laberge after the former NDP MLA resigned (Canadian Press Newswire 1999). Her win catapulted the Liberals from third party to official opposition status. The change brought with it not only more attention for Duncan and her colleagues but also greater scrutiny and criticism from their political opponents.

The economy formed the highest profile issue at the time in Yukon. The Faro Mine, once the largest open pit lead-zinc mine in the world, closed for the last time in February 1998. Global commodity prices declined to the point that gold fell below US$300 an ounce – the lowest it had been since the 1970s (Kitco 2017). These patterns constituted very bad news for a jurisdiction that was highly dependent on mineral resources. Families moved away as work opportunities evaporated (Tobin 2000a).

As opposition leader, Duncan promised to challenge the NDP government on its plan to fix the economy. She believed the strengthened Liberal presence in the legislature would make the tenor of debate less acrimonious since her party had never been a governing party in Yukon and had a less hostile history with the NDP than did the Yukon Party (Small 1999a). Yet NDP MLAs were quick to go on the offensive, attacking the Liberals for criticizing the government without presenting innovative economic ideas of their own. Duncan insisted that if the NDP wanted to know the Liberals' plan to revive the economy, then the premier should call an election (Small 1999c).

One particular legislative exchange made headlines. NDP tourism minister Dave Keenan responded, using extremely stereotypic imagery, to a question Duncan posed about how he was handling consultations on a tourism strategy. In Keenan's words, "This is not a little hen session around a coffee table, my dear." Keenan later apologized publicly for the remark, "to the legislature and women in general" (Small 1999b).

In February 2000, Duncan introduced a legislative motion to open debate on a possible pipeline along the Alaska Highway that would carry natural gas from Alaska's Prudhoe Bay to the continental United States. The plan had been in gestation for decades but was being seriously considered at this point by Alberta-based Foothills Pipe Lines Ltd., which owned exclusive rights to build the Canadian portion of the line. Duncan wanted to see the pipeline built before the Northwest Territories constructed its own line south through the Mackenzie Valley (Small 2000a). Her enthusiasm for the project as opposition leader presaged her focus as premier on the pipeline as the solution to Yukon's economic woes. As of this writing, the pipeline has not been built.

The NDP government used the opportunity to attack Duncan and her former connection to the Progressive Conservatives, saying the two parties were "joined at the hip" (*Whitehorse Daily Star* 2000a). Shortly thereafter, in March 2000, Government Leader Piers McDonald called an election for mid-April (Small 2000b).

Becoming Premier

By many accounts, the Liberals' election victory in 2000 was more a result of frustration with the NDP and the Yukon Party than a vote of confidence for Duncan and her party (Canadian Press 2000a). The territorial economy had not improved under the NDP; in fact, reports suggested that twenty-five hundred people had moved away under their watch (*Whitehorse Daily Star* 2000b). The Yukon Party had not sufficiently recovered from losing to the NDP in 1996 to be a credible alternative. This scenario left only the Liberals, a party that had never governed in Yukon and had mostly been relegated to third-party status in the legislature. "I don't know that voters were overwhelmed with the Liberals. There were three options, and that was the best one," said Jason Cunning, who became Duncan's principal secretary (Cunning interview 2017).

Duncan was widely criticized for not presenting platform specifics during the election campaign (Small 2000c; Small 2000d; Mostyn 2000). She promised to kick-start the territory's economy and mining industry by finalizing a devolution agreement with the federal government under the terms of a proposed accord that would see the territory gain more control over its natural resources. She also promised to complete land claim agreements with several Yukon First Nations, a move that was seen as offering greater certainty for mining companies. Aside from Yukon Party leader John Ostashek's view that land claims should be prioritized over devolution, few differences characterized the Liberal, NDP, and Yukon Party approaches to economic development. Duncan also promised a 20 percent increase to the Yukon grant, a postsecondary education subsidy for Yukon students (Duncan 2000a).

Despite public disenchantment with the NDP, few observers expected the Liberals to win the 2000 Yukon election – let alone secure a majority government. On election day, one newspaper article began by predicting the NDP would return to power (Mostyn 2000). Even Duncan was unprepared for the results. In her words: "I had hoped, definitely, that we were going to win, but was there a transition team plan in place well in advance of the final election day? No, no. We weren't that sophisticated at the time" (Duncan interview 2017).

On the night the Liberals carried ten of the territory's seventeen seats, Duncan delivered her victory speech. "It's a great night to be a Liberal," she said. "I feel like it's Game 7 of the Stanley Cup finals and I feel we've just gone through double overtime" (Small 2000e). Her party won every seat in Whitehorse and two in areas just outside the capital city. Every rural constituency went to the opposition parties, with the result that the NDP won six seats and the Yukon Party held a single riding in Dawson City. Observers were quick to note the urban-rural divide. One columnist described it as a "glaring schism," a "yawning chasm," and an "unhealthy development" (*White-horse Daily Star* 2000b).

Duncan stood out as the only party leader to win re-election in her home constituency. John Ostashek and Piers McDonald both lost to Liberal new-comers, and Ostashek resigned immediately (Small 2000e). Duncan became one of four women in the Liberal caucus – a record high in the Yukon legis-lature. Duncan claims, however, that she never deliberately sought women to run for office. In her words: "It was a matter of the folks who came to the fore, that we knew, that we worked with, and that were ultimately able to get elected. It was the way it worked out" (Duncan interview 2017). One colum-nist observed that it was encouraging to see a number of women elected "in a campaign where women's issues were woefully underplayed" (*Whitehorse Daily Star* 2000b). Still, the win wasn't without its small indignities, includ-ing a *Globe and Mail* article that repeatedly referred to the new leader as "Mr. Duncan" (Canadian Press 2000b).

Policy Impact

Duncan's Liberals came to power with not just enormous expectations that they would improve Yukon's flagging economy but also with a dearth of creative ideas about how to reach that goal. Given this singular focus on the territorial economy, the situation with respect to women's issues resembled what had evolved during the 1990s in the NWT under Premier Nellie Cournoyea (see Chapter 2). As in the case of the NWT, little evidence sug-gests that the Yukon Liberals under a female leader paid particular attention to issues emphasized by feminist social movements, including child care, poverty, and violence against women.

The Liberals began by passing a budget that had been tabled before the election by the previous NDP government. The new government added a promised 20 percent increase in the Yukon grant for postsecondary stu-dents. The decision not to craft a new Liberal budget was made, Duncan said at the time, to cause "as little disruption as possible to the economy and government operations" (Tobin 2000b).

As Yukon premier, Duncan remained a fierce champion of the Alaska Highway natural gas pipeline. She advocated the project during meetings across the country, including with the federal government in Ottawa. NWT premier Stephen Kakfwi pressed for a pipeline along the Mackenzie Valley at the same time. Even as media reports pointed to a rift between Kakfwi and Duncan over the issue, Duncan insisted that both pipelines could proceed. She simply wanted the Alaska Highway project built first

(Duffy 2001). In July 2001, Prime Minister Jean Chrétien said he favoured the Mackenzie Valley route, and, a month later, natural gas producers in Alaska suggested neither project was economically viable (Scoffield and Nguyen 2001; Small 2001e). Thereafter, the Yukon Liberals were roundly criticized for, in the words of one MLA, having put "all their eggs in the pipeline basket" (Small 2002i).

Duncan's government faced additional criticism for its handling of other dossiers. The aim of the controversial Yukon Protected Areas Strategy, introduced by the former NDP government, was to limit development in parts of all twenty-three of the territory's ecosystems. The plan faced serious trouble before the Liberals took office. In 1999, industry leaders withdrew support for the strategy after the first protected area was set aside. They claimed not enough had been done to keep areas of high mineral potential open for development. The Liberals supported the plan, however, and promised to bring industry back to the table. But, despite Duncan's connections to the business community from her time at the Whitehorse Chamber of Commerce, she was unable to restore faith in the project. In February 2001, seven industry groups walked out of a meeting that the government had arranged (Tobin 2001). The Liberals accomplished little else on the file, and the strategy died after the Yukon Party won power in 2002 (Tobin 2003). Jason Cunning, Duncan's principal secretary as premier, reflects as follows: "I think we miscalculated how much of a bogeyman it had become for the industry and for investors" (Cunning interview 2017).

Parallel with Cournoyea's accomplishments on intergovernmental affairs and land claim matters, Duncan was effective with respect to both the devolution and land claim files. As in the NWT, these issues were seen as important for the economic development of Yukon. The formal devolution of power from the federal government to Yukon only took effect on 1 April 2003, after the Liberals were back in opposition, but much of the final work was completed under Duncan's watch (*Whitehorse Daily Star* 2003). The Devolution Transfer Agreement set out the transfer of land and resource management responsibilities to the territory; Duncan signed it in October 2001 (Small 2001h).

As territorial premier, Duncan also concluded a land claim settlement in January 2002 with the Ta'an Kwach'an Council, one of two First Nations in Whitehorse and the eighth Yukon First Nation to sign a final agreement. In Cunning's words, "I like to think when the history books are written that she gets some credit for [those] two pretty significant accomplishments during her term" (Cunning interview 2017). The Liberals also signed memoranda of understanding with four other Yukon First Nations in April 2002, agreeing to complete negotiations and prepare their settlements for ratification (Tobin 2002). However, only three of those four bands have successfully signed final agreements to date.

In her second year as premier, Duncan decided to restructure parts of the Yukon government so that institutions would be in place for the anticipated devolution. This renewal project, as it came to be known, turned out to be politically disastrous. As a large part of the Yukon electorate, government employees are a powerful group. They grew concerned that jobs would be eliminated, and Duncan herself conceded that some positions might be cut (Small 2001d).

As part of the renewal project, Duncan replaced five existing departments with new ones. She eliminated the Women's Directorate as an independent department and absorbed it into the Executive Council Office – a move that drew withering criticism. At the time, Sue Edelman was the cabinet minister responsible for the directorate. As one columnist commented, "It is absolutely startling that the directorate survived the reigns of such right-of-centre ministers as John Ostashek and Doug Phillips, yet was slain by a female premier while headed by a female sponsoring minister, Sue Edelman" (*Whitehorse Daily Star* 2001b).

In addition to Duncan's decision to eliminate the directorate, Edelman courted controversy in the same area. In March 2002, Edelman sent an e-mail to cabinet staff that was titled "women's movement dying." The text, which was later made public, read in part as follows:

> I don't know when I started noticing that the mainstream women's groups were disappearing and that the femi-nazis who have very narrow points of view about most issues – suddenly got the right to say that because I disagreed with them – then I was no longer a feminist – because I disagreed with their radical point of view – I no longer was interested in women's equality ... Perhaps the feminism of my mother's time ... is outdated or not needed anymore. (Small 2002e)

Amidst accusations that her comments reflected a negative attitude towards women on the part of the Liberal government, Edelman resigned her ministerial position (Small 2002f).

This controversy reinforced older claims that Duncan's government was ignoring files of particular concern to women. In 2000, the Liberals held back funds for a number of budget initiatives, including one to build a new

school in Mayo (one of Yukon's smaller communities), one to purchase a
new CT scanner for the Whitehorse General Hospital, and one to raise social assistance payments (Small 2000i). When Duncan's government tabled
its own budget in 2001, the Yukon Anti-Poverty Coalition accused the
Liberals of not spending enough to address social issues like poverty and
substance use, even though the budget increased funding for women's shelters (Hale 2001). The government seemed to create headlines for critics
when it announced that the Whitehorse Public Library would be closed on
Friday evenings and Sundays, a move that was quickly reversed after public
outcry. By the time of the 2002 election, the Liberals again faced criticism
for their lack of progress on poverty, social assistance, and child care programs (Small 2001a; Small 2002j).

Nevertheless, Duncan introduced some policy changes that were particularly important to women. In her first year as premier, she helped to
negotiate an increase in the federal health and social transfer payment to
provinces and territories, which included funding for early childhood development (Small 2000g). She eliminated evening legislative sessions, which
had run from 7:00 p.m. to 9:00 p.m. on Mondays and Wednesdays, in part
because they were a challenge for MLAs with young children (Skikavich
2006a). And she tried to ensure the reconstruction of the Grey Mountain
Primary School in Whitehorse. That intervention likely contributed to her
downfall in 2002 as opposition parties claimed the construction costs were
not justifiable (Small 2002h).

In general, Duncan's government did not stand out for generous spending on social policy. Looking back, Duncan says she was hamstrung by the
territory's fiscal situation and often hadn't been able to spend money where
she had wanted to: "The finances were our biggest issue, and there was no
money when we were in government. No money" (Duncan interview 2017).

Tone in the Legislature

What is perhaps most noteworthy about Duncan's time in government is
the negative tenor of legislative debate during her two and a half years as
premier as well as the infighting in her party, which eventually led to the
defection of three Liberal MLAs. Though Trimble (1997, 145) suggests female politicians tend towards a more cooperative approach than their male
counterparts, little evidence supports that theory in this case. Duncan herself may have believed that women would alter the climate of political discussion. In *Yukon's Women of Power*, published before Duncan became
premier, former Yukon MLA Joyce Hayden (1999, 633) writes: "[Duncan]

believes that most women do their homework, work harder and are better team players than men." She then quotes Duncan as stating: "As Sue Edelman sometimes says, we're all legislators. Ultimately, we're all in there for the same reason. I believe that women just work differently" (Duncan as quoted in Hayden 1999, 634).

In Hayden (1999, 634), Duncan offers an example of working cooperatively with another woman on the Girl Guides council. According to Duncan, the two collaborated well despite their divergent political outlooks: "I see that kind of atmosphere being fostered when there are more women present in any organization. The high testosterone level in our Legislative Assembly gets to me at times."

The tenor of the Yukon Legislative Assembly was divisive before Duncan's Liberal government took over, as evidenced by her stated desire to improve the tone after her party became the official opposition in 1999 (Small 1999a). Yet little headway was made despite Duncan's personal beliefs about how well women work together. Part of the problem rested in persistent male comments that diminished women's contributions, including the infamous "hen session" remark by NDP cabinet minister Dave Keenan in 1999, for which he apologized later the same day (Small 1999b).

Shortly after Duncan became premier, NDP leader Trevor Harding said: "Oh, I see the premier rolling her eyes. She loves to do that. She bats her eyes and sniffs everything off and taunts across the floor, 'We won, you lost; we won, you lost,' as she gloats about the election results." One week later, NDP MLA Dennis Fentie highlighted a trip Duncan was planning to take. In his words: "Well, we hope that the premier's trip to Calgary and Vancouver is a trip to aggressively promote the Yukon, and not just a chance to showcase a wardrobe. We expected that that's what she'd be doing" (Tenove 2000).

Perhaps the most egregious example of sexist male taunting was voiced by Yukon Party leader Peter Jenkins, his party's lone representative in the legislature. In July 2000, when Duncan refused to consider a suggestion from Jenkins, he replied in a manner that appeared to condone the abuse of women: "Well, I say again that the nicest thing about a lady who says no – it's always a pleasure when they change their mind, and I am sure that at the end of the day, our premier is going to change her mind on this very, very important issue" (Jenkins as quoted in Tenove 2000). Jenkins apologized for the remark the same day, but within about a year remarked as follows on the premier's travels outside the territory: "The premier's been flirting all over" (Jenkins as quoted in Small 2001g).

Duncan remembers many additional instances when male lawmakers targeted the weight and appearance of female MLAs. In her words, "It was sexist, it was demeaning, the style was just horrific" (Duncan interview 2017). Liberal backbencher Scott Kent responded to the situation when he introduced a motion in July 2000 urging all MLAs "to use gender-neutral, non-sexist and non-violent language at all times" (Small 2001g).

Duncan describes her governing style as "inclusive." In her swearing-in speech, she declared: "It is our intention for this legislature to become a place of inclusion" (Duncan 2000b). Despite this promise, Premier Duncan was frequently criticized for not adopting a collaborative tone either in the legislature or in her own party. At the end of the first sitting, Duncan told reporters she thought she'd improved the level of decorum in the legislature. Jenkins scoffed, saying, "There's probably more arrogance now than there's ever been" (Small 2000f).

Setting aside the views of opposition MLAs, Duncan developed a wide reputation for being heavy-handed and dictatorial. By spring 2001, one columnist concluded that she had "come to wear the mantle of 'it's my way or the highway'" (Loverin 2001). Later that year, an editorial suggested she was "brusque, strong-minded, impervious to wise advice from outside her circle, and a micro-manager" (*Whitehorse Daily Star* 2001a). Duncan conceded to a reporter that her "tone of voice need[ed] some work." She said: "I do get frustrated and my lack of patience shows and that's not right; it's not fair" (Duncan as quoted in Small 2000h). In the autumn of 2001, the Liberals brought forward a motion to introduce time allocation measures to the territorial legislature for the first time, which would have permitted the government to end debate when it saw fit. In response, opposition parties likened Duncan's regime to a "dictatorship" and a "totalitarian government" (Small 2001i).

Kirk Cameron served as Duncan's cabinet secretary during her initial time in office. He maintains she was not always interested in listening to other people, even those on her own side of the legislative aisle. As he recalls: "She had her approach, she had things she wanted to accomplish. And when she made up her mind on things, she drove them completely" (Kirk Cameron, telephone interview with author, 5 August 2017 [hereafter Cameron interview 2017]).

Concern over the substance as well as the style of Duncan's leadership reached a boil on 2 April 2002. Three of the ten MLAs in the government caucus announced they were leaving to sit as independents, citing concerns similar to those of Cameron. "It was her way or no way. That was it; bottom line," said Wayne Jim, one of the departing MLAs (Small 2002d). The defections proved disastrous for Duncan's government since they tipped the scales dramatically in a legislature that only held seventeen seats. The Liberals fell to minority government status, which drove Duncan to call an early election in fall 2002.

Not all observers blame the departures entirely on Duncan. Two of the three former Liberal MLAs were demoted from cabinet shortly before they decided to leave the government caucus. All three were men, and at least one of them seemed unprepared to return to the backbenches (Small 2002c). Jason Cunning, Duncan's principal secretary at the time of the defections, notes that Dennis Fentie, the Yukon Party premier who succeeded Duncan, also lost three MLAs during his first term – albeit for different reasons and not all at once. Cunning observes that Fentie "doesn't wear any of that, because he was a smooth, tough guy. But it's either she was a bitch or she was weak, you know ... She never wins that comparison argument." Moreover, Cunning does not believe the three Liberal defectors "ever would have done that to a man" (Cunning interview 2017).

Writing about the incident, Trimble and Arscott (2003, 90) assert: "Party infighting and desertions of this sort are unusual in majority government situations, leading us to wonder whether female leaders face higher levels of dissent and even public challenges to their authority because of their gender." They also cite former Manitoba Liberal leader Sharon Carstairs, who once observed that, when women leaders "fall from grace, we do it with a thud that the male candidates don't seem to do. There seems to be very little tolerance for women's failure" (Carstairs as quoted in Trimble and Arscott 2003, 82).

Overall, the tone in the Yukon legislature did not become more collaborative under Pat Duncan despite her hopes for a change. At the same time, little evidence suggests the tenor was more aggressive during her time as premier than it was during the time of preceding or subsequent premiers. In fact, as the lone remaining Liberal MLA, Duncan herself remarked in 2005 that she'd "not seen [the tone] this bad in a decade in the legislature" (McElheran 2005).

Appointments

Fifteen years before Prime Minister Justin Trudeau famously proclaimed that he'd named Ottawa's first gender-balanced cabinet, "Because it's 2015," Pat Duncan quietly named the first cabinet in Canadian history with half men and half women. The numbers were small: Duncan, Sue Edelman, and

Pam Buckway formed 50 percent of a six-person cabinet. Still, Duncan's gender-balanced political executive stands as a first for the country.

Duncan claims the move was not intentional. Before the 2000 election, three of the four Liberal MLAs were women, so it made sense to include them in the cabinet. As Duncan notes: "Realistically, the only people who had any kind of legislature experience were Pam, Sue and I. So it's kind of like, okay, there's a starting point, and then we kind of went from there. And we just did not have the experience to select from. So it wasn't deliberate. You play the hand you're dealt, right?" (Duncan interview 2017). Kirk Cameron, Duncan's cabinet secretary at the time, recalls the situation differently. He claims Duncan was aware of having the country's first gender-balanced cabinet and was "very pleased" about it (Cameron interview 2017). No Yukon government since Duncan's has replicated her achievement.

When Duncan promoted Scott Kent to the economic development portfolio in June 2001, her cabinet briefly lost its gender balance (Glen 2001). The cabinet tilted to more women than men in January 2002, when Duncan demoted Don Roberts and Wayne Jim to the backbench and promoted Cynthia Tucker and Jim McLachlan to the political executive. From that point, Duncan had a majority of four women in her seven-member cabinet (Small 2002b). Kirk Cameron believes the high proportion of women in cabinet affected discussions in that economic issues were, given the presence of so many women, analyzed through a social lens. "The economy is looked at from a different perspective when you take into account impacts on people as opposed to just economic trends," he observes. "It created a discussion that would not have been there with a bunch of middle-aged white guys" (Cameron interview 2017). However, Cameron believes that the human perspective that dominated cabinet debate rarely made its way into policy decisions. Instead, the main message communicated to the public was that the territorial government wanted to reverse the dismal fiscal reality of the time and reorganize a number of key departments in anticipation of the devolution process.

It is hard to know whether gender played a role in decisions affecting Duncan's other appointments. The premier's closest advisors comprised a group of men and women, including Principal Secretary Jason Cunning, Chief of Staff Debbie Hoffman, Policy and Legislative Advisor Wendy Randall, and Executive Assistant Keith Halliday. Duncan named Angus Robertson as deputy minister of economic development and energy, mines and resources; Dan Brennan as deputy minister of tourism; and John Stecyk as deputy minister of infrastructure (Small 2002a; *Whitehorse Daily Star* 2000c; *Whitehorse Daily Star* 2002). More controversially, Duncan appointed former Liberal leader Ken Taylor, who had originally recruited her to the party, as associate deputy minister of education (Small 2001c).

Overall, Duncan did not appear to champion the promotion of women to senior positions in the bureaucracy. Cameron is unable to recall many of the appointments she made (Cameron interview 2017). Halliday, Duncan's executive assistant during part of her time in office, recalls that she had some "strong female officials" in her ranks. In Halliday's words: "I think their point of view was respected and they were treated appropriately as senior officials regardless of gender. I'm not sure that's always the case with some male leaders" (Keith Halliday, interview with author, 10 May 2017).

Losing Power

Within two and a half years of arriving in the premier's office, Duncan called an early election that saw her government decimated in what was called "the worst electoral defeat in Yukon history" (McArthur 2002). Duncan was the lone Liberal MLA to win her seat in 2002, when the Yukon Party rode a wave of public frustration that brought the party to majority government status.

A number of factors led to the dramatic defeat of the Liberals in November 2002. Yukon's economy had not improved. In fact, by May 2001, the number of people employed in the territory had dropped by one thousand – from 13,400 to 12,400 – in the preceding year (Small 2001b). Duncan's government renewal project was deeply unpopular as public servants feared their jobs would be cut just as the territory faced an economic slump.

Above all, Duncan's personal reputation was tarnished by a conflict of interest allegation that was later found to be without merit but that nevertheless damaged her public standing. The debacle began in April 2001, when Yukon Party leader Peter Jenkins read aloud in the legislature the text of an e-mail message from a source that was not identified. The text suggested that Duncan wanted to draw attention away from an incomplete contract worth $150,000 between the territorial government and her brother's company, Total Point Communications. The e-mail also claimed that Duncan sought to highlight $160,000 that Jenkins owed the Yukon government. In the words of the e-mail sent to Jenkins, Duncan "knew from the first day the score on her brother's loan and wanted it deep-sixed, but she wanted yours called in" (Small 2001f).

Jenkins eventually took the matter to Ted Hughes, the territory's conflict of interest commissioner. In November 2001, Hughes completely exonerated Duncan in a report that found that the anonymous e-mail "was not true, and the conduct attributed to the premier was both false and malicious" (Hughes 2001, 76). But the damage was done, as one editorial writer pointed out: "In truth, reputations have been instantly trashed and permanently tainted" (*Whitehorse Daily Star* 2001a).

Each of these challenges weakened the Liberal government's popularity. But the spring 2002 defection of three MLAs, who cited "the centralizing of control and government in the premier's office," was arguably the final nail in the coffin (Small 2002d). After that point, the Liberals had a legislative caucus of only eight members and faced the threat of a non-confidence vote that would have triggered a new election. Duncan's government made it through the spring sitting because some of the MLAs who defected from Liberal ranks decided to support the government (Small 2002g). By the summer, however, Duncan realized she was unlikely to win passage of the fall capital budget, in part because of opposition to the reconstruction of Grey Mountain Primary School (Small 2002h).

In the end, Duncan chose to call an election before tabling the budget rather than letting the opposition pick a time to topple the government. Both the NDP and Yukon Party had just selected new leaders, and observers speculated that the Liberals hoped to secure a new mandate while the other parties were unprepared for a territory-wide contest (*Yukon News* 2002a). In hindsight, Duncan says the decisions to call an election and to insist on a government reorganization project were serious mistakes. In her words: "I had to sign a letter to Bob Nault [at the time federal minister of Indian affairs and northern development] asking to call the election. And I can remember signing it and saying, 'You know what? I feel like I just signed a suicide note'" (Duncan interview 2017).

Duncan's choice proved highly unpopular. Yukoners did not want to go to the polls. Opposition politicians suggested they might have supported the budget, which made the election seem unnecessary (McArthur 2002). In a scathing editorial, the *Yukon News* said the election could have been avoided had the Liberals been more collaborative:

They refuse to make compromises or concessions. Neither are they willing to admit that others might have ideas worth pursuing, or at least seriously considering, even though they themselves have been woefully light in the ideas department since winning the last election. Not once since the

Liberals lost three upstart MLAs to the opposition benches at the start of this year, reducing their smug majority to a smarting minority, did they truly try to make their minority government work in the best interests of all Yukoners. (*Yukon News* 2002a)

Still, the scale of Duncan's defeat was unexpected. The *Yukon News* claimed the Liberals' odds of winning were very good given the state of the opposition parties, and it predicted a Liberal minority government (Mostyn 2002b). The Canadian Press predicted the closest vote in Yukon history (Small 2002k).

Yet the Yukon Party swept back into power, winning twelve of eighteen seats under the leadership of Dennis Fentie, who had crossed the floor from the NDP. Electoral boundary changes since 2000 had resulted in the legislature growing from seventeen to eighteen seats. The NDP, under new leader Todd Hardy, won five seats. Duncan was the only Liberal MLA elected (Maddren 2002). The *Whitehorse Daily Star* called the outcome "the most catastrophic political miscalculation in the history of party politics here." Consistent with Duncan's status as a pioneering leader from a long-time opposition party, the newspaper pointed to the inexperience of many of Duncan's cabinet ministers and the party's "spectacular alienation" of many voters as explanations for the defeat (Butler 2002).

Duncan reflects on the events as follows: "It was a hard day. It was even harder the day I was sworn into the legislature as the last [Liberal] man standing" (Duncan interview 2017). The former premier lost the party leadership to Arthur Mitchell in June 2005 but continued to serve as an MLA (Canadian Press Newswire 2005). She joined with other female lawmakers to form a non-partisan women's caucus that pressed the legislature to adjourn at 5:30 p.m. instead of 6:00 p.m. to help legislators with young families (Butler 2002). Duncan announced she would not seek re-election in 2006 (Skikavich 2006b).

Once Duncan announced she was leaving politics, local media coverage became more sympathetic and paid particular attention to her role as the territory's first female premier. Patrick Michael, clerk of the Yukon Legislative Assembly, was quoted in the *Whitehorse Daily Star* as saying that Duncan's career "was a high point in our political success for women and politics in the Yukon" (Skikavich 2006b). A column in the same paper claimed Duncan broke "new ground for the benefit of future female party leaders and premiers, regardless of their political stripe" (*Whitehorse Daily Star* 2006).

Conclusion

Pat Duncan clearly cared about the place of women in politics and believed that gender influenced her approach to leadership. Yet it remains difficult to link her status as the first and only female premier of Yukon with her actions in office. Her priorities were largely economic, and her government made little headway on such issues as child care, poverty, or violence against women. The tone in the Legislative Assembly under Premier Duncan was generally adversarial and aggressive. One notable accomplishment with respect to gender was her appointment of the first gender-balanced cabinet in Canadian history, although Duncan maintains that outcome was unintentional.

At the same time, the evidence shows Duncan paid a price for her gender. A variety of offensive, gendered comments were directed at her and her government in the legislature. Close observers believe the three male MLAs who defected from her party might have behaved differently had she been a man.

Echoing the argument in Chapter 1 concerning the challenges that face pioneering premiers, Duncan led the first Liberal government Yukon had ever seen. Given that she not only had to manage a caucus of legislators without cabinet experience but also MLAs who had never before held territorial office, it is not surprising that her leadership came under intense scrutiny. Once the criticisms reached a crescendo, Duncan's government fell apart. How much of that result was attributable to gender, and how much to the unseasoned nature of the Yukon Liberals, is hard to know. Clearly, the

FIGURE 3.1

Number of female MLAs in Yukon Legislature, by party, 1978–2016

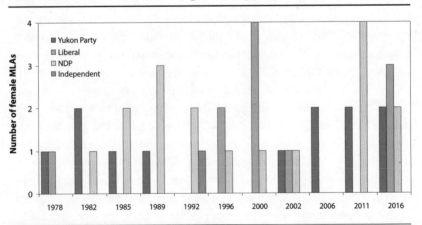

Source: Elections Yukon website, www.electionsyukon.gov.yk.ca.

two factors combined in a manner that was not helpful to Duncan's longevity in office.

Pat Duncan's legacy raises questions that merit further exploration. Though she is Yukon's only female premier to date, the territorial NDP has traditionally elected more women to the legislature. A comparative analysis of

FIGURE 3.2
Number of female candidates for Yukon Legislature, by party, 1978–2016

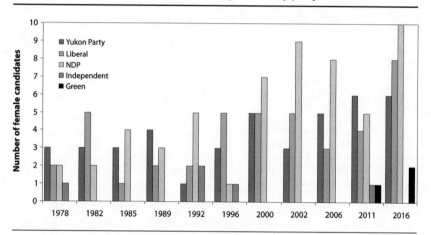

Source: Elections Yukon website, www.electionsyukon.gov.yk.ca.

FIGURE 3.3
Percentage of female MLAs in Yukon Legislature, 1978–2016

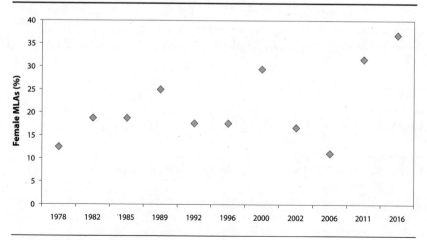

Source: Elections Yukon website, www.electionsyukon.gov.yk.ca.

FIGURE 3.4

Percentage of female candidates for Yukon Legislature, 1978–2016

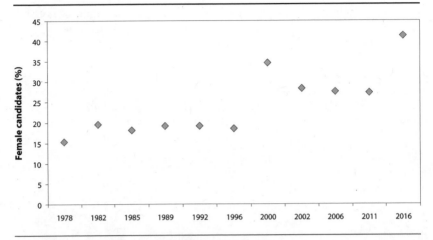

Source: Elections Yukon website, www.electionsyukon.gov.yk.ca.

Duncan's influence on feminist policy issues with the NDP's track record in that area would illuminate the relative impact of a female leader versus the influence of consistently high proportions of female legislators in a caucus.

Yukoners elected their second-ever Liberal government in November 2016. Premier Sandy Silver led his party under conditions that resemble those facing Duncan in 2000: commodity prices were low, the economy was a major issue, and voters were disenchanted with the governing Yukon Party. Once again, the Liberals swept eleven ridings with a slate of rookie candidates, a vast increase from just one MLA. A comparison of Silver's fortunes with Duncan's could provide valuable insight into the role gender played during the leadership of Yukon's "accidental premier" (*Yukon News* 2002b).

Note

1 Duncan was later appointed to the Senate of Canada by Prime Minister Justin Trudeau in December 2008.

References

Butler, Jim. 2002. "An Alienated Electorate Takes Its Revenge." *Whitehorse Daily Star*, 5 November.

Canadian Press. 1996a. "NDP Win Majority in Yukon Election." *Toronto Star*, 1 October.

–. 1996b. "Yukon Opposition Still Up in Air." *Montreal Gazette*, 8 October.

—. 2000a. "Liberals to Take Power after Stunning Upset in Yukon Election." *Sault Star,* 18 April.

—. 2000b. "Liberals Win Majority in Yukon Election." *Globe and Mail,* 18 April.

Canadian Press Newswire. 1996a. "Yukon Party Doesn't Want to Share Opposition Role." *Western Regional General News,* 1 November.

—. 1996b. "Speaker Names Yukon Opposition." *Western Regional General News,* 10 December.

—. 1997a. "Yukon Liberal Leader Quits, Again." *Western Regional General News,* 3 September.

—. 1997b. "Duncan Gets Nod by Acclamation." *Western Regional General News,* 17 November.

—. 1999. "Liberal Win Changes Yukon Opposition." *Western Regional General News,* 26 October.

—. 2005. "Members Hope New Leadership for Yukon Liberals Will Boost Support for Party." *National General News,* 5 June.

Duffy, Andrew. 2001. "Territories Tussle for Pipeline." *Ottawa Citizen,* 16 May.

Duncan, Pat. 2000a. "We'd Re-examine Project." *Whitehorse Daily Star,* 12 April.

—. 2000b. "For the Record: The Premier's Address." *Whitehorse Daily Star,* 10 May.

Glen, Sarah. 2001. "Spokesman Ridiculed for Remark, Asked to Say Sorry." *Whitehorse Daily Star,* 19 June.

Hale, Michael. 2001. "Budget Is 'Stand Pat,' Says Social Activist." *Whitehorse Daily Star,* 23 February.

Hayden, Joyce. 1999. *Yukon's Women of Power: Political Pioneers in a Northern Canadian Colony.* Whitehorse: Windwalker Press.

Hughes, the Hon. Ted, QC. 2001. Decision pursuant to s. 17 of the Conflict of Interest (Members and Ministers) Act of a complaint brought by Peter Jenkins, MLA, Klondike, against the Hon. Pat Duncan, MLA, Porter Creek South, 29 November, 1–76. Document in author's possession.

Kitco. 2017. "Historical Charts & Data." *Kitco Metals Inc.* 4 July. http://www.kitco. com/charts/historicalgold.html.

Loverin, Gordon. 2001. "The Duncan Regime Is Failing Its Electors." *Whitehorse Daily Star,* 9 March.

Maddren, Judy. 2002. "Yukon Party to Form Majority Government." *World Report.* Canadian Broadcasting Corporation. 5 November. Radio.

McArthur, Donald. 2002. "'They Don't Want to Compromise,'" Says NDP Leader Todd Hardy." *Yukon News,* 4 October.

McElheran, Graeme. 2005. "Report Zeroes in on Lack of Decorum." *Yukon News,* 15 April.

Mickleburgh, Rod. 2000. "Looking beyond Gender." *Globe and Mail,* 24 April, A3.

Mostyn, Richard. 2000. "Tight Margin of Victory Expected in Yukon Vote." *Yukon News,* 17 April.

—. 2002a. "The Question Is Answered." *Yukon News,* 11 October.

—. 2002b. "Liberals Will Squeak Through." *Yukon News,* 4 November.

Scoffield, Heather and Lily Nguyen. 2001. "Chrétien Prefers Canadian Route for Arctic Gas." *Globe and Mail,* 21 July.

Skikavich, Julia. 2005. "Pat Duncan: 'I'm Working to Win.'" *Whitehorse Daily Star,* 3 June.

—. 2006a. "MLAs to Debate House Sitting Hours." *Whitehorse Daily Star,* 11 May.

—. 2006b. "'She Kept the Flame Alive after 2002.'" *Whitehorse Daily Star,* 8 August.

Small, Jason. 1999a. "Liberals to Scrutinize Economy." *Whitehorse Daily Star,* 1 November.

—. 1999b. "Fowl Joke Triggers Ministerial Apology." *Whitehorse Daily Star,* 22 November.

—. 1999c. "Century-Ending Awards for Yukon MLAs." *Whitehorse Daily Star,* 17 December.

—. 2000a. "1970s Pipeline Scenario Resurfaces in Legislature." *Whitehorse Daily Star,* 24 February.

—. 2000b "Voters to Choose a 'Vision,' NDP Says." *Whitehorse Daily Star,* 13 March.

—. 2000c. "Hey, Libs – Where's the Beef?" *Whitehorse Daily Star,* 24 March.

—. 2000d. "Duncan: Not Running to Finish Second." *Whitehorse Daily Star,* 14 April.

—. 2000e. "Big Red Machine Steamrolls the NDP." *Whitehorse Daily Star,* 18 April.

—. 2000f. "Parties Offer Differing Takes on Session." *Whitehorse Daily Star,* 14 July.

—. 2000g. "Ottawa Enriches Territory's Social Programs." *Whitehorse Daily Star,* 12 September.

—. 2000h. "Premier Looks Back on Lessons from Legislature." *Whitehorse Daily Star,* 15 December.

—. 2000i. "Politics: The Year of the Big Red Machine." *Whitehorse Daily Star,* 29 December.

—. 2001a. "Sitting Called Liberal Learning Experience." *Whitehorse Daily Star,* 10 May.

—. 2001b. "Far Fewer People Working Here Now." *Whitehorse Daily Star,* 11 May.

—. 2001c. "Job Created for Ex-Liberal Leader." *Whitehorse Daily Star,* 14 May.

—. 2001d. "Jobs May Be Lost in Gov't Restructuring." *Whitehorse Daily Star,* 15 June.

—. 2001e. "Pipeline Scheme Called 'Too Expensive.'" *Whitehorse Daily Star,* 24 August.

—. 2001f. "Pat Duncan: From Conservative to Liberal." *Whitehorse Daily Star,* 27 August.

—. 2001g. "Jenkins Challenges Budget Consultations." *Whitehorse Daily Star,* 19 September.

—. 2001h. "Details of Historic Devolution Deal Out." *Whitehorse Daily Star,* 30 October.

—. 2001i. "Liberals Branded as 'Fascist, Dictatorial.'" *Whitehorse Daily Star,* 1 November.

—. 2002a. "Duncan Fires Three Deputy Ministers." *Whitehorse Daily Star,* 9 January.

—. 2002b. "Premier's Axe Claims Two Ministers." *Whitehorse Daily Star,* 14 January.

—. 2002c. "MLA Philosophical about New Status." *Whitehorse Daily Star,* 21 January.

—. 2002d. "Defections Tip Grits into Minority." *Whitehorse Daily Star,* 2 April.

—. 2002e. "Premier Weighs Minister's Offer to Quit." *Whitehorse Daily Star,* 12 April.

—. 2002f. "Premier Calls e-mail 'Judgment Error.'" *Whitehorse Daily Star,* 15 April.

–. 2002g. "How the MLAs Voted on the Six Vital Bills." *Whitehorse Daily Star*, 31 May.

–. 2002h. "School May Become Liberals' Waterloo." *Whitehorse Daily Star*, 26 July.

–. 2002i. "Premier Broke Her Word, NDP Charges." *Whitehorse Daily Star*, 4 October.

–. 2002j. "Business Audience Quizzes Party Leaders." *Whitehorse Daily Star*, 30 October.

–. 2002k. "Closest Result in History Expected in Yukon Election Vote Monday." *Canadian Press Newswire*, 4 November.

Tenove, Chris. 2000. "MLAs Urged to Clean Up Sexist Ways: Degrading Comments." *National Post*, 15 July.

Tobin, Chuck. 2000a. "Opposition to Turn up Heat under NDP." *Whitehorse Daily Star*, 13 March.

–. 2000b. "Liberals Table Maiden Speech, Budget." *Whitehorse Daily Star*, 5 June.

–. 2001. "Groups Stage Mass Walk-Out on Premier." *Whitehorse Daily Star*, 8 February.

–. 2002. "Eleventh-Hour Claim Deals Signed." *Whitehorse Daily Star*, 1 April.

–. 2003. "Opposition Raps YPAS Decision." *Whitehorse Daily Star*, 28 January.

Trimble, Linda. 1997. "Feminist Politics in the Alberta Legislature, 1972–1994." In *In the Presence of Women: Representation in Canadian Governments*, ed. Jane Arscott and Linda Trimble, 128–53. Toronto: Harcourt Brace.

–. 2004. "Why a Woman Won't Be Chosen as Leader of Alberta's Liberals." *Edmonton Journal*, 31 January.

Trimble, Linda, and Jane Arscott. 2003. *Still Counting: Women in Politics across Canada*. Toronto: University of Toronto Press.

Vincent, Isabel. 2001. "Yukon's Suburban Premier." *National Post*, 3 February.

White, Graham. 2013. "In the Presence of Northern Aboriginal Women?" In *Stalled: The Representation of Women in Canadian Governments*, ed. Linda Trimble, Jane Arscott, and Manon Tremblay, 233–52. Vancouver: UBC Press.

–. 2016. "The Territories." In *Big Worlds: Politics and Elections in the Canadian Provinces and Territories*, ed. Jared Wesley, 184–205. Toronto: University of Toronto Press.

Whitehorse Daily Star. 2000a. "Liberal's Conservative Roots Recalled in Yukon Legislature." 25 February.

–. 2000b. "A Split Territory Bleeds Liberal Red." 18 April.

–. 2000c. "New Deputy Tourism Minister Appointed." 10 November.

–. 2001a. "'Closure' Rests Only in Hughes' Pages." 30 November.

–. 2001b. "Liberals Owe Yukon Women an Explanation." 19 December.

–. 2002. "New DM Named." 22 April.

–. 2003. "The Territory Sheds Its Adolescence." 14 April.

–. 2006. "Upright through the Roar, She Departs." 11 August.

Yukon News. 2002a. "Are You Ready to Rumble?" 4 October.

–. 2002b. "Should She Stay or Should She Go?" 6 November.

4

Eva Aariak

Strong Nunavut Leader, Reluctant Politician

SHEENA KENNEDY DALSEG

Eva Qamaniq Aariak, Nunavut's second premier, was elected to the Legislative Assembly in the territory's third election on 27 October 2008. Just a few weeks later, Aariak was selected by her fellow members of the Legislative Assembly (MLAs) to lead the government as premier, making her Nunavut's first female premier and Canada's fifth woman to lead a provincial or territorial government.

Aariak assumed the role when Nunavummiut (residents of Nunavut) were reflecting on the territory's first decade of existence. Aariak's predecessor, Paul Okalik, had worked to establish the new government amidst high expectations. Despite a general recognition that it was still early days, Nunavummiut were frustrated by what they perceived to be slow progress. There were concerns about Okalik's leadership style and the culture of the territorial government. Okalik was seen as too aggressive and too authoritarian. Many observers found that the new territorial government, which was supposed to bring together both Inuit and Euro-Canadian ways of governing, did not reflect this blended approach. After ten years of Okalik at the helm, voters felt it was time for a change.

Aariak was the sole woman elected to the nineteen-member Legislative Assembly. Prior to Aariak's election, only four female MLAs had served in the Nunavut Assembly. Despite being a newcomer to legislative politics, Aariak was chosen as premier by her fellow MLAs – who included some well-known veteran politicians. She arrived with a wide range of profes-sional and personal qualifications, and was clear from the outset that she intended to do things differently. Unlike her predecessor, she would be open and collaborative. She would lead but she would not dictate. Aariak believed that if everyone – elected officials, bureaucrats, and citizens alike – worked together, then Nunavut's social and economic challenges could be over-come. To some readers, this commitment might sound naïve. Yet, after a lifetime of community and government work, Aariak realized that large-scale change would not be possible in just one term; rather, she hoped to remind Nunavummiut that Nunavut was theirs – that the government was *their* government, put in place to work on their behalf.

This chapter examines Aariak's leadership style and her impact on Nuna-vut politics. While the people who call the Eastern Arctic home have a long and rich history, the political history of Nunavut as a territory in the Canadian federation began in 1999. Since being carved out of the NWT, Nunavut has seen five elections and four premiers. That one of the four is a woman is encouraging but masks the reality that in Nunavut – and indeed across Canada's North – relatively few women contest or win territorial office.

Since little has been written about women and politics in Nunavut, this chapter is among the first scholarly accounts of Aariak's record as premier.[1] It draws primarily on academic sources, media accounts as well as publicly available government documents, and territorial *Hansard* records. In addi-tion, I conducted six semi-formal interviews with members of Aariak's staff and advisors, government employees at the time she was premier, long-time observers of Nunavut politics, and Aariak herself.

The discussion begins with an overview of Nunavut and its political sys-tem, as well as gender and politics in the territory, before turning to the de-tails of Aariak's premiership. Particular attention is devoted to her leadership style, policy priorities and impact, influence on the tenor of debate in the Legislative Assembly, and contribution to fostering women's leadership in Nunavut. I conclude with some reflections on what we can learn from the Aariak years about women in Nunavut politics and women's leadership in the territory.

I find that, since its creation in 1999, Nunavut has had a fairly stable num-erical representation of women in politics. Inuit women have held nearly all the highest offices and occupy a higher proportion of public service pos-itions than do men in the territory.[2] Eva Aariak brought to her role as first

minister wide-ranging professional experience, a strong sense of public service, firm grounding in Inuit culture and language, and a deep commitment
to openness and collaboration. She became premier at a time when citizens
were calling for significant changes in leadership and a return to basic principles underlying Nunavut's establishment.

Throughout her mandate, Aariak remained committed to an inclusive and
collaborative approach to governing. Like other female premiers, she was
convinced it was possible to do politics differently. Despite these starting
points, however, Aariak was criticized for lacking clear direction as premier
and for being weak and naïve.

I argue that Aariak displayed the key qualities Nunavummiut said they
wanted in their leaders. That Aariak was, by her own admission, relatively
unsuccessful in changing the tone of politics in Nunavut challenges Nunavummiut – and all Canadians – to think about how we define strength in
leadership. The following discussion thus raises important questions about
the relationship between institutions and the actors who animate them.

Nunavut in Review

Nunavut, meaning "Our Land" in Inuktitut, comprises one-fifth of Canada's
land mass and one-third of its coastline. The territory's thirty-six thousand
residents, about 85 percent of whom are Inuit, live in twenty-five communities spread across three regions. Each locale can claim its own history in
addition to distinctive social, cultural, and linguistic characteristics. No inter-
community roads or rail lines exist in Nunavut; travel to and between communities is possible only by plane, ski-doo, dog team, or boat. Once a year,
supplies ranging from household goods to school buses are transported to
communities by sealift.

Although Nunavut stands as a relatively new polity, the context within
which it was created and exists has a rich and important background. Inuit
and their predecessors have called this part of the Arctic home for thousands of years. Long before the founding of Canada or the small settlements
that punctuate the territory's vast landscape, Inuit lived in small family
groups. This centuries-old way of life was interrupted first by explorers and
missionaries, and then by the expanding Canadian welfare state in the postwar years. Through the rapid introduction of colonial policies, including
housing and education programs, Inuit families were drawn off the land
into permanent settlements. Very quickly, Inuit began to organize to regain
control over all aspects of their lives and communities. The burgeoning
Indigenous rights movement across Canada in the 1970s led to the creation

of several Inuit political bodies, which, in turn, planted the seeds for what became Nunavut.

The Nunavut Land Claims Agreement (now called the Nunavut Agreement) was signed in 1993 after two decades of negotiation among the federal government, the NWT government, and Inuit representatives.[3] It confirms Inuit title to 350,000 square kilometres of land in the Eastern Arctic, 10 percent of which includes subsurface mineral rights. To compensate for ceding the rest of traditional Inuit lands, the territory received a capital transfer from the federal government of $1.9 billion paid over fifteen years. The Nunavut Agreement also provides Inuit with priority rights to harvest wildlife for domestic, commercial, and sporting purposes and creates five co-management boards that oversee how the land and waters in the Nunavut Settlement Area are used.[4] Members of the co-management boards are appointed by Nunavut Tunngavik Incorporated (n.d.) – the body responsible for coordinating and managing Inuit responsibilities under the Nunavut Agreement – as well as by the federal and territorial governments. Finally, the parties to the Nunavut Agreement made provisions for the 1992 Nunavut Political Accord that set out the conditions and process for creating a new territory with a public government in 1999. On 1 April 1999, Nunavut officially came into being.

Like the NWT, Nunavut has a non-partisan legislative system that is often referred to as consensus-style government. Members of the Legislative Assembly in both jurisdictions run for public office as independents. Once MLAs are elected, they hold a leadership forum to select the premier as well as cabinet ministers by secret ballot. Consistent with language used in other Westminster parliamentary systems, the premier and cabinet in Nunavut together form the government.

Given this system, the power of Nunavut premiers is limited. They can assign portfolios only to MLAs who won election to cabinet and cannot easily remove ministers from cabinet. Premiers do set the agenda for cabinet meetings.[5] The absence of political parties, however, means premiers arrive in office without a formal platform, which is the vehicle that forms the official mandate for party governments in other Westminster systems. In Nunavut, members of cabinet develop the government's mandate with the support of other MLAs during the six to twelve months following a leadership forum. This official statement of government intentions follows from priority issues identified during the last territorial election campaign.[6]

Nunavut's political system was designed to mesh principles of parliamentary democracy with Inuit values of "maximum cooperation, effective use of leadership resources and common accountability" (Government of Nunavut n.d.). Early on, a set of eight core governing principles was developed, known as *Inuit Qaujimajatuqangit*, or Inuit traditional knowledge. These principles are meant to infuse an Inuit way of thinking and being into all aspects of public governance in Nunavut. The non-partisan nature of Nunavut's system is one of its defining features and was meant to encourage consensual decision making as a central tenet of traditional Inuit practice (see Williamson 2006; Cohn and Kunuk 2012).

Gender and Politics in Nunavut

Even though a substantial literature focuses on Nunavut political development, little has been written about gender and politics in the territory. Public debates about gender in recent years have tended to focus on Inuit men's participation in "modern" society – that is, a society that tends to devalue skills and knowledge traditionally held by men in Inuit society. In Nunavut, women make up the bulk of the paid labour force, especially in full-time, year-round jobs. For example, two-thirds of the territory's public servants are women (Government of Nunavut 2017). One explanation for this pattern is that, while women's roles have expanded as a result of colonization, the position of men has diminished. According to Williamson:

> When Inuit were forced to move into permanent settlements, it was difficult for men to reach their familiar hunting grounds. Also, many of the traditionally male tasks have been mechanized (e.g., dog teaming was replaced with snowmobiling, iglu-building with pre-fabricated housing, etc). With this mechanization, hunting itself became an expense. Women therefore expanded their role from housekeepers to income generators so that they could subsidise their men in their traditional duties as providers of food and men have become less busy while women have become more so. (Williamson 2006, 60; see also Altarimano-Jimenz 2013; Condon and Stern 1991)

In Nunavut, politics forms one area in which men have consistently outnumbered women.[7] For many women, entering politics means either leaving behind their families and their paid employment or adding a new role to a growing list of responsibilities.

Much as in the NWT, women face significant challenges in Nunavut's political scene despite their ties to the paid labour force. Although they remain numerically underrepresented from local councils to the territorial legislature, the members of an impressive group of Inuit women have dedicated their lives to promoting and securing Inuit self-determination. The appendix to this chapter provides the names, positions held, and years of service for seventeen Nunavut women leaders in territorial, national, and international politics.[8]

Gender was a subject of sustained public debate in the lead-up to Nunavut's parity plebiscite in 1997. The Nunavut Implementation Commission, formed in 1994 to advise on the institutional design of the new territory, recommended a dual-member constituency system that would have seen one man and one woman elected from each riding.[9] Under the terms of the Gender Parity Proposal, the Nunavut legislature would have been gender balanced. As Minor (2002, 66) points out, the commission believed Nunavut had a rare opportunity to institutionalize gender balance from day one in the Legislative Assembly. According to Young (1997, 308), proponents argued that parity would "reestablish a partnership between Inuit women and men that would be essential to achieving healing of social problems in Nunavut communities."

Prominent Nunavut women, including Manitok Thompson and Nancy Karetak-Lindell, firmly opposed the idea that parity would reinforce traditional Inuit values. Thompson believed political leaders should be chosen based on merit, not gender (see Young 1997; Williamson 2006; McComber and Partridge 2010). Having served as an MLA and cabinet minister in the NWT during the late 1990s, Thompson became Nunavut's first female MLA and first female cabinet minister.[10]

In a non-binding territorial plebiscite on gender parity in 1997, 57 percent of voters opposed the proposal. Turnout was low at only 38 percent, which is notable given that future citizens of Nunavut had a chance to shape their own government. Some analysts attribute the results to limited public interest in and minimal desire for electoral reform (Henderson 2005). Others cite voter inexperience as well as a lack of understanding of the proposal and the political process in general (Gombay 2000; Williamson 2006). Still others note the timing of the vote (Dahl 1997) and a general distaste for the bitter debate over the issue (Hicks as quoted in Williamson 2006, 59). It is unclear which of these explanations comes closest to the truth.

While Nunavut's creation was seen as potentially encouraging more Inuit women to enter politics, that hope has not yet been realized. Many Inuit women have held senior positions – both elected and appointed – at territorial, national, and international levels. Yet the number of women entering

FIGURE 4.1

Number of candidates and MLAs in Nunavut's Legislative Assembly, by sex, 1999–2021

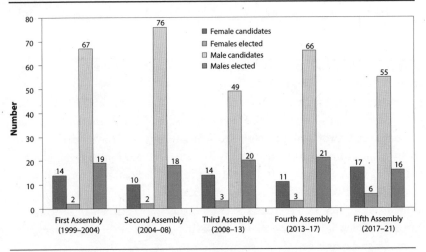

Note: Although Aariak was the only woman elected in the 2008 territorial election, by-elections in 2010 and 2011 added two more women to the Third Assembly.

Source: Elections Nunavut records, http://www.elections.nu.ca/apps/authoring/dspPage.aspx?page= tree-docs#.

politics in Nunavut has changed little since before the territory was created, and it has never come close to parity. As of this writing, Eva Aariak remains one of only fifteen women MLAs ever elected in Nunavut, and one of only sixty-six ever to have run for office in territorial elections.

In the years immediately before Nunavut's creation, the ten MLAs representing Eastern Arctic electoral districts in the NWT legislature included one woman, Manitok Thompson. Figure 4.1 summarizes the gender breakdown of candidates and Nunavut MLAs after 1999.[11] The number of women running for office has remained similar over time, in the range of ten to seventeen, and no more than six women MLAs have ever held legislative office at the same time. Even when the size of the Legislative Assembly grew from nineteen to twenty-two seats before the 2013 election, the numbers of women candidates and MLAs hardly changed.

Personal Background

Eva Aariak was born on the land near what is now the community of Arctic Bay, located on northern Baffin Island in the Qikiqtaaluk (formerly Baffin) region of Nunavut. Her family moved to Arctic Bay when she was five years old so her father could take a job with the Hudson's Bay Company. Eva's early years were immersed in community life, surrounded by extended family. She was a keen student from the beginning, attending federal day school in Arctic Bay and then, like many Inuit of her generation, the Churchill Vocational Centre (CVC) in Churchill, Manitoba. When CVC was slated to close in 1973, students from the Eastern Arctic were given the option to attend either the newly established Gordon Robertson Educational Centre in Frobisher Bay (now Iqaluit) or school in Ottawa. Aariak chose to move to Ottawa to complete her education; she lived with a family and attended Algonquin College.

After earning postsecondary certificates in teaching and business, Aariak returned North and worked as an adult educator. Parallel with Nellie Cournoyea's background in communications and public service, Aariak worked as a journalist with the CBC and in human resources with the NWT government. She then served as communications manager for the Interim Commissioner of Nunavut before becoming Nunavut's first languages commissioner in 1999. Aariak opened her own business – an Inuit art and craft shop called Malikkaat – in 2006, and in 2007 she returned for a short time as the territory's languages commissioner. In 2008, she stepped down from that position to run for territorial office.

Aariak was a first-time territorial politician when she was elected premier in 2008, but her background in community service was already well known. Parallel with research on the strong local profiles of female legislators in the US (see Chapter 1), Aariak had served as a hamlet councillor in Pond Inlet – where she was the only woman on council at the time. Aariak also won a seat on the local education authority and, similar to Pat Duncan in Yukon, served as chair of the Baffin Regional Chamber of Commerce (Eva Aariak, personal interview with author, 12 March 2017 [hereafter Aariak interview 2017]; Gregoire 2011).

Becoming Premier

After years of encouragement from friends and neighbours, Aariak decided to run in her home riding of Iqaluit East in the 2008 territorial election. Aariak had long thought of entering territorial politics but the timing was never quite right. In her words, the "stars aligned" in her life that year:

> As election day was approaching, I thought about it a lot – my children were grown and my new child was my business but I could get someone to look after the business and see what happens if I put my name forward. I

was very humbled and proud to get good numbers in the election, and [was] chosen to lead the government as premier. I was the only female – that was an accomplishment as a woman to say, "Hey, women can do this." I felt that I had opened the door for women to show that anyone can do it. I'm not a super person but once you set out your desire to serve, strive to make a change, you can do it. I really was hoping that more women would come forward saying that if she can do it, I can do it. (Aariak interview 2017)

Like other territorial candidates in Nunavut, Aariak contested office as an independent.

As Nunavut's first decade was coming to a close, citizens reflected on the accomplishments of that period. Many hoped for a change in leadership – and a change in tone – at the Legislative Assembly. As Aariak (interview 2017) recalls: "People were saying to me – there is not enough consensus even though we have consensus government. [It's] too much of a single person making decisions that may not necessarily [reflect] consensus within the government. That's one of the reasons that people were looking for change." Paul Okalik had served two terms as premier from 1999 through 2008, leading the new government through the foundational years of Nunavut's first decade. Okalik oversaw the introduction of several "made-in-Nunavut" laws, including the territory's Official Languages Act, which established Inuktitut as one of Nunavut's official languages, and the territory's first Education Act. His vision and accomplishments for the territory, however, were gradually overshadowed by a leadership style that was seen as autocratic. Reports pointed to a culture of fear and intimidation in the Nunavut public service as well as a sense that Nunavut's government was less responsive and less transparent than the NWT government (see, for example, *Nunatsiaq News* 2007a, 2007b, 2007c; Bell 2008).

Reflecting widespread disappointment with Okalik and his government, voters in 2008 elected ten new MLAs to the nineteen-member Legislative Assembly. Aariak was one of fourteen women candidates that year and secured the seat of Iqaluit East. Aariak's lone-woman status in the assembly garnered some attention from the local media; for instance, she was quoted as saying it might be time to revisit the 1997 gender parity proposal (CBC 2008). As summarized in Figure 4.1, more women MLAs arrived thanks to by-elections in 2010 and 2011.

In mid-November 2008, MLAs gathered for the Nunavut Leadership Forum to select a premier and cabinet ministers from among their ranks.

The three candidates nominated for premier were: Eva Aariak; Tagak Curley, who had served as a national Inuit leader, land claim negotiator, and NWT cabinet minister; and Paul Okalik, the only Nunavut premier to that point. Remarks delivered at the leadership forum indicate Aariak was, by far, the best prepared nominee. All three candidates stressed the need for change. Each highlighted policy challenges facing Nunavut and pointed to the need for a more inclusive government. The main difference among them rested in Aariak's avoidance of general statements about priorities; instead, she offered MLAs a thoughtful, clear, and transparent plan for her premiership.

Aariak tied community-level challenges with national and global circumstances. She emphasized deep connections among social, economic, and political development. While her colleagues spoke in broad terms about improving territorial government, Aariak proposed the direct engagement of citizens in a formal evaluation of Nunavut. Her goal was explicit: to identify what was being done well and what could be done better. The "Report Card," as Aariak called it, would become a defining feature of her tenure as premier.

Aariak's election as premier offered opportunities for both renewal and stability. Although new to territorial politics, she was well known in Iqaluit and across Nunavut from her work as an educator, journalist, and successful business owner. Her status as the only female MLA had little to do with the outcome of the leadership forum. As White (2013, 238) observes, "Aariak's emergence as premier should not be interpreted as a gesture to compensate for the paucity of women in the assembly; rather it is better seen as the victory of a moderate, competent candidate, who, at a time when public opinion seemed to favour a change in Nunavut's political direction, did not carry the political baggage of her male opponents." Aariak made no reference to her gender, and she maintains that she did not run for office or the premier's job because she was a woman. She believed she was well qualified and felt eager to serve her community both as an MLA and a premier (Aariak interview 2017).

The next sections outline her approach, policy priorities, and influence.

Aariak as Reluctant Politician

Words and phrases used to describe Eva Aariak include "principled," "consensus-building," "pragmatic," "quiet and steadfast," "collaborative," "open," "inclusive," and "leading by example." In many ways, Aariak was the anti-politician. According to her former principal secretary, she was "among the most principled and least ego-driven leaders I've worked with ... Eva really and honestly believes that the good sharing of ideas will lead to the best solution" (Paul Crowley, personal interview with author, 15 February 2017). Like NWT premier Nellie Cournoyea, Aariak sometimes frustrated her aides and colleagues because she practised politics differently than did many other leaders – that is, she remained committed to the principles of consensus and collaboration. Emily Woods (personal interview with author, 26 March 2017 [hereafter Woods interview 2017]), who served as her communications director, recalls: "At times, it could be a challenge for us, working in the machinery of politics where many leaders would have adapted to that style, and yet she never would. Kudos to Eva because she was very principled in that regard. She will be remembered for that."

Aariak stated at the leadership forum that she believed strongly in the consensus model of governance and that she would work inclusively and collaboratively not only with cabinet ministers and MLAs but also with the citizens of Nunavut. Consistent with some sources discussed in Chapter 1, Aariak sees women as employing a consensus model of leadership more regularly than men. When asked to describe her approach, Aariak (interview 2017) explains: "I was open to listen to everybody. I was hoping to gain collaboration, to have dialogue, to be open. I didn't really get that unfortunately. I think that's the difference between male and female. I tend to believe that women look for collaboration and working together."

Aariak felt so strongly about openness, accountability, and hearing the ideas of local people that she quickly introduced a territorial report card. Its purpose was to determine "what was working, what needed improvement, and what was not working at all" (Legislative Assembly of Nunavut 2008, 5). Her action was bold both in purpose and scope – and made sense given the mood of the electorate and the fact that neither Aariak nor many of her ministers had served in the previous government. Despite scepticism about the process, Aariak was committed to it, as were many new MLAs who won their seats in 2008 with a promise of change. For Aariak (interview 2017), the exercise was crucial: "Because the territory was so new – only ten years old – over the last decade so many positive things had happened and [my thinking was] 'ok, now what should we be concentrating on some more?' Elected members can brainstorm all they want but we need to hear from the ordinary people who are members of the community."

Aariak's government hired NorthSky Consulting, led by former Yukon NDP leader and premier Piers McDonald, to carry out the work. Consultants reviewed hundreds of government documents, interviewed many civil servants, visited all twenty-five Nunavut communities, and convened public consultations with more than twenty-one hundred citizens via meetings, surveys, interviews, and radio call-in shows. As Hicks and White (2015, 287) note, independent reviews of this nature are rare in Nunavut, especially when they are as sweeping and open-ended as the one commissioned by Aariak. The final report was entitled *Qanukkanniq? The GN Report Card.* Released on 1 October 2009, it contains dozens of recommendations covering multiple policy and governance issues. The document, which Jack Hicks (personal interview with author, 20 January 2017) describes as "disarmingly transparent," confirmed a widely held impression: the performance of the new territory's government was disappointing and left significant room for improvement in all areas.

Former Nunavut premier Paul Okalik criticized the quality of the report and the amount of money spent on the initiative (see Legislative Assembly of Nunavut 2009). By contrast, most citizens welcomed the opportunity to share their experiences and provide feedback in such a direct way. Unfortunately for Premier Aariak, the report created impossibly high expectations of rapid and fundamental change – parallel with the challenges that greeted Pat Duncan as Yukon's first woman and first Liberal premier.

Aariak (interview 2017) acknowledges that no leader in a single term could address all the issues raised in the report card. She maintains that the Tamapta Action Plan, the policy framework developed for her mandate from the findings of the report, reveals innovative thinking that had the potential to turn things around. The plan is broad in scope and identifies many different priorities – perhaps too many. Unlike the primarily economic focus of Cournoyea's government in the NWT and Duncan's in Yukon, Aariak's emphasis was clearly social policy, notably education, poverty, housing, health, and well-being. The action plan permitted Aariak and her cabinet to demonstrate to citizens that the new territorial government had heard them loud and clear. Aariak's attempt to keep the lines of communication open between government and citizens was also clear in the creation of *eva's e-newsletter* (see Office of the Premier 2010).

The process followed in producing Nunavut's report card testifies to Aariak's open and collaborative leadership style. She views the purpose of the exercise not just as hearing what was wrong but also as trying to engage local people in identifying solutions and renewing their faith in Nunavut. Echoing her general approach to leadership, Aariak (interview 2017) believes in taking the long view: "My style was [that] I was not campaigning to be re-elected. I was doing my job, looking far ahead whether I was elected again or not. With so much change needed, one has to be looking farther ahead than four years! Sometimes we get too greedy. Short-term solutions are like patchwork solutions ... bandages. I believe in long-term solutions."

Tenor of Legislative Debate

In general, the tenor of debate among lawmakers in Nunavut is different than it is in most other Westminster-style parliaments. As in the NWT, the absence of political parties means Nunavut MLAs are not openly divided along party lines. Aggressive displays of partisanship that occur in many other Canadian legislatures do not typify the Nunavut Legislative Assembly. In particular, Inuit cultural norms associated with group discussions and meetings have considerable influence over legislative behaviour. Generally speaking, lawmakers avoid open conflict as well as statements that directly oppose the positions of other members. This does not mean, however, that Nunavut MLAs reject passionate debate or that they always resist the temptation to slight other people.

In terms of embracing the ideals of consensus government, Aariak led by example. Her collaborative and inclusive approach extended beyond cabinet and the Premier's Office to the floor of the Legislative Assembly. No evidence exists that Premier Aariak ever lost her temper or spoke in a disrespectful manner to any other legislator. According to Emily Woods (interview 2017), Aariak's communications director: "Eva made the Legislature a very respectful place. She listened, took views into consideration [and] I think people noticed that behaviour. I think it's difficult to act differently when there is someone with that style of leadership running things. Bad behaviour is reflected back at you pretty quickly when someone like Eva is in the room."

At the November 2010 mid-term leadership review, Aariak acknowledged and responded to criticisms that she was not forceful or politically savvy enough. In her words:

I became Premier of this great territory without a lot of political experience, but this is not a weakness. Let's be honest. This is a reality for many of us. What I have brought to this role is of equal or even more value than political experience. I bring a strong moral compass, firmly rooted in Inuit culture and values. By keeping one side firmly rooted in Inuit culture and values, I believe that the judgement and wisdom required for a political role comes more naturally. The day-to-day skills of a politician can be learned by anyone, but a strong moral compass is not a learned skill and it is what takes and makes me a strong and capable leader. (Legislative Assembly of Nunavut 2010, 2–3)

Aariak led a relatively non-hierarchical cabinet. One former advisor refers to her as a "first among equals" rather than as a domineering first minister (Paul Carson, personal interview with author, 20 March 2017). Compared with Okalik, Aariak offered ministers and other senior officials considerably more latitude to make decisions and set their own priorities.

Although this approach brought valuable advantages, it also decentralized power such that cabinet members and bureaucrats were able to act unilaterally. Consistent with criticisms of other women leaders (see Chapter 1), Aariak faced perceptions, both inside and outside government, that she did not fully control the levers of power. However, just because Aariak was not interested in practising politics in conventional ways does not mean that other people had put away their game boards.

Policy Impact

What role did gender play in Aariak's policy legacy? This question must be considered in light of the newness of Nunavut as a jurisdiction: only one premier governed before her and, to date, three afterwards. Much of her predecessor's time and energy was directed towards establishing the new territory. Okalik's government produced a set of operational and policy priorities known as the *Bathurst Mandate*, which addressed four main areas – healthy communities, simplicity and unity, self-reliance, and continuous learning. The document provided a vision for the Nunavut of 2020. Each subsequent premier developed a plan for governing: Aariak's in 2009 was known as *Tamapta/CLᶜC: Building Our Future Together, 2009–2013* (Government of Nunavut 2009a), and her successor Peter Taptuna's in 2014 was known as *Sivimut Abluqta: Stepping Forward Together, 2014–2018* (Government of Nunavut 2014). In March 2018, the newly elected premier, Paul Quassa, released his government's mandate, which is titled *Turaaqtavut: Where We Are Aiming to Go, 2018–2021* (Government of Nunavut 2018).

Despite differences in style, these four documents share considerable overlap. In Nunavut, basic infrastructure, safe and affordable housing, educational attainment, language, culture, and economic development remain ongoing issues facing every government. With limited revenue-raising capabilities, Nunavut leaders work largely with a fixed budget based on federal transfer payments. These financial constraints plus high costs of living, deteriorating infrastructure, insufficient housing, as well as social and economic challenges resulting from the legacies of colonialism and historical trauma confront all premiers and ministers in Canada's North. In addition, decision makers need to balance the reality of climate change with economic development opportunities. In this context it is difficult, if not impossible, to govern in a proactive rather than a reactive way. Aariak's desire to involve citizens in finding solutions to the territory's complex web of challenges was motivated in no small part by this reality.

Aariak set out to address social problems, particularly poverty, by working with a wide variety of stakeholders. After twelve months of public consultation, her government signed a memorandum of understanding in 2012 with Nunavut Tunngavik Incorporated to implement the *Makimaniq Plan: A Shared Approach to Poverty Reduction* (Government of Nunavut 2012b). The Nunavut Roundtable for Poverty Reduction, which oversees the plan, hosts regular gatherings and coordinates more than sixty community projects and programs related to housing and homelessness, education and training, food security, and supporting traditional and land-based activities (Nunavut Roundtable for Poverty Reduction n.d).

In order to foster a more responsive approach inside the civil service, Aariak opened government liaison offices in every community. They were staffed by bilingual officers to serve as points of contact between citizens and the territorial government. Both the liaison offices and poverty reduction strategy were continued by Aariak's successor.

Like Cournoyea, Aariak did not emphasize gender in her public statements but, as noted earlier, viewed female politicians as having a more consultative style than their male counterparts. Aariak's reticence to discuss being a woman and her unwillingness to speak of "women's issues" using that terminology reflected neither a lack of awareness of her own achievements nor a lack of interest in other women; rather, these practices reflect Aariak's desire to be open to and inclusive of all citizens of Nunavut. The fact that she dedicated so much attention to matters of social policy and, especially, poverty reduction – as contrasted with the economic development priorities of Cournoyea and Duncan – speaks to Aariak's deep concern for human well-being and her appreciation of the ways in which economic and social challenges intermingled in the lives of Nunavummiut.

Appointments Record

Although women form the majority of Nunavut public servants, most senior appointments are held by men. This pattern remained largely in place while Aariak was premier. Three women, one promoted by Aariak, served as deputy ministers during her tenure.[12] Aariak appointed women to the board of governors of Nunavut Arctic College and to the Qulliit Nunavut Status of

TABLE 4.1

Women leaders in Nunavut while Aariak was premier

Position/Role	Name	Years
Member of Parliament, Nunavut	Leona Aglukkaq	2008–15
President, Inuit Tapiriit Kanatami	Mary Simon, O.C.	2006–12
President, Nunavut Tunngavik, Incorporated	Cathy Towtongie	2010–16
President, Qikiqtani Inuit Association	J. Okalik Eejeesiak	2008–14
Mayor, City of Iqaluit	Elisapee Sheutiapik	2006–10
	Madeleine Redfern	2010–15

Women Council, and she named women as chief medical officer, information and privacy commissioner, and board chair for the Nunavut Development Corporation (Government of Nunavut 2009b, 2010, 2011, 2012a).

Her Premier's Office staff consisted of a principal secretary, director of communications, executive assistant, and executive secretary. All three principal secretaries who served Aariak were men, while, throughout her term, the other staff positions were held by women. Inside cabinet, the premier named herself to the position of status of women minister.

As summarized in Table 4.1, when Aariak became premier nearly every major political post in Nunavut was held by a woman. This trend sparked a territory-wide discussion about gender and leadership. In 2010, in her role as minister responsible for the status of women, Aariak co-hosted the first women's leadership summit with Okalik Eejeesiak, president of the Qikiqtani Inuit Association, and Donna Adams, president of the Qulliit Nunavut Status of Women Council. Prior to the summit, Nunavut Arctic College published a collection of short memoirs by twelve Inuit women leaders as part of its Northern Leaders and Governance series.[13] Aariak wrote the foreword to the volume.

The premise of the summit was that "the concept of leadership is experienced differently by all women in Nunavut" (Arnait Nipingit Women's Leadership Summit 2010, 4). The event, which attracted about two hundred participants, did not focus specifically on political leadership, even though some of the prominent Inuit women listed in Table 4.1 were in attendance. The record of the sessions identifies many similarities between the leadership qualities valued by women who attended the summit, on one side, and Aariak's approach as premier, on the other:

- Being open-minded
- Being an example for others
- Not being afraid to make mistakes and fix them
- Being confident but humble
- Not letting go of moral values
- Taking an interest in your community
- Being a good listener and advisor
- Working with men and not competing
- Not being afraid to talk about challenges
- Not limiting yourself by adhering to a specific gender role.
  (Arnait Nipingit Women's Leadership Summit 2010, 10)

Summit organizers asked participants to identify barriers that women must overcome to become leaders. The main obstacles they cited were issues of culture and identity, lack of economic resources, the limited availability of supports such as child care, few role models, limited recognition of women's contributions, and personal and family obligations. Participants also saw predefined gender roles, including the perception that only men can be leaders and that women, especially young women, must constantly prove themselves, as significant hindrances to public leadership (Arnait Nipingit Women's Leadership Summit 2010, 11).

Concluding Thoughts

Aariak was elected as a change agent. To her credit, she carried through on promises to implement a territorial report card and reform social policy. As discussed in Chapter 1, however, a conciliatory approach left her open to criticisms that she had too many priorities and lacked a coherent vision.

This chapter demonstrates that Aariak did indeed hold a vision for Nunavut that extended beyond her own term in office. After Okalik led Nunavut through its formative years, Aariak faced the daunting task of engaging citizens in a new territorial political system with which many of them were already frustrated. Hicks and White (2015, 1) quote a young Inuk woman from Nunavut as saying that, in creating a new territory, citizens did not just want a *different* government, they also wanted a *better* government.

Aariak seems to have genuinely shared this view: she consistently worked towards objectives that had been reached via consultation and modelled her own behaviour as a political leader on the norms she sought to elevate in public life. She actively brought decision makers, bureaucrats, community leaders, and citizens together. Aariak listened closely and tried to incorporate the ideas of others into policy and governing practices. However, her approach as a leader probably did not serve her well as a politician.

As premier, Aariak demonstrated qualities that Nunavut residents said they preferred in their leaders. Compared with her predecessor and successor, Aariak was more committed to governing by consensus and to embodying the principles upon which the new territory was built. Nevertheless, a deep commitment to consensus meant that some of Aariak's colleagues, members of the bureaucracy, citizens, and commentators began to see her as weak and naive. Jim Bell (personal interview with author, 1 April 2017) attributes the perception of Aariak as weak to the fact that she "never showed or attempted to display the toughness that Okalik did."

In their account of the Aariak years, Hicks and White (2015, 324) observe:

> Aariak's government lacked direction and consequently accomplished very little. Some observers attribute this to Aariak's leadership style, which was far more consensual in the sense of being based on extensive consultations than was Okalik's. Other observers noted that in the absence of a strong leader, the cabinet was particularly fractious, rendering the government vulnerable to individual personalities and conflicts between them reflecting the absence of shared political values.

Notwithstanding Hicks and White's assessment, Aariak's premiership produced noteworthy accomplishments. The report card initiative was imaginative and necessary. Her government led important initiatives on poverty reduction, food security, suicide prevention, and the creation of an independent child and youth advocate office. Moreover, after several years pressing the issue, Aariak secured a promise from Prime Minister Stephen Harper to begin devolution negotiations – a long-term goal that would involve the transfer of control over Nunavut's public (Crown) lands and resources to the Government of Nunavut. Devolution would allow Nunavummiut to make decisions as to how public lands and resources are used and developed.

Most of the issues that Aariak was passionate about – the same ones that Nunavummiut clearly identified in the report card exercise – required sustained attention during more than one term in office, no matter who was premier. Nunavummiut are disproportionately affected by complex social challenges and unique governance circumstances that are interwoven with colonialism. It constitutes an act of leadership to identify these problems and to create opportunities to discuss them openly and candidly. That Aariak did both and made attempts to engage Nunavummiut in decision-making processes about them stand as important accomplishments in their own right.

Aariak acknowledges that she was unable to achieve the collaborative results she hoped for – despite never straying from her approach. Aariak ran unsuccessfully in the 2013 territorial election.[14] What does this outcome mean for ideas about consensus government and, in particular, responsive politics as practised by an Aboriginal woman in a polity with a majority Aboriginal population? If an Inuit woman who so closely adhered to the principles underlying the cooperative model had such a difficult time under those circumstances, then can any woman hope to lead in a consensus-based manner? Does the perception of Aariak as weak reflect sexist interpretations of what constitutes a strong leader?

Given Nunavut's specific cultural and political context, and given how few women have been involved in electoral politics in the territory, it is too early to reach firm conclusions. All Nunavut politicians operate in a system that tries to bridge Inuit with non-Inuit forms of decision making. Perhaps Aariak's experiences reveal the irreconcilable difference between Aboriginal ideals of social consensus, on one side, and conflicts inherent in Westminster parliamentary institutions, on the other.

We know Aariak was steadfast in her commitment to a consensus-oriented approach. Yet how much of her experience can be explained by gender is unclear in the absence of more comparators. Although Aariak believed men and women lead differently, she maintained that the collaborative values she was trying to uphold as premier were Inuit values, not female values.

Future research needs to ask crucial questions. What is the longer-term impact of female premiers in Canada's North? Do women leaders practise politics differently? Can women leaders be perceived as both collaborative and effective? In the case of Nunavut, exploring the contributions of women like those listed in the appendix to this chapter would shed light on how leadership in land claims or international organizations differs from leadership in public office.

Although a record six women were elected to the Legislative Assembly in 2017, Aariak (interview 2017) believes the gender parity proposal should be reconsidered. Informal observation indicates that the vast majority of Nunavut municipal councillors continue to be men. One step towards increasing the number of women running for territorial office may be increasing women's presence in municipal government.

As Nunavut premier, Aariak will be remembered for her bold decision to engage citizens in evaluating their government and for her unwavering commitment to governing collaboratively. Aariak was not a skilled politician in the conventional sense. That her reluctance to practise politics as usual ultimately resulted in her losing the next election may reveal more about the system and the electorate than it does about her.

Appendix: Nunavut women in territorial, national, and international politics

Name	Position	Years
Eva Aariak	Premier of Nunavut	2008–13
Leona Aglukkaq	Member of the Legislative Assembly (Nattilik) *Minister of Health and Social Services and Minister Responsible for the Status of Women*	2004–08
	Member of Parliament (Nunavut) *Minister of Health; Minister of Environment*	2008–15
Pat Angnakak	Member of the Legislative Assembly (Iqaluit-Niaqunnguu) *Minister of Health, Suicide Prevention (2017–18)*	2013–present
Levinia Brown	Member of the Legislative Assembly (Rankin Inlet South/Whale Cove) *Deputy Premier; Minister of Community and Government Services*	2004–08
Okalik Eegeesiak	President ITK President, QIA Chair, ICC International	1998–2000 2008–14 2014–present
Jeannie Hakongak Ehaloak	Member of the Legislative Assembly (Cambridge Bay) *Minister of Justice; Minister Responsible for Qulliq Energy Corporation; Minister Responsible for Democratic Institutions; Minister Responsible for Human Rights Tribunal; Minister Responsible for Labour*	2017–present
Edna Elias	Commissioner of Nunavut Mayor, Kugluktuk	2011–15

Name	Position	Years
Hon. Monica Ell-Kanayuk	Member of the Legislative Assembly (Iqaluit-Manirajak) *Deputy Premier; Minister of Economic Development and Transportation; Minister Responsible for Mines; Nunavut Business Credit Corporation; Minister Responsible for the Nunavut Development Corporation; Minister Responsible for the Utility Rates Review Council; Minister Responsible for the Status of Women*	2011–17
Ann Meekitjuk Hanson, O.C.	Commissioner of Nunavut	2005–10
Rhoda Innuksuk	President, ITC	1985–88
Mila Adjukak Kamingoak	Member of the Legislative Assembly (Kugluktuk)	2017–present
Nancy Karetak-Lindell	Member of Parliament (Nunavut) President, ICC Canada	1997–2006 2016–present
Aluki Kotierk	President, Nunavut Tunngavik Inc.	2016–present
Nellie Kusugak	Commissioner of Nunavut	2010; 2015–present
Helen Maksagak	Commissioner of Nunavut	April 1, 1999–April 1, 2000
Margaret Nakashuk	Member of the Legislative Assembly (Pangnirtung)	2017–present
Elisapee Sheutiapik	Member of the Legislative Assembly (Iqaluit-Sinaa) *Government House Leader; Minister of Family Services; Minister Responsible for Status of Women; Minister Responsible for Homelessness; Minister Responsible for Immigration; Minister Responsible for Poverty Reduction*	2017–present
Manitok Thompson	MLA (Rankin Inlet South/Whale Cove) *Minister of Community Government and Transportation and Minister Responsible for Sport Nunavut (2001); Minister of Public Works and Services and Minister Responsible for the Nunavut Housing Corporation (2003–04)*	1999–2004

Name	Position	Years
Cathy Towtongie	President, NTI	2001–04; 2010–16
	Member of the Legislative Assembly (Rankin Inlet North-Chesterfield Inlet)	2017–present
Jeannie Ugyuk	Member of the Legislative Assembly (Nattalik, Netsilik)	2010–15
	Minister of Family Services (2013–15)	
Rebekah Uqi Williams	Member of the Legislative Assembly (Quttiktuq)	2000–04

Note: Where cabinet ministers held their portfolios for only part of their time in office this has been indicated by putting the years in parentheses.

Notes

1 Among the only existing sources is Gregoire's (2011) profile of Aariak in *The Walrus*. Aariak is working on a book about her life with Alexander McAuley of the University of Prince Edward Island.

2 Data from the 2016 Nunavut Government Employee Survey show that two-thirds of all government employees were women. This figure includes both territorial and federal government employees working in Nunavut (Statistics Canada 2017).

3 Nunavut Tunngavik Inc., or NTI, represents Inuit under the land claims agreement. NTI coordinates and manages Inuit responsibilities set out in the agreement and ensures that the federal and territorial governments fulfill their obligations. More information about NTI is available at http://www.tunngavik.com/about/.

4 The five co-management boards are: the Nunavut Wildlife Management Board, the Nunavut Planning Commission, the Nunavut Impact Review Board, the Nunavut Water Board, and the Nunavut Surface Rights Tribunal.

5 Premiers set the cabinet agenda, have some power over the order in which legislation is introduced, and speak for Nunavut in intergovernmental meetings.

6 For example, Aariak became premier on 3 November 2008. Her mandate, titled *Tamapta: 2009–2013, Building Our Future Together* (2009), was not tabled until 7 December 2009.

7 Men have outnumbered women in elected politics at the municipal, territorial, and federal levels, and in land claims organizations and national Inuit politics. Although women were actively engaged in the Inuit rights movement from the 1970s onward, most of the high-profile positions in the land claims negotiation process were held by men.

8 In addition to the women listed here, several prominent Inuit women from outside Nunavut have held significant regional, national, and international roles. They include Nellie Cournoyea (see Chapter 2), Mary Simon, and Sheila Watt-Cloutier (see Watt-Cloutier 2015). They have paved the way for other Inuit women to assume

important positions across Canada. As well, multiple women have served as municipal leaders in Nunavut, including in Iqaluit, which has had three women mayors: Elisapee Sheutiapik (2003–10), Madeleine Redfern (2010–12; 2015–present), and Mary Wilman (2014–15). At the time of writing, two other women mayors served in Nunavut: Jeannie Ehaloak in Cambridge Bay and Mary Killiktee in Qikiqtarjuaq.

9   The Nunavut Implementation Commission was established in 1994 to prepare research on the design of the new government, civil service, and electoral system. The NIC published two major reports called *Footprints in New Snow* and *Footprints 2* as well as a number of supplementary reports.

10 For more about Thompson, Karetak-Lindell, and other Inuit women leaders, see McComber and Partridge (2010).

11 To this point, Nunavut has held general elections in 1999, 2004, 2008, 2013, and 2017.

12 Deputy ministers from the previous government were Kathy Okpik (Department of Education) and Aluki Rojas (Department of Intergovernmental Affairs and Department of Social Services). Janet Slaughter, appointed as deputy minister in the Department of Justice in 2010, resigned in 2011. Rojas resigned in 2014 and became president of NTI in early 2017. Okpik served as deputy minister of education at the time of writing.

13 Seven other books were published in this series, all of which offer full-length autobiographies of prominent male leaders in the Inuit rights movement.

14 Aariak lost her seat to Georges Hickes by just forty-three votes. By all accounts, he ran a strong campaign. Since the electoral map was redrawn prior to the 2013 election, Aariak contested a new seat – which may have affected her numbers. As well, Aariak declared in 2013 that she would not be a candidate for premier, citing family reasons and a desire to focus on her constituents (Eva Aariak, personal interview with author, 12 March 2017).

References

Altamirano-Jimenez, Isabel. 2013. *Indigenous Encounters with Neoliberalism: Place, Women, and the Environment in Canada and Mexico*. Vancouver: UBC Press.

Arnait Nipingit Women's Leadership Summit. 2010. *Collecting, Connecting and Creating Women's Voices in Nunavut, Summit Report September 2010*. Iqaluit: Government of Nunavut, Qulliit Nunavut Status of Women Council, Qikiqtani Inuit Association and Nunavut Tunngavik, Inc.

Bell, Jim. 2008. "Candidates Take Aim at the Okalik Government: In Iqaluit, It's Seven against One on Oct. 27." *Nunatsiaq News*, 24 October. http://nunatsiaq.com/stories/article/Candidates_take_aim_at_the_Okalik_government/.

CBC News. 2008. "Banner Year for Inuit Women in Politics." *CBC News North*, 18 November. http://www.cbc.ca/news/canada/north/banner-year-for-inuit-women-in-politics-1.748266.

Cohn, Norman, and Zacharias Kunuk. 2012. "Our Baffinland: Digital Indigenous Democracy." *Northern Public Affairs* 1, 1 (Spring): 50–52.

Condon, Richard G., and Pamela R. Stern. 1991. "Gender Preference, Gender Identity and Gender Socialization amongst Contemporary Inuit Youth." *Ethos* 21, 4: 384–416.

Dahl, Jens. 1997. "Gender Parity in Nunavut?" *Indigenous Affairs* 3–4 (July-December). Copenhagen: International Working Group for Indigenous Affairs.

Gombay, Nicole. 2000. "The Politics of Culture: Gender Parity in the Legislative Assembly of Nunavut." *Études/Inuit/Studies* 24, 1: 125–48.

Government of Nunavut. N.d. *Consensus Government Information Package.* http://www.gov.nu.ca/sites/default/files/final_gn_info_package_-_consensus.pdf.

–. 2009a. *Tamapta 2009–2013: Building Our Future Together – The Government of Nunavut's Action Plan.* Iqaluit: Government of Nunavut.

–. 2009b. *Nunavut Gazette* 11:6. Iqaluit: Territorial Printer of Nunavut.

–. 2010. *Nunavut Gazette* 12:3, 12:8. Iqaluit: Territorial Printer of Nunavut.

–. 2011. *Nunavut Gazette* 13:3, 13:7. Iqaluit: Territorial Printer of Nunavut.

–. 2012a. *Nunavut Gazette* 14:9–11. Iqaluit: Territorial Printer of Nunavut.

–. 2012b. "Government of Nunavut and Nunavut Tunngavik Inc. Commit to Moving Forward on Poverty Reduction." http://gov.nu.ca/edt/news/government-nunavut-and-nunavut-tunngavik-inc-commit-moving-forward-poverty-reduction.

–. 2014. *Sivumut Abluqta: Stepping Forward Together, 2014–2018.* Iqaluit: Government of Nunavut.

–. 2017. *Public Service Annual Report, 2015–2016.* Iqaluit: Government of Nunavut. Tabled Document 20233-4(3) http://assembly.nu.ca/sites/default/files/TD%20233-4(3)%20EN%202015-2016%20Public%20Services%20Annual%20Report.pdf.

–. 2018. *Turaaqtavut: Where We Are Aiming to Go, 2018–2021.* Iqaluit: Government of Nunavut.

Gregoire, Lisa. 2011. "Madam Premier: How Eva Aariak Is Reinventing the Politics of the North." *Walrus,* 12 January. https://thewalrus.ca/madam-premier/.

Henderson, Ailsa. 2005. "Support for (Quasi) Self-Government: Assessments of Northern Political Life Ten Years after the Nunavut Land Claim Agreement." Paper presented at the Canadian Political Science Association annual meetings, University of Western Ontario. http://assembly.nu.ca/library/Edocs/2005/001486-e.pdf.

Hicks, Jack, and Graham White. 2015. *Made in Nunavut: An Experiment in Decentralization.* Vancouver: UBC Press.

Legislative Assembly of Nunavut. 2008. *Nunavut Leadership Forum: Election of the Speaker, Premier and Ministers of the Nunavut Legislative Assembly.* 14 November.

–. 2009. "Question 091-3(2)." *Hansard,* 2nd Session, 3rd Assembly. 24 November, 551.

–. 2010. *Nunavut Leadership Forum.* 3 November.

McComber, Louis, and Shannon Partridge, eds. 2010. *Arnait Nipingit Voices of Inuit Women in Leadership and Governance.* Iqaluit: Nunavut Arctic College.

Minor, Tina. 2002. "Political Participation of Inuit Women in the Government of Nunavut." *Wicazo Sa Review* 17, 1 (Spring): 65–90.

Nunatsiaq News. 2007a. "Fear and Loathing in Nunavut," 18 May.

–. 2007b. "Is the Nunavut Premier's 'Divisive, Juvenile Leadership Style' the Real Problem?" 20 July.

–. 2007c. "Should the Premier Go?" 27 July.

Nunavut Roundtable for Poverty Reduction. N.d. http://www.makiliqta.ca/en/re-sources/news/community-projects-spotlight.

Nunavut Tunngavik Incorporated. N.d. http://www.tunngavik.com.

Office of the Premier. 2010. *eva's e-newsletter.* Issue 3 (May/June). http://assembly.nu.ca/library/GNedocs/2010/000253-e.pdf

Statistics Canada. 2017. *Initial Findings from the Nunavut Government Employee Survey, 2016.* Ottawa: Government of Canada, 27 March 2017. https://www.statcan.gc.ca/daily-quotidien/170327/dq170327c-eng.pdf

Watt-Cloutier, Sheila. 2015. *The Right to Be Cold: One Woman's Story of Protecting Her Culture, the Arctic, and the Whole Planet.* Toronto: Allen Lane Canada.

White, Graham 2013. "In the Presence of Northern Aboriginal Women? Women in Territorial Politics." In *Stalled: The Representation of Women in Canadian Governments,* ed. Linda Trimble, Jane Arscott, and Manon Tremblay, 233–52. Vancouver: UBC Press.

Williamson, Laakkuluk Jessen. 2006. "Inuit Gender Parity and Why It Is Accepted in the Nunavut Legislature." *Etudes/Inuit/Studies* 30, 1: 51–68.

Young, Lisa. 1997. "Gender Equal Legislatures: Evaluating the Proposed Nunavut Electoral System." *Canadian Public Policy* 23, 3 (September): 306–15.

PART 2

ATLANTIC CANADA

5

Striking a Balance

Catherine Callbeck as Premier of Prince Edward Island

DON DESSERUD and ROBIN SUTHERLAND

Striking a balance is not an easy task.

– CATHERINE CALLBECK SPEAKING IN 1977
(AS QUOTED IN MacKINNON 2012, 120)

As the Prince Edward Island legislature convened following the 1993 provincial election, the "First Five" photograph was taken. This now famous picture shows PEI's lieutenant-governor, premier, legislative speaker, deputy speaker, and opposition leader. All are women.[1] Catherine Callbeck, the premier in the photograph, was the first woman ever elected as a provincial leader in Canada. Her success was no small feat, particularly in a province often described as socially conservative. Yet, in the end, just how important was this moment? Neither Callbeck's victory nor the ascent of her colleagues resulted in anything approaching a radical shift in PEI politics or public policy – at least with respect to women's issues. As John Crossley's (1997, 280–81) study of women in PEI politics concludes, "there is no clear evidence to suggest that the presence of women in the Assembly has affected agenda setting, issue processing, or policy outcomes."

Perhaps we are looking at this picture through the wrong lens. Trimble and Arscott (2003, 23) argue that by focusing on some women's accomplishments as "firsts," we risk analyzing these achievements "in isolation from each other, making it difficult to see larger patterns such as the recent decline in the number of women leaders." Furthermore, a corollary to this observation is that some women's achievements, which might not seem unique or trail-blazing, end up being overlooked. Catherine Callbeck was a businesswoman who brought considerable skill to her work in public office. Her case does not fit with stories of a lone woman's triumph over social and financial hardship or with tales whereby the heroine becomes a champion of such issues as women's reproductive health or child care. Instead, Callbeck's career suggests a far more nuanced narrative of political agency.

Callbeck won the PEI Liberal leadership in what was widely referred to as a coronation – under circumstances that Chapter 1 terms politically empowering since the outgoing premier and his governing party remained extremely popular. Like Kathy Dunderdale's situation in Newfoundland and Labrador, but unlike the imperiled situation of other women elites in Canada, Callbeck was not an example of what Trimble and Arscott (2003, 83) call "partisan CPR," whereby a new leader must "resuscitate the party's electoral prospects after the last breath has gone from a once vital partisan body." Indeed, the PEI Liberals in 1993 stood near the pinnacle of popularity, holding all but two of the legislature's thirty-two seats. Under Callbeck's leadership, the party improved its standing by winning thirty-one of thirty-two seats in the 1993 provincial election.

Despite this strong showing, Callbeck's tenure as premier was anything but a smooth ride. Indeed, her own demise, which culminated with her resignation from the party leadership in 1996, appeared to follow directly from pressures exerted by members of the provincial Liberal Party executive. Much like Alison Redford's exit in Alberta, Callbeck's departure was attributed to the "shadow men" (MacDonald 2000, 369), or male backroom operatives, who are invariably blamed for all political machinations on the Island – usually for good reason. Would the "backroom boys" have pushed aside a male leader quite so eagerly? Perhaps not. We will never know.

This chapter focuses primarily on Catherine Callbeck's time as premier of Prince Edward Island from 1993 through 1996. We set the stage by considering her earlier service as an MLA and cabinet minister (1974 to 1978). Our goal is to assess Callbeck's influence on Island public policy and, specifically, on issues affecting women. We evaluate her legacy in light of her own claim that she strove to "strike a balance" among competing policy priorities that often implicated divergent public and private interests (Callbeck as quoted in MacKinnon 2012, 120). We argue that, using this criterion, Callbeck succeeded.

Personal Background

Catherine Sophia Callbeck was born on 25 July 1939 in Central Bedeque, a village in rural Prince Edward Island. At this time, as elsewhere in Canada, few women held formal roles in politics or the workforce. Little support was available to those who sought change. A few days before Callbeck was born, the staunchly PC Charlottetown newspaper known as the *Guardian* published an editorial declaring that working wives were "a menace to the general welfare, to the public health and to the morals of the nation" (editorial as quoted in MacDonald 2000, 200; see also Baldwin 1985, 329).[2]

In the summer of 1939, Canada was still suffering from hard times. Nevertheless, PEI had escaped the catastrophic shock of sudden and massive unemployment that the Great Depression inflicted elsewhere (MacDonald 2000, 170). Moreover, the diligence and business acumen of William Callbeck, Catherine's grandfather, allowed the family to prosper. William had opened a tailor shop in Central Bedeque in 1899, which he later expanded to include a general store and sawmill (Beck 2014). By the time Catherine was born, the family enterprise had grown to the point that "the Callbeck store eventually became the largest country store of sales and shipping in Prince Edward Island, and quite possibly the Maritimes" (MacKinnon 2012, 20).

Catherine Callbeck initially embraced what she saw as her destiny: together with her brother Bill, she worked in – and eventually ran – the family business. To that end, she enrolled in 1956 in Mount Allison University's bachelor of commerce program. Callbeck was the only female student to select the program in her entering year and, upon graduating in 1960, became the second woman to complete the degree at Mount Allison (MacKinnon 2012, 31).

As an undergraduate, Callbeck joined the campus Liberal club and ran for the position of residence representative, two activities that had a profound impact on her future. As Callbeck later told biographer Wayne MacKinnon (2012, 81), "Politics got in my blood at Mt. A and has never left," and her time at Mount Allison brought her into contact with a number of politically well-connected people. Her friend Harriet was the daughter of former PEI premier Thane Campbell and the sister of Alex Campbell, who was PEI's premier from 1966 until 1978 (Callbeck served in his cabinet in 1974). Callbeck also met two highly engaged young Progressive Conservatives, Libby Burnham and Brian Mulroney, at a model parliament; Mulroney, the model parliament's prime minister, would become prime minister of Canada in 1984, while Burnham went on to play prominent roles in the New Brunswick, Ontario, and federal PC organizations (MacKinnon 2012, 37).

After graduating, Callbeck taught business in New Brunswick at the Saint John Institute of Technology, but when her father died in 1967, she returned to Central Bedeque to help her brother run the family business. Following a long family tradition, Callbeck was not just successful in business but also deeply immersed in community activities.

Elective Office

Callbeck's route to elective office can be traced to an offer she received in 1973 to chair a committee in Bedeque that was tasked with organizing local celebrations of the hundredth anniversary of PEI's joining Confederation. Callbeck impressed officials with her administrative abilities, together with an understated but effective speaking style and general panache. Both Liberals and PCs approached her to run in a general election expected the next year. Callbeck chose to seek the Liberal nomination in the solidly Liberal constituency of 4th Prince. Nevertheless, and despite being endorsed by Premier Alex Campbell – the candidate in the neighbouring seat of 5th Prince – Callbeck faced a mixed reaction from local partisans. One Liberal polling captain told her he couldn't support her because she was a woman (MacKinnon 2012, 83). Ironically, Callbeck's two rivals for the seat were PC candidate Doris MacWilliams and NDP nominee Doreen Sark. No matter their prejudices, voters in 4th Prince – including the polling captain – faced the reality that their next "Assemblyman," as members of the provincial legislature were known, was going to be a woman.

A brief word about PEI's unique electoral system. Since 1996, it has resembled that of other Canadian provinces, with twenty-seven single-member constituencies. However, prior to 1996, PEI's legislature combined its Legislative Assembly and Council. Like New Brunswick and Nova Scotia, pre-Confederation PEI had both an elected Assembly (Lower House) and an appointed Council (Upper House). In 1861, PEI's Legislative Council became an elected chamber (MacKinnon 1951, 99–104). This meant that when the Island entered Confederation in 1873, both legislative houses were elected. In 1893, the two bodies merged. Each of PEI's three counties (Kings, Queens, and Prince) was divided into five districts, with one assembly and one council seat per district. Queens County gained an extra district because it included Charlottetown, the provincial capital. Since assembly and council members were elected separately, it is more accurate to describe the system as having two legislators per district as opposed to dual-member

constituencies. Until the 1966 provincial election, a modest property quali-
fication remained for council elections.

Except for this property rule, no clear distinctions characterized council
versus assembly positions. Candidates often ran for one post, and then the
other. The existence of two positions per district, however, allowed parties
to consider matters of balance with respect to religion in areas that contained both Catholics and Protestants. Parties could also use the two positions to field male and female candidates.

Such was the case in 4th Prince in 1974, with the Liberals, PCs, and NDP
fielding male candidates for the Councillor seat, and female candidates for
the Assemblyman seat. That year, Campbell's Liberals were re-elected to a
majority government of twenty-six seats, while the opposition PCs secured
six. Callbeck won the 4th Prince Assemblyman position with 55 percent of
the votes cast. This result impressed the *Guardian*, which termed the significant mandate given to Catherine Callbeck as the election's "most stunning success." Described as a "Bedeque merchant," she was the second
woman ever elected to the PEI legislature (*Guardian* 1974a). The *Guardian*
said Callbeck ranked among the new Liberal MLAs who were being considered for cabinet (*Guardian* 1974b). The account proved prescient, since
the next day Campbell announced the appointment of five new ministers,
including Callbeck in the health and social services portfolios.

Callbeck thus became only the second woman in a PEI cabinet and the
first to hold a portfolio (in her case, two), the significance of which was recognized in a front-page *Guardian* headline that read "Second Woman Joins
Cabinet." The accompanying text reported that Callbeck "said she prefers to
be referred to as Miss Callbeck instead of 'Ms'" and noted that the "34-year
old minister, second youngest in the 10-member cabinet, said although she
is not a strong supporter of women's liberation, she supports recommendations contained in the [federal royal commission] report on the status of
women" (*Guardian* 1974c).

Callbeck thus became responsible for health and social services at a time
when PEI was beginning to modernize both departments. She dealt with
many contentious issues, including hospital closures and mergers, as well as
a transition from service delivery by religious orders and other private organizations to service delivery by public institutions. Perhaps, given reduced
federal transfer payments, her greatest challenge was financing the province's health care system (see Smiley 1972, 76; Maioni 1997, 414). Callbeck
described these challenges in words that would later guide her actions as
premier:

The dilemma facing Prince Edward Island then is to ensure that we are spending enough and allocating these funds appropriately to avoid the cost of an unhealthy population and at the same time to make sure we are not devoting a disproportionate amount of resources to health care so that other needs such as education or job creation programs are neglected. *Striking a balance is not an easy task.* (Callbeck as quoted in MacKinnon 2012, 120; emphasis added)

Not surprisingly, striking a balance between managing the family business and handling two portfolios also proved challenging. After one month on the job, Callbeck asked Campbell to be temporarily relieved of her health portfolio; he supported her request, although he reassured the public that Callbeck would resume her duties as soon as she could "rearrange her private commitments" (*Guardian* 1974d).

Callbeck soon resumed her position as health minister but still felt torn between business and public commitments. Beck (2014, 180) claims that, as early as December 1974, Callbeck had confided to family members that she would not seek re-election and would return to being a full-time businesswoman.[3] By 1978, she appears to have settled on her decision when she told her political colleagues that the family business needed her, and that she would not be running in the election slated for later that year. Interestingly, six other Liberal incumbents also declined to run in 1978.[4] While the family business was a compelling reason to leave politics, did Callbeck (and the six other Liberal incumbents) also sense that the fortunes of the PEI Liberals were about to change? Regardless of the full reasons why she decided to step aside, Callbeck seemed to disappear from public life at the youthful age of thirty-nine.

Becoming PEI Premier

Ten years later, Callbeck decided to return to public life and declared her candidacy for the federal Liberal nomination in the constituency of Malpeque. She had spent the intervening decade as a member of the Board of Governors of the University of Prince Edward Island and the Board of Regents of Mount Allison University. She served on the Maritime Provinces Higher Education Commission (MPHEC) and the Board of Directors of the Prince County Hospital. Callbeck had co-chaired the 1984 federal Liberal campaign in PEI. These contributions did not go unnoticed: Callbeck was acclaimed as candidate for Malpeque, won the seat with 52 percent of the vote, and joined the Liberal opposition to Mulroney's PC government in Ottawa in 1988.

However, Callbeck soon felt frustrated as an opposition MP, sensing that she could accomplish more for PEI at the provincial rather than at the federal level (*Guardian* 1993c; MacKinnon 2012, 171). When Premier Joe Ghiz announced his resignation in fall 1992, all eyes turned to Callbeck. The Liberals remained the party of choice for PEI voters, and their popularity only increased with the prospect of Callbeck as leader. One opinion poll asked voters whether they would prefer Callbeck or PC leader Patricia (Pat) Mella as premier. Seventy-five percent chose Callbeck (MacKinnon 2012, 171).

So Callbeck announced her candidacy for the provincial Liberal leadership in November 1992. Her entry into the race, together with Mella's position as PC leader, inspired at least one Island woman, Montague town councillor Bonnie MacLean-Peardon. As the only female councillor in Montague, Peardon faced considerable resistance from male colleagues who, according to one news account, labelled her interpersonal style as "bristling." Apparently, her "persistent questioning" so "enraged" her colleagues that the "council voted to eliminate question period from the monthly council agenda." Peardon credited her willingness to push back against the men on town council to the confident examples set by Callbeck and Mella; she predicted that 1993 would be "the year for women in politics" (Sharratt 1993b).

Callbeck faced no serious opposition in the Liberal leadership race: her opponents were Bill Campbell and Larry Creed, neither of whom had political experience and both of whom were seen as "fringe" or "rebel" nominees (see Sharratt 1993a). One national newspaper story contended that Callbeck's entry "scared away many leadership hopefuls" (*Globe and Mail* 1993). Cusack (2013, 264) agrees, writing that "when [Callbeck] entered the race, all the other leadership contenders decided not to run."

Callbeck immediately set the agenda for her term as premier. In a speech delivered in Summerside in January 1993, she outlined an economic strategy that built "on traditional strengths" but that nevertheless embraced new technologies to add value to old products. "The further development of our provincial economy will be the preoccupation of any government that I lead," she promised (Lambe 1993).[5] Newspaper editorials referred to Callbeck's certain "coronation" and described the race as a "comic opera" (*Guardian* 1993a). On 23 January 1993, more than fifteen hundred PEI Liberal delegates voted; 79 percent endorsed Callbeck. Reports persisted throughout the campaign that delegates were being pressed to vote for the two male candidates – not because the "backroom boys" opposed Callbeck but, rather, because Liberal insiders feared the appearance of a coronation (Sharratt 1993c). But a coronation it was, nevertheless.

Callbeck was sworn in as premier two days after the convention. Speaking at a party nomination meeting on 1 March, she announced her decision to hold an election at the end of the month. Many of the criticisms of her leadership during the 1993 campaign were ostensibly presented as praise, but the subtext was usually clear. For example, Callbeck was said to lack decisiveness, which prompted an editorial writer for the *Guardian* to write that, despite "all the fuss, flurry and criticism, it turns out that Catherine Callbeck does answer questions and does have an opinion." The same author noted her "firm position on a number of issues," arguing that, "agree or disagree, Ms. Callbeck does appear to have a mind of her own" (*Guardian* 1993b).

Opposition parties tried to exploit the claim that Callbeck was indecisive. One PC radio ad aired in 1993 featured a chuckling male voice that asked: "If you put identical glasses of water in front of Catherine Callbeck, which one would she choose?" The answer was: "Neither – she'd die of thirst before she could make a decision!" (quoted in Spears 1993). This allegation is ironic given that, after she left public office, Callbeck was accused of having a decisive personality that some said bordered on stubbornness but that others referred to as "assertiveness and decisive leadership" (Green 2006, 447).

The PEI Liberals won thirty-one of thirty-two legislative seats in 1993, a victory that the *Guardian* credited mainly to Callbeck and described as a "crushing" blow to the Conservatives (Townshend 1993a). The next day, Callbeck announced she would fly to Toronto to sell PEI as a good place to do business. The *Guardian* drew parallels between Callbeck's strategy and that of New Brunswick premier Frank McKenna, noting with approval that, like McKenna, Callbeck planned on courting the telecommunications industry (McDougall 1993).

Six Liberal women besides Callbeck were elected in 1993: Roberta Hubley, Libbe Hubley, Nancy Guptil, Rose Marie MacDonald, Marion Murphy, and Jeannie Lea.[6] All except Lea were incumbents and two (Roberta Hubley and Nancy Guptil) had served as cabinet ministers. As premier, Callbeck reduced the political executive from eleven to ten members and appointed Lea as minister responsible for government reform and the status of women as well as minister responsible for higher education, adult training and learning (see Green 2006, 446–47). Lea ended up as the sole woman besides Callbeck around the cabinet table.

Fiscal Challenges

Crossley (2000, 194) reports that, in 1994, a "single theme dominated public affairs in Prince Edward Island: change." This generalization could be applied to Callbeck's entire time as premier. Transitions often bring conflict and protest, both of which dominated Callbeck's term as she tried to lower the deficit, streamline government services, and reduce the size of the bureaucracy.

In preparing her first throne speech and budget, Callbeck saw PEI's debt as approaching a crisis point. It had reached $352 million in 1993, almost twice the level of 1989, in part because a new accounting system included some unfunded liabilities in the calculation. This explanation offered little comfort to Callbeck, whose business career had centred on managing a successful family enterprise. Since servicing the provincial debt accounted for 14 percent of PEI's annual budget,[7] funding for social programs was in jeopardy. To make matters worse, bond rating agencies threatened to downgrade PEI's borrowing status, a move that would raise interest rates and debt-servicing costs.

In the 1990s, many politicians and media commentators called for drastic measures to cut debt and eliminate deficits in order to prevent a fiscal crisis (see McQuaig 1996; Workman 1996; and Kelsey 2000). PEI was no exception, with newspaper headlines highlighting "skyrocketing deficits" and "record-breaking debt" (see, for example, *Guardian* 1993d), and the *Guardian* began to track the growth of the provincial deficit following the March 1993 election. By early June, the figure had surpassed $9.8 million. Editorials and commentaries suggested PEI would soon face a financial catastrophe of epic proportions. One deputy minister claimed the very existence of the province was in jeopardy (see McKenna 2015, 72–73n30).

Within this crisis atmosphere, Callbeck began implementing significant reforms to the province's health and education systems, economic development plans, land policy, electoral system, and, of course, the provincial budget. While local media and opposition politicians dismissed Callbeck's first throne speech as "short on specifics," her vision was clear to anyone who paid close attention to the text (see *Guardian* 1993e). Lieutenant-Governor Marion Reid delivered the speech on 7 June 1993. PEI, she read, had become "economically dependent on the rest of the country," a pattern that has "sapped our confidence and our drive to become more self-reliant." Moving forward, Reid continued, the province needed to "rethink the role and purpose of our government, and to remodel our institutions and structures to better address the needs of Islanders in this rapidly-changing world." The new government would reduce the size of the provincial civil service and streamline access to public services. The throne speech called for a reorganization of the civil service so that bureaucrats could operate with efficiency, transparency, and coordinated follow-through. Callbeck's government, said the lieutenant-governor, was committed to "sound financial management" (*Guardian* 1993e).

At the time, New Brunswick's Frank McKenna was being celebrated for his aggressive deficit reduction policies – to the point that popular magazines such as *Reader's Digest* profiled his approach (Magill 1994).[8] Callbeck followed suit. Her first budget of June 1993 pledged to cut PEI's deficit by two-thirds, primarily by reducing capital and program expenditures by nearly $55 million over three years. While headlines in the *Guardian* expressed disappointment that Callbeck had not gone further, stating "Budget Lacks Real Bite" (Townshend 1993b), the strategy was seen as too radical by many PEI voters. Almost immediately, the tide of public opinion turned against Callbeck.

The initial Liberal budget also called for three fewer government departments and for reduced spending on departments, Crown corporations, MLA offices, capital projects, and public-sector salaries. The budget imposed cuts of as much as 30 percent on departmental spending. This seemed extreme; however, Callbeck's approach was consistent with recommendations by many leading economists and fiscal planners at the time, who argued that governments should impose cuts quickly, across the board, and all at once.

New Zealand finance minister Roger Douglas toured the Maritimes in this period to promote a "blitzkrieg" approach to debt reduction, which he claimed would soon eliminate government debt (Douglas 1993; Desserud 1995). The parallels between New Zealand and PEI were not lost on the editors of the *Guardian*, who compared PEI's situation with that of New Zealand before Douglas' reforms (see McKenna 2015, 58; MacAleer 1994). Other provinces tried to implement Douglas's recommendations (see Kelsey 2000; McQuaig 1996), and, in PEI, the task fell to Finance Minister Wayne Cheverie. As he explained to the *Guardian*: "There's no death like a slow death. It's gotta be done and it's gotta be done quickly" (Cheverie as quoted in Crossley 1999, 207).

Energy Policy

An arguably bright spot in Callbeck's record as premier involved a plan for the New Brunswick and PEI governments to purchase Maritime Electric, a utility company that provided electricity to the Island. Maritime Electric was privately owned by Fortis Inc., a Newfoundland and Labrador-based firm that, in 1990, purchased majority shares in the utility. Most of the electricity used by PEI was generated by NB Power and transmitted from NB to PEI via power cables under the Northumberland Strait (see Stuart 2016).

In March 1994, Callbeck's government surprised observers, including Maritime Electric, by announcing the two provinces would purchase the shares owned by Fortis and then hand over operation of the utility to NB Power. Callbeck claimed this decision would secure the Island's energy future, create efficiencies, and potentially reduce power rates by as much as 25 percent (Day 1994a). While this proposal would have made PEI dependent on power delivery and rates set in NB, it sparked none of the outrage voiced in the latter province in 2009 when an attempt was made to sell NB Power to Hydro-Québec (see Desserud 2015).

One *Guardian* editorial called the co-ownership plan "a brilliant move," linking the possibility of lower power rates to improved employment prospects for young people that could, in turn, slow down the exodus of Island youth (*Guardian* 1994a). In the end, however, the deal proved too complicated to be concluded before Callbeck resigned as premier, and it was dropped in 2000 by the PC government of Pat Binns (MacKinnon 2012, 229).

Social Policy and Electoral Reform

Callbeck undertook major reforms to health and community services, most notably the creation of a health and community services agency to oversee and coordinate health and social services. Five regional boards were made responsible for the delivery of those services. Callbeck's government reduced PEI school boards from five to three, cut board budgets, and reduced school bus routes. Her government also established an office of higher education, training, and adult learning, as well as a commission on municipal reform tasked with recommending municipal amalgamations.

Callbeck's time as premier also saw the passage of the Victims of Violence Act, which made it possible for a person accused of domestic abuse to be removed from his or her home before trial. Yet the government's budget cuts seriously weakened programs directed towards, or specifically of benefit to, women. Cuts were implemented across the public bureaucracy in such a way that they affected all departments and agencies, including education and welfare units. While across-the-board strategies appear to share budget reductions evenly, they often have a far greater impact on vulnerable populations than do selective cuts.

Finally, Callbeck would be the last premier to be elected under the old two-member riding system, and her government oversaw the most radical reform of the province's electoral system since the Legislative Assembly and Council were merged in 1893. A court challenge alleged extreme population variance among voting districts in PEI (see *MacKinnon v. Government of Prince Edward Island* 1993). Callbeck's government responded by passing a new election act and creating an electoral boundaries commission, which concluded that the province should adopt single-member constituencies based on population. While the commission recommended a total of thirty constituencies, the legislature settled on twenty-seven single-member ridings (MacKinnon 2012, 206–12). One consequence of these changes was that many Liberal MLAs found themselves in the same constituency as others in the same caucus. When Callbeck was urged to call an early election in 1996, she hesitated in part because there was still confusion over who would run where.

From Empowered to Imperiled

Callbeck's economic reforms and two successive balanced budgets were arguably her greatest accomplishments. They entailed cuts, however, that carried politically disastrous implications. In particular, Callbeck seemed to misread the mood of voters in rural areas and in organized labour. Institutions that received public funding – including hospitals, schools, the provincial bureaucracy, Holland College, and UPEI – were ordered to reduce wages immediately by 7.5 percent. As MacKinnon (2012, 213) writes, "the magnitude and speed of the reform initiatives outpaced their acceptance by Islanders." Budgetary decisions were seen as evidence that Callbeck and her colleagues did not respect Island communities and Island ways of life. Decades later, people affected by the rollbacks remained bitter (Walker 2018).

From another perspective, Callbeck's good intentions may have simply backfired. In April 1994, MLAs agreed to lower their salaries – a move considered as too little, too late. An attempt to cut MLA pensions was described by the *Guardian* as "a last-ditch effort to spike the public outrage" (Beazley 1994a), and it may have even stoked discontent because it placed lucrative MLA retirement benefits in the limelight. According to Mella, pensions for provincial legislators were "the richest ... in North America" (as quoted in Cusack 2013, 269; see also MacKinnon 2012, 216).

Policy as well as fiscal reforms were condemned by critics who said that, taken together, these decisions reflected Callbeck's disregard for Island norms. Plans to amalgamate municipalities, eliminate school boards, and downgrade some hospitals were considered as evidence that Callbeck did not respect local communities. Worse yet, the premier's policies were seen as direct threats to Island life. The fact that some of these reforms might have been needed was not the point.

As resistance to Callbeck's actions escalated, photographs of citizens protesting budget cuts and municipal amalgamations featured in the *Guardian*'s provincial news coverage. "Say No to [Finance Minister] Cheverie, Labor [sic] Leader Urges" read a front-page headline in the 22 April 1994 edition. "Protestors Call for Resignations of Callbeck, Cheverie, [Education Minister] Milligan" was a page-three story lead on the same day. The 4 May 1994 front-page headline read: "Protestors Storm [Province] House" (Day 1994b). Meanwhile, investment agencies pressured the government to act faster and more decisively in the opposite direction. The Canadian Bond Rating Service downgraded its rating of PEI debentures to triple B (from triple B plus) and lowered the government's short-term credit status to A-1 low from A-1 (Beazley 1994b).

Consistent with the argument presented in Chapter 1, Callbeck's leadership style became a pivot for critics. *Guardian* editorials moved from emphasizing how the Liberal government should make the hard decisions needed to bring the deficit under control towards portraying Callback as captain of "a rudderless ship caught in the ice floes of the Northumberland Strait" (*Guardian* 1994b). The newspaper's associate editor, Walter MacIntyre, went so far as to question Callbeck's ability to get the job done. In his view, her "low key style" contrasted unfavourably with the aggressive approach of Alberta premier Ralph Klein (MacIntyre 1994).

Given her sense that speaking with protestors would only enflame passions, Callbeck declined an opportunity to address the critics. So some observers labelled her behaviour as cowardice. But when Callbeck did address protesters, the *Guardian* reported that she was "seen nervously rehearsing a brief speech" and that crowds "booed and hissed as she spoke" (McKenna 1994).

In the same period, tensions between Callbeck and Mella reached a breaking point. Callbeck chastised Mella, the leader and sole member of the opposition, for smiling on one occasion when the premier was explaining details of civil-service wage cuts. "It's really difficult when I'm trying to address this serious question and the leader of the Opposition sits there and smiles" (Callbeck as quoted in Beazley 1994c). Mella then "stalked out and shut herself in her caucus room," declaring she would not return to the chamber unless the premier apologized. Callbeck did not apologize, at least not in the chamber, but she did send a note to Mella asking to meet in an anteroom behind the speaker's chair. According to media reports, the two women then engaged in a rather "loud conversation." The two returned together, and the premier explained to MLAs that she had accepted Mella's contention that she had not been smirking and that the misunderstanding had been resolved. "Certainly," Callbeck told her fellow MLAs, "everybody here's been under a great deal of stress" (Beazley 1994c; see also Cusack 2013, 268–69).

Given that rollbacks to civil service wages required the Callbeck government to break union contracts, labour interests were incensed. The president of the PEI Union of Public Sector Employees, Mike Butler, claimed that violating contracts was worse than cutting wages. "Islanders are noted for dealing by your word," he said. "A handshake is a contract, and she [Callbeck] broke a collective agreement. That upset a number of Islanders." Butler also criticized what he termed Callbeck's "aloofness." Speaking just after Callbeck announced her resignation in August 1996, Butler said he had already held more meetings with the new PC leader, Pat Binns, in the previous three months than he had had with Callbeck during the nearly four years she was premier (Canadian Press 1996).

Protests continued to escalate. In one incident, Callbeck was rumoured to have fled a noisy demonstration through a tunnel connecting the legislature with a nearby office building. It remains unclear whether she had in fact fled, but the five thousand or so protestors believed she had. "Flood the tunnel!" they shouted (Cusack 2013, 268). In short, Callbeck's circumstances had deteriorated rapidly from empowered leadership of a successful governing party in 1993 to imperiled status at the helm of a deeply unpopular government.

Resignation

Waves of protest and weakened poll numbers concerned Liberal strategists, as did the arrival in May 1996 of a new provincial PC leader, Pat Binns. He had served in the cabinets of Premiers Angus MacLean and James Lee from

1979 to 1984 and then as federal MP for Cardigan from 1984 to 1988. Binns enjoyed a popularity that crossed party lines, and so was seen as a more serious threat to Callbeck than his predecessor.

Binns might have been popular, but he did not have recent provincial political experience, nor had he ever been a party leader. Thus Callbeck was urged to call a snap election for spring 1996. The call was to be announced on 28 May. Signs were printed, and some were even hammered into the lawns of eager Liberals. Newspaper advertisements were designed, and an election headquarters was rented. "They even had a campaign song," writes MacKinnon (2012, 256).

However, a new poll was released just before the scheduled announcement, and this changed everything. Data showed the PCs ahead of the Liberals by five points, 47 to 42 percent. Binns was the declared choice of 36 percent of voters surveyed, compared with Callbeck at 26 percent. The Liberal premier had experienced a 14 percentage point drop from a poll conducted the previous November (see Cusack 2013, 276; DeMont 1996).

Liberals who crowded into the Bluefield High School gymnasium and expected an election call were in for a shock. Callbeck took the stage, acknowledged the cheers, and announced the following: "I've given it careful consideration and I've concluded that Islanders do not want an election at this time" (as quoted in MacKinnon 2012, 255). Her decision to stop the election campaign before it officially began raised alarm bells in the Liberal caucus and among party power brokers. Murmurs of discontent grew louder as Liberals saw their opportunity to win slip away (see MacKinnon 2012, 256–57).

Still, observers expected the election call to come fairly soon. Summer 1996 saw a "phoney campaign" as Callbeck and her team criss-crossed PEI to meet voters. Yet, by August, it was clear to the premier that she had lost the confidence of many citizens. At a news conference in Charlottetown, Callbeck announced her resignation. In her words, "I've reached a turning point in my life, and I choose to move on" (as quoted in MacKinnon 2012, 260).

Three years and eight months after reaching top office, Callbeck presumably understood the consequences of persistent protests and weak poll numbers. To what extent, however, was she forced to resign by fellow Liberals? Trimble and Arscott (2003) argue that Callbeck's declining popularity convinced powerful party insiders that she had to go, and they maintain that this was not simply the result of a premier facing a drop in popularity. In

Callbeck's case, they argue, the decision to resign was likely the result of "a leadership *putsch*" from "Backroom Boys" who believed her weak approval ratings were the direct result of her gender (Trimble and Arscott 2003, 91, emphasis in original).

Similarly, *Globe and Mail* columnist Robert Sheppard sees a double standard at play. Given rumours that Liberal backroomers were frustrated because Callbeck did not call an election when she was more popular, Sheppard (1996) asks whether it was fair "to label as fainthearted someone who has balanced the provincial budget, twice now, when former Liberal and Conservative premiers didn't; who has changed the island's school system, converted hospitals to clinics, pressed ahead with the controversial fixed-link to the mainland, and reformed the province's stumpy old two-member districts electoral system?"

Following Callbeck's resignation, Liberals chose Keith Mulligan as their new leader. He called an election for November 1996, at which point Binns's PCs won a majority government with eighteen seats. The Liberals held eight constituencies and the NDP one. About a year later, Prime Minister Jean Chrétien appointed Callbeck to the Senate, where she remained until her retirement in 2014.

Assessing the Record

Upon her induction into the Canadian Women in Politics Hall of Fame, Callbeck reflected: "I did not set out to blaze a trail for women in politics. I hope that my career will serve as an inspiration to all women throughout Canada. I hope it will give them the confidence that their participation is not only possible, but needed as never before" (as quoted in MacKinnon 2012, 236). Callbeck's assessment of her time in public service offers an honest appraisal: while perhaps not a trailblazer for substantive feminist policies, she stands nevertheless as a political pioneer who enabled women to believe they could hold top public office.

Whether Callbeck measurably supported other women remains a contentious subject. On the one hand, she has been praised for championing women's ascent to positions of influence. Dianne Porter served as chair of the Prince Edward Island Advisory Council on the Status of Women from 1986 to 1989, and in 1991 became deputy minister responsible for the newly created provincial Women's Secretariat. In an interview, Porter pointed out that Callbeck named "many women to significant appointments," which included "roles as chairs of government committees" and appointments to "government boards and agencies." Callbeck was also credited with "advance[ing] women in the party executive." As a result, Porter maintained, under Callbeck, "there were more women in senior management" than under previous premiers (Porter as quoted in Bernard 2002, 57–58).

On the other hand, policies designed to advance women were never Callbeck's top priority. As Sharpe (1994, 198) explains, "Callbeck does not bring what the Ontario New Democrats call 'a feminist analysis' to politics. Her priorities are not driven by sexist language, male behaviour in the legislature, or gender inequities in society."

The controversy over Callbeck's legacy invariably centres on her fiscal policies. In PEI, economically vulnerable women were often the most drastically affected by serious budget cuts. According to the National Council of Welfare, the Callbeck years saw a loss of provincial social assistance benefits to the level of "$2,568 a year for a single employable person, $542 for a disabled person, $815 for a single parent with one child, and $1,125 for a couple with two children." As the report explains: "Prince Edward Island entered the 1990s with a series of improvements that made the province's welfare system one of the most progressive in Canada. All that changed in 1993, however, with a series of freezes and cuts that reduced welfare entitlements noticeably over the next several years" (1997 National Council of Welfare Report as quoted in Bernard 2002, 53n11).

Yet, to Callbeck's credit, the PEI economy was in better shape when she left office than when she arrived. The 1995 economic growth rate of 2.6 percent was the second highest in Canada, and provincial GDP rose with the employment rate. Some of this growth came from the construction of the Confederation Bridge, a fixed link to Canada's mainland via New Brunswick. Once the fixed link was completed, the province's economic growth stalled (see Buker 2002, 189). In short, it is hard to know the extent to which Callbeck-era reforms improved economic circumstances in PEI.

PEI historian Ed MacDonald writes that Callbeck "could hardly be described as a feminist icon," although he concludes that she "would not have been elected had she been one" (MacDonald 2000, 363). MacDonald is being neither glib nor apologetic: Catherine Callbeck's career unfolded within a specific social, cultural, and political context. She grew up in a financially comfortable family, enjoyed a high-quality education in business, was well connected with the political elites of her time, and developed a range of practical skills by running the family store. This background shaped the policies she chose to follow, and it meant that she approached the challenge of governing with the steely eye of a successful businesswoman. Overall, her focus as premier was reforming government organization, processes, and infrastructure.

Hers may not be a particularly exciting legacy, but it remains solid and worthwhile. Many a male premier has been praised for precisely Callbeck's approach to economic management, including her New Brunswick contemporary Frank McKenna. So while Callbeck might not have intended to stake a claim for feminism, she did strike a balance that, as she said, was no easy task. Seeking compromise often meant Callbeck's contributions were not widely recognized, let alone celebrated.

To quote Baldacchino (2005, 248), "an island is a nervous duality." Perhaps Callbeck's attempt to strike a balance between public and private interests, and between fiscal prudence and social justice, revealed a tenuous "nervous duality." As Bernard (2002, i) writes, Callbeck did things "quietly, without praise but also without backlash." Obviously, there was backlash. But overall, Callbeck stopped short of taking radical action that would have created even more conflict than was already in play.

Catherine Callbeck succeeded in a world then and now dominated by men, and she did so in a manner that often drew harsh appraisals – including from inside her own party. Her gender was a defining part of her identity as a politician because it was often used as a means of undermining her credibility and competence. Yet Callbeck's experience as a successful businesswoman equipped her to make informed fiscal decisions that were in line with leading economic doctrines of the time. She participated – bravely – in the political life of PEI when many women did not, or could not. This in itself stands as a major accomplishment.

Notes

1 The photo was taken by Brian L. Simpson, provincial photographer, and shows Nancy Guptill (speaker), Marion Reid (lieutenant-governor), Pat Mella (leader of the opposition), Catherine Callbeck (premier), and Elizabeth Hubley (deputy speaker).

2 Island newspapers at the time made no pretense of being politically neutral. In 1935, the Liberals under Walter Lea won all thirty-two seats. The headline in the *Guardian* the next day read: "Island Votes for Liberal Dictatorship."

3 MacKinnon (2012, 122) reports that Callbeck's decision was made in 1977: "Following a long discussion with her brother Bill in early December 1977, she made up her mind to retire from politics."

4 In 1974, 25 other Liberals won their seats in an assembly of 32 members. In 1978, 11 Liberal candidates from 1974 chose not to run – including Callbeck. The Liberals won 17 of 32 seats in 1978. In 1979, the Liberals secured only 11 seats and the PCs 21.

5 The headline for Lambe's (1993) story read: "Callbeck Says PEI Needs Salesman [sic]." In the story, Callbeck is quoted as saying, "I believe that a province's foremost, and certainly most visible *salesperson*, is its premier" (emphasis added).

6 The only Liberal candidate to lose in 1993 was Betty Jean Brown, who lost to PC leader Pat Mella in 3rd Queens, Assemblyman seat.

7 In 2018, servicing the debt accounted for 10 percent of the PEI budget.

8 Whether McKenna's policies worked remains a controversial subject. See, for example, Milne (1996) and Savoie (2001).

References

Baldacchino, Godfrey. 2005. "Islands: Objects of Representation. *Geografiska Annaler. Series B, Human Geography*. 87: 247–51.

Baldwin, Douglas. 1985. *Abegweit: Land of the Red Soil*. Charlottetown: Ragweed Press.

Beazley, Doug. 1994a. "Liberals Roll Back MLA's Pension Benefits." *Guardian* (Charlottetown), 28 April.

–. 1994b. "Bond Rating Service Downgrades PEI." *Guardian* (Charlottetown), 4 May.

–. 1994c. "Pat Mella Storms out of Chamber as Stress Shows on Both Leaders." *Guardian* (Charlottetown), 14 May.

Beck, Boyde. 2014. *Callbeck's of Bedeque: A Century of Island Enterprise*. Charlottetown: Prince Edward Island Museum and Heritage Foundation.

Bernard, Gina. 2002. "More Than Meets the Eye? Women's Leadership, Women's Organizations and Public Policy in Prince Edward Island, 1993–1996." MA thesis, Carleton University.

Buker, Peter E. 2002. "Prince Edward Island." In *Canadian Annual Review of Politics and Public Affairs, 1996*, ed. David Mutimer, 189–97. Toronto: University of Toronto Press.

Canadian Press. 1996. "Callbeck's Fall from Grace No Surprise to Labor." *Canadian Press NewsWire*, 9 August, https://search.proquest.com/docview/359486910?accountid=14670.

Crossley, John. 1997. "Picture This: Women Politicians Hold Key Posts in Prince Edward Island." In *In the Presence of Women: Representation in Canadian Governments*, ed. Jane Arscott and Linda Trimble, 278–307. Toronto: Harcourt Brace.

–. 1999. "Prince Edward Island." In *Canadian Annual Review of Politics and Public Affairs, 1993*, ed. David Layton-Brown, 204–11. Toronto: University of Toronto Press.

–. 2000. "Prince Edward Island." In *Canadian Annual Review of Politics and Public Affairs, 1994*, ed. David Layton-Brown, 194–201. Toronto: University of Toronto Press.

Cusack, Leonard. 2013. *A Party for Progress: The P.E.I. Progressive Conservative Party, 1770–2000*. Charlottetown: Retromedia Publishing.

Day, Jim. 1994a. "PEI Moves to Buy Power Utility." *Guardian* (Charlottetown), 3 March.

–. 1994b. "Protestors Storm House." *Guardian* (Charlottetown), 4 May.

DeMont, John. 1996. "An Island Stunner." *Maclean's*, 109, 34 (19 August): 27.

Desserud, Don. 1995. "Roger and Me." *Beacon* (Atlantic Institute for Market Studies), 1: 10–13.

–. 2015. "The Political Economy of New Brunswick." In *Transforming Provincial Politics: The Political Economy of Canada's Provinces and Territories in the Neoliberal Era*, ed. Bryan Evans and Charles Smith, 110–34. Toronto: University of Toronto Press.

Douglas, Roger. 1993. *Unfinished Business*. Auckland, NZ: Random House New Zealand.

Globe and Mail. 1993. "PEI Liberals Expected to Choose Callbeck." 23 January.

Green, John Eldon. 2006. *A Mind of One's Own: Memoirs of an Albany Boy*. PEI: Tangle Lane.

Guardian (Charlottetown). 1974a. "Liberals Win 26 Seats in Third Term Victory." 30 April.

–. 1974b. "New Cabinet Slate Today." 2 May.

–. 1974c. "Second Woman Joins Cabinet." 3 May.

–. 1974d. "New Health Minister Callbeck Temporarily Relieved of Duties." 24 May.

–. 1993a. "Great Ideas Make Leaders." 5 January.

–. 1993b. "The Callbeck Approach." 13 January.

–. 1993c. "Callbeck Woos West Prince." 15 January.

–. 1993d. "Deficit Skyrockets, Welfare Rolls Swell." 5 June.

–. 1993e. "Speech Opens Legislature." 8 June.

–. 1994a. "Electric Deal Brilliant Move." 4 March.

–. 1994b. "Speech Ignores One Big Problem." 10 March.

Kelsey, Jane. 2000. *Reclaiming the Future: New Zealand and the Global Economy*. Toronto: University of Toronto Press.

Lambe, Sandra. 1993. "Callbeck Says PEI Needs Salesman." *Guardian* (Charlottetown), 13 January.

MacAleer, J.W. 1994. "Debt and Our Destiny." *Guardian* (Charlottetown), 10 May.

MacDonald, Edward. 2000. *If You're Stronghearted: Prince Edward Island in the Twentieth Century*. Charlottetown: Prince Edward Island Museum and Heritage Foundation.

MacIntyre, Wayne. 1994. "Callbeck Style Low-Key." *Guardian* (Charlottetown), 11 May.

MacKinnon v. Government of Prince Edward Island (1993) 101 D.L.R. (4th) 362.

MacKinnon, Frank. 1951. *The Government of Prince Edward Island*. Toronto. University of Toronto Press.

MacKinnon, Wayne. 2012. *Catherine Callbeck: The Politics of Principle*. Charlottetown: JHB Publishing.

Magill, Charles. 1994. "Frank McKenna, Hands-On Premier." *Reader's Digest*, 144: 49–55.

Maioni, Antonia. 1997. "Parting at the Crossroads: The Development of Health Insurance in Canada and the United States, 1940–1965." *Comparative Politics* 29: 411–31.

McDougall, Tom. 1993. "Callbeck Launches Sales Job in Toronto." *Guardian* (Charlottetown), 31 March.

McKenna, Barb. 1994. "Premier Seen Nervously Rehearsing Brief Speech." *Guardian* (Charlottetown), 12 May.

McKenna, Peter. 2015. "Politics on Prince Edward Island: Plus ça change." In *Transforming Provincial Politics: The Political Economy of Canada's Provinces and Territories in the Neoliberal Era*, ed. Bryan Evans and Charles Smith, 49–76. Toronto: University of Toronto Press.

McQuaig, Linda. 1996. *Shooting the Hippo: Death by Deficit and Other Canadian Myths*. Toronto: Penguin.

Milne, William J. 1996. *The McKenna Miracle: Myth or Reality?* Toronto: University of Toronto Press.

Savoie, Donald J. 2001. *Pulling against Gravity: Economic Development in New Brunswick during the McKenna Years*. Montreal: Institute for Research on Public Policy.

Sharpe, Sydney. 1994. *The Gilded Ghetto: Women and Political Power in Canada*. Toronto: HarperCollins.

Sharratt, Stephen. 1993a. "Dark Cloud or Silver Lining?" *Guardian* (Charlottetown), 2 January.

–. 1993b. "1993 – Year for Women in PEI Politics." *Guardian* (Charlottetown), 11 January.

–. 1993c. "Pressure Tactics Emerge in Race." *Guardian* (Charlottetown), 13 January.

Sheppard, Robert. 1996. "Premier Callbeck's Departure." *Globe and Mail*, 14 August.

Smiley, Donald. 1972. *Canada in Question: Federalism in the Seventies*. Toronto: McGraw-Hill Ryerson.

Spears, John. 1993. "Liberals Cocky about Prospects in PEI." *Toronto Star*, 8 March.

Stuart, Kathleen. 2016. "Two Centuries of Energy on Prince Edward Island." In *Time and a Place: An Environmental History of Prince Edward Island*, ed. Edward MacDonald, Joshua MacFadyen, and Irené Novaczek, 264–87. Montreal: McGill-Queen's University Press.

Townshend, Geoff. 1993a. "Rout Puts Callbeck in History Books." *Guardian* (Charlottetown), 30 March.

–. 1993b. "Budget Lacks Real Bite." *Guardian* (Charlottetown), 18 June.

Trimble, Linda, and Jane Arscott. 2003. *Still Counting: Women in Politics across Canada*. Peterborough: Broadview Press.

Walker, Gary. 2018. "Bullied by Government: The 1994 PEI Public Sector Wage Rollback Will Not Go Away after 24 Years." *Guardian* (Charlottetown), 17 April.

Workman, W. Thom. 1996. *Banking on Deception: The Discourse of Fiscal Crisis*. Halifax: Fernwood.

6

In the Wake of Male Charisma

Kathy Dunderdale and the Status
of Women in Newfoundland and
Labrador Politics

DREW BROWN, ELIZABETH GOODYEAR-GRANT,
and AMANDA BITTNER

This chapter examines how women's leadership in Newfoundland and Labrador has shaped women's numerical representation as well as the public policy and legislative process dimensions of politics in the province. In terms of numerical representation, the political history of NL is not one in which women play a central role, despite the fact that women briefly headed all three parties in the provincial legislature from 2010 to 2011 (see Bittner and Goodyear-Grant 2013). The arrival of women party leaders and the province's first woman premier, Kathy Dunderdale, who led a Progressive Conservative government, presents a chance to assess their effect on women's descriptive and substantive representation. These questions have been unduly overlooked as "female leaders and ministers have largely been studied in isolation from one another, and little is known about the relationship between the two" (O'Brien et al. 2015, 690).

Focusing on Dunderdale's period as premier, we ask whether she appointed more women and whether she followed a more women-centred, or indeed feminist, policy agenda than her male counterparts. The chapter offers mixed conclusions. Dunderdale appointed more women to the senior civil service than her predecessors, particularly to deputy minister positions. Women were only 20 percent of deputy ministers at the start of Dunderdale's premiership, and, over the course of four years in office, Dunderdale increased this figure to half, or gender parity.

In terms of promoting women MHAs to cabinet, Dunderdale fared less well than her charismatic predecessor as PC leader, Danny Williams. One reason for this decline was women's reduced proportions as candidates and legislators. On the policy front, Dunderdale was a strong proponent of women's rights and gender equality, but she devoted so much time in office to the Muskrat Falls hydroelectric project in Labrador and a series of other political crises that gender-related issues seemed to fall off the radar screen.

Dunderdale's record reminds us that, even under what Chapter 1 terms "empowered circumstances," executive agendas can be profoundly shaped by the turbulent times in which premiers govern rather than by the values and priorities they bring to public office. Consistent with other chapters, we find that the presence of a woman premier failed to shift the tone of political debate in NL from one of conflict toward consensus – which makes sense given the contentious period in which Dunderdale governed.

Women's Leadership in Newfoundland and Labrador

Lynn Verge, the province's first woman party leader, led the opposition PCs from 1995 to 1996. In the 1989 provincial election, Verge defeated provincial Liberal leader and premier Clyde Wells in the constituency of Humber East. Kathy Dunderdale, who would later become premier, co-chaired Verge's 1995 party leadership campaign. Lorraine Michael served as leader of the provincial NDP from 2006 to 2015, while Yvonne Jones led the Liberals from 2007 to 2011 – when both parties were in opposition.

Given Williams's sustained popularity as premier, Dunderdale took over as PC leader in empowered circumstances with large boots to fill (see Chapter 1). Dunderdale was hand-picked by her predecessor in 2010 and led the PCs to a majority government victory in the 2011 provincial election. As the first woman to lead a governing party in NL, Dunderdale held the premier's office from 2010 to 2014. For a short time in 2010–11, all three parties in the provincial legislature were headed by women. This milestone marked an important departure for NL from its history as a place where women's representation in formal politics was often less visible than elsewhere in Canada (see Bittner and Goodyear-Grant 2013).

Dunderdale attributes her political career to a desire to serve the community and to make a difference in the world. Interviewed after leaving elective office, she reflected, "For me, it was always about the work and making a difference and trying to remember who I work for and why I put my hand up to do that" (Bird 2016). This motivation rings true given that, at the time of writing, Dunderdale served as volunteer coordinator at the Gathering Place, a charitable organization in St. John's that provides people in need with food, shelter, and clothing. We often see former premiers re-enter the business world, join corporate boards, and so on. Rarely do they coordinate volunteers in the social welfare sector.

Dunderdale's commitment to feminism and gender equality was visible from the start. A CBC (2011a) news story notes she was a social worker before entering politics and "had been active in women's groups and feminist causes for many years before being elected to the house of assembly in 2003." When sworn in as premier, Dunderdale emphasized the historic moment for women in NL: "I am reminded of how different life was for my own grandmother. Until 1925, a woman could not even vote in Newfoundland and Labrador and today for the very first time in our province's history, a woman serves as premier" (CBC 2011a). In short, Dunderdale recognized the gendered nature of politics and her own position as a trailblazer.

Dunderdale became the third woman in Canada to lead her party to victory in a general election, after Callbeck in PEI and Duncan in Yukon. In 2011, the NL PCs won thirty-seven of the province's forty-eight seats, only six fewer than under Danny Williams and a commanding majority by any metric. As Bashevkin (2009, 44) points out, patterns of women's leadership in Canadian politics suggest that they are generally more likely than men to lead wilderness parties and once-popular parties now on the decline, something that she refers to as the "loser syndrome" (see also Bashevkin 1993). Plainly, Dunderdale was no "loser," which is all the more reason to examine her record on women's representation and policy. She had a strong mandate and her party had a winning record that made her an empowered successor to Williams, permitting bold action had she chosen such a course.

Dunderdale had a reputation for taking gender equality seriously. In private conversations, many civil servants said she appointed women in larger numbers than had been the case in the past. Data obtained from the NL legislative library and the province's Women's Policy Office suggest that women were placed in senior roles more often over time but that this pattern was much more apparent in the civil service than in cabinet. Indeed, Dunderdale presided over a decidedly less equal governing caucus and cabinet than did Williams. We examine appointments first, moving later in the chapter to the more complicated task of assessing how women and gender influenced Dunderdale's policy agenda.

FIGURE 6.1

Proportion of women in cabinet and in governing caucus in NL, 2003–16

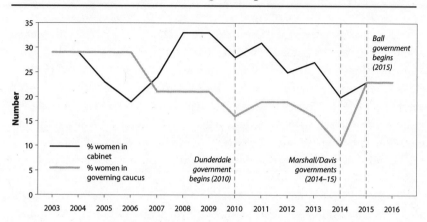

Women in Cabinet

In their account of women's descriptive representation in NL, Bittner and Goodyear-Grant (2013, 123) observe that "women's representation in cabinet has exceeded their legislative presence for more than a decade." In part, this reflects the fact that, for most of the province's postwar history, very few women served in the House of Assembly compared with elsewhere in Canada (see Trimble et al. 2013). The dramatic underrepresentation of women in the House of Assembly continues. Women were approximately 25 percent of sitting members at the time this research was conducted.

Figure 6.1 tracks the proportion of women in both cabinet and governing caucus from 2003 to 2016. It shows that women's presence in cabinet over the last ten years has generally been high relative to proportions in the governing caucus, suggesting that premiers have tended to draw heavily on women caucus members to fill cabinet positions. In 2007, four years after winning a landslide election, Danny Williams began to elevate women in his caucus more so than during his first term as premier from 2003 to 2007, when his cabinet was considerably less gender balanced than the PC caucus.

During Dunderdale's term as premier, the proportion of women in the cabinet dropped from its 2009 zenith. Figure 6.1 shows that levels declined from a high of 33 percent to a low of 20 percent. Under Dunderdale's leadership, the proportion of women in the PC caucus also dropped dramatically as women resigned their legislative seats.[1] Indeed, in 2014 Susan Sullivan was the only female in the PC caucus and the only woman in cabinet until newly elected party leader Paul Davis appointed Judy Manning (see CBC 2014).[2]

Overall, women's share of governing caucus seats dropped to 10 percent, or one female member, after Dunderdale's resignation in 2014. This situation underscores the extent to which gender underrepresentation and patterns of change over time in women's numbers follow from many different factors. We cannot assume a simple linear relationship between women's executive leadership and women's legislative presence. Data from NL show more women in legislative politics under a male premier (Williams) than under his female successor (Dunderdale). Williams led a party caucus and cabinet with higher proportions of women than did the province's first female premier.

The fact that women's representation in caucus and cabinet declined after a female leader was chosen is consistent with O'Brien et al.'s (2015, 690) hypothesis concerning the relationship in right-wing parties between women's executive leadership and cabinet appointments: "the presence of female leaders – especially in nonleft governments – will result in the nomination of fewer women to (high-prestige) portfolios." Part of their explanation rests on the relatively shallow demands for gender representation in right-wing parties and governments, which can easily be met when a woman leads the organization. Her ascent, in turn, reduces pressures for the party to recruit more women to legislative candidacies.

The pattern of appointing women to cabinet in higher proportions than their presence in the governing party caucus ended with the 2015 provincial election, when Liberal leader Dwight Ball secured a majority government. In 2015, ten women were elected to the legislature, three in opposition and seven in the governing caucus. As of mid-2017, the provincial cabinet contained thirteen members, including three women (Cathy Bennett, Siobhan Coady, and Sherry Gambin-Walsh), from a caucus of twenty-nine Liberals. Premier Ball was thus under-utilizing the female members of his caucus in comparison to premiers of the recent past.

This trend is notable given that Ball presides over a party of the centre, while the two previous premiers headed a party on the right in the NL political spectrum. Parties of the centre and left typically have higher proportions of women candidates and legislators than do conservative formations (see Kittilson 2006; Lovenduski and Norris 1993). Figure 6.1 shows the stronger numerical representation of women in the Liberal caucus following the 2014 PC defeat. In cabinet, however, the PCs appointed more women than the Liberal governments that preceded Williams and followed Dunderdale.

How do we interpret the promotion of women to cabinet by PC as compared with Liberal premiers? Did Williams and Dunderdale use appointments to enhance the representational credibility of their governments amid the low and often declining proportions of PC women candidates (see Bittner and Goodyear-Grant 2013) and legislators (see Figure 6.1)? We suggest that women's cabinet appointments may have been part of an effort to draw attention away from shrinking numbers of female candidates and caucus members.

At the same time, comparative research shows that right-wing parties have in some cases been "feminizing" – that is, catching up on representation and policy making with formations on the left (see Celis and Erzeel 2015; Childs and Webb 2012; Piscopo 2014). Conservative parties may explain their willingness to appoint women by referring to a merit-based approach that rewards achieving individuals. Such actions may respond to "contagion" from the centre and left of the political spectrum (see Kittilson 2006; Matland and Studlar 1996). As noted in Chapter 1, the UK's first two female prime ministers, Margaret Thatcher and Theresa May, were both Conservatives. Canada's only female prime minister, Kim Campbell, was a Progressive Conservative, and multiple women premiers – including Dunderdale, Alison Redford in Alberta, and Christy Clark in BC – came from parties of the right. Moreover, Conservative Stephen Harper was the first Canadian prime minister to reach the 30 percent mark in women's cabinet representation (Bittner and Goodyear-Grant 2013).

Civil Service Appointments

This section assesses women's presence as senior civil servants in four categories used by the Women's Policy Office in NL: deputy ministers (DMs), assistant/associate deputy ministers (ADMs), directors, and other managerial positions. Deputy ministers are the highest-ranking civil servants in their departments, and they represent the link between cabinet ministers and the rest of the departmental bureaucracy. DMs and ADMs in NL are order-in-council appointments made by the political executive. Figure 6.2 tracks women's presence in these roles in the period from 2003 to 2016.

The proportion of women in all four civil service categories increased over time, from about 20 to 30 percent in the early 2000s to roughly 40 to 50 percent in 2016. Parity has been reached in several categories, including at the DM level. While different explanations undergird these changes, two points are worth noting: first, since directors and other management team members are hired through competitions held by the Public Service

FIGURE 6.2

Senior civil service appointments of women in NL, 2003–16

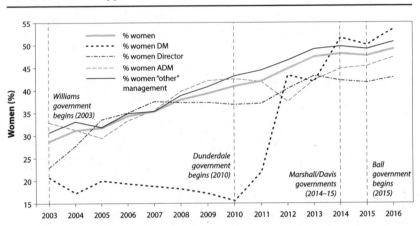

Commission rather than through order-in-council decisions, we expect the premier's influence to be substantially less than in DM and ADM categories. Second, as illustrated in Figure 6.2, increases in proportions of women in the DM and ADM categories occurred at the same time as the total number of DMs and ADMs stayed about the same (about thirty and seventy, respectively). Therefore, the number of men holding senior civil service posts actually declined between 2003 and 2016. This produced an overall net increase in women's share of deputy and assistant deputy minister positions.

In the other categories, numbers of bureaucrats increased over the period studied from 209 to 243 directors and from 633 to 981 other managers. Therefore, the number as well as the percentage of women in those roles could have increased without affecting the absolute number of men in the same positions. Data reported in Figure 6.2 show the overall presence of women in senior civil service positions rose in part because, over time, more jobs opened at the lower two levels. By contrast, representation in senior positions increased because political executives chose to appoint more women than men to a static number of positions. Recent announcements of layoffs and budget cuts in NL may change the number of women and men in the civil service, meaning patterns of appointments need to be followed closely during the next few years.

The consequences of Dunderdale's election as premier can be seen most clearly in data on DMs and ADMs. As revealed in Figure 6.3, Dunderdale

FIGURE 6.3
Number of DM and ADMs appointed in NL, 2003–16

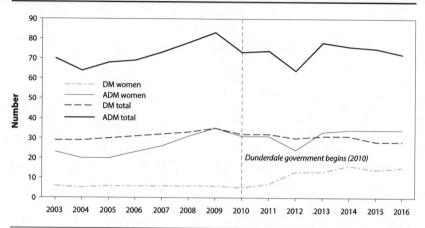

raised the number of women DMs shortly after becoming premier in 2011, following a long period of stasis. By the end of Dunderdale's term in 2014, the gender gap in DMs had closed. The proportion of women ADMs dropped slightly after 2003 before beginning a gradual increase in 2012. The number of female ADMs stayed about the same from 2013 onward, but the overall number of ADMs decreased slightly from that point. This trend indicates that some of the men who held ADM posts either retired or moved on, meaning that women held a higher proportion of ADM posts by 2016.

Figure 6.4 shows that the largest growth in senior women civil servants occurred in two categories that did not require cabinet approval. Among the four categories considered, the number of women recruited at the director level and in other managerial positions increased the most in terms of raw numbers. The rise was greatest in proportional terms in the "other" management group. Since these changes began gradually and before Dunderdale's arrival as premier, they may reflect broader cultural shifts in hiring practices and priorities. Yet the increase in women holding manager jobs from about 30 to 50 percent in the years between 2003 and 2016 is substantial, especially given that it was accompanied by significant growth in female representation at the director level as well. Put simply, between 2003 and 2016 lower-level civil servants became much more accustomed to answering to female supervisors.

FIGURE 6.4
Number of directors and managers in NL civil service, 2003–16

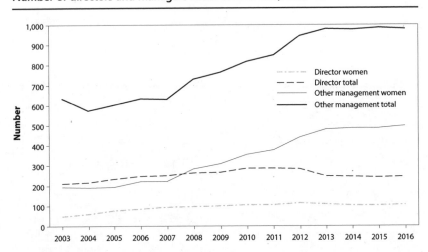

Agenda, Policy, and Legacy

The political institutions and culture established by Danny Williams profoundly shaped Kathy Dunderdale's term as premier. His shadow was initially for the better but, in the end, it was for the worse. As the politics of the province got in the way, Dunderdale found it hard to implement many of the feminist principles she espoused before taking the reins of leadership.

Dunderdale achieved some progress on gender equity in public administration and provincial politics. For example, her government worked to close the gender gap in DM appointments. Yet that accomplishment was often obscured by a sustained focus on Dunderdale herself, who, as leader and "brand," was at the centre of the political universe (see Carty 2004). Many of the challenges she faced illuminate a larger crisis in NL's political system.

Carty (2004, 11) maintains that parties embody and sustain a brand that defines their place in the political spectrum and serves as the locus of voter loyalty. Typically, central party organizations provide the basic product line (policy and leadership), devise and direct the major communication line (the campaign), and establish standard organizational management, training, and financing functions. In practice, parties focus more on communications and promoting leaders than on policy platforms, which parallels Bittner's (2011) argument that voters pay close attention to party leader personalities.

This thesis suggests that Dunderdale may have been the first victim of an effective PC branding strategy that unfolded in the Williams years. Beginning in 2003, the provincial PCs developed a successful approach to personalized politics: the party stage-managed a charismatic male premier who dominated public life. Williams commanded strong approval ratings during most of his time in office, generally in the 75 to 85 percent range. His disposition was famously combative. By the time Williams resigned in 2010, both the cabinet and the caucus had been emptied of anyone willing to challenge his authority.

When Williams anointed her as his successor in 2010, Dunderdale faced a cabinet, caucus, and public who were accustomed to his intense popularity as well as to his reliance on a bombastic, populist governing style. In hindsight, it seems unavoidable that the more subdued Dunderdale would be evaluated harshly (see Goodyear-Grant 2013). She had a tough, if not impossible, act to follow.

As suggested in Chapter 1, being a woman likely limited the extent to which Dunderdale could be perceived as charismatic. Moreover, had she tried to mimic Williams's bluster and bombast, she would have likely faced criticism for adopting a style not her own. Dunderdale chose right away to make the premier's office her own – in part by distancing herself very publicly from Williams soon after her swearing in (CBC 2011b).

She made excellent use of the finely tuned PC communications machine and appeared virtually untouchable during the 2011 election campaign. The Liberals nearly fell to third place behind the NDP, which had long been irrelevant to provincial politics. Although the NDP made impressive gains in St. John's, the two opposition parties together won only eleven seats as compared to thirty-seven for the PCs.

Even if the Tories were slated to win by default, the Dunderdale campaign went above and beyond coasting into office on Williams's afterglow. The party ran a slick operation using the slogan "New Energy," which linked the economic prosperity of the province, a promised hydroelectric project at Muskrat Falls, and the new party leader. Dunderdale helped to reinforce images of "new energy" by regularly posting Twitter feeds about her morning runs in communities across the island and a dramatic weight loss that followed (Bartlett 2011). In short, the provincial PCs mounted a remarkably lively campaign for a governing party seeking its third consecutive term in power – and with little to say about public policy beyond Muskrat Falls.

It was precisely the party's fusion of partisan, legislative, and executive power in the office – and person – of the premier that its greatest strength and greatest weakness lay. The leader holds together the machinery of the NL state by sheer strength of personality. If and when perceptions of the premier begin to deteriorate, so too does the government. Once Dunderdale's public image began to decline, the momentum leading towards collapse quickly became irreversible.

Cracks begin to appear early in Dunderdale's mandate. Shortly after becoming leader in October 2011, she announced the House of Assembly would not re-open until spring and dismissed the legislature as being dysfunctional to the point of being useless (CBC 2011b). In January 2012, a young boy named Burton Winters perished in Labrador when he became lost on the sea ice near Makkovik. It remains unclear how the tragedy could have been prevented. Dunderdale rejected calls for a public inquiry into the role of provincial search and rescue services in Winters's death. She refused to meet the boy's family, which *Telegram* reporter James McLeod suggests created a public perception that she was heartless (McLeod 2016, 61). By rejecting an inquiry as well as a meeting with relatives, Dunderdale proved she was capable of self-inflicted communications blunders. These decisions foreshadowed the rest of her time as premier.

Dunderdale took two additional missteps in 2012 that may have been irreparable. Both involve themes raised in Chapter 1 concerning the tenor of public debate under women leaders. The first and most significant was the decision to champion the Muskrat Falls project. Dunderdale's government was so confident of the venture's promise that it exempted the project from scrutiny by the province's Public Utilities Board. PC leaders treated any concerns or criticism as illegitimate and refused to allow legislative debate on the subject.[3] Government House leader Jerome Kennedy derided the opposition parties as so useless that debate would be pointless (McLeod 2016, 62). As chief public advocate for the project, Dunderdale came across as contemptuous of the democratic process. Given that many problems have since plagued Muskrat Falls, Dunderdale's decision to prevent systematic scrutiny of the megaproject will likely stand as her defining – and damning – legacy.

The PCs also introduced changes that curtailed public access to information in 2012. Known as Bill 29, the legislation gave the government vast powers to redact any document that could be used as source material for a cabinet paper. This move placed virtually all internal provincial documents under the control of censors. The same bill also granted ministers the seemingly arbitrary authority to deny any requests to information that they deemed "frivolous and vexatious."

Given that Bill 29 was introduced at the same time as the government refused to subject Muskrat Falls to review or oversight, it was difficult to escape the impression that the premier and her government were imperious, condescending, and hostile to criticism. James McLeod's (2016) study of NL under Dunderdale makes precisely this point. Yet, as argued in Chapter 1, perceptions of how a woman leader operates can be highly gendered. Indeed, a critique by Hans Rollman (2016) in the *Independent*, a newspaper in St. John's, notes the problematic tone and language used by McLeod (2016) in his assessment of Dunderdale.

Fall from Power

Dunderdale's approval ratings continued to decline for the rest of her premiership. In 2013, she lurched from one political disaster to another. When members of her caucus were found to have orchestrated the manipulation of public opinion polls on provincial news websites and radio shows, Dunderdale dismissed all criticism of the practice by claiming: "there's no story here." She later had an NDP member, Gerry Rogers, removed from the legislature because an unknown third party had posted a death threat against the premier in a Facebook group to which Rogers had been added without her knowledge or consent. The government's view was that people are responsible for the behaviour of their online associates no matter how tenuous those connections may be. When a CBC investigation the next day revealed that Dunderdale's Twitter account was following an X-rated pornography site, the premier refused to alter her view about Rogers's eviction and simply deleted her Twitter account.

This confluence of events would be damaging at the best of times. The fact that it unfolded during a period of economic contraction made the premier's situation exponentially worse. When Dunderdale delivered the 2013 provincial budget – which involved massive layoffs due to falling oil prices – she faced widespread criticism. One business owner wrote "DUNDERDALE BOO HISS" on a roadside billboard outside his office in Conception Bay South (CBC 2013). At the end of 2013, the St. John's *Telegram* published a front-page editorial calling on the premier to resign (Wangersky 2013). The implosion of the government had become a public spectacle, and, in economic terms, the 2013 budget accurately foreshadowed financial calamity.

But the real darkness was yet to come. In January 2014, the premier further undermined confidence in her government during a province-wide blackout that became known as #DarkNL. Many parts of the province were without power for several days during a bitter cold snap. Dunderdale appeared live on television and radio to argue with journalists about the definition of the word "crisis." She maintained that the sudden collapse of the province's electrical grid vindicated her strong support for the Muskrat Falls development. McLeod (2016, 74) tellingly characterizes this moment as "the final nail in Dunderdale's coffin ... it was a trainwreck ... she [came] across as arrogant, dismissive, and nasty."

Similarly, Newfoundland novelist Ed Riche (2014) argued in the *Globe and Mail* that the episode was symptomatic of Dunderdale's overall tenure:

> Kathy Dunderdale has proven a competent and honest premier but a dreadful communicator. She comes off as a vice principal hectoring a dim and fidgety grade four boy. Over the radio (blackouts become radio events) you can hear her wagging a finger at you. She told a dirty, agitated populace that there was no "crisis" when they were shivering in the dark watching their pipes burst. It was semantics; "crisis" for Premier Dunderdale is the Fall of Khartoum with giant spiders. For the electorate it was hours of cold gloom, elderly residents rescued from chronic care facilities, carbon monoxide poisonings and school closures ... Ms. Dunderdale wasn't popular going into this mess and handled it poorly. It's consensus that her latest failure to hear the citizenry and respond will be one of her last.[4]

It was indeed the end. By the time all the lights were restored, backbencher Paul Lane – one of the PC government's fiercest partisan bulldogs – had defected to the Liberals.

In January 2014, Premier Dunderdale abruptly resigned. She offered a short speech that emphasized the achievements of suffragists as well as her own feminist hopes:

> In concluding, I want to recall the many women who could neither vote, nor run for office, who did not let that stop them from working tirelessly so that women like me could vote, run, serve and lead. Let us give them the ovation they deserve. I, in turn, have derived enormous satisfaction from working to clear paths of opportunity for others. As the first woman to serve as premier, I hope I have stoked the fires of imagination in young girls in our province, and inspired them to consider running for public office. For the sake of our province and everything we hope to collectively achieve, let us continue to teach our children that there is no greater honour than to serve others. Let us teach them to take ownership of the challenges they see, and

step forward to make a difference whenever they can. (Dunderdale as quoted in McLeod 2016, 60)

Dunderdale, indeed, quietly made great strides for gender equity throughout her career. Before contesting public office, she was a member of the Advisory Council on the Status of Women as well as the Women in Resources Development Committee. As natural resources minister under Danny Williams, she was instrumental in pressing for more gender-based employment targets that enabled many women to attain high-paying jobs in the skilled trades (McLeod 2016, 59). As discussed earlier in this chapter, Dunderdale oversaw increased representation of women in the upper echelons of the provincial civil service.

These efforts to advance the status of women, however, have thus far made little impact on public evaluations of her legacy. Here, the Progressive Conservative Party was hoisted by its own post-Williams petard, and Dunderdale was the first casualty. In NL politics, where institutions and culture long defined by partisan strongmen are lately dominated by the language and practice of marketing, the leader is a branded product manufactured and sold to voters-turned-passive consumers. It necessarily positions the leader at the centre of the political universe. This approach works exceptionally well as long as the product remains popular. But once perceptions of the product deteriorate beyond a certain point, nothing can go well, and the void left at the centre of politics pulls down everything around it.

Following from Carty (2004), the contemporary practice of business marketing-driven politics can be advantageous at some level. It masks all manner of political foibles and vacuous policy, including by obscuring the details of public issues in order to emphasize the positive affect generated by leader and party brands. In the case of Dunderdale, negative (and highly gendered) perceptions of her leadership overshadowed many important accomplishments. Her personal image was bound above all to the Muskrat Falls project rather than to other political commitments, such as gender equity. As a result, her legacy in the public consciousness is firmly associated with the megaproject's many problems – and her own communications failures – instead of the manifest good she did for women in public life.

It might be cold comfort for Dunderdale that the recent history of NL shows that the difficulties she faced were largely institutional rather than individual – that is, her troubles in office were symptomatic of broader problems in the province's executive, legislative, and partisan institutions.

Following Dunderdale's resignation, the PCs held two consecutive leadership contests, and it took nine months for the party to choose a new premier.[5] Narrowly elected as leader in 2014, Paul Davis held office for less than a year before the party was crushed by the Liberals in the 2015 election.

Almost immediately, Liberal premier Dwight Ball proved himself more gaffe-prone than Dunderdale. Ball stumbled from one crisis to another. Premier Dunderdale governed for at least three years before public calls for her resignation appeared. In contrast, demonstrators and posters urging Ball to resign appeared around St. John's within his first six months as government leader.

Conclusion

Newfoundland and Labrador is not traditionally known as a leader in the area of gender equity in politics (Bittner and Goodyear-Grant 2013). Yet major strides were made over the past ten years as women became leaders of all three major parties (all at the same time) and major increases took place in female cabinet and senior bureaucratic appointments. In part, we believe, these advances were thanks to the leadership of Kathy Dunderdale as the province's first female premier.

The story that emerges here is one that reflects Dunderdale's commitment to gender equality and to promoting women to senior positions. Indeed, in the case of cabinet, she promoted them in numbers greater than their proportion in caucus, thus ensuring that, despite the dearth of women in the legislature, they had a seat at the decision-making table. Whether or not the gender equity that emerged in cabinet and in the civil service under her leadership will continue over time remains to be seen. NL politics needs to be followed closely in the future to understand Dunderdale's lasting legacy.

In reflecting on the Dunderdale years, McLeod (2016, 60) writes: "She was in politics for the right reasons. It's just a shame that she wasn't a very good politician." Although perceptions of what makes a good politician are gendered, this account shows how Dunderdale made mistakes that were highly consequential for her leadership, her party, and NL politics more generally. It is unlikely that history will be kind to Kathy Dunderdale. But, if nothing else, we hope this chapter shows that, for all her flaws, Premier Dunderdale – working quietly in the background, away from the spotlight – made a positive and appreciable difference for women in Newfoundland and Labrador.

Acknowledgments

An earlier version of this chapter was presented at a workshop titled "Women as Provincial and Territorial Leaders in Canada," which was held at the University of Toronto in May 2017. The authors wish to thank Andrea Hyde, legislative librarian in the Newfoundland and Labrador House of Assembly; Brenda Grzetic in the Women's Policy Office; and Linda Ross and Dana Aylward in the Provincial Advisory Council on the Status of Women for providing some of the data used in this chapter. We also wish to thank Brooke Steinhauer for excellent research assistance.

Notes

1 Men left the caucus as well, but there were many more of them than women. When women left the House and were not replaced with new women, proportions dropped dramatically.

2 Data from 2014 in Figure 6.1 reflect the Tom Marshall cabinet, in which three women held portfolios, rather than the Paul Davis cabinet, in which there were either one (Susan Sullivan) or two (Susan Sullivan and Judy Manning) women.

3 In late 2012, the opposition managed to filibuster two bills related to Muskrat Falls in order to hold a symbolic debate about the merits of the project before the Dunderdale government moved to close debate (CBC 2012).

4 This critique of Dunderdale as a matronly school marm is decidedly gendered, as are other evaluations of her tenure as premier.

5 Only three candidates came forward in the first race, all with little or no political background. Wayne Bennett was removed from the race. Bill Barry quit early in the campaign. Frank Coleman, a businessman opposed to women's reproductive choice, was set to be acclaimed as premier when he abruptly quit. The party called a second contest, this time featuring current or past legislators Paul Davis, John Ottenheimer, and Steve Kent. That the premier's job was considered to be so undesirable for so long reflects the malaise in provincial politics.

References

Bartlett, Steve. 2011. "Dunderdale, 'Almost 100 Pounds Lighter,' Set to Run Tely 10." *Telegram* (St. John's), 22 July.

Bashevkin, Sylvia. 1993. *Toeing the Lines: Women and Party Politics in English Canada*. 2nd ed. Don Mills: Oxford University Press.

–. 2009. *Women, Power, Politics: The Hidden Story of Canada's Unfinished Democracy*. Don Mills: Oxford University Press.

Bird, Lindsay. 2016. "Former Premier Kathy Dunderdale Opens up on Life after Politics, and Her New Career." *CBC*, 24 August. http://www.cbc.ca/news/canada/ newfoundland-labrador/kathy-dunderdale-life-after-politics-1.3733970.

Bittner, Amanda. 2011. *Platform or Personality? The Role of Party Leaders in Elections*. Oxford: Oxford University Press.

Bittner, Amanda, and Elizabeth Goodyear-Grant. 2013. "A Laggard No More? Women in Newfoundland and Labrador Politics." In *Stalled: The Representation of Women in Canadian Legislatures*, ed. Linda Trimble, Jane Arscott, and Manon Tremblay, 115–34. Vancouver: UBC Press.

Carty, R. Kenneth. 2004. "Parties as Franchise Systems: The Stratarchical Organizational Imperative." *Party Politics* 10, 1: 5–24.

CBC. 2011a. "Dunderdale Earns Place in History Books." http://www.cbc.ca/news/canada/newfoundland-labrador/dunderdale-earns-place-in-history-books-1.1026878.

–. 2011b. "Tories Prepare for Williams-less Tribute." http://www.cbc.ca/news/canada/newfoundland-labrador/tories-prepare-for-williams-less-tribute-1.1065386.

–. 2012. "Marathon Muskrat Falls filibuster winds down." http://www.cbc.ca/news/canada/newfoundland-labrador/marathon-muskrat-falls-filibuster-winds-down-1.1131424.

–. 2013. "Chiropractor Gets Back up with Anti-Dunderdale Sign." http://www.cbc.ca/news/canada/newfoundland-labrador/chiropractor-gets-back-up-with-anti-dunderdale-sign-1.1399763.

–. 2014. "Tom Rideout Calls Paul Davis Appointments 'Political Madness.'" 1 October. http://www.cbc.ca/news/canada/newfoundland-labrador/tom-rideout-calls-paul-davis-appointments-political-madness-1.2784227.

Celis, Karen, and Silvia Erzeel. 2015. "Beyond the Usual Suspects: Non-Left, Male and Non-Feminist MPs and the Substantive Representation of Women." *Government and Opposition* 50, 1: 45–64.

Childs, Sarah, and Paul Webb. 2012. *Sex, Gender and the Conservative Party: From Iron Lady to Kitten Heels.* Basingstoke: Palgrave.

Goodyear-Grant, Elizabeth. 2013. *Gendered News: Media Coverage and Electoral Politics in Canada.* Vancouver: UBC Press.

Kittilson Miki Caul. 2006. *Challenging Parties, Changing Parliaments: Women and Elected Office in Contemporary Western Europe.* Columbus: Ohio State University Press.

Lovenduski, Joni, and Pippa Norris, eds. 1993. *Gender and Party Politics.* London: Sage.

Matland, Richard E., and Donley T. Studlar. 1996. "The Contagion of Women Candidates in Single-Member District and Proportional Representation Electoral Systems: Canada and Norway." *Journal of Politics* 58, 3: 707–33.

McLeod, James. 2016. *Turmoil as Usual: Politics in Newfoundland and Labrador and the Road to the 2015 Election.* St. John's: Creative Publishers.

O'Brien, Diana Z., Matthew Mendez, Jordan Carr Peterson, and Jihyun Shin. 2015. "Letting Down the Ladder or Shutting the Door: Female Prime Ministers, Party Leaders, and Cabinet Ministers." *Politics and Gender* 11, 4: 689–717.

Piscopo, Jennifer. 2014. "Feminist Proposals and Conservative Voices: The Substantive Representation of Women in Argentina." In *Gender, Conservatism and Political Representation*, ed. Karen Celis and Sarah Childs, 209–30. Colchester: ECPR Press.

Riche, Edward. 2014. "In Newfoundland, It's More Than a Polar Vortex." *Globe and Mail*, 7 January.

Rollman, Hans. 2016. "Turmoil and the Politics of Journalism." *Independent.* 5 February. http://theindependent.ca/2016/02/05/turmoil-and-the-politics-of -journalism-book-review/.

Trimble, Linda, Jane Arscott, and Manon Tremblay, eds. 2013. *Stalled: The Representation of Women in Canadian Legislatures.* Vancouver: UBC Press.

Wangersky, Russell. 2013. "Premier, It's Time to Go." *Telegram* (St. John's), 7 September.

PART 3

CENTRAL CANADA

7

Pauline Marois's Paradoxical Record as Quebec Premier

PHILIPPE BERNIER ARCAND

In her autobiography, Pauline Marois (2008, 51–52) tells the following anecdote. When she was hired in 1979 as chief of staff to Lise Payette, then Quebec's minister for the Status of Women, Marois said, "Listen, Madame Payette, I'm not a feminist." Payette replied, "Don't worry! With me, it's a matter of weeks before you become one!"

Not only did Pauline Marois subsequently identify herself as a feminist, there is no doubt that she became one. Throughout her career as an activist in the sovereignist party known as the Parti Québécois (PQ) and as a cabinet minister in PQ governments, Marois endorsed progressive feminist policies. This chapter reviews Marois's personal background before she entered public life and assesses her impact as Quebec's first and, thus far, only female premier.

Following from the argument presented in Chapter 1, Marois is considered an "imperiled leader" in that she took on the PQ's top post during a time of sustained weakness, when the party was for the most part in opposition and the Liberals governed Quebec for an extended period. Marois served as premier only briefly, for about nineteen months between 2012 and 2014, in a minority government situation that ended when she called a snap election that was won by the Liberals.

The paradox referred to in the title of this chapter follows from the fact that, although Marois consistently pursued feminist policies as a member of early PQ governments, she appointed fewer women to cabinet than did her

Liberal predecessor as premier, Jean Charest. Moreover, I detail below how the historically stronger recruitment of female candidates and legislators by the PQ as compared with other Quebec parties reversed while Marois served as leader. In addition, during most elections contested by the PQ while she headed the party, female legislative candidates were less successful than their male colleagues. Marois as PQ leader made no significant appointments of women to party positions and, unlike her earlier time in cabinet, championed no major policy initiatives as premier that were applauded by leading feminist organizations. Paradoxically, her mandate as premier was marked above all by heated debate over a proposed secularist charter that feminist organizations strongly opposed.

This chapter explores in detail how Marois's term as provincial leader is remembered for that controversy, which concerns what was called the Quebec Charter, or Bill 60. Although the document was supported in some quarters for provisions that defended secular values and gender equality, it was condemned in others as opportunistic and divisive. Given that debates over social norms during her time as premier were highly charged because of their racial and religious content, Marois was unable to convince leading voices of organized feminism in Quebec that the core purpose of the charter was to defend women's rights (see Radio-Canada 2013). Moreover, the heated tone of public debate during her time as premier meant that the presence of a female government leader did not bring about greater consensus as opposed to conflict in the tenor of political discussion.

I conclude that, even though she built a left-of-centre as well as a feminist track record from her time as a member of the National Assembly (MNA) and cabinet minister, Premier Marois advanced a nationalist agenda that can be considered politically exclusionary. When she became party leader in 2007, she promoted an assertive *québécois* identity strategy that undermined the older, more inclusionary approach of her party. Under Pauline Marois, the PQ sought not to defend disadvantaged interests (including immigrant women) but, rather, to elevate the status of a dominant group of Quebec-born francophones – using a controversial "us" (*nous*) versus "others" discourse (see Robitaille 2007).

In line with the argument presented in Chapter 1, I do not consider Marois as a critical actor who, as Quebec premier, made sustained contributions to advancing women in numerical terms or to pursuing feminist interests in politics. I do, however, demonstrate that Marois was deeply committed to her own understanding of pro-equality positions and that she made significant contributions to a women's rights agenda prior to becoming PQ leader.

Feminism and the PQ

Among older parties in Quebec politics, the PQ stands out for the strong presence of women members and activists. According to Tardy (2003), the PQ's emergence in 1968 in the midst of student, anti-war, and feminist mobilization attracted younger people who supported social change. Efforts to gain sovereignty for Quebec thus corresponded in chronological terms with the era of feminism and sexual liberation even though, as discussed below, large numbers of Quebec women were active during referendum campaigns on the pro-independence side as well as on the pro-federalism side.[1]

In Quebec as elsewhere, the overlap between left politics and women's rights was clear because feminist struggles tended to be associated with anti-colonial struggles.[2] The PQ's association with women also stems from the fact that it originated as a grassroots party with a mass membership. At times when the PQ held power, however, the party was criticized by feminist organizations for imposing budget cuts that had particularly negative effects on women's lives.[3]

Within one year of winning a majority mandate in 1976, the PQ created an internal Comité national de la condition féminine. The committee was resolutely feminist, and had no equivalent at the time in the provincial Liberal Party. PQ feminists proposed policy positions and legislative initiatives that they believed would benefit women.

In the 1980 referendum on Quebec independence, the PQ lost to federalist interests, which included thousands of women who mobilized under the umbrella of the Yvette movement.[4] The internal party committee re-emerged in 1981 as the Comité d'action politique des femmes.[5] Tardy (2003) reports that the new committee experienced peaks and valleys: heightened activity occurred after the PQ returned to power in 1994, while engagement was weaker after 2000. The PQ dissolved a series of internal units, including those for women, at the April 2011 party convention, when Pauline Marois was leader.[6] At the same convention, party members voted to ensure gender parity on the PQ's National Executive Board.[7]

Was the PQ women's committee effective? According to Legault, Desrosiers, and Tardy (1988), the PQ and Liberals had fairly similar patterns of internal participation by women until the late 1990s. After that point, Tardy (2003, 49) argues, the Comité d'action politique des femmes helped to bring gender parity to many of the PQ's governing structures.

The PQ's role as the leading proponent of gender equality was threatened beginning in 2006, when a new left sovereignist party known as Québec solidaire (QS) emerged. QS established its own internal Commission nationale des femmes and, once the PQ abolished its women's unit in 2011, became the only Quebec party with such a structure. QS was openly feminist and had a number of prominent women leaders, including Françoise David, the former president of the Quebec women's federation. Therefore, even though, as of 2007, the PQ was led for the first time by a woman, it was no longer the provincial political party most closely associated with organized feminism.

Although PQ constituency associations select candidates on a decentralized basis, the central party can encourage local activists to recruit women. The fact that candidates were long chosen locally means that the party – unlike the federal New Democrats and some provincial NDP organizations – has resisted using targets or quotas to improve women's representation as candidates. When Marois served as PQ leader between 2007 and 2014, no specific measures were adopted to recruit more women. However, Marois said in one interview that, as PQ leader, she had succeeded in imposing women candidates (see Elkouri 2013). Marois (2008, 207) also writes that, as head of the PQ committee preparing for the 2003 election campaign, she was "proud to have recruited ... the highest number of women candidates in the entire history ... [of the] party." Data in Figure 7.1 confirm that female PQ candidates were indeed numerous that year relative to other major parties and relative to the PQ's record since the 1970s.

If and how numbers translate into policies remains a significant question for political scientists. Although the PQ never identified itself as a feminist party, the organization generally had a progressive image and was seen as pro-gender equality. Yet its main political opponent, the Quebec Liberals, could boast that it was a Liberal premier, Adélard Godbout, who made the controversial decision in 1944 to enfranchise women at the provincial level. Moreover, the Liberal government of Jean Lesage in 1964 sponsored legislation granting married women full legal status in terms of property rights and professional employment. A subsequent Liberal premier, Robert Bourassa, created a provincial council on the status of women in 1973 and made Lise Bacon the first ever female deputy premier in 1986. As mentioned earlier in this chapter, the Liberal government of Jean Charest pioneered gender parity in Quebec cabinets. Charest-era legislation also mandated equal numbers of men and women on the boards of directors of Crown corporations.[8]

Despite Liberal contributions to improving women's status in Quebec, it was largely the PQ that elevated the profiles of political women and organized feminism in the province. The PQ's first election victory in 1976 saw a significant increase in women MNAs from one to five; four of the five were

FIGURE 7.1

Percentage of women as major party candidates for Quebec National Assembly, 1970–2014

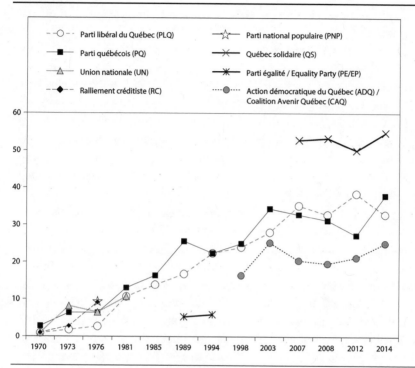

Source: Directeur général des élections du Québec, n.d.

PQ members with strong feminist credentials (see Tremblay 1989). Two PQ women, Francine Lalonde and Pauline Marois, contested the party leadership in 1985. The first woman vice-president of the National Assembly (Louise Cuerrier in 1976) and the first woman president of the National Assembly (Louise Harel in 2002) were both PQ lawmakers. Marois's acclamation as leader in 2007 made the PQ the first major party in Quebec with a woman leader.

At the substantive level, important PQ policies dating from the party's 1976 campaign platform can be considered feminist (see Tremblay 1989). The initial PQ government of René Lévesque established a government department devoted to women and, in 1978, appointed Lise Payette as Quebec's first minister of state for the status of women. The PQ introduced progressive changes to maternity leave legislation and enacted family law provisions that were based on spousal equality, with the result that husbands lost their traditional status as heads of household. Wives were mandated to retain their surnames after marriage rather than take their husbands' names, and parents were permitted to give their children a name composed of the mothers' and fathers' surnames.

Under direction from a series of PQ governments, the provincial Department of Education analyzed textbooks in order to remove gender stereotypes and introduced sex education courses in schools beginning in 1981 (see Payette 1982, 88). The Quebec Charter of Human Rights and Freedoms, dating from 1975, was amended in order to prohibit discrimination based on pregnancy as well as all forms of harassment. The charter was also altered in 1985 to permit positive, or affirmative, action programs that gave women access to equal opportunities under the rubric of what were called programmes d'accès à l'égalité.

After the PQ returned to power in 1994, the government faced sustained protest from the Women's March against Poverty. Organized in spring 1995 by the Fédération des femmes du Québec (FFQ), the march gained significant public support and drew fifteen thousand people to a demonstration outside the National Assembly in Quebec City (see Gagnon 1996). The following fall, the PQ held a second province-wide referendum on independence in which it argued that the status of women was better protected in the Quebec Charter of Human Rights and Freedoms than in the Canadian Charter of Rights and Freedoms. Pro-sovereignty campaigners maintained that federal provisions for maternity leave were less generous than were those in Quebec and promised that equal numbers of women and men would write the constitution of a newly sovereign Quebec.[9] Feminist groups, including the FFQ, endorsed the sovereignty option.[10]

After the PQ narrowly lost the 1995 referendum vote, the party moved forward under Premier Lucien Bouchard with new pay-equity legislation as well as a landmark social policy initiative that created an extensive network of subsidized child care services in Quebec. As minister of education in Bouchard's government, Pauline Marois was responsible for this high-profile and extremely popular program, which created a network of early childhood centres, known as centres de la petite enfance, that cost parents five dollars per day. The Quebec day care model pioneered by Marois in 1997 made it possible for every family, including those of new immigrants and single parents, to enrol their children in reliable, affordable, locally accessible programs that had not been universally available prior to her taking on the education portfolio.

Bouchard's successor as premier, Bernard Landry, named Marois to top posts as minister of finance and deputy premier. In those positions, she oversaw the establishment of a specific fund, based on employer and employee contributions, to support parental leave (including for adoptions) known as the Quebec Parental Insurance Plan. At the point that the PQ lost power in 2003 to Jean Charest's Liberals, Pauline Marois was a veteran government minister who had served in fifteen different cabinet portfolios under four major PQ premiers (Lévesque, Parizeau, Bouchard, and Landry).

Personal Background

After completing a bachelor's degree in social work at Laval University, Pauline Marois worked briefly before undertaking an MBA in Montreal. She met Jacques Parizeau and became his press secretary while he served as Quebec's minister of finance. Marois then became chief of staff to Lise Payette before running successfully for a seat in the Quebec National Assembly in 1981. That same year, she became a junior minister in the PQ government of René Lévesque – where she worked hard to promote women's participation in the paid labour force, notably through improved family services.

As a rookie MNA and cabinet minister, Marois stood out as a woman who gave birth to her second child less than two weeks after being elected to the legislature. She lost her seat in the 1985 provincial election and became active in Quebec's peak feminist organization, la Fédération des Femmes du Québec. Returning to the National Assembly in 1989, she was appointed by Parizeau in 1995 as Quebec's first female minister of finance. The fact that she championed government support for women workers as an activist, MNA, and cabinet minister demonstrates that Marois placed feminism at the heart of her political career.

Marois consistently denounced sexism in politics. When questions were raised about her fitness to serve as PQ leader in 2008, she responded as follows: "We look at women a bit differently. When we are less well coiffed, wearing less makeup, we look tired. A man, he looks as if he has worked very hard. Draw your own conclusions" (Marois as quoted in Chung 2008).

Much like Geraldine Ferraro's experiences as a member of the US House of Representatives and later as a candidate for vice-president, Marois drew attention because her husband Claude Blanchet had built a successful career in real estate. Marois was seen as wealthy, given Blanchet's assets, and was affected by scandals surrounding his perceived conflicts of interest (see Lavoie 2009). While it remains difficult to compare her situation with that of male politicians because few of the latter are married to successful businesswomen, we do know that little attention was directed towards the financial affairs of Marois's former cabinet colleague, Coalition Avenir Québec (CAQ) leader François Legault – himself a multimillionaire.

Marois's physical appearance also drew scrutiny. When she wore silk scarves and other accessories, observers made a point of noting her choices. Yet when PQ leaders such as Jacques Parizeau and André Boisclair dressed in striking suits, they drew no such attention. Marois recognized these double standards that affect women in politics, and she understood her own role as a pioneer for women in Quebec politics (see Chouinard 2008).

Marois as Premier

Although she brought extensive political experience to the 2005 PQ leadership race, Marois finished behind newcomer André Boisclair. The party's third place standing in the National Assembly after the 2007 Quebec elections led Boisclair to resign and, in the absence of any other candidates, Marois was acclaimed as his successor. Her strong performance in the 2008 Quebec leaders' debate restored the PQ's political momentum and made Marois the first woman elected to lead the province's official opposition.

By 2012, the Charest Liberals were facing serious allegations of widespread corruption. Marois ran a campaign that year focused on cleaning up government and eliminating many unpopular initiatives associated with the Liberals – including higher fees paid by parents for child care. Under her leadership, the PQ secured a minority government victory.

The main policy associated with Premier Marois's term in office, the proposed Quebec Charter of Values (known in French as Charte de la laïcité and initially as Charte des valeurs québécoises), echoed an initiative she took as an opposition MNA. In 2007, Marois proposed the Quebec Identity Act, which would have forced immigrants to learn French in order to gain such rights as citizenship in a sovereign Quebec or the opportunity to contest elective office. Her 2007 draft bill, which was not passed into law and which attracted criticism from both inside and outside the PQ, said the future constitution of an independent Quebec would reflect the province's core values, including gender equality and the dominant status of the French language (see Dutrisac 2007).

The Quebec Charter presented by Marois's government in 2013 did not become law because the PQ held only minority status in the legislature and lost power the next year. The proposal echoed a section of the 2012 PQ election platform that promised to "develop the Quebec Charter of *laïcité*," which we translate as "secularism" (see Parti Québécois 2012). In the platform advanced by the PQ in the subsequent 2014 election, the party reiterated its determination to "adopt the Charter affirming the values of secularity and religious neutrality of the State as well as equality between women and men and framing requests for accommodation (Bill 60)" (see Parti Québécois 2014).

The initial name of the charter explicitly referenced Quebec values while the second made clear the extent to which the PQ elevated the primacy of laïcité. The language of Bill 60 was strongly secularist, an approach consistent with the willingness of the first PQ government to end prayer in the National Assembly in 1977 and, twenty years later, with Marois's decision as minister of education to replace Catholic and Protestant school boards with a system based on language rather than religion. What surprised observers, as discussed below in greater detail, was the PQ's attempt, beginning in 2012, to conflate laïcité with gender equality. What likely caused the greatest public controversy was charter language that would have changed provincial human rights provisions in such a way as to prohibit public-sector employees from wearing any "ostentatious" religious symbols in the workplace (see Nadeau 2013).

While laïcité is sometimes associated with gender equality because women's lives are severely restricted by the fundamentalist streams of many religions, it remains difficult to claim that the raison d'être of religion is women's oppression. Critics of the proposed Quebec Charter saw the document as dangerous and exclusionary because it drew a binary distinction between laïcité and Quebec values, on one side, and religion and outsider perspectives, on the other. In particular, opponents claimed, Bill 60 primarily targeted women in public spaces not as Christian wearers of large crosses but, rather, as Muslim wearers of headscarves and veils (see Porter 2013).

Following from European debates and particularly the rise of radical right parties opposed to immigration, the concept of laïcité has in some instances been used as a carrier of conservative, nativist, and xenophobic messages. These tropes evoke hostility towards perceived outsiders in the name of preserving what is seen as a threatened way of life practised by insiders. What remains curious is that ideas about laïcité and gender equality, typically not embraced by the political right in Western democratic systems, often form the pivot for the exclusionary narratives of traditionalists who claim to be defending liberalism and modernity (see Elkouri 2012).

In debates over the Quebec Charter, some seemingly credible, moderate sources argued that feminism is deeply intertwined with laïcité. Janette Bertrand, a prominent TV host, was one such intervener. She and other women who agreed with her were known as the "Janettes" and were criticized for defending conservative and xenophobic views under the guise of progressivism and feminism. The appeal of the Janettes rested not just in their poise and confidence as public speakers but also in their emotional vocabulary. In one striking statement, actor Denise Filiatrault said that women who claimed to wear the veil by choice were "crazy" (La Presse Canadienne 2013). Without any official link to the governing party, Bertrand and other Janettes participated in PQ activities and demonstrations that aimed to highlight potential threats to secular women's access to facilities such as public pools if the charter were not enacted (see Chouinard 2014).

On the other side of the debate, groups including the FFQ – of which Pauline Marois had once been treasurer – strongly opposed the charter. The leading Quebec women's federation said that Bill 60 could create more vulnerability in disadvantaged segments of the population and erode the scope of fundamental rights. By 2013, like feminist interests in other parts of Canada and internationally, the FFQ had adopted an intersectional approach to women's issues that was sensitive to multiple sources of oppression, notably with regard to women from immigrant backgrounds. The FFQ's rejection of the Quebec Charter thus maintained that the PQ had failed to consider various overlapping sources of marginalization, especially since no systematic effort had been made to study the impact of proposed changes (see La Presse Canadienne 2014).

The FFQ announcement prompted the formation, in November 2013, of a new individualist women's group known as Pour les droits des femmes du Québec (PDF; see Buzzetti 2013). The organization presented itself as pro-feminist but as opposed to any forms of cultural relativism that might jeopardize gender equality. PDF explicitly endorsed a secular Quebec state and the proposed PQ charter but rejected what it termed "any and all new definitions of feminism which serve sectarian or communitarian interests at the expense of women's rights" (Pour les droits des femmes du Québec 2017).

The extent to which self-described feminists were divided became even clearer once the head of Quebec's status of women council announced her opposition to Bill 60.[11] Appointed as council president by the Liberals in 2011, Julie Miville-Dechêne said that the Marois government was interfering with the internal workings of the agency, including the appointment of four new council members. In 2013, together with the FFQ, the status of women council called for closer study of Bill 60's impact on women (see Gagnon 2013).

In short, PQ understandings of Quebec identity became increasingly narrow during the period when Marois served as party leader. Unlike more inclusionary views of social solidarity and national liberation that characterized the party's mainstream during its early years, the Marois vision offered a more exclusionary outlook. Lamoureux (1983) argues that feminism and independentism worked well together when the PQ defended a modernizing nationalism consistent with the ideas of Quebec's Quiet Revolution. As a corollary to her thesis, divisions surrounding Bill 60 showed that many progressive and pro-equality interests found the PQ's defence of traditional nationalism to be abhorrent. Not surprisingly, Marois's decision to move the PQ towards insular positions that pitted "us" versus "them" caused a clear break with leading pillars of the feminist movement as well as with many public intellectuals who had been identified with nationalist and social democratic politics in the province (see Radio-Canada 2013).

Electoral Engagement

For much of its history, the PQ fielded the most women candidates of any major party in Quebec and had the highest percentage of women legislators in the National Assembly. This situation changed as of 2007, when Marois became party leader. Figure 7.1 shows how, from the time it first elected MLAs in 1970 through 2003, the PQ was usually the Quebec provincial party with the most women candidates. As revealed in Figure 7.2, the PQ generally had the highest proportion of women in its caucus in the National Assembly.

However, it was not necessarily advantageous to be a female candidate for the PQ. Using the metric developed in Rasmussen (1981),[12] we report in Figure 7.3 that women often had a success index that was lower than that of men running in the same election. In 1976, for example, 57 percent of PQ women candidates were elected compared with 64 percent of men, while 33 percent of Liberal women won relative to 23 percent of men. This meant PQ women candidates had a success rate of 0.88 while Liberal women had a more favourable rate of 1.42. The worst election for PQ women was that of 1981, when elected women stood at 31 percent and elected men at 71 percent. In most subsequent elections until 2007, gender discrepancies within major Quebec parties were in the range of less than 3 percent, such that the

FIGURE 7.2
Percentage of women legislators in major parties in Quebec National Assembly, 1976–2014

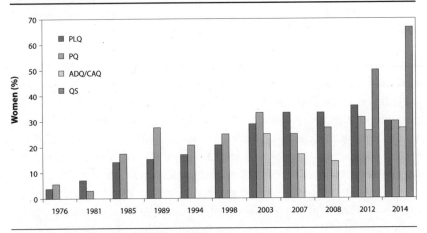

Source: Directeur général des élections du Québec, n.d.

success rate for women ranged from 0.95 to 1.11 percent. In other words, between 1981 and 2007 gender offered little advantage or disadvantage to legislative candidates for major Quebec parties.

The PQ edge with respect to women's engagement changed dramatically in 2007. During the provincial election campaign that year, party leader André Boisclair reached out to "progressives" in an effort to rally support from "pacifists, alter-globalists, feminists, progressives and environmentalists" (see Lacoursière 2007). However, a new left-of-centre formation known as Québec Solidaire (QS) fielded slightly more women than men candidates, thus surpassing the PQ on that measure (see Figure 7.1). At the same time, the Quebec Liberals nominated more women than the PQ. After the ballots were counted, it became clear that the Liberals had elected more women MNAs than had the PQ. With sixteen women comprising one-third of his governing caucus, Liberal premier Jean Charest was in a position to appoint females to half of the cabinet portfolios (see below).

Boisclair's weak showing in 2007 resulted in his stepping down as PQ leader. Marois succeeded him by acclamation that same year. In the 2008 election, as reported in Figure 7.2, QS once again ran more women than men candidates, with the result that both QS and the Liberals fielded more women nominees than did the PQ. The success rate for female PQ nominees

FIGURE 7.3

Success index for female legislative candidates in Quebec, 1976–2014

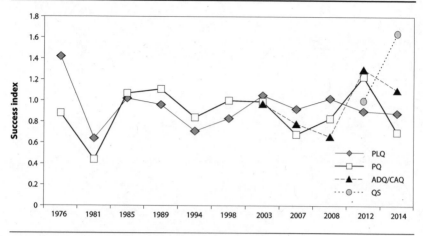

Source: Directeur général des élections du Québec, n.d.

again fell below that of Liberal candidates, although it was better than in 2007. As in 2007, the proportion of women in the Liberal caucus exceeded that in the PQ ranks.

In 2012, Marois led the PQ to minority government status in the National Assembly. Yet, for the third consecutive election, the percentage of female PQ candidates fell below levels in the QS and Liberal parties (see Figure 7.1). Marois's organization fielded thirty-four women candidates (27 percent), which represented a drop relative to PQ levels in the 2007 and 2008 races.

In terms of elected women, the PQ legislative group included seventeen women, or about 32 percent of the caucus. As shown in Figure 7.2, this numerical representation was surpassed by QS, with a caucus of one man and one woman, and the Liberals, with eighteen women (or 36 percent). The success rate for female PQ candidates improved over 2008 levels but remained lower than the rate for female candidates in the CAQ. In 2012, PQ women faced more advantageous circumstances than QS or Liberal candidates.

Under Marois's leadership, the PQ recruited more women candidates than the Liberals for the 2014 provincial election. As summarized in Figure 7.1, QS remained in the lead with 68 women candidates (55 percent) followed by the PQ with 47 (38 percent), the Liberals with 41 (33 percent), and

FIGURE 7.4
Percentage of women in cabinet in Quebec, 1976–2014

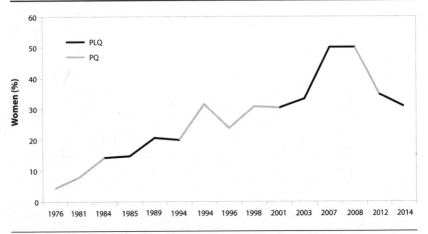

Source: Directeur général des élections du Québec, n.d.

the CAQ with 31 (25 percent). As for caucus representation, QS led with two female MNAs of three (67 percent). Women comprised 30 percent of both the Liberal and PQ legislative groups, and 27 percent of the CAQ caucus. Among Quebec's major parties, women's success rate as candidates was weakest in the PQ (0.7) in 2014 and strongest in QS (1.64), with the CAQ (1.10) and Liberals (0.88) in between. It should be noted that the QS score indicating that women were more successful than men as party candidates is based on the very small number of three elected MNAs.

Cabinet Participation

Data in Figure 7.4 show that, prior to a precipitous rise in 2007, numbers of women in PQ and Liberal cabinets tended to increase gradually. The initial PQ government of 1976 included one woman minister, Lise Payette, among twenty-three cabinet members. The next year, Premier René Lévesque appointed a second female minister. The next breakthrough occurred in the short-lived PQ government of Pierre-Marc Johnson in 1985, when four women were appointed to a cabinet of twenty-eight. This same level of roughly 14 percent female cabinets continued after the Liberals returned to power under Robert Bourassa later in 1985.

A major increase in cabinet representation took place in 1994 under the Parizeau PQ government, when six women joined a cabinet of nineteen ministers (32 percent). Parizeau also revived the Priorities Committee of cabinet that had been abolished by Bourassa, and he ensured that the committee of six members would contain three women.

Women's cabinet representation decreased to five women out of twenty-one ministers (24 percent) in the 1996 government of Lucien Bouchard. In 1998, Bouchard named a record eight female ministers, although the cabinet size of twenty-six meant that the proportion of women (31 percent) stood slightly below the watermark set in 1994 by Parizeau. In the PQ government of Bernard Landry formed in 2001, women held seven of twenty-three cabinet seats (30 percent), but – for the first time – the Priorities Committee contained more women than men, with five women and four men, while the previous Priorities Committee under the Bouchard governments remained below parity with more men than women.

Jean Charest's first government in 2003 featured, for the first time in Quebec history, a cabinet with one-third women. The Liberals' Priority Committee included four women and six men. Charest's major step forward occurred in his second term in 2007, when a path-breaking gender parity cabinet was announced for the province's first minority government in close to 130 years. To that point, the only cabinet with balanced numbers of women and men in Canada had been created in Yukon in 2000. Although Charest's political executive included nine women and nine men, his Priorities Committee consisted of three women and four men. Charest continued with a parity cabinet once the Liberals returned to majority status in 2008, when he appointed thirteen women and thirteen men. His 2008 Priorities Committee gave more space to women than men, with five women and four men.

What stands out from the perspective of gender and politics in Quebec is that cabinet parity ended with the arrival of Premier Pauline Marois. In 2012, she appointed eight women to a twenty-three-member political executive in a minority government – meaning that even if her own presence were counted, the provincial cabinet contained less than 40 percent women (9/24).[13] The arrival of Quebec's first woman premier and first PQ premier in nine years was thus marked not by significant action on numerical representation but, rather, by regress compared to the previous two Liberal governments.

Marois called a surprise election in 2014, which the PQ lost to the Liberals under Philippe Couillard. Couillard gained a large majority mandate that saw the defeat of many veteran PQ legislators, including Marois. He appointed a cabinet of twenty-six ministers, including eight women (31 percent female), and a small Priorities Committee of one woman and one man.

Assessing Marois's Legacy

In her final campaign as PQ leader, Marois fielded a group of candidates that included six more women than did that of the provincial Liberals under Couillard. Couillard's majority government, elected in 2014, had a slightly weaker numerical representation of women in its cabinet than Marois had in hers. At a policy level, it is notable that Couillard's deputy premier and minister for the status of women, Lise Thériault, said in 2016 that she did not consider herself a feminist. According to Thériault and her colleague who held the justice portfolio in the Liberal government, equality is entirely reliant on the individual will of each woman (see Robillard 2016). Feminists were critical not only of these perspectives but also of the austerity policies of Couillard's government (see Lanctôt 2015).

Any assessment of Marois's legacy needs to bear in mind that she won the PQ leadership on her third bid and by acclamation, when the party was weak in the polls and in search of a winning strategy.[14] The PQ by that point no longer looked like a fresh new formation but, rather, like a tired ex-governing party from the 1970s. Compared with other Quebec party leaders of 2007 and following, Marois had been in the political limelight for the longest time.

The PQ was not only in decline as a party but also faced serious competition from new political formations. No longer able to monopolize the Quebec nationalist spectrum, the PQ confronted competition on the left from QS and on the right from the ADQ and then the CAQ. In fact, Marois became head of the PQ just after the 2007 election, when the party had fallen to third party status in the National Assembly behind the ADQ.

Marois's strategy to regain ground lost to the ADQ was based largely on appeals to francophone identity. As argued in this chapter, PQ efforts to insist that it belonged in the political space between competing left and right nationalisms ultimately alienated many party supporters. The identity strategy adopted by Marois was probably suited neither to the social democratic streams within the party nor to its feminist image.

Marois's approach nevertheless allowed the PQ to win the 2012 elections, albeit with a minority government. Like Christy Clark in British Columbia, Alison Redford in Alberta, and Kathleen Wynne in Ontario, Marois inherited a party in dire straits and managed to return it to power. However, the turnaround Marois effected in PQ fortunes was extremely short-lived. She led the briefest Quebec government since Canadian Confederation. The election she precipitated in 2014 produced the weakest showing for the PQ since the party first ran candidates in a Quebec general election in 1970.

During her long political career, Pauline Marois claimed she was a strong advocate of women's rights. Yet leading voices of organized feminism in Quebec took issue with the emphasis that, as premier, she placed on a narrow understanding of nationalism and social values as opposed to a more open-minded reading of the intersectional challenges facing contemporary women. Her priorities as premier and leader of the PQ seemed to be the "us," a francophone and Quebec-born majority, rather than the disadvantaged "other" consisting of cultural, sociological, and sexual outsiders – including diverse immigrant women. Marois sought to defend a politically divided majority of French-speaking Quebeckers inside Quebec, a minority within Canada and North America whom she saw as endangered by newcomers and others who were defined as "not us," or "them."

The paradox of Marois's story is that her immense contributions to the cause of women's equality as an activist, MNA, and cabinet minister may be overshadowed in the history books by the controversies that shaped her time as PQ leader and Quebec premier.

Notes

1 Women participated as much on the sovereignist side as on the federalist side in Quebec referendum campaigns. What distinguished the independentist side both in 1980 and 1995 was the closer association of women's engagement with overtly feminist goals. For example, the poster "Madeleine de Verchères aurait-elle dit oui?" and the Yvette phenomenon in 1980 point towards this overlap. In 1995, the same can be said for the poster with the biological sign for woman forming the "O" of "Oui" and various advertisements specifically targeting feminists.

2 For example, the Front de libération des femmes du Québec in the late 1960s popularized the famous slogan: "Pas de libération des femmes sans libération du Québec et pas de libération du Québec sans libération des femmes."

3 Links between the PQ and feminist movements eroded in the early 1980s following Premier René Lévesque's cuts to social spending as well as in the late 1990s due to Premier Lucien Bouchard's zero deficit policy.

4 In March 1980, PQ minister of state for the status of women Lise Payette described the wife of Liberal leader Claude Ryan as an "Yvette," a name used in some school textbooks to refer to a traditionalist woman. In response to Payette's comments, fourteen thousand federalist women gathered in Montreal during the referendum campaign to inaugurate what became known as the Yvette movement. The mobilization was widely covered in media accounts and is generally viewed as having been more helpful to the PQ's opponents than to the governing party (see MacDonald 2002).

5 The 1981 election did not go well for the PQ among women voters, in part because of the Yvette phenomenon during the referendum campaign of the previous year. When the priorities for a second PQ government were discussed, there was no

mention of any commitment that could be described as feminist. As Fraser (2001, 271–72) points out, in complete contradiction to Lise Payette's speech in the previous government, Corinne Côté-Lévesque (René Lévesque's second wife) maintained that housewives felt depreciated and abandoned. Premier Lévesque promised his government would introduce tax advantages for families with a single wage earner – clearly not an incentive for married women to pursue paid work. The PQ's female candidates were particularly disadvantaged in this election.

6 Other internal groups dissolved at this time included those addressing the elderly and immigrants. See Guay-Dussault (2012).

7 As early as 1971, the PLQ adopted equal access measures that required constituency associations to elect a female vice-president and male vice-president for their Executive Committee.

8 See Act Respecting the Governance of State-Owned Enterprises, L.R.Q., 2006, c. G-1.02, art. 43, which stipulates "that the boards of directors of the enterprises as a group include an equal number of women and men as of 14 December 2011."

9 See the brochure titled *Le Coeur à l'ouvrage*, particularly the chapter titled "Change for a Society of Truly Equal Women and Men."

10 Premier Lucien Bouchard, speaking during the 1995 referendum campaign, claimed *québécoises* were among the white women with the fewest children. Three days later, in a press conference accompanied by FFQ president Françoise David, he expressed regret for his remarks and the feminist movement remained fairly united behind the PQ.

11 I was unable to locate a record of Marois's response to her feminist critics.

12 The index by Jorgen Rasmussen, employed by Pelletier and Tremblay (1992), uses the following formula: (number of women elected / number of women candidates) / (number of men elected / number of men candidates). When the index is greater than 1.0, it indicates that women have achieved greater electoral success than men. See Rasmussen (1981).

13 According to Elkouri (2013), Marois said she preferred a parity cabinet but that circumstances would not allow it. At that time, Marois led a PQ minority government of fifty-four MNAs, including only seventeen women.

14 Marois was a PQ leadership candidate in 1985 in a race won by Pierre-Marc Johnson. She was a potential but not an official candidate in 2003, when Bernard Landry won by acclamation. Marois ran again in 2005 and lost to André Boisclair.

References

Buzzetti, Hélène. 2013. "Un nouveau groupe féministe voit le jour au Québec." *Le Devoir*, 15 November. http://www.ledevoir.com/politique/quebec/392778/pour-les-droits-des-femmes-du-quebec-est-officiellement-cree.

Camp du changement. 1995. *Le Coeur à l'ouvrage: Bâtir une nouvelle société québécoise*. Québec: Le Camp.

Chouinard, Tommy. 2008. "Marois victime d'un sexisme latent?" *La Presse*, 8 November. http://www.lapresse.ca/actualites/elections-provinciales/200811/07/01-37540-marois-victime-dun-sexisme-latent-.php.

–. 2014. "Charte: 'Il y a un danger,' dit Janette Bertrand." *La Presse*, 30 March. http://www.lapresse.ca/actualites/elections-quebec-2014/201403/30/01-4752740-charte-il-y-a-un-danger-dit-janette-bertrand.php.

Chung, Andrew. 2008. "Marois Forced to Battle Sexism, Supporters Argue." *Toronto Star*, 22 November. https://www.thestar.com/news/canada/2008/11/22/marois_forced_to_battle_sexism_supporters_argue.html.

Directeur général des élections du Québec. N.d. http://www.electionsquebec.qc.ca/francais/provincial/resultats-electoraux/elections-generales.php.

Dutrisac, Robert. 2007. "Marois veut une loi 101 de l'identité." *Le Devoir*, 19 October. http://www.ledevoir.com/politique/quebec/161118/marois-veut-une-loi-101-de-l-identite.

Elkouri, Rima. 2012. "Les chauffards de la laïcité." *La Presse*, 14 March. http://www.lapresse.ca/debats/chroniques/rima-elkouri/201203/14/01-4505324-les-chauffards-de-la-laicite.php.

–. 2013. "Une féministe au pouvoir." *La Presse*, 8 March. http://www.lapresse.ca/debats/chroniques/rima-elkouri/201303/07/01-4628867-une-feministe-au-pouvoir.php.

Fraser, Graham, 2001. *René Lévesque and the Parti Québécois in Power*. Montreal and Kingston: McGill-Queen's University Press.

Gagnon, Katia. 1996. "L'équité salariale: Ce sera pour plus tard!" *La Presse*, 1 June.

–. 2013. "Pas de scission à la Fédération des femmes." *La Presse*, 26 September. http://www.lapresse.ca/actualites/politique/politique-quebecoise/201309/26/01-4693354-pas-de-scission-a-la-federation-des-femmes.php.

Guay-Dussault, Charlotte, 2012. "La représentation politique des femmes au Québec: Obstacles et résistances à une égalité de fait." MA thesis, Université du Québec à Montréal.

Lacoursière, Ariane. 2007. "Le PQ n'est pas progressiste, dit Françoise David." *La Presse*, 18 March.

Lamoureux, Diane. 1983. "Nationalisme et féminisme: impasses et coincidences." *Possibles* 8, 1: 43–59.

Lanctôt. Aurélie. 2015. *Les libéraux n'aiment pas les femmes*. Montreal: Lux.

Lavoie, Gilbert. 2009. "Éthique: Claude Blanchet avait des actions chez des partenaires de la SGF." *Le Soleil*, 19 November. https://www.lesoleil.com/actualite/politique/ethique-claude-blanchet-avait-des-actions-chez-des-partenaires-de-la-sgf-3eaa705b961ca5570aeaaa58a16dfd76.

La Presse Canadienne. 2013. "Propos sur les musulmanes: Denise Filiatrault s'excuse." *La Presse*, 18 October. http://www.lapresse.ca/actualites/national/201310/18/01-4700909-propos-sur-les-musulmanes-denise-filiatrault-sexcuse.php.

–. 2014. "Charte: la FFQ incite les opposants à s'exprimer." *La Presse*, 9 February. http://www.lapresse.ca/actualites/dossiers/charte-de-la-laicite/201402/09/01-4737094-charte-la-ffq-incite-les-opposants-a-sexprimer.php.

Legault, Ginette, Guy Desrosiers, and Évelyne Tardy. 1988. "Militer dans un parti provincial: Les différences entre les femmes et les hommes au PLQ et au PQ." Montreal: Université du Québec à Montréal – Centre de recherche féministe.

Marois, Pauline. 2008. *Québécoise!* Montreal: Fides.

MacDonald, L. Ian. 2002. *From Bourassa to Bourassa: Wilderness to Restoration.* Montreal and Kingston: McGill-Queen's University Press.

Nadeau, Jessica. 2013. "Les employés de l'État ne pourront porter de signes religieux ostentatoires." *Le Devoir,* 10 September. http://www.ledevoir.com/politique/quebec/161118/marois-veut-une-loi-101-de-l-identite.

Parti québécois. 2012. *L'avenir du Québec est entre vos mains.*

–. 2014. *Plateforme du Parti québécois, 2014–2018.*

Payette, Lise. 1982. *Le pouvoir? Connais pas!* Montreal: Québec/Amérique.

Pelletier, Réjean, and Manon Tremblay. 1992. "Les femmes sont-elles candidates dans les circonscriptions perdues d'avance? De l'autre examen d'une croyance." *Revue canadienne de science politique* 25, 2: 249–67.

Porter, Isabelle. 2013. "Charte des valeurs: Quel impact sur les femmes?" *Le Devoir,* 14 September. http://www.ledevoir.com/politique/quebec/387451/quel-impact -sur-les-femmes.

Pour les droits des femmes du Québec. 2017. "PDF Quebec." PDFQuebec.org. http://www.pdfquebec.org/index_English.php.

Radio-Canada. 2013. "Pour ou contre la charte des valeurs?" 7 November. http://ici.radio-canada.ca/nouvelle/632374/charte-valeurs-quebecoises-reactions.

Rasmussen, Jorgen. 1981. "Female Political Career Patterns and Leadership Disabilities in Britain: The Crucial Role of Gatekeepers in Regulating Entry to the Political Elite." *Polity* 13: 600–20.

Robillard, Alexandre. 2016. "Féminisme: Stéphanie Vallée préfère se présenter comme une humaniste." *La Presse,* 1 March. http://www.lapresse.ca/actualites/politique/politique-quebecoise/201603/01/01-4956170-feminisme-stephanie-vallee-prefere -se-presenter-comme-une-humaniste.php.

Robitaille, Antoine. 2007. "L'entrevue: Le 'nous', c'est lui." *Le Devoir,* 24 September. http://www.ledevoir.com/politique/quebec/158085/l-entrevue-le-nous-c-est-lui.

Tardy, Évelyne. 2003. "Égalité hommes-femmes? Le militantisme au Québec: le PQ et le PLQ." Montreal: HMH, Cahiers du Québec, Collection Science Politique.

Tremblay, Manon. 1989. "Les élues du 31e Parlement du Québec et les mouvements féministes: de quelques affinités idéologiques." *Politique* 16: 87–109.

8

Activist Outsider Becomes Partisan Insider

Kathleen Wynne as Ontario Premier

SYLVIA BASHEVKIN

First elected to the provincial legislature in 2003 and sworn in as the first woman premier of Ontario ten years later, Kathleen Wynne was a deeply engaged social activist who won municipal and then legislative office before becoming a cabinet minister and party leader. Her trajectory from movement to party politics illuminates many core concerns of the research on women leaders.

As discussed in Chapter 1, scholars have probed the extent to which female elites "make a difference" to the substance and practice of democratic politics. They question how a background in progressive extra-parliamentary or campaigning politics shapes actions in office. Do women leaders introduce significant changes of a pro-equality variety? Or, consistent with the literature on feminist institutionalism, do prevailing norms that govern the operations of parties and legislatures limit opportunities to transform those structures? This chapter details how Wynne pursued increasingly feminist directions as a Liberal premier in Ontario, showing that she demonstrated strong "critical actor" characteristics in the run-up to a watershed provincial election. In June 2018, Wynne had the chance to become Canada's first female party leader to win two consecutive popular mandates.

Kathleen Wynne first gained notoriety during the mid- to late 1990s as a high-profile critic of the Progressive Conservative government of Premier Mike Harris and, more specifically, as a leading campaigner for public education and local democracy in Toronto (see Boudreau 2000). Wynne again drew public attention in 2000 when opponents of her candidacy for a seat on the Toronto school board targeted her sexual orientation – notably in campaign literature that described Wynne as an "extremist lesbian" (Brean 2013). She went on to contest two provincial Liberal nominations in Toronto and, in 2003, won the mixed midtown and inner suburban constituency of Don Valley West.

About ten years later, Wynne announced her candidacy for party leadership. The incumbent Liberal premier, Dalton McGuinty, had secured two successive majority governments but only a minority in 2011. When he stepped down in fall 2012, McGuinty was widely criticized for a failed shift to electronic health records, costly decisions to cancel electricity plants that would have been located in Liberal seats west of Toronto, and the imposition of wage freezes for public-sector workers (see Esselment 2016). Polls conducted towards the end of McGuinty's time as premier found he was the second most unpopular subnational leader in the country (see Benzie 2011; Sibley 2012).

As outlined in Chapter 1, Wynne faced imperiled circumstances on becoming Ontario premier: her predecessor had not only dropped in public approval ratings but also oversaw a shift such that support for the provincial Liberals trailed that of both opposition parties (Sibley 2012). In her campaign to succeed McGuinty, Wynne promised to renew the Liberals as a collaborative and fiscally responsible "social justice premier" (*Toronto Star* 2013).

Within four years of becoming leader, Wynne had also sunk to a remarkable nadir in terms of public approval. Polls by multiple survey organizations in late 2016 found that between 13 and 16 percent of voters endorsed her handling of the premiership, meaning Wynne's popularity after roughly a term in power ranked below that of all other provincial leaders in the country. According to Crawley (2017a), Wynne's ratings in late 2016 were among the lowest ever recorded for any premier. She was widely condemned for privatizing Hydro One, a Crown corporation responsible for transmitting and distributing electricity in Ontario. Her action prompted a court challenge by the Canadian Union of Public Employees. Wynne delayed reforms to fundraising rules that critics said permitted party and government business to be inextricably interwoven – including in the sale of Hydro One (Leslie 2016). Consistent with patterns discussed in Chapters 5 and 6, some Liberal insiders were anxious to find a new leader. Crawley (2017b) writes that, inside the legislative caucus and party executive, "Rumours certainly abound that there is a concerted movement to push Wynne out" (see also Crawley 2017c).

With a provincial election looming, Wynne shuffled her cabinet, with the result that she broke through a high-water mark for female representation that had stood since the 1990s. She announced new rules on pay transparency and promised to fund daycare for children beginning at age two and a half. Ontario Liberals recruited more women candidates than ever before. These actions moved the dial on Wynne's record such that by early 2018 her actions were consistent with a critical actor repertoire. Prior to that time, Wynne had made few significant alterations to policies on pay and child care; moreover, her initial candidate recruitment record was weaker than that of her predecessor.

In short, Kathleen Wynne's actions in 2018 dovetailed more with her background as a social movement campaigner than with her earlier record as premier. Many of Wynne's initial decisions were inconsistent with a progressive stance; for example, she privatized a major public asset and defended traditional fundraising practices. On an urban policy issue that resonated with her own political origins, Wynne ignored Liberal legislation dating from 2006 that offered greater fiscal latitude to Toronto municipal government (see City of Toronto Act 2006). In early 2017, she blocked a plan to introduce road tolls – a plan that was endorsed by Toronto's mayor as well as city council as a means to finance new public transportation infrastructure and, at the same time, reduce traffic congestion and pollution. Her government acted belatedly in spring 2017 to curb foreign investment in the Toronto housing market following rapid price escalation and a decision by the BC government to restrict property speculation in Vancouver.

Wynne's decisions to tax foreign purchasers of real estate and increase the provincial minimum wage helped to improve her approval ratings and widened public support for the Liberals (Giovannetti 2017). Yet Ontario voters chose in June 2018 to elect a majority PC government under the leadership of right-wing populist Doug Ford, an NDP official opposition, and only seven Liberal legislators (see *Globe and Mail* 2018).

Political Background

Kathleen Wynne came to public attention as co-founder of the campaign to block the amalgamation of inner-city Toronto and its surrounding boroughs. The forced creation of what critics called a "megacity" unfolded after the provincial PCs won a majority government in 1995. Leading an anti-megacity coalition known as Citizens for Local Democracy (C4LD) with former Toronto mayor John Sewell, Wynne built her reputation as a passionate, articulate defender of urban civic participation. Wynne's background at that point included volunteer work as founder of a local parents' network that opposed Harris-era changes to public schools. The protests of Wynne, Sewell, and thousands of others were unsuccessful in the sense that amalgamation as well as changes to Ontario schools proceeded as planned. The first elected mayor of megacity Toronto was Mel Lastman, at least initially a Harris ally, rather than Barbara Hall, the candidate whose platform closely resembled the positions of C4LD (see Boudreau 2000).

At another level, however, the campaign to oppose restructuring in Canada's largest city created discernible effects. A group called the Women's Coalition for Local Democracy emerged in early 1997. Comprised of the City of Toronto Committee on the Status of Women (an official body created in 1991) and Women Plan Toronto (a feminist planning project formed during the 1980s), the coalition opposed amalgamation on the grounds that it would weaken provisions crucial for women in such areas as low-income housing, child care, and public transportation and that it would also reduce numbers of elected women at the local level (see Bashevkin 2006, 13).

Wynne thus began her political career at a time of sustained ferment over local democracy and gender equality in Toronto. Moreover, she initially contested public office at a time when the autonomy of urban civic institutions was a major subject of public debate. Wynne lost her first campaign for a school board seat in 1994, tried unsuccessfully to win the Liberal nomination in the provincial constituency of St. Paul's in 1999, and eventually secured a school trustee position the next year. Opponents of Wynne's 2000 candidacy for the Toronto school board circulated a pamphlet that directly targeted her sexual orientation. As Brean (2013) reports, Wynne won public office "after a nasty campaign that saw her called an 'extremist lesbian' in anonymous fliers."

After three years as a trustee, Wynne won the Liberal nomination in Don Valley West. Strong networks developed during the course of anti-amalgamation and pro-public school activities helped her defeat Harris's education minister, David Turnbull, in the 2003 provincial election. With a change of government from majority PC to majority Liberal, Premier Dalton McGuinty named Wynne to a series of parliamentary assistant roles before, in 2006, promoting her to the education portfolio (see Esselment 2016). This appointment made Wynne the first openly lesbian cabinet minister in Ontario history (Raney 2013, 155).

Wynne went on to hold three other cabinet positions in the fields of transportation, municipal affairs and housing, and Aboriginal affairs. She won re-election in 2007 when the Liberals gained a second majority, and again in 2011 when they secured a minority. Wynne announced her candidacy for the party leadership following McGuinty's resignation in 2012.

The race triggered by McGuinty's decision was unusual in that two candidates were publicly declared homosexuals (Wynne and Glen Murray) and both leading candidates were women (see Everitt and Camp 2014, 230). Wynne's main challenger was a former cabinet colleague, Sandra Pupatello, who held a Windsor-area seat until 2011. Pupatello campaigned as a conservative, or business, Liberal while Wynne adopted a progressive, or social, Liberal orientation. Despite Pupatello's closer ties with the party establishment, Wynne won thanks to support from four of the five male candidates who either dropped out or were eliminated in successive rounds of delegate voting (Babbage and Leslie 2013).

In early 2013, Wynne became Ontario's twenty-fifth premier. As the province's first woman and first openly gay chief political executive, she governed for more than a year before returning the Liberals to majority government standing in June 2014. Wynne's ability during that period to establish a distinctive leadership profile resembles what Christy Clark accomplished under similarly imperiled circumstances in British Columbia.

Policy Record

During the party leadership race, Wynne staked out a position to the left of her main competitor. In an interview with the *Toronto Star* editorial board (2013) shortly before the convention vote, Wynne stated her desire to be "the social justice premier" who would demonstrate skills of cooperativeness and fiscal responsibility. She emphasized her status as a political outsider by noting that, compared with the Liberal establishment's support for Pupatello, "the party hierarchy *isn't* circling around me. If we talk about renewal, I'm not someone who has been of the party my whole adult career. I came to politics later in life so I bring a different life experience to it" (Wynne as quoted in *Toronto Star* 2013, emphasis in original).

In the same interview, Wynne was asked about the threat posed to the Ontario government by social movements, including Occupy, a global protest against social inequality that began in 2011, and Idle No More, a mobilization initiated in 2012 by Indigenous women in Canada. She replied that her party had "lost touch with some of the people who actually brought us to power. I want to reconnect with the energy of those people because that's where we can find common ground" (Wynne as quoted in *Toronto Star* 2013).

What conclusions emerge from a comparison of Wynne's record as premier with her stated goals as a party leadership candidate? While it is difficult to compress more than five years of activity into a brief summary, we find that Wynne oversaw important pro-equality directions in provincial policy. This was particularly evident prior to the 2018 election, when she tried to address the electoral threat posed by the NDP by announcing progressive, pro-equality directions consistent with those of a critical actor. As demonstrated below, Wynne's earlier record was more middle-of-the-road and less resonant with a critical actor repertoire.

Government spending data show Wynne overseeing heightened as well as reduced investment in equality initiatives. As reported in Figure 8.1, the McGuinty Liberals initially raised expenditures on the Ontario Women's Directorate (OWD), the bureaucratic unit charged with enhancing women's economic security and reducing violence against women, by about $200,000. Although the OWD budget rose and fell during McGuinty's time as premier, it remained consistently above the level it had held under the preceding PC government. Once Wynne became party leader, the OWD budget grew slightly for the first two years and then increased by more than 10 percent to exceed $20 million for 2015–16.

In early 2017, the OWD changed from a unit of the Ministry of Citizenship and Immigration to a stand-alone status of women ministry. Spending on the separate unit grew significantly, such that by the 2017–18 fiscal year, budget allocations reached close to $26 million (Government of Ontario, Ministry of Finance 2018). On average, spending on the directorate was approximately $17.5 million while McGuinty was premier versus more than $19 million during Wynne's first three budget cycles. Consistent with the argument that, as time passed, Wynne's record resonated more with a critical actor approach, average budget allocations in her later budget cycles exceeded $24 million (see Figure 8.1).

This pattern of placing significantly more investment in one civil service division contrasts with reduced spending on the Ontario Pay Equity Commission. The commission is responsible under the terms of the province's Pay Equity Act for ensuring that women receive fair and equal compensation in the workforce. Its budget exceeded $4 million during most of the McGuinty years but fell to about $3.6 million in 2014–15 and following under Wynne (Government of Ontario, Ministry of Finance 2016, 2018).

FIGURE 8.1

Budgets of Ontario Women's Directorate and Ministry of the Status of Women, 2003–18

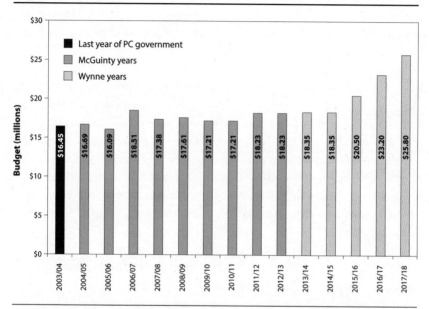

Note: In early 2017, the Ontario Women's Directorate, which had been part of the Ministry of Citizenship and Immigration, became the independent Ministry of the Status of Women with an expanded budget. *Sources:* Government of Ontario, Ministry of Finance (2016, 2018).

In terms of substantive outcomes, we find that pro-equality steps were taken in some sectors at the same time as limited progress occurred in others. Initially, the most visible changes introduced by the Wynne government with respect to women's rights occurred with regard to violence against women, an area in which, due to its primacy in the domain of criminal law, core legislative control rests with the federal government. As Collier (2008, 20) notes, the financial costs associated with tougher antiviolence policies at the subnational level in Canada tend to be far less than expenditures for new or expanded social policy initiatives such as universal child care.

Ontario's Sexual Violence and Harassment Action Plan Act, 2015, raised penalties and mandated measures to lower the incidence of sexual assault in three domains in which provinces hold lead jurisdictional responsibility: universities, workplaces, and rental housing. A total of $41 million was allocated towards the action plan, which included a viral advertising campaign known as #WhoWillYouHelp that was designed to spread awareness of sexual violence and harassment. One video spot drew more than 85 million views worldwide and was later translated into Turkish and Portuguese (Government of Ontario 2015; Benzie 2015; Progress Report 2016). Provincial governments elsewhere, including in Manitoba and Saskatchewan, adopted the anti-violence campaign (Progress Report 2016).

Wynne also altered the sex education curriculum in public schools. Changes initially discussed during her term as education minister were set aside due to vigorous protests by social conservatives. Once Wynne succeeded McGuinty, the Liberals moved forward despite strong opposition from the same interests that had rejected the earlier initiative (Benzie et al. 2015). Wynne-era changes not only introduced information about sexuality and contraception to elementary school students but also widened the provincial curriculum to cover consent in intimate relations, sexual harassment, and diverse sexual orientations (Government of Ontario, Ministry of Education 2016).

In terms of policies that would make an obvious difference for working women and their families in such areas as equal pay, child care, and guaranteed annual income, Wynne's government chose at first to delay. Concerted action in these fields is not only more costly in financial terms than the $41 million allocated for the 2015 sexual violence and harassment initiative but also at least as risky at a political level as reforms to sex education. Stated simply, conservative opponents can effectively target direct labour market intervention (via equal pay) as well as expansive child care programs because they entail major budgetary commitments and, at the same time, implicate matters of family organization as well as state/market relations that remain much more contentious at the level of policy ideas than does preventing violence against women.

Ontario's first Pay Equity Act dates from a legislative accord between the Liberals and the NDP that was negotiated after the 1985 provincial election. Pressed by the NDP, David Peterson's Liberal minority government introduced a trail-blazing attempt to address systemic discrimination against women in the workforce. The 1987 legislation required all public-sector employers as well as private-sector employers with ten or more workers to evaluate female versus male job classes, using specified criteria, in order to ensure fair compensation for women (see Todres 1990).

Nearly thirty years after the passage of the law, Statistics Canada reported a wage gap of about 25 percent between women and men employed in full-time, full-year positions in Ontario (Austin et al. 2016, 17). Concerns that fair compensation would be further endangered by patterns of declining unionization as well as the growth of precarious part-time and temporary work led Wynne's government to appoint the Gender Wage Gap Steering Committee. The four-member panel conducted public consultations and issued a final report in August 2016 that recommended creating an early child care system that is "high quality, affordable, accessible, and publicly funded, and geared to income, with sufficient spaces to meet the needs of Ontario families" (Austin et al. 2016, 8). Tracy MacCharles, named by Wynne as minister for women's issues, was given until spring 2018 to respond to this proposal.

Three months before the 2018 election, the Liberals introduced legislation requiring employers to publicly post salaries or salary ranges for advertised positions. The terms of the Pay Transparency Act prevent companies from asking potential workers what they have earned in the past, and they require employers to file pay transparency reports showing differences by gender in employee composition as well as compensation. The bill, passed in April 2018 with NDP support and PC opposition, was widely applauded by equality interests as a way to address wage and salary differentials (Ebner 2018).

Feminist campaigners have long argued that child care availability directly influences women's employment and pay prospects. They raised this claim in Ontario not only during the mid-1980s period of Liberal minority government but also when the Liberals relied on NDP support in a subsequent minority situation beginning in 2011 (Turgeon 2014, 240; Ontario Coalition for Better Child Care 2015). As McGuinty's minister of education, Wynne helped to implement full-day kindergarten in Ontario and held a seat at the cabinet table when, under pressure from the NDP, the Liberals chose to allocate $250 million in additional child care funding in the 2011 budget (Collier 2016, 223).

Under Wynne's leadership in 2013, the Liberals changed regulations affecting child care providers in a manner that the government said would standardize services (Government of Ontario 2016). Wages paid to child care workers rose by one dollar per hour and municipalities gained greater control over how services were administered and delivered (Collier 2016, 223). Ontario's lieutenant-governor delivered a throne speech in 2016 that promised 100,000 more child care spaces within six years (Office of the Premier 2016).

Wynne maintained the Liberals had created fifty-six thousand new child care spaces between 2013 and 2016 (Office of the Premier 2016), but critics saw the government's pledge of 100,000 new slots by 2022 as lacking the necessary budgetary detail to be credible. Moreover, the lead campaigning group in the sector, the Ontario Coalition for Better Child Care, argued that promising additional supply failed to address problems faced by parents who either paid expensive child care fees or, if they were eligible for subsidies, waited on long lists in order to obtain financial aid. Frustration with government inaction was particularly clear in the province's largest city. According to Monsebraaten (2016), "More than 13,000 Toronto children are waiting for child-care subsidies at a time when parents can pay upwards of $20,000 a year for infant care."

In early 2017, the Toronto District School Board announced it would eliminate rental subsidies for 350 child care centres located in board properties – thus saving the City of Toronto about $3.4 million over two years (Alphonso 2017). Given that Wynne-era legislation had granted greater autonomy to municipalities, the immediate blame for what would effectively become a new cost for Toronto parents without daycare subsidies fell on the city and its school board rather than on the provincial government. Two weeks after Wynne denied Toronto leaders the opportunity to impose road tolls, the city's mayor announced that local funds had been found to cover rental subsidies for one year. The mayor insisted, however, that the province needed in future years "to directly fund the full cost of spaces used by all early learning child care and before and after school programs in Toronto" (John Tory, as quoted in Qureshi and Chubb 2017).

Much like actions taken on pay transparency in March 2018, the Liberals announced later the same month that $2.2 billion would be directed over the next three years towards universal, publicly funded daycare for children aged two and a half and up. While child care advocates welcomed this pre-election budget commitment, the finance critic for the opposition PCs condemned it as Wynne's "11th-hour Hail Mary announcement," which used "money she [didn't] have" (Lisa MacLeod as quoted in Giovannetti et al. 2018). NDP leader Andrea Horwath released a more expansive campaign platform that promised to cap daycare fees for younger children at twelve dollars per day for most families, to be funded in part by a luxury vehicle tax and income tax surcharge (Giovannetti 2018b).

Overall, Wynne's track record as premier from 2013 through 2017 included pro-equality policies to prevent violence against women and to reform the province's sex education curriculum. Stagnation or lack of progress characterized the areas of equal pay and child care during that period, when the government convened public consultations and promised action that would unfold years in the future. One mother thus told a *Globe and Mail* reporter that "she might have to quit her job" if public school rental subsidies disappeared and "daycare costs continue[d] to climb" (Alphonso 2017).

An outcome whereby large numbers of women left the paid labour force and faced diminished economic independence was hardly consistent with Wynne's stated intentions to be a "social justice premier" who governed collaboratively and responsively. Weak public approval ratings led the Liberals to try to regain support among progressive voters via a series of actions in 2018 on pay transparency as well as child care (see Radwanski 2018). Yet the provincial election that year saw the Liberals reduced to 20 percent of the popular vote and seven seats, or less than official party status, with far stronger seat and popular vote results for the PCs and the NDP (see *Globe and Mail* 2018).

Cabinet and Civil Service Appointments

Like policy changes, cabinet appointment patterns suggest Wynne broke with precedent in 2018. Before that time, ministerial representation in Ontario had remained at or below a "glass ceiling" of 42 percent women that had been set in the early 1990s. Data in Table 8.1 show that, beginning in 2003, Dalton McGuinty created multiple cabinets that contained, on average, 35 percent female members. Wynne named more women to her early political executives than McGuinty, such that the average level of females in cabinet between 2013 and 2017 reached 42 percent, or about seven points higher than under the previous Liberal premier and the same as in NDP governments of the Bob Rae era.

TABLE 8.1
Women's representation in Ontario cabinets, 2003–18

Year	Number of women	Cabinet size	Percentage
2003	5	25	20
2007	9	28	32
2010	11	28	39
2011	6	22	27
2013	8	27	29
2014	8	27	29
2016	12	30	40
2018	13	28	46

Sources: Collier (2016, 218); Legislative Assembly of Ontario (2018a).

Early increases under Wynne thus fell short of the parity level reached in Justin Trudeau's federal Liberal cabinets beginning in fall 2015 and matched what had been a significant breakthrough in the 1990 NDP provincial government (see Bashevkin 1993, 86; Burt and Lorenzin 1997; Byrne 2009). Therefore, even as Wynne surpassed the record of her immediate predecessor with respect to cabinet representation, her initial appointments as premier returned women's presence to the same level as a quarter century earlier.

By contrast, the Ontario cabinet named in January 2018 contained thirteen women and fifteen men, meaning women held 46 percent of political executive roles. Wynne elevated a number of female backbenchers in order to compensate for decisions by two cabinet stalwarts, Deb Matthews (deputy premier and advanced education minister) and Liz Sandals (Treasury Board), not to seek re-election. In introducing her new cabinet, Wynne said gender diversity had been an important consideration in making the shuffle (Giovannetti 2018a).

Who held which ministerial portfolios under Wynne versus McGuinty? Researchers distinguish between higher-status, or "hard," assignments (notably finance, natural resources, and legal affairs) and lower-status, or "soft," assignments (notably those related to social policy, status of women, and arts and culture). Women in many jurisdictions are typically named to portfolios in the latter rather than in the former area (see Tremblay and Stockemer 2013; Reynolds 1999; Siaroff 2000).

As presented in the appendix to this chapter, Tremblay and Stockemer (2013) distinguish among political, economic, socioeconomic, sociocultural, and other cabinet assignments. Table 8.2 uses their categories to assess the division of Ontario cabinet portfolios and finds that, under McGuinty, men held about three-quarters of the explicitly political portfolios while, under Wynne, women held nearly 60 percent of them. Much of this shift followed from the fact that, as of 2013, Ontario had a female premier who assigned herself the intergovernmental affairs job in each of her cabinets and, until 2018, entrusted the post of deputy premier to Deb Matthews.

While women's numbers rose significantly on the political side of cabinet, their presence increased only slightly (from 29 to 32 percent) in the economic domain. Just as McGuinty relied on Dwight Duncan as minister of finance, so Wynne appointed and relied on Charles Sousa. Consistent with her willingness to appoint more female ministers, Wynne oversaw a pattern whereby women's representation in socioeconomic portfolios grew from 30 percent under McGuinty to 43 percent under her leadership. Percentages of

TABLE 8.2

Ontario cabinet assignments by substantive focus, 2003–18

	Premier			
	Dalton McGuinty (2003–13)		Kathleen Wynne (2013–18)	
	Men	Women	Men	Women
Political	17 (74%)	6 (26%)	5 (42%)	7 (58%)
Economic	22 (71%)	9 (29%)	13 (68%)	6 (32%)
Socioeconomic	28 (70%)	12 (30%)	16 (57%)	12 (43%)
Sociocultural	12 (40%)	18 (60%)	9 (35%)	17 (65%)
Other	7 (70%)	3 (30%)	4 (50%)	4 (50%)

Note: For details on how cabinet positions were categorized, see the appendix to this chapter.
Source: Legislative Assembly of Ontario (2018a).

female political executives also rose in the categories of sociocultural and other departments (see Table 8.2).

In terms of demographic characteristics, Ontario political executives became more diverse on one measure but less varied on others. McGuinty's cabinets had four members of visible minorities, including two women (Margarett Best and Mary Anne Chambers) as well as three declared members of sexual orientation minorities (Wynne, George Smitherman, and Glen Murray). By comparison, Wynne appointed nine visible minority ministers, including four women (Dipika Damerla, Harinder Malhi, Mitzie Hunter, and Indira Naidoo-Harris). Smitherman's decision to leave provincial politics in 2010 left Wynne and Murray as the only openly LGBT cabinet ministers. On the age dimension, census data show the median Ontario resident was thirty-eight in 2003 and forty in 2013 (Statistics Canada 2015; Office of Economic Policy Labour and Demographic Analysis 2012). The average age of McGuinty-era cabinet ministers when initially appointed was fifty-one whereas for Wynne-era cabinet ministers it was fifty-five – indicating that the province's first woman premier named an older rather than a more youthful group of ministers to office.

Parliamentary assistant (PA) positions are widely considered as testing grounds for cabinet roles. They permit premiers to assess a legislator's reliability and skill before awarding full cabinet status. Data not reported in tabular form show that both McGuinty and Wynne named roughly two male PAs for every female (Legislative Assembly of Ontario 2018a).

A similar ratio can be discerned for deputy ministers. Under McGuinty, twenty-six women and fifty men were named to the highest bureaucratic position in their respective departments. Many of them continued to serve after Wynne became premier, with the result that her record saw sixteen women and thirty-five men in deputy minister roles. Wynne's actions included the appointment of Ontario's first Indigenous woman to a DM position: Deborah Richardson, a Mi'kmaq from Pabineau First Nation in New Brunswick, reached deputy status in the Ministry of Aboriginal Affairs in 2015 (Ontario Public Service 2018).

As with McGuinty, female DMs in the Wynne years tended to be clustered in social portfolios such as health, education, and labour. Neither premier named a woman as the senior bureaucrat in what the academic literature portrays as "hard" domains such as finance, energy, or the Attorney General's Office.

Overall, Wynne appointed more women ministers than her predecessor, raised the numerical presence of women in political portfolios, and brought more visible minority women into the political executive. Yet patterns of cabinet and DM appointments after she became premier are consistent with the predictions of the scholarly literature as to where female elites would be clustered, notably in departments with sociocultural as opposed to economic and justice mandates. Moreover, no historic breakthrough occurred during Wynne's initial years in power in either the percentage of women cabinet members or the ratio of female to male deputies.

As with her policy record, the high-water mark for women's representation in Ontario cabinets occurred in 2018, late in Wynne's term. The level of 46 percent reached that year exceeded the previous peak dating from the 1990s.

Legislative Recruitment
Consistent with patterns in most advanced industrial systems, proportions of women parliamentarians in Ontario tended to increase over time – primarily because of concerted candidate recruitment efforts by centre and centre-left parties. As shown in Figure 8.2, percentages of female legislators rose markedly in NDP and somewhat in Liberal caucuses between 2011 and 2016, at the same time as they declined in PC ranks. Overall, women held 30 of 107 seats at Queen's Park following the 2011 provincial election and 38 of 107 after the 2014 contest. These results compare with only 2 female members in the legislature as of 1971, 6 in 1981, and a breakthrough level of 29 with the NDP majority win in 1990 (Bashevkin 1993, 82).

FIGURE 8.2

Percentage of women as Ontario legislators, by party, 2011–18

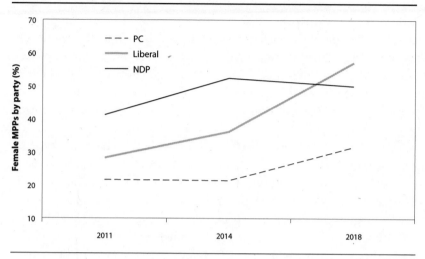

The likelihood that female candidates win seats tends to vary with the electoral fortunes of their respective parties. In 1971, for example, the governing PCs nominated 6 women and elected 2 (33 percent), while the opposition parties nominated a combined total of 11 women and elected none of them. Ten years later, the dominant PCs fielded 13 women and elected 4 (31 percent), the Liberals ran 8 and elected 1 (12.5 percent), and the NDP nominated 24 and elected 1 (4 percent) (Bashevkin 1993, 82).

New Democrats and Liberals faced vastly improved fortunes with the decline of the Ontario Tories in the mid-1980s and following. In the 1987 contest, which produced a Liberal majority, the victorious party fielded 27 women candidates – of whom 16 (59 percent) won seats. The odds were much lower in the NDP, which elected 3 women from a total of 46 candidates (6.5 percent). Only 1 PC woman was elected in 1987 among 22 nominees (4.5 percent). The subsequent election in 1990 of an NDP majority saw that party nominate 39 women, of whom 20 (51 percent) won seats. Liberals in 1990 elected 6 women out of 26 candidates (23 percent), and PCs elected three out of 20 (15 percent) (Bashevkin 1993, 82).

This same period saw feminist interests present a growing challenge to the practice of nominating female candidates in constituencies they had little chance of winning. Beginning in the 1980s in response to pressures from party women as well as from such groups as the Committee for '94, New

Democrats and Liberals introduced strategies to recruit female candidates, subsidize their campaigns, and position them in winnable constituencies (Bashevkin 1993, ch. 4). These efforts reflected the overlap between centre-left and centrist party ideologies, on one side, and the progressive politics of leading Canadian feminist organizations, on the other (see Young 2000, ch. 5). By comparison, Ontario PCs resisted formal quota-based rules adopted in the NDP as well as informal targets used by the Liberals – both of which were seen by conservatives as diluting merit-based recruitment (Bashevkin 1993, ch. 4).

Table 8.3 reveals the ongoing effect of practices adopted in the 1980s in Ontario's three main parties. In 2011 and 2014, when groups such as Equal Voice pressed for women nominees, the New Democratic and Liberal parties fielded more than one-third female candidates – or above the one-quarter range among the PCs (see Raney 2013, 168). Yet in the first provincial election with a female premier, the Liberals nominated five fewer women than they had nominated in McGuinty's last campaign – meaning representation among Liberal candidates dropped from 39 to 35 percent. At the same time, PC proportions increased slightly from 22 to 25 percent while NDP numbers grew from 35 to 41 percent.

Consistent with improved party fortunes, the electability of Liberal women measurably improved between 2011 and 2014. As Table 8.3 shows, Wynne's majority victory brought twenty-one women to government benches at Queen's Park, with the result that they comprised 36 percent of the Liberal caucus – compared with 28 percent after McGuinty's last campaign. The success rate for Liberal nominees increased markedly from 36 percent (15/42) in 2011 to 57 percent (21/37) in 2014.

Table 8.3 also demonstrates the degree to which women's presence in the NDP caucus vastly overshadowed their representation in the other two parliamentary groups. Horwath's efforts to recruit female candidates in promising seats built on internal NDP policies adopted at a 1980 provincial convention (Bashevkin 1993, 97). These practices produced a caucus with 41 percent women as of 2011 and a remarkable 52 percent after the 2014 election. The success rate for NDP candidates also improved over time, from 18 percent (7/38) in 2011 to 25 percent (11/44) in 2014 and 29 percent (20/70) in 2018.

Table 8.3 shows that the PC caucus was comprised of between 21 and 32 percent women throughout this period. The success rate for female PC candidates declined over time from 33 percent (8/24) in 2011 to 22 percent (6/27) in 2014, when the party lost seats and popular vote share relative to

TABLE 8.3

Women as major party candidates and elected MPPs in Ontario, 2011–18

	Election		
	2011	2014	2018
Liberals			
Candidates	42/107 (39.3%)	37/107 (34.6%)	54/124 (43.5%)
MPPs	15/53 (28.3%)	21/58 (36.2%)	4/7 (57.1%)
Progressive Conservatives			
Candidates	24/107 (22.4%)	27/107 (25.2%)	40/124 (32.3%)
MPPs	8/37 (21.6%)	6/28 (21.4%)	24/76 (31.6%)
New Democrats			
Candidates	38/107 (35.5%)	44/107 (41.1%)	70/124 (56.5%)
MPPs	7/17 (41.2%)	11/21 (52.4%)	20/40 (50.0%)

Sources: Elections Ontario (2016); Equal Voice (2014, 2018).

2011. By contrast, Ford's majority victory in 2018 saw 60 percent of PC women win seats (24/40).

Echoing results in the two previous sections, data on candidacies indicate that Wynne's initial actions did not transform party recruitment practices. Absolute numbers of Liberal women candidates declined between McGuinty's final campaign as party leader and Wynne's first run. The higher success rate for Liberal women in 2014 dovetails historical data showing that female nominees from electorally ascendant parties are more likely to win seats than are those from stagnant or declining formations – regardless of the gender of the party leader. Although the growing presence of women in the Liberal caucus after the 2014 election was notable (at 36 percent), it remained significantly below the density in the NDP (52 percent).

Data from 2018 in Table 8.3 show that the NDP continued to lead in proportions of female candidates, followed by the Liberals and then the PCs. New Democrats fielded about 57 percent women nominees, compared with 44 percent for the Liberals and 32 percent for the PCs. Each level represented an increase over earlier figures from the same party such that the Liberals in 2018 reversed an earlier decline that occurred between 2011 and 2014.

Consistent with older patterns, the results of the 2018 race were advantageous for women candidates from successful parties and, conversely, disadvantageous for those in weaker formations. Four Liberal women – of whom Wynne was one – secured seats that year out of fifty-four nominees, creating a success rate of about 7 percent. As reported in Table 8.3, the fact that the party's caucus contained only seven members meant that those four women held 57 percent of Liberal seats.

Tenor of Legislative Debate

Comparative scholarship asks whether women's legislative presence is associated with a more consultative climate of deliberation. While some sources offer support for this thesis (see Blaxill and Beelen 2016; Lovenduski and Norris 2003; Phillips 1995), others maintain that the conflictual norms governing parliamentary institutions will trump women's socialization to consensus-based behaviour (see Kathlene 1998; Krook and Mackay 2011).

The personal backgrounds of two of the three major party leaders after 2013 make this question particularly suitable to the Ontario context. Not only did Kathleen Wynne pledge during her leadership campaign to be a collaborative premier, but she also faced a woman leader of the NDP – which held third-party status at Queen's Park. Andrea Horwath resembled Wynne in that she began her political career as a social activist in the trade union, cooperative housing, and legal education fields before winning a city council seat in Hamilton and, later on, provincial public office. Horwath became leader of the Ontario NDP in 2009. PC leaders in this period came from economics (Tim Hudak), law (Patrick Brown), and business (Doug Ford) backgrounds.

If we use ejections from the legislature to measure the tone of parliamentary debate, then Wynne's tenure was more raucous than that of McGuinty. Official *Hansard* records indicate that a total of twenty-four legislators were ejected during McGuinty's ten years as premier while twenty-nine were ejected during Wynne's first five years in that office. Although men in the PC and NDP caucuses tended to do most of the heckling of the government during both periods, it is worth noting that women in the opposition parties were in some cases ejected on multiple occasions. Among NDP members, Monique Taylor was ejected twice during the Wynne years, Marilyn Churley three times during the McGuinty years, and Andrea Horwath once under each Liberal leader. PC legislator Lisa McLeod was removed by the speaker twice, once during the tenure of each premier.

In particular, Horwath's decision to lead a concerted protest against the privatization of Hydro One casts doubt on the view that female parliamentarians will adopt cooperative and consensus-seeking repertoires. Fourteen New Democrats were ejected from the legislature in April 2015 as part of

TABLE 8.4

Government time allocation motions by provincial legislative session in Ontario, 2007–18

Premier	Legislative session	Government	Time allocation attempts (N)
McGuinty	39:1 October 2007–March 2010	Majority	20
McGuinty	39:2 March 2010–June 2011	Majority	18
McGuinty	40:1 November 2011–October 2012	Minority	1
Wynne	40:2 February 2013–May 2014	Minority	1
Wynne	41:1 July 2014–September 2016	Majority	22
Wynne	41:2 September 2016–March 2018	Majority	19

Note: Most, but not all, time allocation motions were successful.
Source: Legislative Assembly of Ontario (2018b).

the party's larger effort to block the asset sale via petitions, town hall meetings, and a letter-writing campaign directed at Liberal members (Brennan 2015). Eight NDP legislators ejected in 2015 were men and six were women.

Tenor of debate can also be gauged via the use of time allocation measures, typically employed by governing parties to limit discussion of contentious legislation. As shown in Table 8.4, Ontario Liberals resorted to this strategy far less frequently under minority than under majority circumstances. McGuinty tried to invoke time allocation a total of thirty-nine times in the course of three legislative sessions between October 2007 and his resignation five years later. By comparison, Wynne attempted time allocation on forty-two occasions between February 2013 and March 2018. In short, Wynne was more likely than McGuinty to use this instrument to limit debate.

From the perspective of the official opposition, Wynne's actions as premier did not reflect a conciliatory approach to problem-solving. PC legislator Lisa MacLeod, for example, argued in late 2016 that shut-downs of legislative debate had become distressingly regular. In her words: "I think that we have probably voted more on time allocation and closure motions than legislation this past session, and I find that that is disturbing. It's getting to the point where it's actually reaching the ridiculous stage" (MacLeod as quoted in Legislative Assembly of Ontario 2016).

Taken as a group, data on ejections from the legislature and time allocation measures suggest Queen's Park was not a site of calm deliberation during the Wynne premiership – which corresponded with a time when the NDP also had a woman leader. Wynne tried to stop debate more often than McGuinty, and her period in power was marked by the removal of more members on a more frequent basis from the chamber. Female legislators in both the NDP and PC caucuses expressed strong frustration with what they viewed as Wynne's authoritative and conflictual legislative style, as evidenced in their ejections from the Legislative Assembly and comments about the use of time allocation.

We conclude that, with respect to the climate of legislative debate, Wynne fell short of promises she made as a party leadership candidate to operate in a collaborative manner. In particular, data indicate that Wynne's term as premier corresponded with a highly contentious deliberative atmosphere in the provincial parliament.

Conclusion

Considered as a whole, Kathleen Wynne's tenure as premier made a difference to pro-equality developments in Canada's most populous province. Her ascent from social movement campaigner to top political executive constituted a key breakthrough not just for women but also for sexual orientation minorities. The substantive directions she pursued in 2018 included a major overhaul of pay and child care policies. In terms of numbers, her cabinet appointed that year moved women's representation beyond a long-standing "glass ceiling" of 42 percent. Wynne also oversaw a sizeable increase in proportions of female party nominees in 2018.

Yet Wynne's presence was not associated with transformative change in patterns of deputy minister appointments or the climate of legislative debate. This tension within her record offers support for both sides of a core argument in the gender and politics literature. Our results show that even as Wynne, according to some metrics, demonstrated change agent characteristics – particularly in the final months of her term – her record in other respects reinforced older patterns.

In terms of policy substance, researchers ask whether a female decision maker is a critical actor who promotes a significant women's rights agenda or, alternately, is constrained by structural norms that limit such behaviour. In Wynne's case, this debate was eventually resolved in favour of the former position. Her willingness in 2018 to act on pay transparency and child care contrasts with a markedly lower tolerance for risk between 2013 and 2017. The shift Wynne pursued may be attributable to weak poll numbers and an effort by Liberals to court progressive voters in the run-up to the 2018 provincial election (Radwanski 2018).

The less transformative elements of Wynne's record make sense given her move from progressive extra-parliamentary activist to Liberal Party candidate, legislator, minister, and premier. Echoing comparative research, Thomas's account of Rachel Notley confirms that leaders of left-of-centre rather than moderate parties are more likely to behave in a sustained way as critical actors (see Chapter 11). Once Wynne chose to affiliate with the Liberals in a competitive three-party system, she could not change policies or practices too quickly or too dramatically without jeopardizing her standing in her own party organization – not to mention the broader electorate. Weak poll numbers and the fact that at least one prominent Liberal insider was questioning her leadership capabilities by early 2017 may have led Wynne to pursue an assertive progressive agenda in 2018 (see Crawley 2017c).

After raising expectations that a campaigning background meant she would be a collaborative leader with social justice priorities, Wynne built a record as premier that, in part, supported that narrative. Like other centrist politicians in multi-party environments, she was buffeted from all sides. From the left, New Democrats claimed she had irresponsibly sold Hydro One and not gone far enough on such issues as child care. On the right, Progressive Conservatives criticized the new sex education curriculum as radical and portrayed Wynne as a dangerous spendthrift who had overseen unprecedented levels of public debt.

About 40 percent of Ontario voters among the roughly 58 percent who turned out in 2018 chose PC candidates. New Democrats won about 34 percent of the popular vote and Liberals about 20 percent (*Globe and Mail* 2018). The upshot was a strong PC majority, a result that Wynne acknowledged immediately on election night when she resigned as Liberal leader.

The ability of a woman premier in Canada to win a second public mandate had, once again, proven elusive.

Appendix: Cabinet Portfolio Classification

Ontario cabinet portfolios were divided into political, economic, socioeconomic, sociocultural, and other areas using Tremblay and Stockemer's (2013) categories. When department names were changed, or departments in the same area were merged but the minister remained the same, the appointments were not counted separately. When departments from different categories were merged (such as a sociocultural unit combined with an economic unit), the new ministry was classified by the more prestigious, or "harder," of them so that, for example, the Ministry of Citizenship, Immigration and International Trade came to be considered an economic portfolio.

Categories	Departments
Political portfolios *"The political sector refers to the State's traditional missions, such as justice, foreign affairs and defence (at the federal level) and interprovincial relations (at the provincial level), and public safety (at the provincial and territorial levels), constitutional affairs, native affairs, and the first minister" (Tremblay and Stockemer 2013, 535).*	• Aboriginal Affairs/ Indigenous Relations and Reconciliation • Attorney General • Community Safety and Correctional Services • Deputy Premier • Government House Leader • Intergovernmental Affairs • Premier
Economic portfolios *"The economic sector includes portfolios with a clear economic or financial mandate, such as finances and the treasury, revenue, natural resources (including agriculture and fisheries), industry and economic development"* (Tremblay and Stockemer 2013, 535).	• Agriculture, Food, and Rural Affairs/ Agriculture and Food • Economic Development/ Economic Development and Trade/ Economic Development and Innovation/ Economic Development and Growth/ Economic Development, Employment, and Infrastructure/ Economic Development, Trade, and Employment • Energy/ Energy and Infrastructure • Finance • Infrastructure • International Trade/ International Trade and Investment/ Citizenship, Immigration, and International Trade • Natural Resources/ Natural Resources and Forestry • Northern Development and Mines • Revenue • Treasury Board

Categories	Departments
Socioeconomic portfolios *"The socioeconomic sector is based on the sustainable management of human life; the prospect of achieving, on the one hand, the physical, mental and social well-being of citizens, and on the other hand, the economic development of society. Examples of socioeconomic portfolios include education (for example, colleges, universities and research), employment and labour, municipal and urban affairs, and the environment" (Tremblay and Stockemer 2013, 535).*	• Advanced Education and Skills Development • Associate Finance – Ontario Retirement Pension Plan • Consumer and Business Services • Education • Environment/ Environment and Climate Change • Housing • Labour • Municipal Affairs and Housing • Poverty Reduction Strategy • Public Infrastructure Renewal • Research and Innovation/ Research, Innovation, and Science • Small Business and Consumer Services/ Government Services • Tourism/ Tourism, Culture, and Sport/ Tourism and Recreation • Training, Colleges, and Universities • Transportation
Sociocultural portfolios *"The socio-cultural sector also centers on the well-being of citizens, but in view of state-provided services to citizens, thus contributing to building and sustaining a substantive or caring citizenship. Examples of such portfolios are health, social services, family, youth and elderly, housing, communications, culture, citizenship and immigration, and status of women" (Tremblay and Stockemer 2013, 535).*	• Anti-Racism • Accessibility • Associate Education – Early Years and Child Care • Associate Health and Long-Term Care • Children and Youth Services • Citizenship and Immigration • Community and Social Services • Culture • Francophone Affairs • Health and Long-Term Care • Health Promotion/ Health Promotion and Sport • Rural Affairs • Seniors/ Senior Affairs • Women's Issues

Categories	Departments

Other portfolios
"The 'others' (or miscellaneous) cat-
egory is a residual one which covers
topical issues such as democratic,
electoral and parliamentary reform"
(Tremblay and Stockemer 2013, 535).
	• Consumer Services/ Government
	  Services/ Government and Consumer
	  Services
	• Democratic Renewal
	• Digital Government
	• Without Portfolio

Acknowledgments
I am grateful to the Social Sciences and Humanities Research Council of Canada for funding this project, to Jason VandenBeukel for his research assistance, and to my fellow chapter authors for their comments on an earlier version.

References
Alphonso, Caroline. 2017. "Toronto Proposes Ending Daycare Occupancy Grant." *Globe and Mail*, 5 January. http://www.theglobeandmail.com/news/toronto/toronto-proposes-ending-childcare-occupancy-grant/article33518967/.

Austin, Nancy, Linda David, Emanuela Heyninck, and Parbudyal Singh. 2016. "Final Report and Recommendations of the Gender Wage Gap Strategy Steering Committee." Ministry of Labour. June. https://files.ontario.ca/7198_mol_gwg_finalreport_eng_wa_08f_v2_1.pdf.

Babbage, Maria, and Keith Leslie. 2013. "Ontario Liberal's 2013 Leadership Convention: As It Happened." *National Post*, 26 January. http://news.nationalpost.com/news/canada/canadian-politics/ontario-liberal-2013-leadership-convention-live-coverage.

Bashevkin, Sylvia. 1993. *Toeing the Lines: Women and Party Politics in English Canada*. 2nd ed.; Toronto: Oxford University Press.

–. 2006. *Tales of Two Cities: Women and Municipal Restructuring in London and Toronto*. Vancouver: UBC Press.

Benzie, Robert. 2011. "McGuinty Remains Highly Unpopular, Poll Shows." *Toronto Star*, 7 June. https://www.thestar.com/news/canada/2011/06/07/mcguinty_remains_highly_unpopular_poll_shows.html.

–. 2015. "Edgy Ontario Ad Combating Sexual Violence Goes Global." *Toronto Star*, 16 March. https://www.thestar.com/news/queenspark/2015/03/16/edgy-ontario-ad-combating-sexual-violence-goes-global.html.

Benzie, Robert, Rob Ferguson, and Kristin Rushowy. 2015. "New Sex-Ed Curriculum Gets Mixed Reviews from Parents." *Toronto Star*, 23 February. https://www.thestar.com/news/queenspark/2015/02/23/ontario-finally-unveils-revamped-sex-education-curriculum.html.

Blaxill, Luke, and Kaspar Beelen. 2016. "A Feminized Language of Democracy? The Representation of Women at Westminster since 1945." *Twentieth Century British History* 27, 3: 412–49.

Boudreau, Julie-Anne. 2000. *Megacity Saga: Democracy and Citizenship in this Global Age*. Montreal: Black Rose.

Brean, Joseph. 2013. "'A Premier Has to Learn How to Relate to All Ontarians': Wynne's Reputation as a Peacemaker Set Her Apart from Rivals." *National Post*, 28 January. http://news.nationalpost.com/news/canada/canadian-politics/kathleen-wynne-profile.

Brennan, Richard J. 2015. "NDP Campaign to Stop Hydro One Sale Points to Cheaper Power in Public Systems." *Toronto Star*, 27 April. https://www.thestar.com/news/canada/2015/04/27/ndp-campaign-to-stop-hydro-one-sale-cites-cheaper-power-in-public-systems.html.

Burt, Sandra, and Elizabeth Lorenzin. 1997. "Taking the Women's Movement to Queen's Park: Women's Interests and the New Democratic Government of Ontario." In *In the Presence of Women: Representation in Canadian Governments*, ed. Jane Arscott and Linda Trimble, 202–27. Toronto: Harcourt Brace.

Byrne, Lesley. 2009. "Making a Difference When the Doors Are Open: Women in the Ontario NDP Cabinet, 1990–95." In *Opening Doors Wider: Women's Political Engagement in Canada*, ed. Sylvia Bashevkin, 93–107. Vancouver: UBC Press.

City of Toronto Act. 2006. Statutes of Ontario chapter 11, schedule A.

Collier, Cheryl N. 2008. "Neoliberalism and Violence against Women: Can Retrenchment Convergence Explain the Path of Provincial Anti-Violence Policy, 1985–2005?" *Canadian Journal of Political Science* 41, 1 (March): 19–42.

–. 2016. "A Path Well Travelled or Hope on the Horizon? Women, Gender, and Politics in Ontario." In *The Politics of Ontario*, ed. Cheryl N. Collier and Jonathan Malloy, 209–28. Toronto: University of Toronto Press.

Crawley, Mike. 2017a. "Why Kathleen Wynne Is So Unpopular, and What She Can Do about It." *CBC News*, 16 January, http://www.cbc.ca/news/canada/toronto/kathleen-wynne-polling-ontario-approval-rating-1.3932298.

–. 2017b. "No Sign That Liberal Knives Are Truly Out for Kathleen Wynne." *CBC News*, 11 March. http://www.cbc.ca/news/canada/toronto/kathleen-wynne-ontario-liberal-party-1.4017225.

–. 2017c. "'Extremely Unlikely' Liberals Can Win Election under Wynne, Says Greg Sorbara." *CBC News*, 22 March. http://www.cbc.ca/news/canada/toronto/greg-sorbara-kathleen-wynne-ontario-liberals-1.4036033.

Ebner, David. 2018. "Ontario Takes Aim at Gender Wage Gap with Pay Transparency Bill." *Globe and Mail*, 7 March, B1.

Elections Ontario. 2016. "Official Election Results." https://www.elections.on.ca/en/resource-centre/elections-results.html.

Equal Voice. 2014. "Ontario Election 2014." https://www.equalvoice.ca/toronto.cfm.

–. 2018. "Ontario Ranks First in Canada for Women's Representation... but Canada Now Has Just One Female Premier." https://mailchi.mp/equalvoice/bc-is-on-the-cusp-of-electing-the-highest-percentage-of-women-to-a-legislature-in-canada-ever-2096023?e=[UNIQID].

Esselment, Anna. 2016. "An Inside Look at the Ontario Liberals in Power." In *The Politics of Ontario*, ed. Cheryl N. Collier and Jonathan Malloy, 229–50. Toronto: University of Toronto Press.

Everitt, Joanna, and Michael Camp. 2014. "In versus Out: LGBT Politicians in Canada." *Journal of Canadian Studies* 48, 1: 226–51.

Giovannetti, Justin. 2017. "Poll Shows Boost in Support for Liberals." *Globe and Mail*, 5 July.

—. 2018a. "Wynne Shuffles Cabinet Heading into Election Run." *Globe and Mail*, 18 January.

—. 2018b. "Ontario NDP Lists Child Care, Health Care in Electoral Platform." *Globe and Mail*, 16 April. https://www.theglobeandmail.com/canada/article-ontario -ndp-lists-child-care-health-care-in-electoral-platform/.

Giovannetti, Justin, Caroline Alphonso, and Erin Anderssen. 2018. "Ontario Liberals Announce Child-Care Funding," *Globe and Mail*, 28 March.

Globe and Mail. 2018. "Ontario Election Results 2018: A Map of the Results," 7 June. https://www.theglobeandmail.com/canada/article-ontario-election-results -2018-a-map-of-the-live-results/.

Government of Ontario. 2015. "#WhoWillYouHelp." YouTube video, 1:00. Posted March 6. https://www.youtube.com/watch?v=c2ZSZrGc-O8.

—. 2016. "Child Care Modernization." 12 February. https://www.ontario.ca/page/ child-care-modernization.

Government of Ontario, Ministry of Education. 2016. "The Ontario Curriculum Grades 1-8: Health and Physical Education." http://www.edu.gov.on.ca/eng/ curriculum/elementary/health1to8.pdf/.

Government of Ontario, Ministry of Finance. 2016. "Expenditure Estimates (Volume 1 estimates for each fiscal year)." http://www.fin.gov.on.ca/en/budget/estimates/.

—. 2018. "Expenditure Estimates." http://www.fin.gov.on.ca/en/budget/estimates/.

Kathlene, Lyn. 1998. "In a Different Voice: Women and the Policy Process." In *Women and Elective Office*, ed. Sue Thomas and Clyde Wilcox, 188–202. New York: Oxford University Press.

Krook, Mona Lena, and Fiona Mackay, eds. 2011. *Gender, Politics and Institutions: Towards a Feminist Institutionalism*. Basingstoke: Palgrave Macmillan.

Legislative Assembly of Ontario. 2016. *Hansard*, 7 December.

—. 2018a. "Past and Present MPPs." http://www.ontla.on.ca/web/members/members _all.do?locale=en.

—. 2018b. "Debates and Proceedings." http://www.ontla.on.ca/web/house-proceedings/ house_proceedings_home.do?locale=en.

Leslie, Keith. 2016. "CUPE Sues Wynne, Cabinet Ministers over Hydro One Sale." *Globe and Mail*, 7 December. http://www.theglobeandmail.com/news/national/ cupe-sues-wynne-cabinet-ministers-over-hydro-one-sale/article33236128/.

Lovenduski, Joni, and Pippa Norris. 2003. "Westminster Women: The Politics of Presence." *Political Studies* 51, 1: 84–102.

Monsebraaten, Laurie. 2016. "Ontario Parents Welcome New Focus on Daycare." *Toronto Star*, 12 September. https://www.thestar.com/news/queenspark/2016/ 09/12/ontario-parents-welcome-new-focus-on-daycare.html.

Office of Economic Policy Labour and Demographic Analysis. 2012. "Population Counts: Age and Gender." Government of Ontario. 3 August. http://www.fin. gov.on.ca/en/economy/demographics/census/cenhi11-3.html.

Office of the Premier. 2016. "Affordable, Accessible, Quality Child Care for More Families." Government of Ontario. 12 September, https://news.ontario.ca/opo/ en/2016/09/affordable-accessible-quality-child-care-for-more-families.html.

Ontario Coalition for Better Child Care. 2015. "Child Care Matters to Everyone: A Snapshot of Child Care in Ontario." https://d3n8a8pro7vhmx.cloudfront.net/childcareon/pages/1355/attachments/original/1450198905/Child_care_matters_to_everyone_A_snapshot_of_child_care_in_Ontario.pdf?1450198905.

Ontario Public Service. 2018. "DM_Historical_Assignments_with_end_dates_post_Jan1_2003_revised May2018." Government of Ontario, Microsoft Excel File. Retrieved 10 May 2018.

Phillips, Anne. 1995. *The Politics of Presence.* Oxford: Clarendon Press.

Progress Report. 2016. "It's Never Okay: An Action Plan to Stop Sexual Violence and Harassment." Ministry of Women's Issues, 8 March. https://files.ontario.ca/mi-2005_svhap_progress_report_en.pdf.

Qureshi, Momin, and Christine Chubb. 2017. "Tory Calls on the Province to Fund Daycares in TDSB Schools." *CityNews,* 6 February, http://www.citynews.ca/2017/02/06/tory-calls-on-the-province-to-fund-daycares-in-tdsb-schools/.

Radwanski, Adam. 2018. "Can Wynne Convince Voters Government-Funded Daycare Is about Something Bigger?" *Globe and Mail,* 28 March.

Raney, Tracey. 2013. "Breaking the Holding Pattern? Women in Ontario Politics." In *Stalled: The Representation of Women in Canadian Governments,* ed. Linda Trimble, Jane Arscott, and Manon Tremblay, 154–72. Vancouver: UBC Press.

Reynolds, Andrew. 1999. "Women in the Legislatures and Executives of the World: Knocking at the Highest Glass Ceiling." *World Politics* 51, 4 (July): 547–72.

Siaroff, Alan. 2000. "Women's Representation in Legislatures and Cabinets in Industrial Democracies." *International Political Science Review* 21, 2: 197–215.

Sibley, Robert. 2012. "McGuinty Steps Down as Premier after Nine Years in Power," *Ottawa Citizen,* 16 October. http://www.ottawacitizen.com/news/mcguinty+steps+down+premier+after+nine+years+power/7394414/story.html.

Statistics Canada. 2015. "Annual Demographic Estimates: Canada, Provinces and Territories." 27 November. http://www.statcan.gc.ca/pub/91-215-x/2014000/t593-eng.htm#T593FN1.

Todres, Elaine M. 1990. "Women's Work in Ontario: Pay Equity and the Wage Gap." *Ottawa Law Review* 22, 3: 555–71.

Toronto Star editorial board. 2013. "Ontario Liberal Leadership Candidate Kathleen Wynne: 'I Want to Be the Social Justice Premier.'" *Toronto Star,* 15 January. https://www.thestar.com/opinion/editorialopinion/2013/01/15/ontario_liberal_leadership_candidate_kathleen_wynne_i_want_to_be_the_social_justice_premier.html.

Tremblay, Manon, and Daniel Stockemer. 2013. "Women's Ministerial Careers in Cabinet, 1921–2010: A Look at Socio-Demographic Traits and Career Experience." *Canadian Public Administration* 56, 4 (December): 523–41.

Turgeon, Luc. 2014. "Activists, Policy Sedementation, and Policy Change: The Case of Early Childhood Education in Ontario." *Journal of Canadian Studies* 48, 2: 224–49.

Young, Lisa. 2000. *Feminists and Party Politics.* Vancouver: UBC Press.

PART 4

WESTERN CANADA

9
Rita Johnston and Christy Clark as British Columbia Premiers

TRACY SUMMERVILLE

This chapter examines the premierships of Rita Johnston (from April to November 1991) and Christy Clark (from March 2011 to July 2017). Both Johnston and Clark supported women's rights but did so without crossing from the right or centre of the ideological spectrum into left-wing politics and, more specifically, without demonstrating a deeper understanding of multiple sources of inequality – notably those caused by social class and race. Both premiers were constrained by conservative worldviews and, in particular, by a shared emphasis on the personal responsibility of individuals to deal with poverty, discrimination, and other disadvantages.

Their respective views fit neatly within the larger context of British Columbia politics. The province is known for its polarized politics. Both premiers had to aggregate the interests of a broad right-wing coalition, which, in turn, rejected the idea that state intervention was necessary in order to create more equality of results (and not simply opportunities) for women. The argument in this chapter, which is that political ideology matters to the actions of women leaders, is consistent with the larger gender and politics literature discussed in Chapter 1 (see also Collier 2007).

I examine the Johnston and Clark premierships by weaving their respective times in office into a larger narrative about BC politics. The history of the province's right-wing coalition and the dramatic swings that characterize provincial politics form a crucial part of the story. Although Johnston's limited time as premier might seem to warrant much less attention than

Clark's premiership, fulsome discussion of both periods permits us to link women's leadership with major points of change in BC politics. In particular, Johnston reached power on the threshold of the collapse of the Social Credit Party. The Socred demise forced right-wing populists and conservatives to seek a new home, which they largely found in the BC Liberal Party. BC Liberals thus tried to aggregate a broad spectrum of traditionalist interests. Shortly after the Socred collapse, Gordon Campbell became Liberal leader; he worked to entrench the formation as a free enterprise party and the only alternative to the NDP in a two-party provincial system.

Given this environment, both Johnston and Clark framed equity for women as a matter of job opportunity and job creation. Unlike their counterparts on the political left, neither identified the challenge as one of structural inequality and poverty. This chapter outlines the circumstances that brought Johnston and Clark to the premier's office, and it pays particular attention to the growing numerical representation of women in BC politics during the Clark era. I show how both women were associated with once-strong political dynasties that ended in scandal, with the result that the declining fortunes of the party imperiled their leadership (see Chapter 1). Above all, Johnston and Clark headed parties fraught with controversy and expected to lose the next election. As Dan Gardner (2012) of the *Vancouver Sun* writes:

> It may be that people see stereotypically female qualities as those that are necessary to turn an organization around, which isn't entirely a bad thing. But other research suggests the explanation may be more dismal. "Women may be favoured in times of poor performance," wrote Ryan and Haslam, "not because they are expected to improve the situation but because they are seen to be good people managers and can take the blame for organizational failure." The "glass cliff" theory fits Canadian political experience with almost eerie precision.

Johnston's fate was sealed by Bill Vander Zalm's missteps and the perception that she remained too close to him to put a new face on the Social Credit Party.

Clark, by contrast, survived Gordon Campbell's demise as Liberal leader in 2011. Unlike Johnston, Clark had two years prior to the next election in which to prove she could govern effectively – and independent of his influence. Arguing that the Liberals were the only party that could ensure BC's economic well-being, Clark led her party to its fourth consecutive majority win in 2013 – despite polls that predicted otherwise. The ensuing years tested Clark's leadership skills and set up expectations that, as the first popularly elected female premier in BC history, she would do better for women than the premiers who preceded her.

Johnston and Clark appealed to families, and particularly to views that job security and low taxes rather than government intervention create a prosperous society. Their policies, campaign platforms, and budgets were all geared towards advancing these ideas. Johnston had much less time to make any substantive changes than Clark, but it is clear that she was more willing than Vander Zalm to endorse social equity policies. Johnston, for instance, recognized that the lives of women in "the 1990s ... and [at the dawning of] the twenty-first century ...will change" (British Columbia, Legislative Assembly, 1991b). Like Johnston and other BC conservatives, Clark used a "family first agenda" to frame her premiership. What distinguishes Clark is that her advocacy for women was nested inside a broader appeal to a nebulous "middle class" that worked for pay and wanted to get ahead (see Anderssen 2015; Grant 2013; Hodges and Brown 2015). As a result, her approach to problems facing women relied entirely on growing the economy and creating jobs.

Party Politics in British Columbia

Much has been written about the polarization of BC politics. A sharp divide has long distinguished left-wing, union, and environmental interests on one side from right-wing, conservative, and libertarian streams on the other – with a strong populist streak characterizing the second cluster. Except for a brief interruption from 1972 to 1975, the BC Social Credit Party held provincial power for close to forty years, beginning in 1952. In 1991, under the leadership of Rita Johnston, the party not only failed to win re-election but also dropped from seventy-four legislative seats to just seven. Johnston lost her own constituency, and the scale of defeat removed the Socreds from the BC political landscape.

Prior to 1991, the Social Credit Party shaped BC through a style of politics that encouraged a strong relationship among industry, government, and society. Many resource towns were developed as the result of a provincial regulation that forced industry to develop communities close to where resources were extracted. In particular, the W.A.C. Bennett government of 1952–72 transformed the economy and social structure of the province. As Donald Blake (1996, 72) argues, "the labour force doubled during his twenty years as premier ... employment in the public sector expanded along with new demands in the health, education, and social welfare fields." His study connects the provincial NDP's victory over Social Credit in 1972 to the growth of public-sector employment. As Blake (1996, 73) explains, the shift was "in part attributable to dissatisfaction among occupational groups the government had helped to create and nourish."

The short-lived NDP government of Dave Barrett in the early 1970s introduced many reforms that portended a tilt in BC politics towards the left. Yet Barrett lost the 1975 election to Social Credit leader Bill Bennett (the son of W.A.C. Bennett), who served as premier until his retirement in 1986. Bill Vander Zalm, Bennett's successor as Social Credit leader, led the party and the province through 1991. He stepped down only a few months before his successor, Rita Johnston, had to call an election because the provincial government had reached its statutory limit of five years in office.

The late Social Credit years saw a major shift in Western democracies away from Keynesian economics, which endorsed state intervention in markets, towards neoconservative and neoliberal approaches, which called for low taxes, minimal government intervention, and the large-scale privatization of public assets. BC Social Credit tried to pursue many of the latter directions but, as Resnick (1987) and Richmond and Shields (2011) show, strong resistance by the NDP, organized labour, and progressive community groups kept neoconservative policies at bay. Richmond and Shields (2011, 222) describe the rise of the BC Solidarity movement, "comprised of a broad spectrum of interests ranging from professionals to the unemployed, consumers to small business, feminists to ethnic minorities, environmentalists as well as the disabled." According to their account, "the political range within this component of Solidarity was consequently also very broad, ranging from real progressive conservatives to communist and anarchistic elements, united by what they opposed rather than a particular alternative vision" (Richmond and Shields 2011, 222–23).

Social Credit also faced internal discord that pitted older against newer party activists. Blake (1996, 75) views the 1986 party leadership convention as "divided sharply along populist/non-populist and establishment/non-establishment lines, with the candidate favoured by the party establishment (Brian Smith) defeated on the fourth ballot. The result represented a repudiation of Bill Bennett's leader style and his attempts to modernize the party organization." In selecting Vander Zalm, party delegates endorsed a member of the old guard as their new leader. Vander Zalm proved unable to heal the deep split in the party and his own personal failings led to his resignation (Blake 1996, 75). When Johnston became premier on the brink of the

1991 provincial election, she faced many difficult challenges: a divided governing party, Vander Zalm's scandal-plagued reputation, and strong opposition to conservative policies among progressive voters.

Women's Representation through 1991

As discussed in Chapter 1, BC has been the site of important breakthroughs for women in Canadian politics. These include the appointment in 1921 of a Liberal MLA, Mary Ellen Smith, as the first female cabinet minister in the British Empire. More than fifty years later, New Democratic MLA Rosemary Brown was elected to the BC House in 1972. The first black woman to hold a provincial legislative seat in Canada, Brown went on to place second in the federal NDP leadership race in 1975, thus becoming the first woman in the country to mount a competitive campaign for the top post in a major federal party.

A number of women were elected as MLAs in BC during the years 1952 through 1991, and Buda Brown served as minister without portfolio in the W.A.C. Bennett cabinet in 1956. According to Rose (1960, 6), "Premier Bennett told reporters with a twinkle in his eye it would be a shame to tie a woman down to any specific cabinet task." Despite the disparaging nature of that comment, Brown's appointment was seen as a victory for women.

As reported in Table 9.1, women ran more frequently as candidates in BC elections with the rise of second-wave feminism in the 1970s. Their proportions were typically higher in the NDP than in either the Social Credit or Liberal organizations. Even during the Barrett years, however, none of the four women elected to the legislature as a New Democrat, including Rosemary Brown, was assigned a cabinet post.

Between 1975 and 1991, a total of eleven women sat as BC MLAs. Three were appointed to cabinet during that period: Grace McCarthy and Rita Johnston under Bill Bennett, and Carol Gran by Bill Vander Zalm. As Erickson (1996, 118) notes, Gran's appointment as minister for the status of women created "a formal advocacy position for women within cabinet." The Social Credit regime established a bureaucratic unit for women, but, according to Erickson (1996, 118), "its direct program responsibilities were minimal."

Premier Rita Johnston

Born in 1935, Rita Johnston resembled many other female politicians in that her career began in municipal politics (e.g., Kathleen Wynne). Johnston won a seat on Surrey city council in 1969 and then a provincial legislative

TABLE 9.1
Women as party candidates in BC general elections, 1972–91

	NDP	Social Credit	Liberal	Other*	Total
Year	% (*N*)	% (*N*)	% (*N*)	% (*N*)	% (*N*)
1972	14.5 (8/55)	7.2 (4/55)	9.4 (5/53)	15.9 (10/63)	11.9 (27/226)
1975	18.2 (10/55)	3.6 (2/55)	16.3 (8/49)	11.3 (7/62)	12.2 (27/221)
1979	21.1 (12/57)	5.3 (3/57)	(0/5)	18.6 (11/59)	14.6 (26/178)
1983	22.8 (13/57)	8.8 (5/57)	19.2 (10/52)	5.2 (3/58)	13.8 (31/224)
1986	30.4 (21/69)	7.2 (5/69)	23.6 (13/55)	11.4 (5/44)	18.6 (44/237)
1991	33.3 (25/75)	24.3 (18/74)	21.1 (15/71)	26.8 (26/97)	26.5 (84/317)

* Other party candidates as well as independent candidates.
Sources: Erickson (1996, 111); Elections BC (1988, 311–56); Elections BC (2002, 5–14).

seat in 1983. She remained an MLA until her defeat in the 1991 election. Once Vander Zalm resigned as Social Credit leader in April 1991, Johnston became Canada's first female premier.

The circumstances in which Johnston took over the party were extremely imperiled. She became interim Socred leader in April, then had to contest a party leadership race in July and a general election in November. This time frame forced her into an odd contradiction. On one side, she had to demonstrate loyalty to the party's old guard in order to unite the organization; on the other, she needed to show voters that Social Credit was newly refreshed.

Her strongest opponent in the leadership race was Grace McCarthy, who had served since 1975 as a Social Credit MLA. Unlike Johnston, McCarthy pledged to change the party's direction. Johnston defeated McCarthy thanks to support from older populists in the party. According to MacQueen (1991, 2), Johnston's "loyalty was seen as a virtue," while "McCarthy, a Vander Zalm critic, was painted as a party malcontent." According to Oake (1991), McCarthy had "resigned from cabinet in 1988 because of policy disagreements with Vander Zalm." In the end, the fact that more delegates believed Johnston could unite the party meant that she was elected by a slim margin.

These leadership campaign dynamics left Johnston open to criticism that she was too close to the discredited Vander Zalm and would be unable to make any significant changes if she won her own popular mandate. Baldrey et al. (1991) describe Johnston as "a Vander Zalm loyalist whose associations with the former premier go back to their days on Surrey municipal council in the early 1970s. She remained loyal to Vander Zalm through his last hours as premier, standing grimly behind him when he announced his decision to quit immediately."

While Premier Johnston attempted to introduce new policies related to women, she had no time to move them forward. Perhaps most telling is the number of times women were highlighted in the single throne speech for which Johnston was responsible and the number of times women were discussed in the legislature afterwards (British Columbia, Legislative Assembly 1991a). The speech raised a broad set of issues ranging across class and race; it recognized that, as "the twenty-first century dawns on the province of British Columbia, societal values, needs and structures will change [and] the roles and needs of women have changed, and will continue to change, whether they are in the home or employed." The text mentioned wanting to help women "achieve equality in the workplace, economic security and safety, both in the home and in the community."

In flagging plans for a "comprehensive child care strategy," the speech acknowledged that barriers to employment opportunities affect women, visible minorities, Indigenous peoples, and persons with disabilities. It raised the prospect of "fostering the growth of entrepreneurship among women and removing barriers that inhibit business development among women." The text said that Johnston's government would "affirm the central role of the family and underscore the importance of the care of our children to the future well-being of the province." Finally, the speech included a promise to "expand direct services for victims of family violence and sexual assault, giving priority to initiatives aimed at breaking the cycle of abuse" (British Columbia, Legislative Assembly, 1991b).

Writing in the *Ottawa Citizen*, Gerard Young (1991) describes the Johnston government's only fiscal statement as follows:

> It's a motherhood budget. [Finance Minister John] Jansen holds the line on direct taxes on middle-class families, while fulfilling Premier Rita Johnston's throne speech pledge that those who can afford to will pay more. Johnston's influence on the budget is evident ... [S]he has emphasized an increased focus on families, women and the elderly. Jansen committed an additional $12.1 million to day care and another $4 million to fight family violence. Health, education and social services, which take up the biggest chunk of the budget, are also increased by $1.2 billion ... Jansen avoided direct taxes affecting the middle class, which make up the majority of voters.

Young (1991) concludes that the budget was more conciliatory than earlier Social Credit budgets. In his words, "there [was] no outrageous spending and none of the oppressive restraint that bitterly divided the province in the past." Johnston likely took this approach in order to blunt public criticism of earlier Social Credit austerity measures.

As premier, Johnston retained Carol Gran as minister of government management services and minister responsible for women's programs (Legislative Library of British Columbia 1991a, 1991b). Jocelyne Praud (2013, 65) argues that, despite the willingness of Social Credit premiers to appoint a women's minister, the party remained committed to an old style of politics. In her words: "Two decades after the Royal Commission on the Status of Women had identified parties' women's auxiliaries, which separated women from the mainstream party organization and confined them to supportive roles, as a major impediment to women's involvement in politics, the Social Credit Party still had one such body in 1990." She attributes the sudden increase in numbers of women candidates running for the party in 1991 to the weakened state of the Social Credit organization (see Table 9.1). According to Praud, "many fewer men, including a large number of incumbents, were interested in contesting the election under the banner of a badly damaged party that was almost certainly heading for defeat" (ibid.)

Johnston's effort to change gears fell apart in the fall 1991 election campaign. In her mid-fifties at the time, she was widely seen as an aged, even motherly figure in the televised debate against NDP leader Mike Harcourt and Liberal leader Gordon Wilson – both of whom were in their forties. The exchange brought out a personality trait that Johnston herself described as "scolding" (CBC Digital Archive 1991). The premier called Harcourt "gutless" and repeatedly asked him to "produce the numbers" that would show the cost of NDP campaign promises. Wilson burst into the fray by declaring: "Here's a classic example of why nothing ever gets done in the province of British Columbia" (ibid.). In that moment the Liberals effectively turned the tables on Social Credit by offering right-of-centre populists a new party that did not carry the heavy baggage of Bill Vander Zalm. Wilson's barb changed the direction of the election and vaulted the BC Liberals from zero to seventeen legislative seats – enough to become the official opposition to an NDP government.

In hindsight, it is difficult to know whether Johnston would have modernized the Social Credit Party or changed public policies. Her short stint as premier allowed little time to do anything but try to survive the next election. As shown in Table 9.1, Social Credit ran women in about one-quarter of BC constituencies in 1991, which was a major increase from the less than 10 percent level in previous campaigns. Like most other candidates for the party, Johnston lost in 1991 when Social Credit was reduced to third-party status with only seven MLAs.

Between Women Premiers

The 1991 election of an NDP majority government under Mike Harcourt was a major watershed in BC politics. The event not only marked the end of Social Credit as a force to be reckoned with but also shifted the province to the left. Yet Harcourt had to contend with diverse and sometimes competing interests inside the Solidarity coalition, which made progressive policy difficult. Trade union, environmental, and First Nations groups, for instance, were often at odds over the best directions for a resource-based economy.

Harcourt was also pressed by growing national and international demands for fiscal conservatism and austerity. Collier (2007, 15) captures this tension when she writes:

> Activists and party insiders interviewed ... noted that the rhetoric of fiscal conservatism became more prevalent in the NDP in 1994 and following, threatening women's policy issues. Over time, Harcourt found it difficult to "walk the tightrope" between appeasing the core constituencies of the NDP and allaying the fears of business groups that were uncomfortable with a social democratic government.

The full weight of the neoliberal push became evident after Premier Harcourt resigned in 1996 and was replaced by Glen Clark. As Albo (2002, 47) argues, "policies of deregulation, privatization, and social austerity" characterized Canadian governments across the ideological spectrum such that citizens "get neoliberalism even when we elect social democratic governments."

For feminists and other progressive interests, these were trying times. As Carroll and Ratner (2007, 63) maintain, the "economic imperatives of global capitalism make it difficult for social movements to forge effective alliances with social democratic parties and organized labour." The NDP found it hard to formulate policy in a polarized political climate, particularly after Glen Clark won a reduced majority government in 1996. The party's decade in power ended with a stunning defeat in 2001 when Gordon Campbell's Liberals won all but two provincial constituencies. As of 2001, both NDP MLAs were women holding seats in Vancouver: Jenny Kwan and Joy MacPhail.

The overwhelming Liberal victory resulted, in part, from scandals and budget overruns that were associated with BC NDP leaders. As well, the rhetoric of neoliberalism, employed by Campbell and others, framed social democratic policies as unresponsive to citizens because they imposed high taxes to finance "big government" and "special interests." BC Liberals promised to decentralize power and open the province to business and global markets. This pledge enabled the party to win consecutive majority governments under Campbell's leadership in 2001, 2005, and 2009.

The 2011 resignation of Gordon Campbell was a critical, highly strategic move that gave the party new life and extended its term in power until 2017. Despite a series of personal as well as policy scandals, Campbell remained reasonably popular until he broke a major campaign promise not to harmonize the provincial sales tax with a federal levy. Anger over the tax decision reduced his popularity to single digit numbers and opened the BC Liberal Party to a leadership race.

Premier Christy Clark

Born in 1965, Christy Clark entered provincial politics as a Vancouver-area MLA in 1996. She served in opposition until the BC Liberals swept to power in 2001, the same year as Clark gave birth to a son. Among the first mothers of very young children in Canada to hold a political executive role, she held a series of cabinet posts until 2004, when she decided to step back to spend more time with her son. It is notable that as co-chair of the Liberal election campaign in 2001, Clark found it hard to recruit women candidates; she attributed their lack of interest to the fact that women hold politics in "low regard" (Edwards 2008, 118). At the time she left provincial politics in 2004, Clark opposed targets or quotas for female candidates, and suggested that what women need is to be nominated into more winnable ridings. In her words, "they need the encouragement and mentors to bring them along like anybody else does" (Canadian Press 2004).

In 2005, Clark was unsuccessful in her campaign for the Vancouver mayoral nomination in the right-of-centre Non-Partisan Association. However, between 2007 and 2010, she kept a high public profile as a news commentator, columnist, and host of her own radio show. When Clark announced she would run to succeed Campbell as leader of the BC Liberals, her candidacy gained support from only one member of the party's legislative caucus. She had been an early member of the Campbell government but was seen as an outsider who had left provincial politics six years earlier.

Clark's engaging personal style gave her a clear advantage in a hotly contested leadership race against cabinet ministers Kevin Falcon, George Abbott, and Mike de Jong (CBC News 2011). Not only was her victory seen as surprising, but it is also apparent that she was only expected to lead until the Liberals were defeated in the next provincial election. Polls suggested that voters were ready to punish the Liberals and return the provincial NDP to power under Adrian Dix (Ekos Politics 2013).

Clark entered the 2013 election campaign as a highly unpopular premier. In one leaders' debate, John Cummins of the Conservative Party said there was no doubt about the outcome of the campaign: Dix would be the next BC premier (BC Leaders' Debate 2013). According to Cox (2013), "Conservative Leader John Cummins trolled for votes by pointing out the Liberals weren't likely to win the election so casting a vote in his direction would send a message." Clark was in this sense advantaged by there being such low expectations for her performance.

She used that edge to communicate the Liberals' Family First platform, which focused on job creation and debt reduction as contrasted with the bloated government and high taxes implicit in NDP promises. The first question put to Clark in the leaders' debate concerned her decision to run a red light with her son in the car. Clark took responsibility for her behaviour and said she should not have done it. Then she shifted the subject to the difficulties involved in parenting and stressed how families were the "building block" of society (BC Leaders' Debate 2013). Clark ensured that most of her interventions underlined a core argument that individuals and families are better suited to make decisions than governments.

The debate moderator asked Clark about her party's weakness among women voters. Clark responded that, as Election Day approached, both men and women would become more focused on substantive issues – notably the need to expand business in the province. According to Ipsos (2013), Clark was correct in her strategy of reaching out to all voters:

> The BC Liberals improved among both men and women, and almost beat the NDP among women on Election Day. Among men, the Liberals improved by a NET 15 points (from a 2 point deficit to the NDP in [a] pre election poll, to a 13 point advantage in [the] election poll). Among women, the Liberals improved by a NET 11 points (from a 14 point deficit to the NDP in [a] pre election poll, to a 3 point deficit in [the] election poll).

Despite very weak polling numbers at the start of the 2013 campaign, Clark's Liberals won a strong majority government with forty-nine of eighty-five legislative seats.

Comparing Two Imperiled Premiers

How did Clark not just ensure her party's survival but also win a majority government, while Johnston was unable to reach these goals? First, timing matters a great deal. Johnston had less than eight months to turn around Social Credit fortunes whereas Clark had two years. That distinction is crucial because Clark had many opportunities to develop her public persona and create distance between herself and her predecessor's unpopular decisions. In addition, Clark had formidable public speaking skills that allowed her to appear warm and engaged. The fact that NDP leader Adrian Dix said throughout the 2013 election campaign that he was not going to attack Clark worked in the Liberals' favour. Post-election analysis points to Dix's strategy as a reason for the NDP loss (Mason 2013).

Second, Johnston was seen as too close to both Vander Zalm, her predecessor as party leader, and other insiders who were unwilling to update the aging right-wing organization. Modernization would have meant bringing Social Credit in line with newer conservative ideas of the 1980s and after, including shedding older province-building policies that had poured government funds into aging resource towns. Clark, by contrast, could use her earlier resignation from provincial politics to run as a Liberal outsider. Without the shadow cast by the party's old guard, she could claim her leadership would bring something new to provincial politics (Bailey 2010).

A third explanation is that Johnston's defeat marked not just a major setback for Social Credit but also a fundamental realignment of provincial politics. In 1991, BC voters were not so much endorsing the NDP as they were rejecting Social Credit. Research shows that the latter party's failure to modernize created a wholesale shift towards the Liberals that effectively erased Social Credit from the political map (Blake and Carty 1995–96).

For BC voters in 2013, it was not necessary to defeat Clark in order to punish the Liberals. The real culprit was Gordon Campbell, who had already been forced to resign as party leader and premier. Given that she was outside government beginning in 2004, Clark promised to consult the public on the contentious question of a harmonized sales tax (HST). Untarnished by the debacles associated with Campbell's later years, she carried through with a tax referendum that rejected the HST and dissipated a great deal of anger over the issue. In short, because the problem had already been solved, voters did not need to punish her or the Liberal Party.

A fourth explanation is tied to how each leader framed her narrative on social and economic policy. Johnston led during a period of what McMartin (2009) describes as "dramatic, tumultuous swings" in GDP that "were more exaggerated than those of the nation as a whole." Other than her throne speech agenda, Johnston proposed few solutions to this boom-and-bust cycle – in part because, as argued earlier, she had no time to develop a more complete policy platform.

By contrast, Clark used the records of previous NDP governments to develop a story line that demonized social spending and celebrated the Liberals' commitment to creating jobs and eliminating public debt. Her 2013 election platform proposed a women's enterprise centre to encourage new women entrepreneurs and a women's economic advisory council to ensure government policies assisted women in business (BC Liberal Party Platform 2013). Overall, Clark hammered home the message that economic stability was more important than changing the party in power – since her discredited predecessor had been ousted years earlier.

Taken together, these factors shed light on how Clark's Liberals won the 2013 election while Johnston was unable to revive Social Credit in 1991.

Recruitment and Policy Impact

Similar to left-of-centre parties in many other political systems, the BC NDP made consistent efforts to recruit female candidates and voters beginning in the 1970s (Praud 2013, 66). Between 1972 and 1991 the number of female NDP candidates rose steadily from about 15 to 33 percent (See Table 9.1). Data in Tables 9.2 and 9.3 reveal that women became even more numerous as New Democratic nominees after 1991, with levels as high as 51 percent in 2017. The party had three female leaders while in opposition – namely, Joy MacPhail (2001–03), Carole James (2003–11), and Dawn Black (2011).

Compared to the NDP, BC Liberals paid significantly less attention to women's participation in the years between 1972 and 1991, when female Liberal candidates fluctuated from zero in 1979 to about 24 percent in 1986 (see Table 9.1). Yet, as indicated in Tables 9.2 and 9.3, numbers of Liberal candidates tended to grow over time towards the 30 to 40 percent level. This shift was linked much less to formal rules and procedures in the Liberal Party than in the NDP. At a session with his party Women's Commission,

TABLE 9.2
Women as party candidates in BC general elections, 1996–2009

Year	NDP % (N)	Social Credit % (N)	Liberal % (N)
1996	29 (22/75)	11 (4/35)	27 (20/75)
2001	25 (20/79)		24 (19/79)
2005	29 (23/79)		32 (25/79)
2009	48 (41/85)		29 (25/85)

Sources: Praud (2013, 60); Elections BC (1996).

for instance, Premier Gordon Campbell "showed how few ideas he has on improving the role of women in government. When asked how he plans to slay the gender imbalance he said, 'Boy, I wish it was up to government'" (Canadian Press 2004).

Campbell appointed cabinets of no more than 30 percent women and had few women on cabinet committees (BC Office of the Premier 2008). In 2005, however, 45 percent of BC's deputy ministers were women. This level may have been reached because Campbell believed individual civil servants were the most capable for the job and hired them without considering gender. Such an approach would be consistent with BC Liberal practices, which focus on individual responsibility and merit rather than any formal efforts to recruit women.

Numbers of women in BC government rose during Christy Clark's term in office. Between 2011 and 2017, she appointed thirty-seven cabinet members, of whom thirteen, or 35 percent, were women (Legislative Library of British Columbia 2016a, 2016b). Her cabinet committees included nine women chairs or vice-chairs. In 2017, 41 percent (12/29) of BC deputy ministers were women (Government of British Columbia 2017).

Despite these numerical gains, substantive policy changes sought by feminist organizations did not follow. Clark's throne speeches typically focused on families and contained few mentions of women. For instance, the February 2013 throne speech mentioned women twice, once to promise improvements to the BC Women's Hospital and once to encourage women to enter skilled trades (British Columbia, Legislative Assembly 2013a). In policy-related items, the words "family" or "families" were mentioned fourteen times (British Columbia, Legislative Assembly 2013a). The June 2013 throne speech referred to domestic violence but mentioned

TABLE 9.3

Women as party candidates in BC general elections, 2013–17

Year	NDP % (N)	Green % (N)	Liberal % (N)	Conservative % (N)
2013	34 (29/85)	18 (11/61)	28 (24/85)	9 (5/56)
2017	51 (44/87)	38 (30/80)	40 (35/87)	20 (2/10)

Sources: Tyee (2013); Ghoussoub (2017); Elections BC (2017).

women only once, compared to seven mentions of family or families (British Columbia, Legislative Assembly 2013b). In 2014 and 2015, women were mentioned in passages about domestic violence (British Columbia, Legislative Assembly 2014a; British Columbia, Legislative Assembly 2015). In 2016, the speech cited a planned partnership with Ottawa on the National Inquiry into Murdered and Missing Indigenous Women and Girls. Mentions of women were in each case part of the phrase "men and women" (British Columbia, Legislative Assembly 2016).

In 2017, the throne speech mentioned a "healing event" for families of missing and murdered Indigenous women and girls, and it introduced a new safety plan for Highway 16 – known as the Highway of Tears because it has been the site of many women's disappearances. Although Clark introduced a policy document called *Vision for a Violence Free BC* (British Columbia 2015), she was seen as not strongly committed to the issue as it affected Indigenous women in Northern BC. Under Premier Clark, references to the Highway of Tears were deleted from Ministry of Transport e-mail communications (CBC News 2015). Although Clark's government eventually ensured limited bus service along the Highway 16 corridor, problems of violence in Northern BC remained (Talaga 2017).

Between 2013 and 2017, Premier Clark increased licensed child care spaces but refused to implement a ten-dollar-a-day child care plan that would have paralleled the program created by Pauline Marois as a Quebec cabinet minister. While BC Liberals implemented a full-day kindergarten initiative promised in 2010, the government came under scrutiny because of the deaths of multiple children in foster care (Sherlock and Culbert 2017). Critics focused on decisions by Clark's minister of children and family development, Stephanie Cadieux, and on Liberal attempts to privatize foster care (Slattery 2017; Shields 2015). Among the government's most effective critics was Mary Ellen Turpel-Lafond, BC's representative for children and youth. As a First Nations woman, Turpel-Lafond tried to bring the racial-ized nature of the foster care system to public attention (Kines 2016).

As premier, Clark announced that her own personal experience of sex-ual violence led her to support Green Party leader Andrew Weaver's pro-posal to create guidelines on campus sexual assault (Harnett 2016). Clark also accepted Weaver's bill to change the provincial labour code so that women could not be required to wear high heels at work, a decision the party highlighted in its subsequent election platform (BC Liberal Party Platform 2017).

Overall, Premier Clark's singular message was that job creation and a growing economy were the best tools for addressing poverty and struc-tural inequality. The 2017 Liberal election platform reiterated this message and, like throne speeches delivered while Clark was leader, emphasized families (forty mentions) and challenges facing middle-class voters (thirteen mentions) (BC Liberal Party Platform 2017).

Losing Power

During her time as BC premier, Clark was widely acknowledged to be a savvy public speaker. She adeptly handled many controversies, including with Alberta premier Alison Redford over pipeline expansion into BC. Yet, over time, Clark operated in what was increasingly perceived to be an impatient, hard-nosed manner. She was said to admire W.A.C Bennett and drew the same objection he had – namely, that she cared "more about the economy, at times, than people" (Shaw 2017).

Comparing the 2013 and 2017 BC elections helps to demonstrate how public approval of Clark's style, personality, and policy choices declined with the passage of time. In the 2013 race, Conservatives and Liberals com-peted for right-of-centre voters with the result that Clark could position herself as the more progressive, centrist politician. As an incumbent pre-mier in 2017 with no Conservative opponent, Clark had to defend a Liberal record dating back sixteen years. Moreover, BC's Green Party claimed a spot in 2017 as the progressive alternative to the NDP. Since Clark offered few new policy options, her approach seemed stale and she was no longer able to present herself as an outsider ready to challenge the status quo.

Consistent with materials presented in Chapter 1, gender and tone be-came central issues in the 2017 election campaign. In a leaders' debate broadcast on Facebook, Clark reached out and touched John Horgan's arm and told him to "calm down" (Zussman 2017). The exchange brought

Horgan's temperament into question; however, later in the campaign, when the moderator in the televised debate asked Horgan about his temperament, Horgan replied that he gets angry when he sees "government inaction" (BC Leaders' Debate 2017). That rebuttal effectively turned the earlier exchange between Horgan and Clark to his advantage.

At the start of the 2017 campaign, less than 20 percent of BC voters believed Clark was caring, honest, relatable, and trustworthy. About 21 percent found her likeable, and 30 percent thought she was tough (Ipsos 2017). Clark made little effort to change public perceptions.

The sense that Clark failed to comprehend the human dimension of policy challenges came into sharp focus in 2017 during an impromptu campaign visit to a grocery store in North Vancouver. Clark was approached by a woman named Linda Higgins, who told Clark she would not be voting for her. Clark cut her off by saying, "You don't have to – that's why we live in a democracy." Higgins said she was frustrated by a number of issues, including the fact that her two grown children could not enter the expensive Vancouver housing market despite having good jobs (Bailey 2017).

The interaction sparked strong social media interest and demonstrated the limits of Clark's effort to equate economic growth with social well-being. Particularly in BC's major cities, the inequality gap was growing and Liberal support eroding. Moreover, according to Ipsos (2017) polling data, female voters heavily favoured the NDP: "the BC Liberals lead by 8-points among men (44 percent Lib vs. 36 percent NDP), while the New Democrats have a 10-point lead among women (44 percent NDP vs. 34 percent Libs)."

In the 2017 election, Clark's Liberals won both the seat count and the popular vote. Yet the party was unable to maintain the confidence of the Legislative Assembly when the Greens sided with the NDP to topple the government. In a final effort to retain power, Clark crafted a throne speech that read like an opposition manifesto – promising, for example, to expand child care funding by a billion dollars. Moscrop (2017) describes the document as "gruesomely stitched together from the platforms of the party's rivals." The strategy did not sit well with fiscal conservatives in BC. After months of speculation, Clark announced her resignation as Liberal leader in August 2017.

Conclusion

In her study of women's advancement in BC politics, Jocelyne Praud (2013, 57) argues that "three conditions need to be present: (1) gender parity, or the equal representation of women and men in the legislature and cabinet; (2) a governing party that is committed to support women and issues of concern to them; and (3) a progressive and feminist premier who will promote gender parity and policies designed to improve the lives of women." Curiously, data presented in this chapter suggest that, in some respect, these three conditions were met under Clark's leadership. Numbers of women in cabinet and the senior bureaucracy approached parity and the premier claimed to support women.

Christy Clark refused, however, to acknowledge multiple sources of disadvantage facing women and instead adopted policies that ignored structural inequality. She failed to move forward progressive policy change for women even though the number of women in government did increase. In her assessment of women's representation, Praud (2013, 70) concludes that "the tenure of British Columbia's second woman premier may turn out to be an unfortunate example of women's important numerical gains not translating into substantive policy gains for women, families and children." Unfortunately, it appears that her prediction was correct.

Both Rita Johnston and Christy Clark served in the polarized setting of BC politics. Both premiers led right-wing formations in what was essentially a two-party system. The Socreds and Liberals had to aggregate a broad spectrum of interests, including libertarians, populists, and mainstream conservatives in a free-enterprise coalition. This grouping stood in opposition to an equally diverse alliance of social democrats, socialists, and extra-parliamentary progressives on the left. The right-wing ideology of Socreds and Liberals restricted the kinds of policies that Johnston, Clark, or any premier in that part of the spectrum could have introduced.

Echoing the findings of comparative women and politics scholarship, BC women premiers from two different conservative parties stand out for their belief in free enterprise as the key driver of social progress and for their resistance to state-led initiatives that might address structural sources of inequality.

References

Albo, Gregory. 2002. "Neoliberalism, the State, and the Left: A Canadian Perspective." *Monthly Review* 54, 1: 46–55.

Anderssen, Erin. 2015. "The Trouble with Pitching the Middle Class." *Globe and Mail*, 19 September.

Bailey, Ian. 2010. "Clark Enters Race to Replace Campbell." *Globe and Mail*, 8 December.

–. 2017. "#IamLinda Encounter Continues to Plague Christy Clark, BC Liberals." *Globe and Mail*, 1 May. https://beta.theglobeandmail.com/news/british-columbia/ iamlinda-encounter-continues-to-plague-christy-clark-bc-liberals/article 34871610/?ref=http://www.theglobeandmail.com&.

Baldrey, Keith, Justine Hunter, David Hogben, and Jeff Lee. 1991. "Vander Zalm Loyalist First Woman Premier." *Vancouver Sun*, 3 April: A1.

BC Leaders' Debate. 2013. https://www.youtube.com/watch?v=6sHYeu5Fmjg.

–. 2017. http://globalnews.ca/video/3408262/bc-leaders-debate-2017.

BC Liberal Party Platform. 2013. "Strong Economy, Secure Tomorrow." https://www. poltext.org/sites/poltext.org/files/plateformes/bc2013lib_plt.pdf

–. 2017. "Strong BC, Bright Future." https://www.bcliberals.com/wp-content/uploads/ 2017/04/2017-Platform.pdf

BC Office of the Premier. 2008. "Backgrounder: Cabinet Committees." 23 June. https://archive.news.gov.bc.ca/releases/news_releases_2005-2009/2008OTP01 65-000983-Attachment4.htm.

Blake, Donald E. 1996. "The Politics of Polarization." In *Politics, Policy, and Government in British Columbia*, ed. R.K. Carty, 67–84. Vancouver: UBC Press.

Blake, Donald E., and Ken Carty. 1995–96. "Partisan Realignment in British Columbia: The Case of the Provincial Liberal Party." *BC Studies* 108 (Winter): 61–74.

British Columbia. 2015. *Vision for a Violence Free BC*. http://cdhpi.ca/sites/cdhpi. ca/files/A_Vision_for_a_Violence_Free_BC.pdf

British Columbia, Legislative Assembly. 1991a. *Hansard* (7 May, afternoon sitting) Lam, David. https://www.leg.bc.ca/content/Hansard/34th5th/34p_05s_910507p. htm.

–. 1991b. "Speech from the Throne." 34th Legislature, 5th Session.

–. 2013a. "Speech from the Throne." 39th Legislature, 5th Session.

–. 2013b. "Speech from the Throne." 40th Legislature, 1st Session.

–. 2014a. "Speech from the Throne." 40th Legislature, 2nd Session.

–. 2014b. "Speech from the Throne." 40th Legislature, 3rd Session.

–. 2015. "Speech from the Throne." 40th Legislature, 4th Session.

–. 2016. "Speech from the Throne." 40th Legislature, 5th Session.

Canadian Press. 2004. "BC Liberals Need to Nominate More Women." *Globe and Mail*, 8 November. http://www.theglobeandmail.com/news/national/bc-liberals -need-to-nominate-more-women-christy-clark/article1143381/

Carroll, William, and R.S. Ratner. 2007. "Ambivalent Allies: Social Democratic Regimes and Social Movements." *BC Studies* 154 (Summer): 41–66.

CBC Digital Archive. 1991. "Gordon Wilson's Debate Triumph in BC." http://www. cbc.ca/archives/entry/bc-elections-1991-gordon-wilsons-debate-triumph

CBC News. 2011. "Christy Clark Voted BC Liberal Leader." 26 February. http://www. cbc.ca/news/canada/british-columbia/christy-clark-voted-b-c-liberal-leader -1.987130.

–. 2015. "Highway of Tears emails: What happened during those meetings." 23 October. https://www.cbc.ca/news/canada/british-columbia/highway-of-tears -emails-what-happened-during-those-meetings-1.3285046.

Collier, Cheryl. 2007. "How Party Matters: A Comparative Assessment of the Openness of Left- and Right–Wing Governments to Women's Issues in Ontario and British Columbia, 1980–2002." Paper presented at the Canadian Political Science Association meetings, University of Saskatchewan. https://www.cpsa -acsp.ca/papers-2007/Collier-Cheryl.pdf.

Cox, Wendy. 2013. "Cummins, Sterk, Dix, Clark Trade Barbs in TV debate." *CTV News* digital edition. 29 April. http://bc.ctvnews.ca/cummins-sterk-dix-clark -trade-barbs-in-tv-debate-1.1259647

Edwards, Anne. 2008. *Seeking Balance: Conversations with BC Women in Politics.* Halfmoon Bay, BC: Caitlin Press.

Ekos Politics. 2013. "An Unapologetic Analysis of the BC Polling Debacle: What Really Happened?" http://www.ekospolitics.com/articles/FG-2013-05-29.pdf

Elections BC. 1988. "Electoral History of British Columbia 1871–1986." http:// elections.bc.ca/docs/rpt/1871-1986_ElectoralHistoryofBC.pdf.

–. 1996. Statement of Votes 36th Provincial General Election, 28 May. http:// elections.bc.ca/docs/rpt/1996-SOVGeneralElection.pdf

–. 2002. "Electoral History of British Columbia Supplement, 1987–2001." https:// www.leg.bc.ca/content-leglibrary/documents/electhistvol2.pdf.

–. 2017. Interim Statement of Votes 41st Provincial General Election, 9 May. http:// elections.bc.ca/docs/2017-provincial-general-election/2017_GE_Interim_VA_ Results_summary.pdf

Erickson, Lynda. 1996. "Women and Political Representation in British Columbia." In *Politics, Policy, and Government in British Columbia,* ed. R.K. Carty, 103–22. Vancouver: UBC Press.

Gardner, Dan. 2012. "Women in Politics Face 'Glass Cliff.'" *Vancouver Sun,* 13 April.

Ghoussoub, Michelle. 2017. "111 Women Ran in BC's Election, Just 34 Were Elected." *CBCNews,* 11 May. http://www.cbc.ca/news/canada/british-columbia/111-women -ran-in-b-c-s-election-just-34-were-elected-1.4111156

Government of British Columbia. 2017. "Deputy Minister's Council of British Columbia." http://www2.gov.bc.ca/gov/content/governments/organizational-structure/ cabinet/deputy-ministers

Grant, Tavia. 2013. "Five Myths about Canada's Middle Class." *Globe and Mail,* 19 November.

Harnett, Cindy. 2016. "For Premier, Sexual Violence Is Personal." *Times Colonist,* 6 October.

Hodges, David, and Mark Brown. 2015. "Are You in the Middle Class?" *Maclean's* supplement, 27 January.

Ipsos. 2013. "Inside the BC Election: What Happened and Why." https://www.ipsos. com/en-ca/inside-bc-election-what-happened-and-why.

–. 2017. "BC Election: Too Close to Call." https://www.ipsos.com/en-ca/news-polls/ bc-election-too-close-call. https://www.ipsos.com/en-ca/inside-bc-election-what -happened-and-why.

Kines, Lindsay. 2016. "Turpel-Lafond Ends Her Term as Children's Representative." *Times Colonist,* 24 October. http://www.timescolonist.com/news/local/turpel

-lafond-ends-her-term-as-children-s-representative-1.2371957#sthash.Z9b3
wavk.dpuf

Legislative Library of British Columbia. 1991a. "Vander Zalm Cabinet 33rd–34th
Parliament 1986–1991." Prepared by Vivenne Bruce with the assistance of Judi
Bennett. Updated 10 July 1996.

–. 1991b. "Rita Johnston Cabinet 34th Parliament 1991." Prepared by Vivenne Bruce.
Re-issued 2011. http://www.llbc.leg.bc.ca/public/reference/johnstoncabinet.pdf.

–. 2016a. "Christy Clark Cabinet 2011– Present." http://www.llbc.leg.bc.ca/public/
reference/christyclarkcabinet.pdf.

–. 2016b. "Women Members of the Legislative Assembly of British Columbia, 1918–
Present." http://www.llbc.leg.bc.ca/public/reference/womenmembersofthelegis
lativeassembly.pdf.

MacQueen, Ken. 1991. "Rita Wins on Second Ballot." *Prince George Citizen,* 22 July.

Mason, Gary. 2013. "The Only Sure Election Winner: Negative Campaigning." *Globe
and Mail,* 17 May. https://www.theglobeandmail.com/opinion/the-only-sure
-election-winner-negative-campaigning/article11973183/?arc404=true.

McMartin, Will. 2009. "BC's Economy: Whose Was Best." *Tyee,* 23 April. https://
thetyee.ca/Views/2009/04/23/BCEcon/.

Moscrop, David. 2017. "The Foul Cynicism of Christy Clark's Speech from the
Throne." *Maclean's,* 23 June.

Oake, George. 1991. "Socred 'Godmother' Brings Race to Life." *Toronto Star,* 30 June.

Praud, Jocelyne. 2013. "When Numerical Gains Are Not Enough: Women in British
Columbia Politics." In *Stalled: The Representation of Women in Canadian Government,* ed. Linda Trimble, Jane Arscott, and Manon Tremblay, 55–74. Vancouver: UBC Press.

Resnick, Philip. 1987. "Neo-Conservatism on the Periphery: The Lessons from BC."
BC Studies 75 (Autumn): 3–23.

Richmond, Ted, and John Shields. 2011. "Reflections on Resistance to Neoliberalism:
Looking Back on Solidarity in 1983 British Columbia." *Socialist Studies* 7 (Spring/
Fall): 216–37.

Rose, Ron. 1960. "City's Buda Brown Gets Cabinet Post." *Vancouver Sun,* 29 November. https://news.google.com/newspapers?id=jZhlAAAAIBAJ&sjid=TIoNAA
AAIBAJ&pg=2762,5542736.

Shaw, Rob. 2017. "Christy Clark: BC's Modern-Day W.A.C. Bennett." *Vancouver Sun,*
3 May. http://vancouversun.com/news/politics/christy-clark-b-c-s-modern-day
-w-a-c-bennett.

Sherlock, Tracy, and Lori Culbert. 2017. "Number of BC Kids-In-Care Deaths,
Critical Injuries Jump Dramatically." *Vancouver Sun,* 9 February. http://vancouver
sun.com/news/local-news/number-of-b-c-kids-in-care-deaths-critical
-injuries-jump-dramatically.

Shields, John. 2015. "Evaluate Privatization of Child-Welfare Services." *Times Colonist,* 18 December: A15.

Slattery, Jill. 2017. "Mother of Boy Who Died in BC Government Care Confronts
Minister for Apology." *Global News,* 25 March. http://globalnews.ca/news/

3334259/mother-of-boy-who-died-in-government-care-confronts-minister-for
-apology/.

Talaga, Tanya. 2017. "Highway of Tears Partial Bus Service Ready to Roll." *Toronto Star*, 27 January. https://www.thestar.com/news/canada/2017/01/27/highway-of
-tears-partial-bus-service-ready-to-roll.html.

Tyee. 2013. "BC Election 2013 Candidates." http://election.thetyee.ca/candidates

Young, Gerard. 1991. "British Columbia Budget: Treasurer Makes Few Enemies." *Ottawa Citizen*, 22 May.

Zussman, Richard. 2017. "'Don't Touch Me Again': The Moment the Provincial Debate Changed." *CBC News*, 21 April. http://www.cbc.ca/news/canada/british
-columbia/don-t-touch-me-again-the-moment-the-provincial-debate-changed
-1.4078156.

10

Women and Politics in Alberta under Alison Redford

CLARK BANACK

In October 2011, Alison Redford won the leadership of the Alberta Progressive Conservative (PC) party to become the province's first female premier. In April 2012, she became the third woman in Canadian history to lead a provincial party to victory in an election, with the PCs capturing a commanding majority. Yet, in March 2014, facing dismal poll numbers and the makings of a caucus revolt, Redford announced her resignation, which ended the shortest tenure of any elected Alberta premier (two years and 167 days; see Chapter 7 on Pauline Marois's similar record in Quebec).

It is notable that Redford resembles women premiers in Quebec, Ontario, and BC in that she led in imperiled circumstances: a once powerful governing party had measurably weakened. Given the brevity of her premiership, it is perhaps unrealistic to assume Redford could fundamentally alter the place of women and women's issues in Alberta politics. This chapter argues that, while Redford was once dismissed as a "little-known feminist human rights lawyer" (Morton 2013, 32), she moved the needle very little when it came to encouraging more women to enter politics, placing more women in positions of political influence, or ensuring women's issues were a prominent focus of her government. Although she presented herself as a socially progressive politician and won support among women voters, her record as premier suggests she would not have made significant gains in these areas even with more time in office.

Relying on government documents, *Hansard* records, media reports, and seven semi-structured interviews with Alberta politicians and senior bureaucrats who worked closely with Redford,[1] this chapter begins to unpack the relationship between Redford's premiership, on one side, and women and politics in Alberta, on the other. Following an overview of Redford's political career, I examine her record of appointing women to cabinet and deputy minister positions as well as patterns of women's candidacy and legislative participation. The discussion then considers the tenor of debate in the Alberta House under Redford, the attention issues important to women received in the legislature, and policy outcomes with respect to those issues. The final section assesses the role of gender in Redford's sudden resignation.

This chapter shows how Redford's government made incremental advances, especially with respect to domestic and sexual violence. As argued in Chapter 8, policy change in this area is generally less costly in fiscal as well as political terms than are pro-equality interventions in such fields as equal pay and child care. Overall, Redford's approach to women's issues in general and women in politics in particular seemed to be governed by a conservative worldview that limited the possibilities for advancement. Put simply, Redford disavowed the notion that more women in positions of power would necessarily alter outcomes. Furthermore, like her right-of-centre counterparts in British Columbia, she displayed little interest in broad structural factors that affect the lives of many women from diverse backgrounds. Finally, it seems that gender did play an indirect role in Redford's political downfall, although it was but one of several important factors.

Political Career

A lawyer by trade, Redford developed deep connections to the "Red Tory" side of both the Alberta and federal PC parties before she became premier. Long an admirer of the popular centrist provincial premier Peter Lougheed, Redford served as a policy advisor to both Joe Clark and Brian Mulroney at the federal level. She also had extensive experience working on constitutional and human rights issues in the international arena, including stints in South Africa, Afghanistan, Bosnia, Serbia, Vietnam, and the Philippines. Little evidence exists to substantiate the claim, however, that she was an overtly feminist lawyer in such work – as was alleged by Morton (2013, 32) in the quotation cited in this chapter's introduction. In 2008, Redford won a Calgary seat in the provincial legislature and was immediately named

Alberta's first female minister of justice and attorney general. In 2011, she resigned her cabinet post to pursue the PC leadership.

Redford's victory in that race shocked party insiders as well as casual observers. Like Christy Clark in British Columbia and Kathleen Wynne in Ontario, Redford was not the candidate of the party establishment and had little support among PC MLAs. The majority of the party caucus and executive endorsed Gary Mar, a popular cabinet veteran from the PC government of Ralph Klein, who built a commanding first ballot lead over Redford (40.8 versus 18.7 percent).

For the second consecutive time in an Alberta PC leadership contest, however, the establishment candidate and first ballot leader was unable to secure victory.[2] Redford's campaign capitalized on internal party rules that allowed five-dollar PC memberships to be sold in the two-week period between the first and second ballots (see Morton 2013). By campaigning against the record of her own party, Redford used the time between ballots to advance a centrist platform that pledged to restore $107 million in education funding that had been cut by former premier Ed Stelmach's PC government. Promising to reverse an unpopular decision gained Redford a strong base among teachers and parents of school-age children, most of whom were not traditional PC supporters (Ashenburg 2013; Steward 2012). Riding a wave that brought nearly twenty thousand additional voters to the second ballot in the party leadership selection process, Redford narrowly defeated Mar and became Alberta's fourteenth premier.

In the first months of her premiership, Redford implemented many of her centrist campaign pledges. She restored $107 million to the province's education budget, raised monthly supports for severely handicapped citizens, and worked towards more family-centred community health clinics, lower crime rates, and tougher penalties for drunk drivers. After less than six months as premier, Redford called an election for April 2012.

Although the party was slightly ahead in the polls at the time the writ was dropped, PC support quickly eroded – leading many commentators to predict the party would lose an election for the first time since 1967. The right-wing Wildrose Party had grown in popularity since 2007, when Stelmach raised resource royalty rates in an effort to stabilize provincial revenues. Large donations from the oil and gas industry and growing concerns among fiscally conservative citizens over deficits run by the PCs helped Wildrose pull ahead in a series of polls prior to Stelmach's resignation. In fact, the PCs were in such rough shape in the last days of Stelmach's premiership that the choice of Redford as his successor appeared to be a classic "glass cliff" scenario wherein a woman wins the top post in a deeply imperiled party (see Chapter 1; Bruckmuller and Branscombe 2010; Thomas and Young 2014).

Redford's victory in the party leadership vote initially improved PC fortunes thanks in large part to her popularity among women. Indeed, one 2012 survey suggests 48 percent of female voters preferred the PC party while only 18 percent endorsed Wildrose (Cosh 2012). The first few weeks of the PC election campaign were disastrous, however, and polls showed Wildrose in the lead by as much as thirteen points (Grenier 2012). As in her leadership run, Redford defended centrist positions on health and education: she criticized the neoliberal policies of Ralph Klein and won the endorsement of Peter Lougheed – the province's ultimate "Red Tory" (Thomson 2012).

In the waning days of the campaign, Redford received a valuable boost from the decision of Wildrose leader Danielle Smith not to repudiate the homophobic comments of a Wildrose candidate and to question the science behind climate change. These actions allowed Redford to portray Wildrose as a party of social conservatives and climate change deniers, which, in turn, produced a last-minute surge in PC support among centrist and left voters. In the past, many of these voters had supported Liberal or NDP candidates, or perhaps had not bothered to vote at all. Yet in 2012 they feared a potential Wildrose government (Davison 2012; Kellog 2012; Markusoff 2013).

Redford's PCs won a solid majority government with sixty-one of eighty-seven legislative seats. Now with a popular mandate, the premier began to press for a national energy strategy to increase oil and natural gas exports from Alberta. By imposing deep cuts to spending on postsecondary education and limiting the bargaining rights of public-sector unions, however, she disappointed many progressive voters. At the same time, conservative voters who were already suspicious of Redford were dismayed by her willingness to run budget deficits and adopt liberal positions on the rights of sexual orientation minorities.

Rumours of strife inside the PC caucus began to spread. Although 77 percent of party members who participated in an internal review process approved of Redford's leadership in November 2013, most of the talk concerned her governing style (see Chapter 1; Cryderman and Walton 2013). By spring 2014, a series of expense scandals led to a dramatic drop in public support for the premier as well as her party. Redford's decision to spend $45,000 of public money to travel to South Africa to attend Nelson Mandela's funeral drew particularly harsh criticism. Once details emerged of the costs of other international trips, a penthouse under construction for the premier near the legislature, and the use of government jets for questionable purposes, Redford found it hard to escape allegations that she was a profligate spender out of touch with the lives of average citizens.

Sensing their party's electoral vulnerability, PC legislators, constituency association presidents, and eventually the party executive began to denounce Redford publicly. MLA Len Weber quit the PC caucus on 13 March 2014, stating that Redford was "a bully" and "not a nice lady" (Gerson 2014a). Developments in the subsequent week effectively ended Redford's political career: an Edmonton PC riding association president publicly called for her resignation (Canadian Press 2014). Redford was made to sit through a lengthy critical evaluation of her leadership by the party's board of directors (Wood and Varcoe 2014). A group of at least ten backbench MLAs met to discuss leaving caucus (Russell 2014). And, finally, a member of Redford's cabinet, Donna Kennedy-Glans, quit her post and left the PC caucus (Gerson 2014b).

Redford's public approval rating plummeted in two months from 35 to 18 percent – both of which were far below the 58 percent she commanded after winning the PC leadership (Commisso 2014). On 19 March 2014, Redford resigned as premier.

Candidacies and Cabinet Appointments

Did Redford's presence as Alberta's first woman premier alter numerical representation in the governing caucus, cabinet, or civil service? Although slight shifts are noted below, my overall answer is "no."

Unlike the views expressed by women leaders in Yukon and Nunavut, Redford dismissed the notion that the participation of more women would, by itself, lead to a less conflictual political environment or different policy outcomes. In a candid exchange in 2013 on the topic of women in politics, Redford expressed her admiration for Margaret Thatcher as a strong, intelligent, and engaging woman. When asked if meetings of Canada's first ministers had changed given that six of thirteen premiers were female, Redford replied:

> Margaret Thatcher, if you'd asked her that question, she probably would have told you she wasn't going to talk about this issue because from her perspective she was the prime minister of the country and she was the leader of the party and the fact that she was a woman was pretty irrelevant. I've got to say from my perspective ... I am more of that view. I've had some

time to think about whether or not you see those differences. I will say that there is one premier who has said they are very optimistic that having more women around the table will allow for a different dialogue to happen. I am skeptical. I don't think that's a bad thing, I just think that what we have at the table is 13 premiers who are advocates for their provinces and territories ... That's where we've seen success. I'm not so sure that we've seen a different tone around the table simply because there are women at the table. (as quoted in MacDonald 2013, 13)

Implicit in this comment is a view that capable women should have opportunities to rise to leadership positions – a position consistent with Redford's efforts to encourage young women to pursue professional careers.

At the same time, we find a clear resistance in her comments to the notion that women necessarily bring different attributes to the table or that more of them should occupy influential roles in government. As demonstrated below, Redford's record of recruiting candidates, ministers, and senior civil servants shows she held a conservative, individualistic worldview that rejected group identity claims and dismissed calls for affirmative action programs or quotas in order to increase representation from marginalized groups.

As shown in Table 10.1, Redford's time as party leader was associated with a slight improvement in women's participation as PC candidates. Five more women ran as PC candidates in 2012 than in 2008 (25 versus 21 percent). What stands out is the level of representation of women in the PC caucus after the 2012 election as compared with previous as well as subsequent contests. A substantially higher percentage of women sat in Redford's government caucus (30 percent) than in those of her two predecessors (16 and 19 percent) or her successor (10 percent).

TABLE 10.1
Women as PC legislative candidates and MLAs in Alberta, 2004–15

Election	PC leader	% female candidates	% female MLAs
2004	Ralph Klein	14.5 (12/83)	16.1 (10/62)
2008	Ed Stelmach	20.5 (17/83)	19.4 (14/72)
2012	Alison Redford	25.3 (22/87)	29.5 (18/61)
2015	Jim Prentice	25.3 (22/87)	10.0 (1/10)

Source: Elections Alberta (2015).

Did Redford make the recruitment of women candidates a priority? No evidence on the public record indicates that she did so. This finding is consistent with her view that the participation of women in politics does not make a difference (see MacDonald 2013, 13). Yet it remains possible that the presence of a female premier drew more women into the electoral ring and, perhaps indirectly, signalled to voters the legitimacy of female candidates. At the same time, Redford's moderate platform contrasted with Smith's more traditional directions as Wildrose leader – a factor that may have attracted women to become PC candidates and to vote for the party.

Interviews with two female MLAs in the PC caucus lend support to this proposition: both identified Redford's policy positions as a key reason they ran in 2012. As well, research suggests Redford's moderate platform as a leadership candidate and as a premier seeking a public mandate attracted more women and more socially progressive voters than did previous PC campaigns (Ashenburg 2013; Steward 2012). Their support, in turn, helped the party to win in 2012 by preventing a victory for the hard-right Wildrose Party (Kellogg 2012; Davison 2012).

From this perspective, the slight rise in the number of women PC candidates and the larger increase in the number of female MLAs after the 2012 election (see Table 10.1) follow more from Redford's moderate politics than from her gender. Indeed, the same number of PC women ran in 2012 under Redford as in 2015 under Jim Prentice, who also staked out fairly centrist ground. The percentage of PC women candidates who won seats dropped drastically in 2015, however, as a result of the party's poor performance. In 2015, progressive voters flocked to the NDP, which elected a record twenty-four women to the Alberta legislature and formed a majority government under Rachel Notley.

Redford formed three cabinets: one upon winning the leadership in 2011, another after winning the provincial election in 2012, and one in 2013 that tried to improve the government's popularity. As Table 10.2 demonstrates, Redford's initial cabinet sharply reduced both the number and percentage of women ministers relative to the final political executive of her predecessor. In 2008, Stelmach appointed seven women representing close to 30 percent of his cabinet, which was very high compared to other cabinets formed in Alberta between 2004 and 2014. Table 10.2 shows that two of Redford's three cabinets rank among the weakest with respect to percentages of women appointed for the years considered, a pattern that stands out given that she had *more* caucus women to draw from than had

TABLE 10.2
Women in Alberta cabinets, 2004–15

Year	PC premier	Women in cabinet % (N)	Women associate ministers* % (N)
2004	Ralph Klein	22.7 (5/22)	50.0 (1/2)
2006	Ed Stelmach	10.5 (2/19)	N/A
2008	Ed Stelmach	29.2 (7/24)	20.0 (2/10)
2011	Alison Redford	14.2 (3/21)	11.1 (1/9)
2012	Alison Redford	21.1 (4/19)	14.3 (1/7)
2013	Alison Redford	15.8 (3/19)	30.0 (3/10)
2014	Jim Prentice	17.6 (3/17)	33.3 (1/3)

* In 2004, Ralph Klein labelled these members as caucus liaisons. In 2008 and 2011, the same members were labelled parliamentary assistants.
Source: Author's own calculations based on a wide variety of media reports.

the male premiers who preceded and succeeded her. This finding contradicts Tremblay's (2012) argument that, in Canada, the percentage of women in governing party caucuses is positively associated with women's appointment to cabinet.

Furthermore, if we remove Redford from the list of women ministers, the representation picture is even bleaker. In three successive cabinets, Redford appointed two, then three, then two women besides herself. Similar to the situation of Margaret Thatcher, who, as mentioned in Chapter 1, was generally the lone woman in her UK cabinets, the pattern under Redford seems to be a case of a woman leader "shutting the door" as opposed to "letting down the ladder" for other women (O'Brien et al. 2015).

In terms of cabinet clout, Redford named more women to marginal than to influential posts. Diane McQueen, who served in all three Redford cabinets, was both minster of the environment and minster of energy – both important portfolios in Alberta. Heather Klimchuk, who also served in all three cabinets, was minister of culture while Christine Cusanelli, who only served briefly, was minister of tourism (see appendix to Chapter 8 for a detailed discussion of the ranking of cabinet portfolios).

Cabinets appointed by Klein and Stelmach do not score well in terms of numerical representation; however, compared to Redford, these premiers appeared more willing to appoint women to prestigious portfolios. For instance, Shirley McClellan held several top posts under Klein, including finance and deputy premier. Iris Evans held both the health and finance portfolios under Klein and Stelmach, while Redford was justice minister under Stelmach.

Why did the first female premier of Alberta fail to elevate the numerical presence and prestige of women in cabinet? This question seems especially important given that Redford's record differs from that of other PC leaders examined in this volume, including Kathy Dunderdale in Newfoundland and Labrador. One possible explanation follows from the fact that, after the 2012 election, the number of women MLAs in the Alberta PC caucus was far below the number of men (eighteen versus forty-three). Other PC premiers considered in Table 10.2, however, faced even more imbalance in their caucus gender ratio. Another explanation builds on Redford's resistance, noted above, to the notion that political outcomes would necessarily change with more women in positions of influence.

O'Brien et al. (2015) maintain that women leading right-of-centre parties may face a particular set of pressures that militate against appointing other females. More specifically, they may be expected to present a masculine image and avoid the pursuit of "identity politics" – factors that discourage them from including other women in their cabinets. This theme emerged in an interview with a female PC backbencher who served while Redford was premier:

> [Redford's] a very smart woman but I very much had the sense that she doesn't like women very much. She had an opportunity – there are a lot of smart women in the caucus – and she only picked three of them to sit in her cabinet. And really, you know, there were probably six or seven who I think would have been far more capable at the table than some of the men that ended up there. So, it's just an observation on my part that, you know, she didn't go out of her way to establish relationships with any of the women, didn't go out of her way to look at the idea of promoting them, very much the antithesis of what I see in Rachel Notley ... [C]ertainly amongst the members of her caucus there was frustration, you know, amongst the women, that we weren't engaged more. And, you know, she didn't seem to be all that interested in doing that.

A man interviewed for this study who served in Redford's cabinet observed:

> You know, I don't think Alison liked competition from other women. That's total speculation on my part ... [but] ... just observing her interact with people, I would say she got along better with men than women. The women

I know, my female colleagues, were not – they definitely were not fans of her. And other people who worked in the bureaucracy, women, definitely they hated her guts. So, there's something there that … I don't know, I can't explain. There were people who didn't know Alison who thought it was wonderful to have a woman leader, they were fans. The people who knew her, they weren't fans.

Each of these reflections sheds light on the dynamics of O'Brien et al.'s (2015) thesis as it played out in Alberta.

Interviewees repeatedly noted that Redford had especially difficult relationships with women colleagues. This raises the possibility that Redford's appointment record reflected more than simply an ideological outlook grounded in notions of individual merit. Whether it was a personality characteristic or related to pressures on women leaders in right-of-centre parties is unknown. Perhaps the trend reflects a "Queen Bee Syndrome," wherein one woman in a position of authority treats female subordinates more harshly than she does male subordinates (Staines et al. 1974). Additional research is needed to shed further light on these possibilities.

Senior Civil Service Appointments

Redford's record on deputy minister appointments largely mirrors the pattern discussed above with respect to cabinet. As Table 10.3 indicates, she displayed no proclivity towards elevating women to top bureaucratic posts. In fact, the number and percentage of women appointed as DMs while Redford was premier are substantially lower than for Stelmach and Prentice. One woman who held a senior civil service position under Redford said in an interview that expanding opportunities for women bureaucrats was not a priority for the PC government – especially when compared to the emphasis that the Notley NDP government placed on this goal.

Similarly, Redford's inner circle of advisors was also dominated by men. Susan Elliott, a former campaign manager, was reputedly the single woman who wielded significant influence in Redford's advisory group. That network included Stephen Carter, Farouk Adatia, Stefan Baranski, Darren Cunningham, and Lee Richardson – an all-male team that fits with the pattern of cabinet and civil service appointments discussed above.

Tone and Content of Policy Debate

Did the presence of a woman premier alter the tone of the legislature, the

TABLE 10.3
Women deputy ministers in Alberta, 2008–14

Year	Premier	Deputy ministers who were women % (N)
2008	Ed Stelmach	26.9 (7/26)
2011	Alison Redford	14.3 (3/21)
2014	Jim Prentice	25.0 (5/20)

Sources: Alberta Government (2008, 2011, 2014a).

frequency with which women's issues were discussed, or the types of policies passed? These are crucial questions given that, as of fall 2011, not only was the Alberta premier a woman but so were both the leader of the official opposition (Danielle Smith) and the deputy leader of the NDP (Rachel Notley). In response, it is not clear that the presence of so many women in positions of major responsibility altered Alberta politics.

Although previous studies maintain that female MLAs in Alberta tend towards cooperative and issue-based debating styles and males towards adversarial approaches (Arscott and Trimble 1997; Trimble 1997), recent accounts suggest the tone of the 2012 election campaign and subsequent legislative session was as divisive as any in Alberta history (Gerson 2012; Wood 2012). Evidence of the gendered content of this conflictual environment was reflected, for instance, when, on Twitter, a member of Redford's staff questioned Smith's dedication to families – Smith had no biological children (Henton 2012). Redford quickly apologized to Smith.

Yet, throughout the 2012 campaign, the premier continued to misstate Smith's positions on abortion and gay rights in an effort to move moderate voters away from Wildrose and towards the PCs (Canadian Press 2012). Party competition with an overlay of gender content thus underpinned much of the tension in Alberta politics during Redford's term as premier. In the polarized environment of the times, Wildrose as an aggressive opposition party challenged Redford on ideological grounds and hoped to end the PC dynasty in the next election (Thomson 2015).

As shown in Table 10.4, issues brought to the public agenda by feminist movements were raised far more often in legislative debate while Redford was premier than when her predecessor served. Given the total amount of time parliamentarians spent in session, however, these matters were not discussed often. Aside from a handful of easy questions raised by government

TABLE 10.4

Frequency of women's issue mentions by Alberta legislative session

Session	Date	Premier	Opposition leader	Women's issue mentions
3rd Session, 27th Legislature	2010–11	Ed Stelmach (PC)	David Swann/ Raj Sherman (Liberal)	23
1st Session, 28th Legislature	2012–14	Alison Redford (PC)	Danielle Smith (Wildrose)	42
2nd Session, 29th Legislature	2017	Rachel Notley (NDP)	Brian Jean (Wildrose)	61

Note: Although specific topics varied slightly across legislative sessions, issues such as women in politics, violence against women, domestic violence, women's shelters, pay equity, child care, and the recognition of events such as of International Women's Day were included in these calculations.
Sources: Legislative Assembly of Alberta (2011, 2014, 2017).

backbenchers to permit cabinet ministers to highlight modest action on child care or domestic violence, or to mark International Women's Day, Alberta PC lawmakers largely ignored such issues.

Redford herself was literally silent on women's issues. The majority of mentions by PC parliamentarians responded to questions posed by NDP MLAs or by Laurie Blakeman, the lone woman in the Liberal caucus. Table 10.4 demonstrates that women's issues were mentioned twenty-three times under Stelmach through 2011, then forty-two times under Redford. This figure grew dramatically with the change of government in Alberta in 2015. By the second session of the 29th Legislature under Notley, the number of mentions reached sixty-one.

These longitudinal data merit deeper analysis given that, in all legislative sessions, women's issues were overshadowed by debate related to the economy (especially resource industries and hopes for economic diversification), environmental concerns, the rights of land owners, and health and education.[3] The lack of attention to women's issues under PC premiers is notable and is likely more significant than the fact that a woman led Alberta's Wildrose opposition and, briefly, its government as well. Echoing the comparative literature considered in Chapter 1, left/right ideology seemed to make an important difference to what was discussed in the Alberta legislature. As the number of NDP MLAs grew, so did attention to women's issues (see Table 10.4).

With respect to policy outcomes, the Redford government made some progress. Unlike the premier's view that women in leadership roles would not make much difference, a veteran PC cabinet minister commented that Redford "changed the tone of conversations in cabinet and we became much more cognizant of a family perspective on policy." Consistent with promises made in the 2011 leadership race, Redford's first budget provided modest budget increases for foster care, child care subsidies, women's shelters, and family violence prevention. Although the amounts were small when measured against total provincial expenditures, the government's repeated emphasis on them represented something of a new focus in the province (Alberta Government 2012). Similar increases to many of the same programs occurred in the 2013 and 2014 budgets (Alberta Government 2013a, 2014b). Redford also oversaw the creation of the First Nations Women's Council on Economic Security and the Métis Women's Council on Economic Security, both intended to advise ministries on improving economic outcomes for Indigenous women (Alberta Government 2013b).

In mid-2013, Redford appointed MLA Sandra Jansen to the newly created post of associate minister of family and community safety. Jansen was tasked with advancing programs related to bullying, cyber-bullying, and LGBTQ issues in schools as well as issues related to family violence and sexual violence. The government introduced Alberta's first Domestic Violence Framework and took steps towards both a sexual violence framework and a women's equality and advancement framework – two projects that were not fully in place before Redford resigned as premier but served as foundations for similar frameworks adopted by the Notley government (see Alberta Government n.d.[a] and Alberta Government n.d.[b]). The Department of Human Services also introduced a limited version of gender-based budgeting, which was significantly expanded by the Notley government.

Much of the foundational work on these initiatives had been completed earlier by civil servants in the Human Services Department. Yet they had received little support from the governments led by Klein or Stelmach. As a former PC cabinet minister recalled in an interview:

> There were a number of things in that area that had kind of been in a bottle-neck, they hadn't moved anywhere. So, there had been a domestic violence framework that had been sitting there for about five years that the Human Services minister had brought forward and tried to get through cabinet and hadn't been able to ... [B]ehind these initiatives was a wonderful group

doing status of women work within the Human Services Department. And they worked on similar issues for years and they had some great stuff that they wanted to move forward. So, they pitched the idea because they had been working on this for years.

Taken together, these initiatives amount to more than modest advances in pro-equality policy in the province given that they had apparently been endorsed by civil servants for years but were only acted upon once Redford empowered Jansen to bring them forward.

For Redford's colleagues, these pro-equality actions spoke to the importance such issues held for her. Yet women's equality did not rank as an extremely high priority, relatively speaking, for the Redford government. Rather, following the pattern established by previous PC premiers, Redford placed Alberta's economic prosperity at the top of her agenda, especially as it pertained to the extraction and transportation of oil and natural gas and the promise of economic diversification. It was not until she had served as premier for twenty months that she asked Jansen to oversee the changes mentioned above. Moreover, as one former PC cabinet minister notes, Redford was not personally involved in developing these frameworks nor did she frequently comment on them in public.

According to a senior civil servant who worked closely with both Redford and Notley, the broader approach to women's issues by the Redford government was constrained by the traditional ideological commitments of the PC party:

> As an individual, I know that [Redford] supported the idea of equality in a conceptual way. But it wasn't really part of the vernacular. What she cared about, she cared about individual people. So, she cared about children, absolutely. She cared about the elderly. She cared about vulnerable people, vulnerable women, no question about it. But then ... when you look at Alison, she was more concerned about individual women than she was necessarily about structural or systemic issues. She didn't focus her eye, her line of sight, on structural and systemic issues. But individual women, I think that it was the most marginalized women that touched the greatest chord in her.

This same interviewee contrasted PC with NDP governments as follows:

> In terms of actual policy, what I see today in this government [the NDP] and the level of commitment to gender – intersectional policy analysis to

not just equality but equity as the pathway to equality ... Sometimes we have to treat people differently in order to achieve equality. I just never heard dialogue like that in those days [the Redford government]. Now, whether she would or would not describe herself as a feminist, Alison, I don't know the answer to that. I am kind of curious about that myself. But certainly, this gendered perspective where we look at everything now in this [NDP] government – this is the goal – through that gendered lens of, you know, how is this going to differentially impact men and women? That was certainly not present [under the Redford government].

These perspectives reinforce the argument that, while Redford's cabinet initiated important steps on pro-equality policy that previous PC governments had refused to take, Redford-era changes pale in comparison with subsequent innovations introduced in the Notley years.

Overall, Redford's government made some progress in terms of policy outcomes. These included modest spending increases for child care and women's shelters, the introduction of gender-based budgeting, and work on policy frameworks concerning domestic violence, sexual violence, and women's equality. Since most of these developments had been under way within the civil service for some time but only moved through cabinet approval processes in 2013 and 2014, I credit Redford for creating a pathway for this work.

None of these issues, however, was a central priority for either Redford or the wider PC caucus since, for the most part, her government did not highlight equality policies in the legislature. Furthermore, given the attention the Notley government subsequently devoted to these same files, it appears that Redford's political executive was prevented by ideological considerations from doing more. However, additional research must be done to clarify if the failure to adopt a more structural approach to women's issues (parallel with what transpired in BC conservative parties) resulted from Redford's own thinking on the issues or resistance from more right-wing members of her cabinet and caucus. Several decision makers interviewed for this study point towards the strength of the second explanation.

Downward Momentum

What role did gender play in Redford's downfall? A number of commentators suggest Redford's departure from office less than two years after leading her party to a legislative majority was due at least in part to her being a woman (Adkin 2014; Geddes 2014; O'Neill and Stewart 2014).

Clearly, Redford engaged in behaviour that contributed to her fall in popularity. A report by the auditor general confirmed it was reasonable to question Redford's extensive use of government planes (Saher 2014). Redford's relations with her caucus and cabinet were tense; according to insiders interviewed for this study, they followed from a leadership style that was seen as not inclined to consult with people beyond a small circle of advisors. Observers saw her insular approach as compounding larger factional differences inside the PC party that began with Stelmach's selection as leader in 2006.

Some accounts are consistent with perspectives presented in Chapter 1 in that Redford faced much harsher party, media, and public reactions to scandals than did male leaders such as Klein (Adkin 2014). Analysts thus view PC caucus comments on Redford's leadership style, famously captured in the complaint that Redford was "a bully" and "not a nice lady," as highly gendered. From this perspective, mostly male PC politicians and party executives were uncomfortable taking orders from an intelligent and forceful leader who challenged stereotypic views of women as compliant and conflict-avoidant.

What can we make of this interpretation? To what degree can Redford's downfall be attributed to her gender? While it is difficult to answer this question definitively in a short space, I propose that Redford's plunging public approval ratings were not linked to any single factor. Instead, larger patterns beyond Redford's control generated considerable problems for her party even before spending scandals came to light.

Having been in power for more than forty years, Alberta PCs faced a growing public sense that it was time for a change – a change perceived as a legitimate possibility given a well-funded and increasingly popular official opposition, the Wildrose Party. In addition, declining resource revenues led to PC budget cuts in 2013 that angered many of the same centre and centre-left voters who had supported Redford and her party a year earlier (Kellogg 2012). In other words, Alberta PCs were losing support on both the left and the right before news spread about questionable spending by Redford.

An additional factor in this mix relates more to power politics than to gender. From the outset, Redford was the outsider candidate to succeed Stelmach. One PC MLA endorsed her in the 2011 leadership contest, and she was not the first choice of the party executive. Redford points to this factor as crucial in her political demise (Mason 2015). It is notable that Redford followed Stelmach as the second consecutive outsider to win the

Alberta PC leadership, only to be pushed aside once poll numbers tumbled – despite impressive general election results. Rumours suggest that some PC MLAs and party executive members fanned the flames of public discontent towards her by sharing "insider accounts" with the media (Adkin 2014).

Two former PC MLAs who sat in Redford's cabinet endorse this interpretation. In the words of one interviewee:

> The PC executives hated her; they loathed her with every fibre of their being. So she wasn't just fighting the public perception; she was fighting the PC executive. And they were a nasty old boys club, nasty. And they had it in for her from the start. They wanted Gary Mar to be their premier, they were looking forward to him stepping into that role and then when she won it, they felt that she'd stolen it from him and she never got an inch of slack from any of them.

A second interviewee with a similar background added: "So, definitely ... sabotage, you know, took place. There were people that were actively working on getting her out. On the inside and the outside. The problem was that she was making it very easy on them." This account is similar to stories of what occurred inside the PEI Liberal Party towards the end of Catherine Callbeck's term, with the important caveat that Callbeck was the insider candidate to succeed a very popular predecessor.

All seven interviewees for this study emphasized Redford's poor relationship with the PC caucus and cabinet. They portrayed Redford as an intelligent and articulate leader who was prone to fierce and angry outbursts that turned many colleagues against her. As summarized by a member of Redford's cabinet:

> She's extremely bright and extremely capable. I think in a lot of ways she ran a very good meeting. You know, she definitely is a strong personality and has leadership qualities. But just by her, kind of by virtue of some of those strengths, she could stifle debate. I can remember getting my head chewed off for just a mild questioning of, you know, it was just kind of, "Gee, are we sure we want to do that?" And bam, she put the boots to me. And so, people weren't looking for opportunities, you know, to be contrary.

Unlike party executive members who resented her defeating their favoured candidate for PC leader, cabinet ministers were arguably more open to building constructive relations with a new premier who had appointed them to the political executive. In this respect, Redford failed to build a solid cabinet base that might have insulated her from other sources of opposition.

Growing tensions between Redford and the PC caucus led to threats of floor-crossing. As one Redford-era MLA reflects:

> There is this natural frustration [to being a backbencher] and then add on top of that you're treated like dirt, literally like dirt, from time to time by kind of a volatile personality who's in the chair and might bite your head off if you say something out of line. And then you go home to your constituency and people are just tearing a strip off of you for stuff that you have no control over because she's made announcements that we're doing this or we're doing that. And you're not even consulted. And, you know, put that together month after month after month and pretty soon people start to think, "Well, what do I have to lose here?"

While PC MLA Len Weber used highly gendered language in describing Redford as "not a nice lady," material in these interviews suggests others shared the view that it was hard to work with her. In 2014, Weber left the PCs to sit as an independent to protest Redford's leadership style. Gerson (2014a) reports that his sentiments were shared by other PC MLAs, including women. That sentiment was politically significant given that it was the threat of caucus revolt in response to the spending scandals and subsequent drop in the polls that ultimately forced Redford to resign.

Consistent with the argument advanced in Chapter 1, many political insiders interviewed for this study believe Redford's gender may have played a role in her relationship with the PC caucus and cabinet. According to a female cabinet minister:

> Arrogance in a man is much easier to take for a lot of people. I saw it first-hand for years. When she dressed somebody down, if you were getting a dressing down from – you know, and I saw this in my colleague's faces, getting a dressing down from her was humiliating and they were not happy about it in a way that if they had gotten a dressing down from a male politician I think they would have shrugged it off and walked away. She made people very angry and they didn't like it.

In the words of a male minister:

You know, I also wonder ... if you're a woman and you kind of had to be extra tough to get to that position and you know everybody's against you, some of that is probably almost a defensive thing. It seems aggressive and offensive but it might also be a defensive mechanism to kind of almost survive and to move anything along. And I mean we had some very strong personalities in our cabinet that probably weren't used to being told what to do by a woman. So, you'd have to kind of, you know, make your presence felt in order to get anything done.

Another man who served in Redford's cabinet offered the following:

I do say that we judge female politicians with a different gauge than male politicians. I think she, as a female leader, already enters with a handicap. Without a doubt. And I think she had to be more forceful, that's why she was the way she was. She had to be more forceful, more determined. Not showing any weakness or indecisiveness ... because it would have been seen as a weakness, as incompetence at a boardroom table. So, she very much acted masculine ... and yet I know her to be a very feminine, nice person. But definitely she had to put on what I would call a front, but you know, it may have been something she had to do all her life to get to where she got.

This minister saw particularly gendered dimensions to the way Redford was criticized and scrutinized. In his view, specific discussions involving such matters as Redford's attention to her young daughter would not have arisen had a man won the PC leadership race:

But no, I don't think she got a fair shake. Alison has made a lot of mistakes, at a variety of levels. And as a public figure, she needed to be chastised for them, and consequently punished for them. Fair game. The manner in which it happened was different because of the fact that she's a female. [And] she had to deal with issues like no other [politician]. People were wondering about her mothering skills. As a matter of fact, it even came up in cabinet once. Someone asked how she would deal with [her daughter]. You would have never asked a male cabinet member that. As a matter of fact, you sort of expect them not to be fathers or to be negligent, neglectful fathers. But because she's a female, you know ...

This observation regarding Redford as a mother is noteworthy given that, at the height of her public downfall, she faced significant scrutiny for government-funded flights that involved having her daughter on board (Ibrahim 2014). The public backlash she faced speaks to larger challenges faced by mothers in politics (see Thomas and Bittner 2017).

Each of these insights sheds light on how Redford's gender shaped her ties with the PC caucus and cabinet. A similar dynamic may have affected her ties to the PC executive as well. The academic literature on barriers facing women in politics, especially women who act with strength and determination, points to an important question: Would the PC caucus have rallied behind an equally assertive male premier who was not the establishment choice as party leader and who became entangled in the same spending scandals as Redford? There is no way to know. Yet the uncertainty surrounding this question in the eyes of many close observers suggests gender was a factor that, directly or indirectly, led to Redford's downfall.

Conclusion

In general, Alison Redford's time in office presents a mixed record. Although she neither actively recruited women candidates nor increased the representation of women in influential posts, her socially progressive positions likely encouraged more women to run as PC candidates and more female voters to support the party. Parallel with results from Ontario under Wynne, the tone of debate in the Alberta legislature under Redford became more rather than less divisive. Mentions of equality issues increased in the legislature and, more important, measurable progress on actual policy outcomes occurred relative to previous Alberta PC governments.

The accomplishments of the subsequent NDP provincial government in terms of the representation of women in the legislative caucus and cabinet as well as the embrace of pro-equality policies significantly overshadow steps taken by Redford's PCs. This pattern reinforces the argument cited in Chapter 1 that stresses the impact of left/right party ideology. Although evidence from Alberta supports the view that Redford's fall from grace was related to gender, it also suggests that gender was neither the only factor nor necessarily the most important.

Two questions deserve attention in future research. One involves the observation, made by several interviewees, that Redford disliked competition from other women. Did this phenomenon lead her to appoint relatively few women to cabinet? Perhaps the various barriers women face when seeking to advance their careers may condition them to interact differently with women than with men and, further, to perceive men as crucial allies whose support they require in order to move up.

Second, interviewees consistently identified Redford's temperament, notably her tendency towards displays of anger and lack of trust in her colleagues, as key reasons she lost caucus support. Future studies can explore how such characteristics are perceived differently when they are exhibited in the same environment by men as opposed to women. As well, scholars can consider how these repertoires might result from the frustrations of leaders who have long been on the outside of political organizations, who find themselves, perhaps by surprise, in positions of authority on the inside.

Acknowledgment

The author acknowledges financial support from the Council for Research in Social Sciences at Brock University.

Notes

1 Interviewees included four PC MLAs who sat in Redford's cabinet (two female and two male), two senior bureaucrats (one male and one female) who worked closely with Redford, and one long-time opposition MLA (male). Interviews took place in person or by telephone in December 2016 and January 2017.
2 Ed Stelmach, a long-time rural MLA with little name recognition outside the PC caucus, shocked observers by defeating establishment choice Jim Dinning for the PC leadership in 2006. Stelmach finished third on the first ballot of the contest.
3 For a helpful reference point, consider that, during the legislative session of Premier Redford reported in Table 10.4, the Responsible Energy Development Act was mentioned more than three hundred times.

References

Adkin, Laurie. 2014. "The End of Alison." *Alberta Views*, 22 April. https://alberta views.ab.ca/2014/05/27/the-end-of-alison-2/.

Alberta Government. 2008. "New Provincial Deputy Minster Team Ready to Deliver." 13 March. https://www.alberta.ca/release.cfm?xID=23175A92C82A8 -0628-8509-8F128A5A2B91E56C.

–. 2011. "Premier Announces New Deputy Minister Line-up." 13 October. https:// www.alberta.ca/release.cfm?xID=31369FE5C54BD-BCC7-88C3-135C 16532AB5E605.

–. 2012. "Budget 2012 Provides Close to \$5 Billion in Supports for Vulnerable Albertans and Seniors." 9 February. https://www.alberta.ca/release.cfm?xID= 31916644672F3-F3A1-2051-D18381AF304D7615.

—. 2013a. "Human Services Business Plan 2013–16." 20 February. https://open. alberta.ca/dataset/cab94fc3-1368-4065-ab36-1317175fd1e1/resource/4d769699 -feb6-4d8a-92d0-29ea95888890/download/5084443-2013-Human-Services -Business-Plan-2013-2016.pdf.

—. 2013b. "Alberta Establishes Aboriginal Women's Councils." 9 December. https:// www.alberta.ca/release.cfm?xID=3552471A4D81A-C496-0D97-C0C88135 3154D3F4.

—. 2014a. "New Deputy Minister Lineup Unveiled." 15 September. https://www. alberta.ca/release.cfm?xID=37063D478BC23-CCD6-EC08-89ABBEDAA 883872D.

—. 2014b. "Budget Delivers Programs and Services Albertans Need." 6 March. https://www.alberta.ca/release.cfm?xID=35989FC4D207D-FAEA-A4E8 -B8107E268F5B10DD.

Alberta Government. N.d.[a]. "Family Violence Hurts Everyone: A Framework to End Family Violence in Alberta." http://www.humanservices.alberta.ca/documents/ family-violence-hurts-everyone.pdf.

—. N.d.[b]. "Preventing Violence against Women and Girls." https://www.alberta.ca/ violence-against-women.aspx.

Arscott, Jane, and Linda Trimble. 1997. "In the Presence of Women: Representation and Political Power." In *In the Presence of Women: Representation in Canadian Governments*, ed. Jane Arscott and Linda Trimble, 1–17. Toronto: Harcourt Brace.

Ashenburg, Katherine. 2013. "Her Way." *Walrus*, 11 March. https://thewalrus.ca/ her-way/.

Bruckmuller, Susanne, and Nyla E. Branscombe. 2010. "The Glass Cliff: When and Why Women Are Selected as Leaders in Crisis Contexts." *British Journal of Social Psychology* 49, 3: 433–51.

Canadian Press. 2012. "Wildrose Leader Affirms Stance on Abortion, Gay Rights." *CTV News*, 11 April. http://www.ctvnews.ca/wildrose-leader-affirms-stance-on -abortion-gay-rights-1.794947.

—. 2014. "Redford Facing More Criticism, Riding President Calls on Her to Quit." *CTV News*, 14 March. http://www.ctvnews.ca/politics/redford-facing-more -criticism-riding-president-calls-on-her-to-quit-1.1730219.

Commisso, Christina. 2014. "Alison Redford's Approval Rating Plunges to 18%: Poll." *CTV News*, 19 March. http://www.ctvnews.ca/politics/alison-redford-s-approval -rating-plunges-to-18-per-cent-poll-1.1736943.

Cosh, Colby. 2012. "One Wild Rise for One Wild Rose." *Maclean's*, 20 April. http:// www.macleans.ca/news/canada/one-wild-rise/.

Cryderman, Kelly, and Dawn Walton. 2013. "Premier Redford Facing Strife from Within Alberta PCs." *Globe and Mail*, 16 April. http://www.theglobeandmail. com/news/politics/premier-redford-facing-strife-from-within-alberta-pcs/ article11253238/.

Davison, Janet. 2012. "Alberta Election Saw 'Fear' Win Over 'Anger'." *CBC News*, 24 April. http://www.cbc.ca/news/canada/manitoba/alberta-election-saw-fear-win -over-anger-1.1267615.

Elections Alberta. 2015. *Summary of Results by Electoral Division, 1905–2015.* Edmonton, AB. https://www.elections.ab.ca/wp-content/uploads/Summary-of -Results-by-ED.xlsx.

Geddes, Lisa. 2014. "Did Sexism Play a Role in Alison Redford's Downfall?" *Global News,* 20 March. http://globalnews.ca/news/1221870/did-gender-politics-play-a -role-in-alison-redfords-downfall/.

Gerson, Jen. 2012. "Alberta Election Campaign Is One of the Meanest Ever, Observers Say." *National Post,* 4 April. http://news.nationalpost.com/news/canada/ alberta-election-campaign-is-one-of-meanest-ever-observers-say.

–. 2014a. "Tory MLA Laid Bare Alberta's Worst Kept Secret: Alison Redford's Greatest Weakness – She's Just 'Not a Nice Lady.'" *National Post,* 14 March. http://news.nationalpost.com/news/canada/canadian-politics/alison -redfords-greatest-weakness-is-that-shes-not-a-nice-lady.

–. 2014b. "Alberta PC Associate Minister Donna Kennedy-Glans Quits in Another Blow to Alison Redford's Already Shaky Leadership." *National Post,* 17 March. http://news.nationalpost.com/news/canada/canadian-politics/alberta -pc-associate-minister-donna-kennedy-glans-quits-in-another-blow-to-alison -redfords-already-shaky-leadership.

Grenier, Eric. 2012. "Alberta Election Results 2012: Why Were the Polls so Wrong and What Does the Vote Mean for Alberta." *Huffington Post,* 24 April. http:// www.huffingtonpost.ca/2012/04/24/alberta-election-results-2012-polls_ n_1448602.html.

Henton, Darcy. 2012. "Election Takes Another Nasty Turn as Calgary PC Staffer Throws out Personal Dig at Wildrose Leader." *Calgary Herald,* 31 March. http:// calgaryherald.com/news/local-news/election-takes-another-nasty-personal -turn-as-pc-staffer-throws-out-dig-at-wildrose-leader.

Ibrahim, Mariam. 2014. "Former Premier Redford Brought Daughter on Dozens of Government Flights." *Edmonton Journal,* 14 April. http://www.edmontonjournal. com/Former+premier+Redford+brought+daughter+dozens+government +flights/9737339/story.html.

Kellogg, Paul. 2012. "Alberta Election – Party of Big Oil Defeats Party of Big Oil." *Europe Solidaire Sans Frontières,* 11 May. http://www.europe-solidaire.org/spip. php?article25142.

Legislative Assembly of Alberta. 2011. *Alberta Hansard Subject Index: 27th Legislature, 3rd Session (2010–2011).* Edmonton, AB. http://www.assembly.ab.ca/net/ index.aspx?p=hansardindex&docid=29305&type=subject&record=hansard& mode=summary&letter=A.

–. 2014. *Alberta Hansard Subject Index: 28th Legislature, 1st Session (2012–2014).* Edmonton, AB. http://www.assembly.ab.ca/net/index.aspx?p=hansardindex& docid=40558&type=subject&record=hansard&mode=summary&letter=A.

–. 2017. *Alberta Hansard Subject Index: 29th Legislature, 2nd Session (2016–2017).* Edmonton, AB. http://www.assembly.ab.ca/net/index.aspx?p=hansardindex& docid=55927&type=subject&record=hansard&mode=summary&letter=A.

MacDonald, L. Ian. 2013. "Q&A: A Conversation with Alison Redford." *Policy Magazine,* (June – July): 7–13.

Markusoff, Jason. 2013. "Our Surprising Premier." *Alberta Views*, 15 January. https://
albertaviews.ca/our-surprising-premier/.

Mason, Gary. 2015. "One Year Later, Alison Redford Looks Back: 'I'm a Polarizing
Figure.'" *Globe and Mail*, 20 March. http://www.theglobeandmail.com/news/
national/one-year-later-alison-redford-looks-back-im-a-polarizing-figure/
article23546195/.

Morton, Ted. 2013. "Leadership Selection in Alberta, 1992–2011: A Personal Perspective." *Canadian Parliamentary Review* (summer): 31–38.

O'Brien, Diana Z., Matthew Mendez, Jordan Carr Peterson, and Jihyun Shin. 2015.
"Letting Down the Ladder or Shutting the Door: Female Prime Ministers, Party
Leaders, and Cabinet Ministers." *Politics and Gender* 11, 4: 689–717.

O'Neill, Brenda, and David Stewart. 2014. "Redford's Tenure Follows a Familiar
Script for Women in Politics." *Globe and Mail*, 24 March. http://www.the
globeandmail.com/opinion/redfords-tenure-follows-a-familiar-script-for
-women-in-politics/article17634215/.

Russell, Jennie. 2014. "Alison Redford Uproar: Tory MLAs Consider Leaving
Caucus." *CBC News*, 17 March. http://www.cbc.ca/news/canada/edmonton/
alison-redford-uproar-tory-mlas-consider-leaving-caucus-1.2575314.

Saher, Merwan. 2014. *Report of the Auditor General of Alberta: Special Duty Report
on the Expenses of the Office of Premier Redford and Alberta's Air Transportation
Services Program*. Government of Alberta. https://www.oag.ab.ca/webfiles/
reports/August%202014%20Report.pdf.

Staines, G., C. Tavris, and T.E. Jayaratne. 1974. "The Queen Bee Syndrome." *Psychology Today* 7: 63–66.

Steward, Gillian. 2012. "Alberta Premier Alison Redford Is Winning over Women."
Toronto Star, 13 February. https://www.thestar.com/opinion/editorialopinion/
2012/02/13/alberta_premier_alison_redford_is_winning_over_women.html.

Thomas, Melanee, and Amanda Bittner, eds. 2017. *Mothers and Others: The Role
of Parenthood in Politics*. Vancouver: UBC Press.

Thomas, Melanee, and Lisa Young. 2014. "Women (Not) in Politics: Women's
Electoral Participation." In *Canadian Politics* 6th ed., ed. James Bickerton and
Alain-G. Gagnon, 373–93. Toronto: University of Toronto Press.

Thomson, Graham. 2012. "Peter Lougheed Was a Player in Alberta Politics to the
End." *Edmonton Journal*, 15 September. http://www.edmontonjournal.com/news/
thomson+peter+lougheed+player+alberta+politics/7245649/story.html.

–. 2015. "Progressive Conservatives the Wallflowers in Alberta's Post-Budget Dance."
Edmonton Journal, 29 October. http://edmontonjournal.com/news/politics/
graham-thomson-progressive-conservatives-the-wallflowers-in-albertas-post
-budget-dance.

Tremblay, Manon. 2012. "Women's Access to Cabinets in Canada: Assessing the
Role of Some Institutional Variables." *Canadian Political Science Review*, 6, 2–3:
159–70.

Trimble, Linda. 1997. "Feminist Politics in the Alberta Legislature, 1972–1994," in
In the Presence of Women: Representation in Canadian Governments, ed. Jane
Arscott and Linda Trimble, 128–53. Toronto: Harcourt Brace.

Wood, James. 2012. "Alberta Politics Turns Nasty as Opposition Hammers and Redford Attempts Damage Control." *Calgary Herald*, 4 December. http://www. calgaryherald.com/news/Alberta+politics+turns+nasty+Opposition+ hammers+Redford+attempts+damage+control/7646379/story.html.

Wood, James, and Chris Varcoe. 2014. "The Trials of Alison Redford." *Calgary Herald*, 22 March. http://www.calgaryherald.com/news/trials+alison+redford/ 9648255/story.html.

11

Governing as if Women Mattered

Rachel Notley as Alberta Premier

MELANEE THOMAS

Many important "firsts" for women in Canadian politics come from Alberta. In 1916, Emily Murphy became the first woman appointed as a magistrate in Canada and the British Empire. While not the first province to extend the right to vote, Alberta became, in 1917, the first province to conduct an election in which (white) women were enfranchised (Janovicek and Thomas 2018). That same year, Annie Gale was elected to Calgary city council and Louise McKinney to the Alberta legislature – making them the first women in Canada to win these offices.

Although women and feminism have a fraught political history in Alberta, the story of important breakthroughs continues (see Harder 2003). In 2012, the two major parties contesting the provincial election were both led by women.[1] Following a PC majority victory under Alison Redford in 2012, voters elected a majority New Democratic Party government led by Rachel Notley in 2015 – making Alberta the first province to elect a woman-led party to government two elections in a row.

Unlike what's been presented in many other chapters in this volume, which show women leaders not pursuing or securing significant pro-equality changes, Notley's career both as an MLA since 2008 and as premier demonstrates her importance as a critical actor (see Cavanaugh 1993; Childs and Krook 2008; Janovicek and Thomas 2018). This chapter examines how Notley's contributions reshaped numerical representation and public policies in Alberta. Notley was long committed to equity and social justice, and consistently raised gender issues. Under her leadership, the Alberta NDP committed to and delivered on a promise to nominate women candidates in half the province's ridings. This action created a near parity government caucus in 2015 (47 percent women) as well as Alberta's first parity cabinet.

The coming to power of the NDP brought Alberta from laggard status to innovator on gender-based policy (Harder 2003). Because much of this change is the direct result of Notley's leadership, I argue that she is a critical actor with respect to equality issues. Consistent with findings about the Wynne years in Ontario and the Redford period in Alberta, I conclude that Notley's presence did not alter the tone of provincial politics; rather, in Alberta, ideological and partisan changes sparked by the 2015 election reinvigorated a constituency already hostile not just to women and feminism but also to progressive politics generally. This pattern increased hostility in the tone of legislative debate and politics in general.

Growing Up in Politics

Rachel Notley was born into an Alberta political dynasty. Her father, Grant Notley, was the first leader of the Alberta NDP and its first MLA. He died in a plane crash in 1984 when Rachel was twenty years old. Grant was often away from home, organizing for the party across the province and dedicating time to being the "social conscience of Alberta" in the legislature (Leeson 2015).

Rachel felt pressure to build on her father's legacy. Yet she also sensed her own connection to the political universe. In her words: "I got involved in politics because I enjoyed the camaraderie and the issues. I grew up in a campaign office ... I loved these elections and our family watching the results come in was a bit like *Hockey Night in Canada*, made even more important because winning and losing was about issues that mattered" (Notley as quoted in Leeson 2015, xii). The most salient message Notley took from her father's political career was that "political victory worth having rarely comes easily" (Notley as quoted in Leeson 2015, xii).

Although one might assume Notley's father was her political inspiration, her mother offered as much, if not more, of an influence. The gruelling schedule Grant maintained as party leader meant he was not present for Rachel's birth. The first news he received of it came at a political rally the next day (Leeson 2015, 111). As an activist who worked on poverty, voter registration in the American South, and peace and social equity issues, Sandra Notley directly shaped Rachel's political development (Harper 2015). Sandra brought her daughter to protest marches in Edmonton in the early

1970s. As Rachel recalls: "I remember walking across the High Level Bridge and thinking,[2] 'Wow, this is a very long walk.' You know, I was a kid" (Notley as quoted in Canadian Press 2015).

Notley credits both her parents for establishing her political priorities and work ethic. In her words: "Dad taught me about political work and, together with my mom, taught me my political values: justice, determination, and integrity. Through both my parents I learned that if you actually care about something, you better get up and do something about it" (Notley as quoted in Leeson 2015, xii).

After completing her legal training in Ontario, Notley worked in labour law and as an advisor to the BC attorney general (at the time a New Democrat) on changes to occupational health and safety as well as sexual orientation rights (Canadian Press 2015). The experience of writing rules that changed people's lives led Notley to return to Alberta and run for public office. Elected in 2008, she intervened in Question Period and delivered her first statement as an MLA on the high cost of child care in Alberta (Alberta *Hansard* 2008). Her initial legislative speech supported a vibrant, participatory democracy:

> Good leadership is about recognizing that the public interest is the government's obligation. Good leadership is about defining the public interest with reference to the quality of life experienced by regular citizens instead of looking only at corporate profit margins. Good leadership is about making hard decisions now for the benefit of future generations. I would venture to say that good leadership equates with what one might describe as activist government. (Alberta *Hansard* 2008)

Notley became leader of the Alberta NDP in October 2014. She secured 70 percent of the vote in a race against two men, David Eggen and Rod Loyola. In her first legislative session as party leader, she pressed for progressive action on poverty, government integrity, gay-straight alliances in schools, violence against women, child protection, health care, the environment, and tax policy (Alberta *Hansard* 2014). This record indicates that, before becoming premier, Notley was already a pro-feminist critical actor in the Alberta legislature. She used her positions as an MLA and opposition party leader to advocate for women, diversity, and equity – even though she did not have the power to legislate on these issues.

Notley unabashedly campaigned to win in 2015. She opened most of her campaign speeches, including in the leaders' debate, with the following statement: "My name is Rachel Notley, and I'm running to be your premier" (Canadian Press 2015). By contrast, other opposition parties appeared to concede the election to the governing PCs.

Notley's strategy may reflect her early exposure to campaigns in her father's constituency in northwestern Alberta, where he consistently won elections between 1971 and his death in 1984. Rachel Notley approaches politics as a left populist. Populism is not new in Alberta politics (see Stewart and Archer 2003; Stewart and Sayers 2009, 2013), but Notley's version diverged clearly from what is offered on the political right. She campaigned in 2015 to make "life better for Albertans one family at a time" (Canadian Press 2015). This approach helps to explain why Notley has protected government programs and services during the economic downturn that began before she became premier.

It is unclear whether Notley genuinely expected the NDP to win a majority government in 2015. The party focused its campaign on expanding the size of the legislative caucus by targeting seats it hoped to win (see Thomas 2019). Notley used her strengths as a public speaker in the crucial televised debate with PC leader Jim Prentice (Wells 2015; Thomas 2019). A week before election day, Notley realized she was going to win. She reports that her first thought was: "Oh my Lord. We have so much to do" (Bennett 2015).

Given that Notley was a critical actor for women's representation from the start of her political career, it is important to probe the ways in which she initiated policy proposals or otherwise substantively represented women as premier (see Childs and Krook 2008). Therefore, the question addressed in the next sections is not whether Notley remained a critical actor as premier but, rather, how a government led by a critical actor substantively represented women and gender. I highlight Notley's cabinet and other government appointments as well as her approach to candidate recruitment and policy decisions.

Appointments Record

It is difficult to assess the appointments pursued by a government while it remains in office. Yet, as of this writing, considerable evidence suggests Notley's approach differed from that of previous Alberta premiers. In particular, she seemed substantially more concerned with diversity and transparency than did her predecessors.

When compared to that of previous governments, Notley's first cabinet stood out with respect to gender parity and size.[3] Her initial cabinet included only twelve ministers counting the premier, making it far smaller than most provincial cabinets in Canada. The first cabinets for previous PC premiers – Jim Prentice, Alison Redford, and Ed Stelmach – had twenty or more members. Notley shuffled her cabinet three times between 2015 and the time of writing, increasing its size first to thirteen and then to twenty-one ministers.

Although her cabinets grew to the size of earlier ones in Alberta, they remained distinctive in other ways. First, Notley's cabinet contained equal numbers of women and men. It was the first parity cabinet in Alberta's history and the third in Canada, following those of Pat Duncan in Yukon and Jean Charest in Quebec. Although the 2015 NDP platform did not commit to a parity cabinet, the document included explicit policy initiatives to advance women.

Notley's predecessors Prentice and Stelmach appointed four women to their cabinets while Redford initially appointed two women besides herself. This suggests that gender was seen as a less important representational category by previous Alberta premiers, who tended to name women to no more than about one-fifth of cabinet portfolios. In short, Notley's commitment to gender parity in Alberta cabinet appointments broke from past practice.

Moreover, Notley appointed women to portfolios with considerable power and responsibility (on the categorization of cabinet roles, see appendix to Chapter 8). Her ministers of health, environment and climate change, energy, justice, and solicitor general were all women. Since these ministries are considered influential in Canada, we conclude that women besides Notley wielded significant power in Alberta's NDP cabinet. Consistent with findings from other jurisdictions, many female ministers in the Notley government held social policy and administrative portfolios that are often considered to be less prestigious – notably in the areas of seniors and housing, children's services, and Service Alberta.

Notley's cabinet also stood out because several women members had small children. Multiple ministers in the initial political executive had children under the age of five (Shannon Phillips, Danielle Larivee). When the cabinet was expanded to twenty, one of the appointees (Stephanie McLean) had a small infant while another (Brandy Payne) was pregnant. These appointments led MLAs to address issues that had hitherto been ignored, including child care and paid leave for elected members. McLean was the first MLA in Alberta history to be pregnant while in office. Prior to changes introduced by the NDP government, McLean and Payne would have been penalized one hundred dollars pay per day for their absence from the legislature (Bellefontaine 2015a). By the time the third minister to have a baby in the Notley cabinet delivered her child, the norms had shifted such that Kathleen Ganley took a three-month maternity leave from December 2017 to February 2018.

Other demographic features distinguished the Notley cabinets from previous ones. The NDP premier appointed a political executive that, like her caucus, was younger on average than previous cabinets. One minister in her expanded cabinet was openly LGBTQ (Sinnema 2015a). All NDP ministers had at least some postsecondary education; by contrast, between two and four members of the Redford and Stelmach first cabinets had no formal education beyond high school. Notley's ministers were less likely to have been involved in agriculture or small business prior to their election than were members of PC cabinets. One area where Notley's ministers resembled past cabinets is with respect to racial and ethnic diversity: on balance, cabinets in Alberta remain overwhelmingly white.

Notley faced criticism for what some observers saw as a geographic imbalance in favour of ministers from the Edmonton area (Wood 2017). This view is closely related to the fact that her cabinet was more urban than past ones. Concerns about cabinet composition are not new in Alberta politics; for instance, Stelmach's critics maintained his cabinets were too rural and northern (CBC News 2008). After Redford became premier, her cabinet appointments were seen as attempts to minimize internal party dissent and to promote the status quo (Bennett 2013).

Notley's approach to including equity and diversity in appointments extended beyond cabinet. She effected important changes in appointments to public agencies, boards, and commissions – units responsible for a great deal of policy and governance work (Alberta Government 2017f). These agencies became controversial once independent reviews by the auditor general identified financial mismanagement and pay anomalies (Thomson 2017). Notley campaigned in 2015 on a promise to extend conflict of interest rules to appointees at agencies, boards, and commissions, and to include employee details on public-sector salary lists. Once in government, the NDP opened the appointment process to all Albertans and said that agency members must represent the diversity of the province (Alberta Government 2016a; Alberta Government 2017a).

Notley's approach could have been a rhetorical ploy to highlight opaque or partisan appointments by previous premiers. Yet some evidence suggests the NDP was genuinely committed to ensuring greater diversity. When the University of Calgary requested that terms be extended for three government-appointed board members, the request was denied on the basis of diversity concerns as well as Notley's commitment to a new process (CBC News 2016a). In the end, some existing board members were reappointed while two women and a Métis man were added (UToday 2016).

This example is instructive. Some observers feared the Notley government would fire PC appointees en masse. Yet the NDP made no such move. Instead, when positions become available, an appointment process with a clear emphasis on diversity was employed. This may explain why progress to date was incremental rather than radical. Status of Women Alberta (2017b) reported the representation of women on Government of Alberta agencies, boards, and commissions increased from 32 percent in 2014–15 to 37 percent in 2015–16.

Candidate Recruitment

Rachel Notley was a leader who, in directing her party to ensure a diverse group of MLAs, changed how her party recruited and nominated candidates. As discussed in Chapter 1, the NDP resembles other left parties, which tend to be more concerned with diversity in representation than do organizations of the centre and right. Since 1984, the federal NDP constitution has called for equity in nominations, including 50 percent women candidates, as well as targeted recruiting for visible and sexual minorities, youth, and people with disabilities (Cross 2004). Yet, across Canada, NDP candidates remain less diverse than the general, and particularly the urban, population, sometimes by a large margin.

Notley stated publicly that gender parity would not happen organically; instead, she maintained the need for consistent efforts to create space for women in politics (CBC 2016b). This approach contrasted directly with that of Alison Redford. Alberta NDP organizers credited the parity slate of candidates in 2015 to Notley (Thomas 2019). While no fixed targets or quotas were set, Notley said she wanted (1) NDP nominees to reflect the diversity of Albertans and (2) a gender parity slate of candidates. By investing time and effort beyond that required to find more conventional candidates, she inspired organizers to look for candidates in places they might otherwise overlook. In the words of one organizer: "There's never a shortage of middle to older white males who are able-bodied who put their hands up to run for election. There's a level of comfort there" that needs to be cultivated for women, people of colour, sexual minorities, and people with disabilities (quoted in Thomas 2019).

This approach of using "commitment rather than a directive" (quoted in Thomas 2019) worked since half of the NDP candidates in 2015 were women. Many won, with the result that women comprised 47 percent of the government caucus and 31 percent of all MLAs after the election (Parliament of Canada 2017). NDP candidates and MLAs were considerably younger and more sexually diverse than were their counterparts in other parties. Several members of the government caucus were LGBTQ; some were gender-fluid and requested that they be referred to in *Hansard* by gender-neutral pronouns. It appears that, prior to 2015, no openly identified LGBTQ candidate had won a seat in Alberta (Sinnema 2015a).

On matters of race and ethnicity, the NDP as well as other parties struggled to diversify their candidates (Markusoff 2015). In 2015, opposition parties faced a particular challenge with respect to women's representation. By early 2018, only three women sat as opposition MLAs following the decision of Sandra Jansen,[4] a cabinet minister from the Redford years, to join the NDP because of harassment she had experienced in the PC party (Giovanetti 2016).

Notley's emphasis on recruiting more women extended to local government. The NDP's newly created Status of Women department initiated a program known as Ready For Her, which was designed to increase the number of women running for municipal office (Alberta Government 2017b). The program's six videos include a message from the premier that addressed women's political ambition and confidence; a fundraising tutorial from the provincial minister for the status of women; a message from the federal minister for the status of women; tips from a mayor on raising local profiles; advice from a rural NDP MLA on campaigning in rural areas; and advice from a town councillor on how to balance political work with family.

Notley's message and the video about balancing work and family specifically targeted stereotypes that devalue women's voices and experience in the public sphere. The videos connected directly with a Ready For Her tour by the provincial status of women minister and with information on election rules, campaigning, and fundraising. Much of the motivation for this effort followed from research showing that women candidates need to be recruited more aggressively than men (Young and Cross 2003). As well, studies show that, when women agree to run, they win as often as men (Goodyear-Grant 2010).

One conclusion that can be drawn from comparing Notley's approach to Redford's is that if a party leader genuinely wants representational diversity, her party will make it happen. Future research can assess how leader commitments affect other sources of demographic diversity such as race, age, and sexual orientation – whether in Canada or other parliamentary systems.

Public Policy

Premier Notley's policy actions highlighted the importance of critical actors. The NDP campaign platform contained multiple references to women and gender, including an emphasis on the need to "help women and families" (Alberta's NDP 2015, 3). Party statements used the rhetoric of family to promote policies geared towards women. For example, the platform promised to create a twenty-five-dollar-a-day child care program and maintained that gender equality requires affordable child care (Alberta's NDP 2015, 16). The NDP also promised a women's ministry, full-day kindergarten, compassionate care leave, and more spaces in emergency women's shelters as well as other initiatives directed at ending intimate partner violence. The party promised to support a national inquiry into missing and murdered Indigenous women. Budget details for the women's ministry and shelter spaces were provided in the campaign platform (Alberta's NDP 2015, 25).

Once in office, because of the province's precarious finances, the NDP took little action on full-day kindergarten (Vernon 2016). Changes to compassionate care leave that altered policies from 2014 were scheduled to come into effect in 2018 (Alberta Labour 2017; Alberta Government 2014). In 2017, the government undertook a pilot study for twenty-five-dollar-a-day child care (Alberta Budget 2017; Bellefontaine 2016; Alberta Government 2017e) and expanded it by six thousand spaces in spring 2018 (Bartko 2018).[5] Federal funding created a new unit in the provincial government to support the families of missing and murdered Indigenous women (Stevenson 2017). Legislation added gender identity as a protected category in the Alberta Human Rights Act (Status of Women Alberta 2016) and made it possible for Albertans facing intimate partner violence to break rental leases without penalty (Cole 2016). These initiatives on violence against women demonstrated the importance of gender equality to the Notley government, and they represented new directions as compared with actions undertaken in the Redford years.

While important, these initiatives paled alongside the creation of Alberta's Status of Women Ministry. Though the federal government and other provinces have units dedicated to the status of women, in 2015 Alberta established the first full department with its own deputy minister (see Alberta Government 2017g; Ontario created a women's ministry in 2017).[6] The first minister responsible for Status of Women Alberta announced the ministry was designed to help "build feminism in Alberta" (Southwick 2015). Prior to 2015, for nearly twenty years the province had had no minister responsible for the status of women (Southwick 2015).[7]

Notley's government formed the ministry on a compressed timeline between July 2015 and March 2016, and staffed it primarily with existing members of the civil service. Status of Women Alberta built on an existing desire for this work inside the Alberta civil service, which had been largely frustrated by a series of PC governments, and benefited from explicit support – both fiscal and otherwise – from the Notley government. The new department identified three key policy areas: women's economic security, women's leadership and democratic participation, and violence against women and girls (Alberta Government 2016b; Status of Women Alberta 2016). Each area had its own sense of urgency: relative to the rest of Canada, Alberta had a large gender gap in salaries and wages (Lahey 2016), high levels of intimate partner violence (Burczycka and Conroy 2017), and relatively few women in either municipal public office (Alberta Government 2017b) or corporate leadership positions (Alberta Securities Commission 2016). In short, the Notley government was prepared to engage in gender equality policy across several policy domains rather than focusing only on less expensive and often less contentious areas such as violence against women.

The research and analytics division of the Status of Women department launched a large-scale public consultation project. In July 2016, Minister Stephanie McLean sent an e-mail message to nearly two hundred individuals and organizations soliciting potential research questions for the new unit to pose to Albertans. Questions had to be empirically answerable and policy relevant. The e-mail solicitation generated more than five hundred research questions. At a workshop in September 2016, participants narrowed this list to fewer than thirty questions. An online consultation held in October 2016 created a shortlist of priority research questions to direct the ministry's work in developing new initiatives.

A second division of Status of Women Alberta addressed gender-based policy analysis, which was initially undertaken beginning in 2014 when the PC government contracted Status of Women Canada to train provincial employees (Status of Women Alberta 2016). After 2015, the presence of a dedicated department at the provincial level widened the reach of this policy lens. As of late 2017, more than fifteen hundred government staff had received training and the ministry planned to reach six thousand bureaucrats by 2018 (Status of Women Alberta 2017a). Notley's leadership in cabinet ensured the prominence of gender-based analysis. She required that all presentations to cabinet, regardless of ministry, use a gender lens, and she expected every minister to be prepared to answer questions relating to equity and diversity whenever they presented to cabinet (Status of Women 2017b).

Status of Women Alberta's third division was responsible for community capacity and outreach. It oversaw a series of diverse initiatives to assist women. They included a safe cities program with the city of Edmonton, grants and scholarships, and leadership training for female civil servants.

Although the goals of the new ministry were ambitious, the Notley government seemed committed to ensuring resources were in place to fulfill the unit's mandate. Status of Women Alberta (2017a) was awarded an initial budget in 2015–16 of just over $1 million; this increased to $7.5 million in 2016–17 once the ministry's organizational structure was in place. That investment remained tiny relative to overall government operating expenses, which reached $44.8 billion in 2016.

Yet the difference made by having a government ministry dedicated to the status of women was not easily quantified. Though the department's budget was modest, the allocation exceeded investments in this area by any previous Alberta government (see Harder 2003). NDP government funding supported foundational data collection and information dissemination that reached both the public and other government ministries (Status of Women Alberta 2017b). The unit's presence demonstrated strong commitment to gender equality on the part of the Notley government, which was prepared to use the institutional apparatus of the provincial government to ensure pro-equality outcomes.

What if a subsequent government were to close the new ministry, either by folding it into a different department or eliminating it entirely? Clearly, the knowledge capacity within the provincial public service, especially with respect to gender-based policy analysis, would still exist. From this perspective, Notley's decision to create the department would stand as transformative.

I conclude that the creation of a women's ministry constitutes among the most important actions Premier Notley took on gender in Alberta politics – if not her most important decision. This dimension of Notley's record further confirms her role as a critical actor (see Childs and Krook 2008).

Tenor of Debate

The Notley government consulted more widely than had previous Alberta regimes on gender-based policy initiatives as well as on other issues, including school curricula, Indigenous leadership, labour law, and urban affairs (Alberta Government 2017d). Past provincial governments used the internet to gain public input, but most consultations prior to 2015 sought primarily to inform the public about decisions rather than to seek perspectives before decisions were made (Power 2013). It is unclear at the time of writing whether the Notley government's consultations outside the Status of Women case discussed earlier will produce significant changes.

By contrast, the tenor of debate inside the legislature worsened after the 2015 election. Since ideology tends to underpin a great deal of political hostility in Alberta, it is not surprising that a change of governing party from PC to NDP produced heightened antagonism. Hostility to new actors has been a feature of Alberta politics for some time (see Stewart 2017), and this legacy seemed unlikely to change with the addition of more women MLAs and a second woman premier. That being said, since 2015 gender and sexism have interacted with ideology to produce clear public displays of antagonistic politics.

Two sets of developments help to illuminate this point. At least on the surface, they seem contradictory. At one level, more legislative time was devoted to discussions of women and gender after 2015 than before. MLAs granted unanimous support to expanded sexual orientation rights in provincial human rights provisions. At another level, female legislators faced pernicious sexism, including in relations with their fellow MLAs, and leaders, including Notley, faced unprecedented threats to their physical safety.

Hansard data from the two sessions prior to Notley's election as an MLA show one or no mentions of the word "women." During the same time period, the words "gender" and "diversity" were not used in legislative debate. After the 2008 election, mentions of women and gender in legislative debate increased to 546 and twenty-seven, respectively (see Chapter 10, Table 10.4).

Closer study of who spoke about what reveals the partisan dimension of the story: NDP and Liberal MLAs used the terms to raise substantive policy issues, while PC MLAs disproportionately referred to "men and women in uniform." During Notley's first session as premier, women were mentioned 694 times and gender 468 times. This increase was largely driven by references to the Status of Women department, Notley's parity cabinet, gender identity expression in the Human Rights Act, and the government's acknowledgment of the Transgender Day of Remembrance (Alberta *Hansard* 2008, 2014, 2015).

At least initially, two NDP government bills promoting sexual diversity drew no opposition. One proposed to add gender identity expression as a protected category in the Alberta Human Rights Act. It passed unanimously (Sinnema 2015b), but then opposition politicians challenged the idea when discussion turned to ensuring the right applied to school-aged children (Alberta Education 2016; Bennett 2017).

In the second case, a former NDP MLA sitting as an independent, Deborah Drever, proposed a private member's bill to allow victims of intimate partner violence to break a residential lease agreement without penalty. That bill also passed unanimously (Ibrahim 2015a). Drever had been expelled from the NDP caucus shortly after the 2015 election because of controversial social media posts. Some critics suggested the bill was part of a scheme to permit Drever to rejoin the NDP caucus, which happened in 2016 (Dippel 2016). Commentary of that type abated when NDP MLA Maria Fitzpatrick cited her own experiences as a survivor of domestic violence in a speech endorsing the proposal. Fitzpatrick concluded by stating, "I will be horrified if anybody in this chamber votes against this bill" (Ibrahim 2015b). The abuse Fitzpatrick outlined was so horrific that it effectively silenced any opposition or cynicism other MLAs may have harboured towards the legislation.

Despite these advances, explicit sexism hardly disappeared in Alberta politics. In the last legislative session before the 2015 provincial election, Notley used the turn of phrase "Call me crazy, but..." in a legislative speech. Several members interrupted with shouts of "Crazy" (Alberta *Hansard*, 9 December 2014, 462). Once Notley became premier, members of the PC executive and others routinely disparaged the weight of female cabinet ministers (Bellefontaine 2015b; CBC News 2015a). Some critics simply attacked Notley and members of her government for being women (Huncar 2015). Sandra Jansen, a former PC cabinet minister and leadership candidate, resigned from both the leadership race and her party. After crossing the floor to the government side, Jansen used her first statement as an NDP MLA to detail her experiences of harassment (McConnel 2016; *Edmonton Journal* 2016). She called on all MLAs to oppose sexism in politics.

The treatment of political women by Wildrose Party supporters and MLAs was particularly troubling.[8] By December 2015, the content of the party's Facebook page was so violent that Wildrose issued a statement asking supporters to stop calling for Notley's assassination (CBC News 2015b).

Wildrose MLA Brian Jean quipped that, while he was "beating the drum" for seniors' housing, it was "against the law to beat Rachel Notley." Jean later described his remark as "inappropriate" (Bell 2016). Several Wildrose MLAs, including the party leader, were openly rude to Kathleen Wynne when she visited the legislature as Ontario premier (Bennett 2016). Wildrose legislators suspended one MLA from their caucus after he endorsed a hateful comment about Wynne that was posted on his Facebook page (Ramsay and Heidenreich 2016). Wynne suggested the treatment she received from opposition MLAs in Alberta was motivated by her gender (Berthiaume 2016). Lately, newly selected opposition leader Jason Kenney attributed the hostile tone of Alberta's legislature to heckling by NDP MLAs (Graney 2018).

Data reveal an exponential increase in threats against Alberta women in politics since 2015, suggesting this issue goes beyond heckling. Reports in 2016 by the provincial Department of Justice show Notley was subject to more than four hundred incidents of inappropriate contact and communication. Of them, twenty-six were deemed serious enough to forward to police for investigation. By contrast, during the years between 2003 and 2015, Alberta's premiers faced in total fifty-five threats (Trynacity 2017).

Since the political use of social media platforms predates the 2015 Alberta election, it is hard to link these threats to the mere availability of Twitter and Facebook. Notley's party and gender are arguably key components: detailed reports on these threats show misogyny against women in politics was pervasive among some members of the public. In particular, hostility towards Notley and other NDP women spiked around the one hundredth anniversary of suffrage rights being extended in Alberta (Trynacity 2018).

Many observers saw as problematic the polarized and hateful atmosphere facing women leaders in Alberta. Others, however, claimed female politicians were being overly sensitive (see Boyd 2016). This contentious tenor of debate presented at least one obvious danger: the backlash against women in Alberta politics risked deterring diverse candidates of all varieties from seeking election to public office – at the same time as the NDP government actively promoted pro-equality initiatives in provincial as well as municipal politics.

Notley as a Critical Actor

On balance, the evidence suggests that Rachel Notley was a critical actor who sought to represent feminist positions in politics. As soon as she became an MLA, she spoke frequently and directly to women's issues. As NDP leader, she ensured her party nominated diverse candidates with respect to gender, age, and sexual orientation. As premier, she used the levers of the provincial state to appoint equal numbers of women and men to cabinet, entrench gender identity rights in Alberta's Human Rights Act, and create a ministry dedicated to understanding and promoting the status of women and girls. The only area where gender-based representation did not improve as of this writing was in the tenor of political debate. Material presented in this chapter demonstrates that, beginning in 2015, Notley and other progressive women in Alberta politics became frequent targets of misogynist commentary and physical threat.

One question that follows from this discussion is how Notley's contributions will stand the test of time. It is reasonable to expect that if the NDP wins re-election in 2019, Notley will continue to be a critical actor for women's representation. But if the party loses, it is not clear how willing the next government will be to substantively represent women. A provincial civil service trained in gender-based analysis could be directed by a new premier to stop using that lens. Similarly, Notley's explicit invocation of gender in her political work could be emulated by future premiers or repudiated by them. Will future leaders of the Alberta NDP use the same language?

Consistent with the gender and politics literature introduced in Chapter 1, research on Alberta politics shows that having a woman premier does not ensure either that public policies will advance women or that governments will use a gendered lens in reaching their decisions. Instead, as this chapter highlights, Rachel Notley's record as an MLA, party leader, and NDP premier underlines how coming from a left party and holding a strong personal commitment to gender equality and feminism form the foundations for critical actor practices.

Overall, Notley made considerable gains for women and for sexual diversity groups in Alberta. She ensured that women and non-binary individuals were elected under her party's banner. She actively promoted women and sexual minorities to cabinet and other government positions. She actively pursued gender-based equality in public policy.

Although political debate in Alberta became increasingly hostile after the 2015 election, it is difficult to believe that Notley alone could have changed the situation. As one critical actor working hard for equality, she faced other influential participants – including opposition party leaders – who employed or condoned hateful discourse. Despite the obstacles before her, Notley set forth a valuable template of how to be a critical actor in opposition as well as in government.

Notes

1 In 2012, analysts expected the Wildrose Party led by Danielle Smith to win the most seats. On election day, however, the PCs, led by Alison Redford, were re-elected.

2 The High Level Bridge in Edmonton spans the North Saskatchewan River. It is often the site of protest marches that end at the Alberta legislature.

3 Background references for these cabinet appointees are available from the author upon request. I would like to thank Anna Johnson for her assistance in gathering this information.

4 A common joke circulating in the legislature at the time of writing was that there were more men named Richard in the opposition benches than there were women. Two of the women in opposition – Leela Aheer and Angela Pitt – sat as members of the United Conservative Party (UCP). The third, Karen MacPherson, was elected as an NDP MLA in 2015 and crossed to sit with the Alberta Party in the fall of 2017. In the fall of 2018, a fourth woman, Robyn Luff, left the NDP caucus as a result of alleged bullying, although much of what Luff describes reads as standard party discipline in Canada (see Thomson 2018).

5 Some analysts maintain that subsidized child care in Quebec offered a net revenue gain for the provincial government because it increased the number of mothers who entered the labour force and hence paid personal income and sales taxes (Baker, Gruber, and Milligan 2009). Comparable arguments do not resonate in Alberta because (1) the province has no sales tax and (2) personal income tax rates are significantly lower than in Quebec (Canada Revenue Agency 2017; Revenu Québec 2017). As a result, the revenue generated from increasing the proportion of mothers in the labour force would be considerably less for Alberta. Data from Statistics Canada (2017) also show that Alberta women's labour force participation rate is lower than men's by about twelve percentage points but that is higher than women's participation rate in Quebec by about five points. A more persuasive argument for greater public funding for child care in Alberta is that costs are too high for most families; median monthly fees in Calgary in 2016 exceed one thousand dollars, compared to $164/month in Montreal (Macdonald and Friendly 2016).

6 Status of Women Alberta was a government department with its own deputy minister (Alberta Government 2017c) while Status of Women Canada self-identified as a federal government organization (Status of Women Canada 2017).

7 Although relations were often hostile between Alberta PC governments and organized feminism (see Harder 2003), former PC ministers claimed Notley should have included more women in her parity cabinet if she "actually believed what she said about equality for women" (Southwick 2015).

8 The Wildrose Party merged with the Progressive Conservative Association of Alberta to form the United Conservative Party in July 2017. The merger did not diminish the hostility observed in political debate in Alberta.

References

Alberta Budget. 2017. "2017–20 Fiscal Plan: Expense." http://finance.alberta.ca/"-publications/budget/budget2017/fiscal-plan-expense.pdf.

Alberta Education. 2016. "Guidelines for Best Practices: Creating Learning Environments That Respect Diverse Sexual Orientations, Gender Identities and Gender Expressions." https://education.alberta.ca/media/1626737/91383-attachment-1-guidelines-final.pdf.

Alberta Government. 2014. "Employment Standards: Compassionate Care Leave." https://work.alberta.ca/documents/compassionate-care.pdf.

—. 2016a. "Public Appointments Now Open to All Albertans." https://www.alberta.ca/release.cfm?xID=4345606F7F2A1-06B3-DA8D-479A6C6D3AB72906.

—. 2016b. "Status of Women Ministry Launches Mandate Ahead of International Women." https://www.alberta.ca/release.cfm?xID=4034736BBB060-9843-168F-59498D9E3AFF267C.

—. 2017a. "Current Public Agency Board Opportunities." https://www.alberta.ca/public-agency-opportunities.cfm#.

—. 2017b. "Ready For Her: A Guide for Women Running for Municipal Office." https://www.alberta.ca/ready-for-her.aspx.

—. 2017c. "Ministry of Status of Women." https://www.alberta.ca/ministry-status-of-women.aspx#toc-3.

—. 2017d. "Active Consultations and Engagements." http://www.alberta.ca/consultations.aspx.

—. 2017e. "Early Learning and Child Care Centres." https://www.alberta.ca/early-learning-child-care-centres.aspx.

—. 2017f. "Alberta Boards." https://www.alberta.ca/alberta-boards.aspx.

—. 2017g. "Ministry of Status of Women." https://www.alberta.ca/ministry-status-of-women.aspx.

Alberta *Hansard*. 2008. "The 27th Legislature, First Session." Province of Alberta. http://www.assembly.ab.ca/ISYS/LADDAR_files/docs/hansards/cpl/legislature_27/session_1/20080414_1500_01_cpl.pdf.

—. 2014. "The 28th Legislature, Third Session." Province of Alberta. http://www.assembly.ab.ca/ISYS/LADDAR_files/docs/hansards/cpl/legislature_28/session_3/20141117_1500_01_cpl.pdf.

—. 2015. "The 29th Legislature, First Session." Province of Alberta. http://www.assembly.ab.ca/ISYS/LADDAR_files/docs/hansards/cpl/legislature_29/session_1/20150611_1330_01_cpl.pdf.

Alberta Labour. 2017. "Compassionate Care Leave | Fact Sheet." https://work.alberta.ca/employment-standards/compassionate-care-leave.html.

Alberta NDP. 2015. "Alberta's NDP: Leadership for What Matters." https://d3n8a8pro7vhmx.cloudfront.net/themes/5538f80701925b5033000001/attachments/original/1431112969/Alberta_NDP_Platform_2015.pdf?1431112969.

Alberta Securities Commission. 2016. "Alberta Women on Boards Index: Statistics." http://www.albertasecurities.com/Publications/2016_Alberta%20WOB%20stats_FINALpdf.

Baker, Michael, Jonathan Gruber, and Kevin Milligan. 2008. "Universal Child Care, Maternal Labor Supply, and Family Well-Being" *Journal of Political Economy* 116, 4: 709–45.

Bartko, Karen. 2017. "Alberta $25-a-Day Daycare Expands to 100 More Locations: 6,000 Spaces Created." *Global News.* https://globalnews.ca/news/4166956/alberta -25-dollar-daycare-pilot-program-expansion/.

Bell, Roberta. 2016. "Brian Jean Comment Reflects Alberta's Wider Sexism Problem, Women's Advocates Say." *CBC News.* http://www.cbc.ca/news/canada/ edmonton/brian-jean-comment-reflects-alberta-s-wider-sexism-problem -women-s-advocates-say-1.3743825.

Bellefontaine, Michelle. 2015a. "Premier Rachel Notley Vows MLA Will Not Lose Pay Due to Pregnancy." *CBC News.* http://www.cbc.ca/news/canada/edmonton/ premier-rachel-notley-vows-mla-will-not-lose-pay-due-to-pregnancy-1. 3304765.

–. 2015b. "'What Women Put Up With': Alberta Politician Calls Out Twitter Sexism." *CBC News.* http://www.cbc.ca/news/canada/edmonton/what-women-put -up-with-alberta-politician-calls-out-twitter-sexism-1.3228871.

–. 2016. "$25-a-Day Child Care Coming to 18 Alberta Daycare Centres." *CBC News.* http://www.cbc.ca/news/canada/edmonton/25-a-day-child-care-coming -to-18-alberta-daycare-centres-1.3851628.

Bennett, Dean. 2013. "Alison Redford Remakes Alberta Cabinet in Major Shuffle of Ministers." *National Post.* http://news.nationalpost.com/news/canada/canadian -politics/alison-redford-remakes-alberta-cabinet-in-major-shuffle-of-ministers.

–. 2015. "Rachel Notley Says It Hit Her a Week before Election That She'd Be Premier." *CBC News.* http://www.cbc.ca/news/canada/edmonton/rachel-notley -says-it-hit-her-a-week-before-election-that-she-d-be-premier-1.3068407.

–. 2016. "Fury in Alberta Legislature after Ontario Premier Ridiculed by Wildrose." *Calgary Herald.* http://calgaryherald.com/news/politics/wynne-ontario-ridiculed -by-opposition-wildrose-in-alberta-legislature.

–. 2017. "Alberta's Wildrose and PCs at Odds over Gay-Straight Alliances in Schools." *Globe and Mail.* https://www.theglobeandmail.com/news/alberta/albertas-wildrose -and-pcs-at-odds-over-gay-straight-alliances-in-schools/article34570244/.

Berthiaume, Lee. 2016. "Wynne Blames Sexism for Hostility in Alberta." *Ottawa Citizen.* http://www.pressreader.com/canada/ottawa-citizen/20160530/28166395 9259157.

Boyd, Alex. 2016. "With Female Politicians, You're Either Stupid or a Bitch." *Metro News.* http://www.metronews.ca/news/edmonton/2016/11/16/alberta-women -politics-insults-threats-harassment.html.

Burczycka, Marta, and Shana Conroy. 2017. "Family Violence in Canada: A Statistical Profile, 2015." Statistics Canada: Catalogue no. 85-002-X, ISSN 1209-6393. http://www.statcan.gc.ca/pub/85-002-x/2017001/article/14698-eng.pdf.

Canadian Press. 2015. "What You Need to Know about Rachel Notley." *Calgary Herald.* http://calgaryherald.com/news/politics/next-premier-rachel-notley-takes -up-fathers-ndp-legacy.

Cavanaugh, Catherine. 1993. "The Limitations of the Pioneering Partnership: The Alberta Campaign for Homestead Dower, 1909–25." *Canadian Historical Review* 74, 2: 198–225.

CBC News. 2008. "Stelmach Names Smaller Cabinet." http://www.cbc.ca/news/canada/edmonton/stelmach-names-smaller-cabinet-1.600083.

–. 2015a. "Sarah Hoffman Weight Insults Show Sexism Still an Issue in Politics, Expert Says." http://www.cbc.ca/news/canada/edmonton/sarah-hoffman-weight-insults-show-sexism-still-an-issue-in-politics-expert-says-1.3096679.

–. 2015b. "Rachel Notley Assassination Chatter 'Needs to Stop,' Wildrose Leader Says as Bill 6 Anger Mounts." http://www.cbc.ca/news/canada/calgary/notley-assassination-comments-bill-6-brian-jean-1.33610637.

–. 2016a. "U of C Board of Governors Will Not Have Terms Extended by Alberta's NDP Government." http://www.cbc.ca/news/canada/calgary/university-of-calgary-board-governors-1.3547420.

–. 2016b. "Canada's Female Premiers on Hillary Clinton and Sexism in Politics." http://www.cbc.ca/news/thenational/canada-s-female-premiers-on-hillary-clinton-and-sexism-in-politics-1.3694912.

Childs, Sarah, and Mona Lena Krook. 2008. "Critical Mass Theory and Women's Political Representation." *Political Studies* 56: 725–36.

Cole, Yoland. 2016. "New Alberta Law Gives Victims of Domestic Violence Option to Break Lease." *Calgary Herald.* http://calgaryherald.com/news/local-news/new-alberta-law-gives-victims-of-domestic-violence-option-to-break-lease.

Cross, William. 2004. *Political Parties.* Vancouver: UBC Press.

Dippel, Scott. 2016. "Deborah Drever's Political Redemption." *CBC News.* http://www.cbc.ca/news/canada/calgary/deborah-drever-redemption-1.3489641.

Edmonton Journal. 2016. "'Dead Meat': Full Text of Sandra Jansen's Statement Outlining Harassment since She Joined the NDP." *Edmonton Journal.* http://edmontonjournal.com/news/politics/dead-meat-full-text-of-sandra-jansens-statement-outlining-harassment-since-she-joined-ndp.

Giovanetti, Justin. 2016. "Alberta Tory MLA Sandra Jansen Defects to NDP, Citing Sexism and Personal Attacks." *Globe and Mail.* http://www.theglobeandmail.com/news/alberta/former-alberta-tory-leadership-candidate-sandra-jansen-crosses-floor-to-ndp/article32902968/.

Graney, Emma. 2018. "Kenney Laments Heckling, Nasty Tone in Legislature." *Calgary Herald.* https://www.pressreader.com/canada/calgary-herald/20180503/281608126057059.

Harder, Lois. 2003. *State of Struggle: Feminism and Politics in Alberta.* Edmonton: University of Alberta Press.

Harper, Tim. 2015. "Alberta's Giant Killer Notley Grew Up with NDP Titans." *Toronto Star,* 5 May. https://www.thestar.com/news/canada/2015/05/05/albertas-giant-killer-notley-grew-up-with-ndp-titans-tim-harper.html.

Huncar, Andrea. 2015. "Alberta Female Politicians Targeted by Hateful Sexist Online Attacks. *CBC News.* http://www.cbc.ca/news/canada/edmonton/alberta-female-politicians-targeted-by-hateful-sexist-online-attacks-1.3281275.

Ibrahim, Mariam. 2015a. "Independent MLA's Domestic Violence Bill Gets Unanimous Support from Alberta Legislature." *Edmonton Journal.* http://edmonton

journal.com/news/politics/independent-mlas-domestic-violence-bill-gets
-unanimous-support-from-alberta-legislature.

—. 2015b. "In Her Own Words: MLA Maria Fitzpatrick Recounts Horrors of Domestic Violence." *Edmonton Journal.* http://edmontonjournal.com/news/ politics/in-her-own-words-mla-maria-fitzpatrick-recounts-horrors-of -domestic-violence.

Janovicek, Nancy, and Melanee Thomas. 2018. "Women's Suffrage and Electoral Participation in Canada." In *Global Handbook of Women's Political Rights*, ed. Susan Franceschet, Mona Lena Krook, and Netina Tan, 169–84. London: Palgrave Macmillan.

Lahey, Kathleen. 2016. "Equal Worth: Designing Effective Pay Equity Laws for Alberta." Edmonton: Parkland Institute. http://www.parklandinstitute.ca/equal _worth.

Leeson, Howard. 2015. *Grant Notley: The Social Conscience of Alberta.* 2nd ed. Edmonton: University of Alberta Press.

Macdonald, David, and Martha Friendly. 2016. "A Growing Concern: 2016 Child Care Fees in Canada's Big Cities." *Canadian Centre for Policy Alternatives.* https://www.policyalternatives.ca/sites/default/files/uploads/publications/ National%20Office/2016/12/A_Growing_Concern.pdf.

Markusoff, Jason. 2015. "NDP Falls Short on Ethnic Diversity: Fewest Minority MLAs in Ruling Caucus since 1993." *Calgary Herald.* http://calgaryherald.com/ news/politics/ndp-falls-short-on-ethnic-diversity-fewest-minority-mlas -in-ruling-caucus-since-1993-2.

McConnell, Rick. 2016. "Impassioned Sandra Jansen Calls on Legislature to Stand against Misogyny." *CBC News.* http://www.cbc.ca/news/canada/edmonton/ impassioned-sandra-jansen-calls-on-legislature-to-stand-against-misogyny -1.3863097.

Parliament of Canada. 2017. "Women in the Provincial and Territorial Legislatures: Current List." http://www.lop.parl.gc.ca/ParlInfo/compilations/ProvinceTerritory/ Women.aspx?Province=edad4077-a735-48ad-982e-1dcad72f51b6&Current =True.

Power, Samantha. 2013. "Alberta Fails to Consult on Consultation Policy." *Straight Goods.* http://sgnews.ca/2013/06/03/alberta-fails-to-consult-on-consultation -policy/.

Ramsay, Caley, and Phil Heidenreich. 2016. "Alberta MLA Derek Fildebrandt Suspended from Wildrose Caucus over 'Unacceptable' Social Media Comment." *Global News.* http://globalnews.ca/news/2727371/alberta-mla-derek-fildebrandt -suspended-from-wildrose-caucus-over-unacceptable-social-media-comment/.

Revenue Canada. 2017. "Canadian Income Tax Rates for Individuals – Current and Previous Years." https://www.canada.ca/en/revenue-agency/services/tax/ individuals/frequently-asked-questions-individuals/canadian-income-tax -rates-individuals-current-previous-years.html.

Revenu Québec. 2017. "Income Tax Rates." http://www.revenuquebec.ca/en/citoyen/ situation/nouvel-arrivant/regime-fiscal-du-quebec/taux-imposition.aspx.

Sinnema, Jodie. 2015a. "Gender Variance, Drag Queens and Cisgender: Alberta Legislature's Lexicon Expands." *Edmonton Journal.* http://edmontonjournal.com/

news/politics/gender-variance-drag-queens-and-cisgender-the-language-of
-the-legislature-like-youve-never-heard-before.

—. 2015b. "Gender Identity, Expression to Be Protected in Alberta Human Rights
Code." *Edmonton Journal.* http://edmontonjournal.com/news/politics/gender
-identity-expression-to-be-protected-in-alberta-human-rights-code.

Southwick, Reid. 2015. "NDP Government Will 'Build Feminism in Alberta,' Status
of Women Minister Says." *Calgary Herald.* http://calgaryherald.com/news/
local-news/ndp-government-will-build-feminism-in-alberta-status-of-women
-minister-says.

Statistics Canada. 2017. "Labour Force, Employment and Unemployment, Level
and Rates, by Province." http://www.statcan.gc.ca/tables-tableaux/sum-som/l01/
cst01/labor07b-eng.htm.

Status of Women Alberta. 2016. "Annual Report, 2015–16." https://open.alberta.
ca/dataset/723a2178-45b3-4280-b2bc-506dec99c300/resource/08d1404c-3614
-41dc-9340-c4e39cb2d444/download/Status-of-Women-Annual-Report-2015
-16.pdf.

—. 2017a. "Business Plan 2017-20: Status of Women." http://finance.alberta.ca/"pub-
lications/budget/budget2017/status-of-women.pdf.

—. 2017b. "Annual Report, 2016-17." https://open.alberta.ca/dataset/723a2178-45b3
-4280-b2bc-506dec99c300/resource/efbbf26d-2075-4410-ac48-017aca
6a3caa/download/Status-of-Women-annual-report-2016-17.pdf.

Status of Women Canada. 2017. "Who We Are." http://www.swc-cfc.gc.ca/abu-ans/
who-qui/index-en.html.

Stevenson, Scott. 2017. "Province Announces Support for Families of Murdered
Indigenous Women in Alberta." *CBC News.* http://www.cbc.ca/news/canada/
edmonton/richard-feehan-missing-murdered-liaison-unit-1.4124854.

Stewart, David. 2017. "Where Leaders Matter More Than Party." *Alberta Views.*
https://albertaviews.ca/leaders-matter-party/.

Stewart, David, and Keith Archer. 2003. *Quasi-Democracy? Parties and Leadership
Selection in Alberta.* Vancouver: UBC Press.

Stewart, David, and Anthony Sayers. 2009. "Leadership Change in a Dominant
Party: The Alberta Progressive Conservatives, 2006." *Canadian Political Science
Review* 3, 4: 85–107.

—. 2013. "Breaking the Peace: The Wildrose Alliance in Alberta Politics." *Canadian
Political Science Review* 7, 1: 73–86.

Thomas, Melanee. 2019. "Ready for Rachel: The 2015 Alberta NDP Campaign." In
The Orange Chinook: The Politics of the New Alberta, ed. Duane Bratt, Keith
Brownsey, Richard Sutherland, and David Taras. Calgary: University of Calgary
Press.

Thomson, Graham. 2017. "Partisan Job, Public Pay: Why do leaders need an army of
politicized staff when there's a giant civil service at their disposal?" *Alberta Views.*
https://albertaviews.ca/partisan-job-public-pay/.

—. 2018. "If Only MLA Robyn Luff Had Called Brent Rathgeber before Ending Her
Political Career." *CBC News.* https://www.cbc.ca/news/canada/edmonton/robyn
-luff-mla-ndp-alberta-1.4898256.

Thomson, Stuart. 2017. "Government Cites CEO Pay and Bonuses at Agencies, Boards and Commissions." *Edmonton Journal.* http://edmontonjournal.com/news/politics/government-cuts-ceo-pay-and-bonuses-at-agencies-boards-and-commissions.

Trynacity, Kim. 2017. "Rachel Notley: Alberta's Most Threatened Premier." *CBC News.* http://www.cbc.ca/news/canada/edmonton/notley-threats-alberta-history-1.3982276.

–. 2018. "'A Wake-Up Call': Documents Detail Litany of Threats against Premier Rachel Notley." *CBC News.* http://www.cbc.ca/news/canada/edmonton/notley-premier-threats-security-1.46449898.

UToday. 2016. "Public Members Appointed to University of Calgary Board of Governors." 16 December. https://www.ucalgary.ca/utoday/issue/2016-12-16/public-members-appointed-university-calgary-board-governors.

Vernon, Tom. 2016. "Alberta NDP Platform: What's Done and What's Left to Do." *Global News.* http://globalnews.ca/news/3032583/alberta-ndp-platform-whats-done-and-whats-left-to-do/.

Wells, Paul. "My Name Is Rachel Notley." *Maclean's.* http://www.macleans.ca/news/canada/my-name-is-rachel-notley/.

Wood, James. 2017. "Two Years after Provincial Election, NDP and Calgary Still Have Uneasy Relationship." *Calgary Herald.* http://calgaryherald.com/news/politics/two-years-after-provincial-election-ndp-and-calgary-still-have-uneasy-relationship.

Young, Lisa, and William Cross. 2003. "Women's Involvement in Canada's Political Parties." In *Women and Electoral Politics in Canada*, ed. Manon Tremblay and Linda Trimble, 92–109. Don Mills: Oxford University Press.

PART 5
DRAWING CONCLUSIONS

12

Doing Politics Differently?

SYLVIA BASHEVKIN

The eleven premiers considered in this volume governed a total of six provinces and three territories – diverse jurisdictions ranging from densely ur-
banized to sparsely populated, and from fiercely partisan to officially non-
partisan and consensus-based – extending across Canada's massive latitude
as well as longitude. The challenges female leaders faced varied greatly between 1991, when Rita Johnston in BC and Nellie Cournoyea in the NWT
were sworn into office, and early 2018, when Kathleen Wynne in Ontario
and Rachel Notley in Alberta held power. This chapter focuses on shared
themes that permit us to assess more than twenty-five years of women making history in jurisdictions that directly shape the daily lives of Canadians.

My discussion considers each of the core questions presented in Chapter 1. I begin by examining the circumstances of public leadership. How did
different levels of party competitiveness shape women's access to power at
the subnational level? In what ways has the ideological positioning of parties
influenced women's ability to gain and retain power? How do the empirical
cases explored in this volume illuminate findings concerning the shorter
average tenure of women than men leaders of parties in Canada (see O'Neill
and Stewart 2009)?

I then probe how women lead. Does the tenor of political debate become
more conciliatory when female premiers govern? Or when women lead
multiple parties in a single legislature? Do policy outcomes change with the
presence of female premiers, perhaps to the point that they operate as

critical actors on feminist issues (Childs and Krook 2009)? How, if at all, do women leaders alter patterns of candidate, cabinet, and senior bureaucratic recruitment?

The purpose of Chapter 12 is to address the larger themes that underpin this book, using empirical data available as of spring 2018. Has it made a difference that a handful of women reached top levels of political responsibility in Canada's provinces and territories? If so, what are the main features of that difference? How can future scholarship contribute to our understanding of women's impact?

Assessing Circumstances

One key conclusion is that, despite the many obstacles detailed in the substantive chapters of this volume, more women became subnational leaders across Canada as time passed. As reported in Table 12.1, the opportunity for scholars to undertake a serious comparative assessment of female premiers barely existed prior to 2008. Between 1991 and 2007, a total of four women reached top political executive posts in provinces and territories. Two of the four, Rita Johnston and Pat Duncan, were only in office very briefly: Johnston for about seven months and Duncan for less than 2.5 years. These short tenures help to explain how the average period in power for the first four female premiers in Canada was 2.7 years (see Table 12.1).

Following Eva Aariak's selection as Nunavut premier in 2008, the chance for academics to evaluate female leaders at the subnational level expanded dramatically. Seven premiers, beginning with Aariak, were sworn into office beginning in 2008, and a number of them – notably Christy Clark and Kathleen Wynne – remained in office for much longer periods than Johnston or Duncan. As of April 2018, the average time in power for female premiers since 2008 was 3.8 years, or more than a full year longer than for their predecessors (see Table 12.1).

This finding does not mean that it became easier for women to win and retain power in Canada's provinces and territories. As revealed in Table 12.1, days in office for earlier as well as more recent political executives varied a great deal. Among the earliest premiers, Nellie Cournoyea and Catherine Callbeck held the keys to their respective premiers' suites more than six times longer than Johnston. Among more recent leaders, Christy Clark held the keys nearly five times longer than Pauline Marois.

Table 12.1 also shows that no premier after Johnston, the only leader in this study not to win an electoral mandate of her own, served less than one year. Moreover, the number of leaders who emulated Cournoyea's record of

TABLE 12.1
Women premiers by days in office, 1991–2018

Name	First elected as subnational legislator	Sworn in as premier	Left office as premier	Days in office as premier
Rita Johnston	5 May 1983	2 April 1991	5 November 1991	217
Nellie Cournoyea	1 October 1979	14 November 1991	22 November 1995	1,468
Catherine Callbeck	29 April 1974	25 January 1993	9 October 1996	1,353
Pat Duncan	30 September 1996	5 June 2000	30 November 2002	883
Eva Aariak	27 October 2008	19 November 2008	19 November 2013	1,826
Kathy Dunderdale	21 October 2003	3 December 2010	24 January 2014	1,147
Christy Clark	16 May 2001	14 March 2011	18 July 2017	2,316
Alison Redford	3 March 2008	7 October 2011	23 March 2014	897
Pauline Marois	13 April 1981	19 September 2012	23 April 2014	581
Kathleen Wynne*	2 October 2003	11 February 2013	29 June 2018	1,872
Rachel Notley*	3 March 2008	24 May 2015	n/a	1,039

* Days in office calculated as of 1 April 2018. First four premiers spent an average of 970 days in office, compared with 1,383 for seven premiers in office beginning in 2008.

Source: "List of female first ministers in Canada," *Wikipedia*, https://en.wikipedia.org/wiki/List_of_female_first_ministers_in_Canada.

surpassing four years in power grew over time to include Aariak, Clark, and Wynne. This increase in the number of premiers and the length of their terms in office permits comparative research within Canada since it enriches the pool of evidence concerning the policies of women premiers, their recruitment strategies, and the impact they had on the tenor of political debate.

Many factors shape the political longevity and legacy of government leaders. Consistent with the larger academic literature on women and politics, Chapter 1 pays close attention to party competitiveness. That variable distinguishes among premiers who led parties in empowered, imperiled, or pioneering circumstances. Table 12.2 summarizes outcomes for the nine women who were active in party- as opposed to consensus-based systems, meaning all jurisdictions considered in this volume except for the NWT and Nunavut. It shows that the two Atlantic Canadian leaders who succeeded charismatic men leading popular governing parties, Callbeck in PEI and Dunderdale in Newfoundland and Labrador, indeed won majority mandates in the next general election.

Yet Tables 12.1 and 12.2, along with material in Chapters 5 and 6, reveal that neither Callbeck nor Dunderdale served a full term as party leader despite having secured a strong electoral mandate of her own. In addition, Table 12.2 shows that both the PEI Liberals and the NL PCs lost power in the election that followed the woman premier's resignation: voters in PEI chose a PC majority government while in NL they elected a Liberal majority. Callbeck led her party through a general election campaign two months after becoming party leader, while Dunderdale had the writs dropped ten months after being sworn in.

Detailed case studies in Chapters 5 and 6 suggest that leaders in empowered circumstances were challenged by the impatience of political insiders. As members of veteran governing formations, PEI Liberals and NL PCs were accustomed to holding power and falling in line behind charismatic men who secured adherents of those organizations with advantages that accrue from being in power. Chapters 5 and 6 demonstrate how party elites as well as journalists and members of the attentive public lost patience with women leaders who were in charge when the proverbial cookie began to crumble.

Although Callbeck and Dunderdale succeeded popular leaders in what looked like empowered circumstances, it seems they were not personally empowered by those scenarios. Both women left provincial politics under a shadow that followed neither from a scandal that was associated with them

TABLE 12.2

Women premiers by party circumstances and election results, 1991–2018

Year sworn in	Name	Party	Favoured to lead party	Party circumstances	Months before next election*	Election result	Subsequent election result
1991	Rita Johnston	BC Social Credit	No	Imperiled	7	NDP majority	NDP majority
1993	Catherine Callbeck	PEI Liberal	Yes	Empowered	2	Liberal majority	PC majority
2000	Pat Duncan	Yukon Liberal	Yes	Pioneering	–	Liberal majority	Yukon Party majority
2010	Kathy Dunderdale	Newfoundland PC	Yes	Empowered	10	PC majority	Liberal majority
2011	Christy Clark	BC Liberal	No	Imperiled	26	Liberal majority	NDP minority
2011	Alison Redford	Alberta PC	No	Imperiled	6.5	PC majority	NDP majority
2012	Pauline Marois	Parti Québécois	Yes	Imperiled	–	PQ minority	Liberal majority
2013	Kathleen Wynne	Ontario Liberal	No	Imperiled	16	Liberal majority	PC majority
2015	Rachel Notley	Alberta NDP	Yes	Pioneering	–	NDP majority	n/a

* For parties in power when a woman became party leader.

Source: Materials on public record.

as individuals nor from any other allegation of malfeasance on their part. The main problem Callbeck and Dunderdale faced was, as the authors of Chapter 6 suggest, the need to operate in the wake of male charisma. Simply put, it was hard for any woman to fill the "big shoes" left by the "big man," whether Joe Ghiz in PEI or Danny Williams in NL.

Could a male successor have lasted a full term and won power again? That question remains unanswerable. What stands out on the historical record is that when Ghiz and Williams stepped down, PEI Liberals and NL PCs saw Callbeck and Dunderdale as the best candidates to succeed them. As shown in Table 12.3, both women brought extensive legislative and cabinet experience to the role of premier. Yet being the favoured candidate to succeed a strong party leader, having lots of prior service in parliament and government, and then winning a majority government of one's own were not sufficient to keep women premiers in office for a full term.

Callbeck and Dunderdale thus fell from grace despite, from the perspective of party competitiveness, arriving under promising circumstances. This shared turn of events offers a salutary perspective on leadership in Canada. Even though they reached the premier's suite in what seemed like a best case scenario, Premiers Callbeck and Dunderdale departed the public stage amidst sustained public as well as internal party criticism. Both resigned, but the narratives suggest that they were strongly pressed to do so. And, as reported in Table 12.1, their average time as premiers in empowered circumstances was only slightly longer (1,250 days) than that of leaders at the helm of imperiled parties (1,143 days).

Considerable variation exists among the five premiers who led parties facing hard times. As Tracy Summerville argues in Chapter 9, it was often beneficial in imperiled circumstances for new leaders taking over a governing party to have a significant period in office before going to the polls. That time offered women an opportunity to distinguish themselves from their embattled predecessors. Summerville's account of BC politics shows that seven months were insufficient for Rita Johnston to build a profile independent of former Social Credit leader Bill Vander Zalm. By comparison, twenty-six months offered Christy Clark far more time to create a reputation distinct from that of departed Liberal leader Gordon Campbell (see Table 12.2). Neither Johnston nor Clark was favoured to win her respective party leadership race, but Johnston's long association with Vander Zalm made it harder for her to establish distance than it was for Clark – who had resigned from Campbell's cabinet years before contesting the top post.

TABLE 12.3

Occupational and public service backgrounds of women premiers, 1991–2018

Name	Occupational background	Public service background
Aariak	Language teacher, retail store owner	Nunavut Languages Commissioner; Chamber of Commerce president
Callbeck	Business teacher, co-owner of family business	PEI legislator; PEI cabinet minister; federal MP
Clark	Newspaper columnist, radio show host	BC legislator; BC cabinet minister
Cournoyea	Radio journalist, radio station manager, land claims specialist	NWT legislator; NWT cabinet minister
Duncan	Small business owner	Chamber of Commerce director; assistant to federal cabinet minister; Yukon legislator
Dunderdale	Social worker	President of NL PC Party; local councillor; NL legislator; NL cabinet minister
Johnston	Co-owner of family business	City councillor; BC legislator; BC cabinet minister
Marois	Social worker, launched community TV station	Active in Quebec feminist federation; Quebec legislator; Quebec cabinet minister
Notley	Labour lawyer	Worked for trade unions; Alberta legislator
Redford	Constitutional law and human rights advisor	Advisor to federal cabinet minister and prime minister; Alberta legislator; Alberta cabinet minister
Wynne	Mediator, adult educator	Community activist; school trustee; Ontario legislator; Ontario cabinet minister

Source: Materials on public record; data presented in Chapters 2 through 11 of this volume.

Summerville's thesis helps to explain Kathleen Wynne's ability to return the Ontario Liberals to majority government status sixteen months after becoming leader. Like Johnston and Clark, Wynne was not seen as the most likely candidate to become party head. Parallel with Clark's trajectory, she used the time between securing the premier's job and winning her own electoral mandate to reshape public images of the provincial Liberal Party.

The passage of time can also benefit the leader of an imperiled party in opposition. Chapter 7 shows how Pauline Marois contested the Parti Québécois leadership multiple times and won on her third try – by acclamation in late 2008. In the next provincial election, she led the PQ from third-party status to a higher share of the popular vote, more legislative seats, and official opposition status in the National Assembly. In the subsequent 2012 election, nearly four years after Marois became party leader, the PQ won a minority government. The period between 2008 and 2012 thus provided Marois with opportunities both to make her mark as PQ head and to benefit from the collapse of the governing Liberals.

The case of Alison Redford stands out because it deviates somewhat from the thesis proposed by Summerville. As leader of the Alberta PCs for less than seven months when she went to the polls, Redford won a majority government for a party that had already held power for more than forty years. As Clark Banack argues in Chapter 10, Redford successfully portrayed the leading Alberta opposition party at the time – the Wildrose Party – as a greater threat to the province's future than the faltering PC dynasty. Consistent with Summerville's thesis, Redford held a valuable advantage similar to that of Clark and Wynne: she was an outsider candidate for party leadership and not expected to win. These factors were helpful in that they served to distance Redford from her predecessor, Ed Stelmach.

The fact that Marois and Redford became the elected premiers of their provinces with the shortest ever tenures in office reveals another way in which timing shapes leaders in imperiled circumstances. Whatever legislative and cabinet experience women brought to the top job in these formations – and here Marois stood out for having been the "Minister of Everything" in PQ governments dating back to the Lévesque years, they nevertheless faced a clock that was not ticking to their advantage (see Mercier 2012). In short, parties facing what looks like an imminent political expiry date might be in a downward spiral that is not recoverable no matter how much talent, experience, and commitment new leaders bring. Internal factional splits are often loud and intense, as Philippe Bernier Arcand shows was the case inside the PQ regarding issues of "reasonable accommodation" while Marois was premier (see Chapter 7).

Voters in these situations often insist on regime change – a circumstance that Redford's PC successor faced in Alberta in 2015, when the provincial election yielded an NDP majority. As discussed in Chapter 1, pioneers lead long-term opposition parties that come to power in surprising turns of events. Rachel Notley in Alberta was one such premier, as was what Maura

Forrest terms the "accidental premier" of Yukon, Pat Duncan (see Chapter 3). Pioneers operate with neither the shadow cast by a previous premier from the same party nor the experience that comes from long years as a government backbencher or cabinet minister. Duncan's record of less than 2.5 years in office suggests that the absence of governing experience can severely limit the ability of pioneers to retain power.

Notley's popularity rating at 28 percent in 2017 constituted the second weakest among all Canadian premiers. Wynne in Ontario stood at the top of the unpopularity rankings with a 15 percent public approval rating (Wood 2017). Low resource prices and struggles over moving those products to tidewater created serious problems for Notley – as they likely would have for any Alberta premier. Future analysts will be able to examine Notley's full record in office in order to assess the significance of her leading a long-term opposition party.

What remains noteworthy is the clustering of female premiers in the lowest tier of public approval ratings. In 2017, Wynne had served as government leader for more than four years and had brought to the job extensive experience in diverse cabinet posts. By comparison, Notley had no track record in cabinet prior to becoming premier in 2015. She led the major party of the left in Alberta politics, while Wynne's party roots rested in the progressive wing of the Ontario Liberals. The fact that both became party leaders reinforces research findings to the effect that left and centre-left parties are often more congenial to women's ascent than are right and centre-right parties (see O'Neill and Stewart 2009).

Yet conditions that permit women to become leaders of progressive and moderate parties appear to co-exist with other, highly disadvantageous circumstances. Voters and political analysts were harshly critical of Wynne and Notley – to the point that both faced heightened threats of physical harm. As Melanee Thomas documents in Chapter 11, Notley received an unprecedented number of violent threats. Media reports indicate Wynne faced dozens of serious "security incidents" after becoming premier based on her gender and sexual orientation (Dawson 2017).

Like most other premiers addressed in this volume, Notley and Wynne were mothers at the time they held top office.[1] The threats women face as mothers and politicians are examined in Thomas and Lambert (2017, 148), who report that, because of safety concerns, federal MPs in Canada avoided posting the names and photographs of their children on the internet. The fact that two contemporary provincial premiers were widely and often intensely disliked is also consistent with international data gathered by the

National Democratic Institute (NDI), a non-profit organization based in Washington, DC, that seeks to strengthen democratic political institutions. According to NDI research, violence and threats of violence against women in politics are specific, targeted phenomena that try to exclude female participants in order to restore a traditional hierarchy of male public leaders. Consistent with patterns revealed in Chapters 5 and 6, NDI data indicate insiders in women's own political parties are often major contributors to efforts to marginalize them.[2]

These trends lead me now to consider how women lead and, more significantly, how they are perceived to lead.

Tone and Style

For women and girls, socialization processes typically stress nurturing other people and finding common ground with them. These emphases can be seen as encouraging behaviour that differs from the norms of political interaction in Westminster parliamentary systems. Divergent patterns of professional employment offer an additional basis for expectations that female and male leaders will vary: women politicians tend to come from occupational backgrounds such as teaching, journalism, and social work that are unlike the usual ones for men – namely, law and business. As summarized in Chapter 1, expectations that women leaders will operate in less conflictual ways than their male counterparts contrast with institutional arguments. The latter suggest that parties and legislatures are highly gendered, with the result that strong pressures to conform make it hard even for change-oriented leaders to be transformative, including with respect to the climate of political debate (see Krook and Mackay 2011).

Table 12.3 summarizes the occupational backgrounds of women premiers in Canada. It shows that six of the eleven had work experiences that resembled those of many men in politics: Aariak, Callbeck, Duncan, and Johnston all owned or co-owned businesses while Notley and Redford practised law. The other five came from fields that historically were more welcoming towards women than law and business – namely, communications (Clark, Cournoyea), social work (Dunderdale, Marois), and mediation/education (Wynne). The fact that a majority of female premiers worked in business and law, the same fields that long dominated the backgrounds of male politicians in Canada and elsewhere, suggests their occupational training would tend to support rather than unsettle the ways in which politics was practised.

Eight chapters of this volume consider party-based systems outside the NWT and Nunavut. As summarized in Table 12.4, they indicate that the

TABLE 12.4

Women premiers by tenor of debate, public policy, and recruitment measures, 1991–2018

Sworn in	Name	Tenor of political debate	Policy record	Recruitment record
1991	Johnston	Polarized climate remains	Throne speech contains promises but party loses next election	More women candidates for party than under predecessor
1991	Cournoyea	Tries to avoid personal attacks when criticized	Limited attention to social policy	Emphasizes individual merit over group representation
1993	Callbeck	Challenged by media and own party insiders	Major cuts to social spending	One other woman in cabinet
2000	Duncan	Highly partisan environment remains	Fiscal pressures divert attention from social policy	Unintentional gender parity cabinet
2008	Aariak	Tries to avoid personal attacks when criticized	Extensive consultation process yields few results	Little change in women's participation
2010	Dunderdale	Highly partisan environment remains	Sustained focus on energy projects diverts attention from other areas	Parity among deputy ministers, decline in female candidates and cabinet ministers
2011	Clark	Polarized climate remains	Emphasizes economic growth over social spending	More women candidates and cabinet ministers, little change on deputy ministers
2011	Redford	More acrimonious tenor of debate than earlier	Incremental progress on violence, gender-based budgeting	More women candidates but fewer female cabinet ministers and deputy ministers

▶

Sworn in	Name	Tenor of political debate	Policy record	Recruitment record
2012	Marois	Extremely contentious tenor including internal party divisions	Feminist federation condemns proposed Quebec charter of values	Fewer women as cabinet ministers and party candidates
2013	Wynne	Elevated security threats; legislative climate remains contentious	Some spending on violence, action on pay transparency, promise of action on child care	More women ministers and candidates, little change on deputy ministers
2015	Notley	Extremely hostile environment with threats to premier's security	Separate women's department and gender policy lens introduced	Gender parity in candidates as well as cabinet appointments

Source: Data presented in Chapters 2 through 11 of this volume.

presence of female premiers did not shift the climate of political debate in a conciliatory direction. Provinces such as BC and Alberta, long characterized by strong ideological polarization, remained deeply split along left/right lines while Johnston, Clark, Redford, and Notley governed. Legislatures in Yukon, PEI, and NL, where strong personalities historically clashed across the aisle, continued to feature heated partisan exchanges under Premiers Duncan, Callbeck, and Dunderdale. In Ontario's three-party system, tense divisions between opposition parties and government continued while Wynne served as premier. In Quebec, conflicts between pro-federal and pro-sovereignty interests as well as among independentists were sharply defined during the tenure of Premier Marois.

The presence of female opposition leaders did not seem to moderate these directions and might, at some level, have exacerbated them. As Banack argues in Chapter 10, Redford won a majority government by portraying Danielle Smith and her Wildrose Party as right-wing extremists. Don Desserud and Robin Sutherland suggest in Chapter 5 that Callbeck's ability to prevail over Pat Mella led the PEI PCs to recruit a strong male leader who defeated the Liberals in the next election. Bashevkin reports in Chapter 8 that the climate of the Ontario legislature during Wynne's tenure was not at all conciliatory: more MPPs were ejected more frequently from the house than under her predecessor, and women opposition members expressed particular frustration with what they saw as Wynne's unyielding approach.

Kim Campbell, as a federal PC leadership candidate, held that women "do politics differently"; some female premiers, including Cournoyea in the NWT and Aariak in Nunavut, stated similar views (see Campbell 1996). Yet the need to move legislation forward, to lead a cabinet, and to steer a bureaucracy required premiers in party as well as consensus systems to wield power in structures not of their own creation. Given that they were responsible for making these institutions work, women premiers tended to adopt many of the same repertoires as did the men who preceded and succeeded them.

This trend seems to apply not just to women with backgrounds in business and law but also to those coming from "pink collar," or female-dominated, professions. For instance, Chapter 8 reveals that Wynne's background as a mediator and adult educator did not prevent her from closing off debate in the Ontario legislature through the use of time allocation measures. Nor did it lower the heat of discussion, at least as measured by the number and frequency of ejections of MPPs from the legislature while she served as premier.

In order to gauge the tenor of debate, we also need to consider what happens outside legislatures. Data in this volume on party systems are consistent with NDI findings cited earlier in that they indicate fewer constraints on the targeting of female than on the targeting of male politicians (see National Democratic Institute 2018). Journalists' accounts of Premier Dunderdale, for example, seemed more harsh and unforgiving than the norm in the already rough-and-tumble world of NL politics. The number and severity of violent threats directed at Rachel Notley stood out because they required heightened security protection. As Thomas argues in Chapter 11, the hostility directed in Alberta at female politicians was not limited to Notley – other women (including Wynne as a visiting Ontario premier) were also targeted. Patterns examined earlier in this chapter confirm that Wynne and Notley tended to be judged more negatively by voters than did male premiers who held office at the same time.

Did the situation differ in consensus-based systems? In the NWT and Nunavut, both female premiers came from Indigenous backgrounds. In Chapter 2, Graham White describes the ways in which Cournoyea led a productive NWT government despite challenging political and economic circumstances. Her governing style combined collective, or team, effort with listening to the general public and strong personal leadership. In Chapter 4,

Sheena Kennedy Dalseg discusses Aariak's efforts to consult widely on improvements to governance in Nunavut, also within a context of major constraints on what territorial leaders could accomplish. Like Cournoyea, Aariak was a collaborative leader who actively sought other perspectives.

As reported in Table 12.1, the average time in office for women premiers in the NWT and Nunavut was about 4.5 years (1,647 days), or more than a usual parliamentary term. Table 12.3 shows that Aariak had been Nunavut languages commissioner and Chamber of Commerce president before her political career, while Cournoyea had worked as a land claims specialist, NWT legislator, and NWT cabinet minister before becoming premier. Even these experienced women leaders from Indigenous backgrounds, however, were limited in their ability to foster political cooperation in consensus-based systems within which they held power for significant periods of time. As Chapter 2 reports, Cournoyea was criticized as tough and demanding and, at the same time, as indecisive because she failed to remove underperforming members of her cabinet. Chapter 4 notes that Aariak was seen as lacking direction and not accomplishing much.

These examples illustrate the dangers for women leaders of being seen as too collaborative – including in environments that emphasize cooperation and empowering local communities. No matter how well-developed their consultative skills, Cournoyea and Aariak were still seen as deficient. Critics considered them either as too meandering and not sufficiently decisive or else as too demanding and too tough. In some instances, the conclusion that they were ineffective decision makers was grounded in highly contradictory portrayals of their leadership skills.

Women leaders in party systems were subject to similarly mixed messages. In Yukon, Duncan was condemned for consulting too much and also for being autocratic. Marois was criticized as a populist who paid too much attention to public demands that immigrants integrate into the host society. After expanding her party's electoral base beyond its usual parameters, Redford was chastised for relying too heavily on advice from beyond the PC establishment.

Premiers examined in this volume thus confronted critics who questioned not just their likeability but also their core competence and suitability. Given a sustained level of scrutiny both inside and outside the legislature, women who led party- as well as consensus-based systems needed to find ways to steer legislation through a contentious parliament, build cabinet solidarity, reach out to political insiders, and win favourable press coverage. At each step along the way, female premiers contended with the reality that few of the individuals with whom they interacted had ever dealt with women at the apex of power. The people they faced likely felt uneasy or – at the very least – inexperienced in the presence of a powerful woman (see Bashevkin 2009). This discomfort revealed itself in varied ways documented in the preceding chapters, ranging from inappropriate and intemperate remarks by other lawmakers to biased accounts by political observers to hostility and violent threats directed against women leaders by outraged citizens.

Overall, leaders considered in this book did not make the tenor of debate in Canada's provinces and territories either more conciliatory or less divisive; instead, some of the dynamics suggest it was remarkable that women premiers had the courage to step forward day after day onto the public stage. Looking to the future, the presence of more female decision makers seems unlikely to change the ways in which powerful women are viewed by fellow parliamentarians, political analysts, or voters. In particular, the anger and hateful threats directed against progressive leaders in Alberta and Ontario appear not just beyond the ability of individual women to mitigate but also deserving of much closer public attention and censure.

Public Policies

Parallel with comparative research on the ideological correlates of policy action, contributors to this book find that leaders on the centre-left and left were more likely than those on the right to "act for" equality interests. As detailed in Chapter 11, Notley's record as an Alberta New Democrat stands out for its consistent attention to the gender dimension of social and economic policies. Notley introduced a gender lens to government decision making and created a separate women's department with its own deputy minister. These changes unfolded at the same time as the NDP increased spending on violence against women policies and created a pilot child care program. Given Notley's commitment to women's equality considerations, Thomas finds her priorities to be consistent with those of a critical actor.

Moving towards the centre-left of the ideological spectrum, Wynne's record as a social Liberal in Ontario included efforts on violence against women and sex education. With respect to equal pay and child care, her government initially held public consultations and promised action at some point in the future. On the brink of a 2018 provincial election that their party lost, Ontario Liberals announced a bill to promote greater pay transparency as well as a plan to fund daycare for children beginning at age two and a half (Ebner 2018; Giovannetti et al. 2018). Given that the Ontario Liberals had been in power for about fifteen years at the point of those announcements, Wynne's willingness to press ahead in the areas of employment and child care was portrayed as an electoral strategy to sway progressive voters (Radwanski 2018). It can also be seen as continuing previous Liberal policies that stood between more consistently interventionist NDP platforms and more laissez-faire conservative positions. In terms of the machinery of government, Wynne increased spending on the Ontario Women's Directorate but reduced expenditures for the Pay Equity Commission. In short, she pursued some actions that resonated with a critical actor repertoire.

As Chapter 7 demonstrates, Marois's centre-left and critical actor record as minister of education contrasted with more traditionally nationalist directions as premier. Having developed and implemented a five-dollar-per-day child care scheme in the late 1990s, Marois ranked among North America's most transformative social policy actors. Feminist positions as a minister on child care and women's labour market participation, however, contrasted with her opposition as premier to intersectional understandings of discrimination against women. Many progressives opposed Marois's proposal for a Quebec charter of secular values – including feminists with whom she had once worked in the province's women's federation. This contrast reflects not only the changing currents of women's movement politics but also the divergence between her actions as a minister versus as a premier.

Three business-oriented Liberals – Callbeck, Clark, and Duncan – all expressed concern at some point for women and families but were less inclined than social Liberals such as Wynne to channel public resources in those directions. Duncan and Callbeck faced fiscal pressures that limited their ability to allocate new monies: tough times pressed both leaders to consider contentious budget reductions in such fields as health and education. Clark was arguably the most conservative of the five Liberal premiers considered in this book: she led BC's party of the right, which fiercely opposed the NDP on the left. Clark's consistent message was that creating jobs and a prosperous economy offered the best support for women and families.

PC premiers Dunderdale and Redford resembled the three business-oriented Liberals. Both sought to expand or at least to stabilize resource-based economies, a priority that took precedence in their governments over social policy. While Redford made incremental progress on violence against women and gender-based budgeting, her emphasis on these issues was measurably less than what occurred under Alberta's subsequent NDP government. As BC premier for about seven months, Johnston had little opportunity to act on rhetoric contained in her government's throne speech. Moreover, the conservative values of BC's Social Credit Party mean Johnston was unlikely to alter policies in ways demanded by pro-equality interests – even if she had secured more time in office.

The two premiers in consensus-based systems, Cournoyea and Aariak, differed somewhat in ideological terms. As a strong individualist who elevated personal initiative above group rights, Cournoyea emphasized economic development rather than social policy. By contrast, Aariak seemed more concerned about social policy. The extensive consultation process Aariak convened to produce a report card on Nunavut, however, ultimately yielded few policy results.

As reported in Table 12.4, our finding that the actions of only a minority of women premiers consistently advanced equality policies may surprise some readers. Campaigns by Equal Voice and other organizations for more women in politics tend to link gender representation of a substantive variety with the election of more female legislators. Yet data reported in this volume suggest the physical presence of a woman in the Office of the Premier is far from sufficient to create significant action on equality issues.

Echoing comparative scholarship on women in politics, this volume recalls the legacy of leaders such as Margaret Thatcher. Women politicians on the political right, like Thatcher, tend to be strong individualists who do not identify with progressive group-based interests such as organized feminism. Conservatives usually favour approaches to problems that are grounded in personal responsibility, human initiative, and unfettered markets as opposed to expansive, often expensive, government programs (see Bashevkin 1998). Canadian conservatives such as Redford may admire, resemble, and emulate Thatcher – notably by rejecting the idea that gender matters to the style or content of policy action. In some instances, their track records in office support that view.

For centrist politicians, gender sometimes makes a more significant difference – although not necessarily at the pinnacle of leadership, as the Marois case demonstrates. Gradations within the moderate middle can also be relevant, as is shown by our comparison of Kathleen Wynne as a social Liberal with Catherine Callbeck, Christy Clark, and Pat Duncan as more business-oriented Liberals. The experiences of Marois and Wynne in social movement politics is likely influential as well in this calculus. Both were active in their early years in progressive mobilizations that sought to change government agendas from the outside. This campaigning background probably made Marois and Wynne more open than others in their respective parties to extra-parliamentary influences and hence more responsive, at various points, to feminist claims.

Notley's initial record reinforces earlier research on the overlap between left parties and equality policies. As Alberta's first NDP premier, she made clear upon arriving in power her commitment to substantive as well as to procedural change. Notley reorganized the provincial cabinet and bureaucracy in order to deliver on her promises, including by insisting on the use of a gender lens in policy discussions.

Data presented by chapter authors show a number of women premiers talked about doing politics differently, yet few produced results that measurably transformed the daily lives of women and girls. Notley stands alone as the only NDP premier considered in this study, and she was a critical actor who placed equality considerations at the core of her government's priorities. Yet eco-feminists concerned with the environmental consequences of energy development in Alberta – especially critics of building more pipelines to carry those resources – would not endorse core elements of her agenda. Researchers in the future will be able to probe the consequences of Notley's decisions in greater depth, having a lengthier track record as well as knowledge of how her legacy fared under subsequent Alberta governments.

Recruitment Patterns

Did premiers promote other women? This volume divides that question into three component parts concerning political candidates, cabinet members, and deputy ministers. We find the following: first, early female leaders in Canada's provinces and territories did significantly less on the recruitment front than more recent leaders; second, Premiers Clark, Wynne, and Notley were alone in raising women's numbers in at least two categories.

In terms of the longitudinal story, Premiers Johnston, Cournoyea, Callbeck, Duncan, and Aariak did not champion women's engagement in the senior civil service or elective office. Female candidates for the BC Social Credit Party were more numerous when Johnston was leader than under her predecessor, but Johnston did not publicly intervene to facilitate such an outcome. Duncan led Canada's first parity cabinet but insists that those appointments were a function of political experience as she never sought out women for half her political executive seats. Little positive change in numbers occurred under Cournoyea, Aariak, or Callbeck. Each of these premiers took office in 2008 or earlier.

Leaders who took the oath of office in 2010 and following were more likely to oversee improvements in women's representation as candidates, ministers, or deputy ministers. Dunderdale's government reached gender parity in the ranks of deputy ministers, even though the numbers of female PC candidates and cabinet members declined. Wynne appointed more women to cabinet, but candidacies in 2014 were lower than under her predecessor. The latter pattern reversed for the 2018 election, when Ontario Liberals ran record numbers of female nominees.

In BC, Clark named more women to her cabinet and ran with more women on her party slate. Redford's term in office saw fewer women ministers and deputy ministers than the previous premier, but more women candidates for the governing party. Accounts of these leaders suggest that some, such as Redford, made no conscious effort to achieve these goals, while others, such as Wynne, stated publicly that they were trying to diversify the composition of their political executives (see Wynne as quoted in Giovannetti 2018).

For divergent reasons, Marois and Notley stand out from other leaders who took office in 2010 and later. Marois led a PQ government with a lower proportion of female ministers than the preceding Liberal regime – which had reached numerical parity. Moreover, women's representation as PQ candidates in the provincial elections when she led the party in 2008 and 2012 was weaker than in earlier contests when the PQ typically eclipsed all Quebec formations on that score (see Table 12.4).

Notley is unusual in that she intervened actively to ensure the NDP ran a parity slate of candidates in 2015. The Alberta premier went on to name a series of parity cabinets after winning power. Like Wynne, Notley seemed open to intersectional arguments about varieties of exclusion and discrimination given that she considered demographic differences along such lines as Indigeneity and sexual orientation. In announcing a cabinet shuffle before the 2018 Ontario election, Wynne said: "It is important to have a diversity, in gender, regional and background diversity, at the cabinet table" (as quoted in Giovannetti 2018).

Clark, Wynne, and Notley were the only premiers who oversaw significant gains in women's public presence on at least two measures. Despite their ideological differences, these leaders headed parties that nominated more female candidates and governments that appointed more women ministers than had earlier ones in their provinces. Wynne came to party politics from a background in social movement activism, while Clark and Notley were born in the mid-1960s and seemed to work well with other women, a variable that distinguished them from Redford – another western premier born in the same period who was reputed to prefer the company of men.

How does party ideology figure in this story? Wynne and Notley's actions are consistent with comparative findings about the openness of centre-left and left parties to women's upward mobility. Clark's record is harder to explain using such arguments since she led a right-wing formation in BC. Moreover, the weaker recruitment records of Marois and early Liberals such as Callbeck and Duncan show that, at the subnational level in Canada, not all women leading centre or centre-left parties took major strides in this area.

Our results on cabinet appointments can be considered in light of comparative research by O'Brien et al. (2015, 690), which finds the presence of female leaders outside the political left tends to weaken women's ministerial representation. In Canada, Clark and Wynne remain important exceptions to this pattern given that they elevated numbers of women on the political executive. Their records are at odds with results from other systems, which show that female leaders of the centre and right tend not to promote other women because they face minimal demands for diversity given their own presence at the pinnacle of power. While some leaders of moderate and conservative parties at the subnational level in Canada held individualist principles that were not conducive to the idea of representing groups in senior positions, we find that this view was not universally held by female elites outside the political left.

Conclusion

This volume stands as the first not only to compare women political executives in Canada with the men who preceded and succeeded them but also to contrast female leaders across jurisdictions. Material presented here enriches multiple academic literatures at the same time as it informs ongoing public debates about the relevance of demographic diversity to executive decision making. More specifically, we set out to learn what difference, if any, nearly a dozen women have made at the highest level of political responsibility in Canada's provinces and territories.

We conclude that, while more women became subnational leaders across Canada as time passed, they faced difficult challenges in empowered, in imperiled, and in pioneer circumstances. Expectations that the presence of female premiers might shift the climate of political debate in a conciliatory direction were not confirmed by the data we collected, nor were propositions to the effect that the presence of female opposition leaders and premiers together would have such an impact. In consensus-based systems in the NWT and Nunavut, Indigenous women faced the danger of being seen as too collaborative or too consultative – even though they worked in environments that placed a strong emphasis on the values of cooperation and empowering local communities.

Did women premiers "act for" other women and, in particular, for equality interests? Consistent with the comparative literature on gender and politics, leaders from left and centrist parties were more likely than those from the political right to carry forward feminist claims. One critical actor identified in this collection, Rachel Notley, was also the only female NDP premier at the time of writing, while another, Kathleen Wynne, led the Ontario Liberals as a social (as opposed to business) Liberal. Pauline Marois made crucial pro-equality contributions as minister of education in an early PQ government.

Yet we also report important deviations from left/right ideological patterns. These include the willingness of Alison Redford as a PC premier in Alberta to strengthen violence against women policies and to expand the machinery of government in the field of women's issues. Christy Clark, as leader of BC's right-of-centre Liberals, took important steps forward in the recruitment of women to senior posts.

We note the extent to which leaders' records with respect to promoting other women as candidates, ministers, and senior bureaucrats seemed to vary by chronological period. Early premiers in Canada's provinces and territories did significantly less on the recruitment front than more recent leaders – notably Christy Clark in BC, Kathleen Wynne in Ontario, and Rachel Notley in Alberta, all of whom raised women's numbers in at least two of the three categories. The fact that Clark led the major party of the right in BC politics reminds us that, as in the case of Redford's policy actions in Alberta, ideological positioning was not a rigid determinant of what premiers accomplished in office.

Like any study that opens new scholarly terrain, our volume risks raising more questions than it answers. One area that merits closer attention in the future is the climate faced by female political executives. In particular, researchers would do well to systematically investigate party, media, and public narratives about leaders, which sometimes seem more impatient, harsh, and threatening for progressive women than for other premiers. Valuable opportunities exist to compare the treatment of federal versus provincial and territorial party leaders in Canada, and to compare Canadian elites with their counterparts in other countries.

As well, analysts might probe the legacy of leaders considered in this account after they were more distant from power. What is the "stickiness," or longevity, of the innovations they introduced in patterns of recruitment and government policy? Under what circumstances did premiers introduce expansive programs such as universal and affordable child care, parallel with the policy adopted by Quebec in 1997? Finally, future scholars will be able to evaluate premiers who were sworn in after the period analyzed in this volume – perhaps as the first woman to head a government in Nova Scotia, New Brunswick, Manitoba, or Saskatchewan.

The following question often confronts scholars in this field: Is it worth electing more women to public office? Given the track records of Canadian premiers, the answer to that question depends on how citizens define what is worthwhile. The symbolic value of seeing women in top leadership positions is important to many people but we do not address it directly. Political justice arguments for basic fairness also matter in a democratic society, and, again, they are beyond the purview of our analysis. In terms of actions in office, contributors to this volume show that not all women leaders seek to promote other women or to implement expansive social programs in fields such as child care. Readers holding similar perspectives can take comfort from the election of premiers who pursue no such goals.

By contrast, Canadians who normatively desire more women decision makers and a more robust set of social policies can read the data presented here as evidence that, for women as for men, left/right ideology generally matters. For citizens who want critical actors in power so they can promote significant, pro-equality changes – the answer is clear. Elect more leaders whose backgrounds and priorities resemble those of Rachel Notley, Kathleen Wynne, or the early Pauline Marois.

Notes

1 Biographical data on *Wikipedia* indicate that Clark (1), Dunderdale (2), Marois (4), Notley (2), Redford (1), and Wynne (3) were all mothers at the point they became premiers, with the number of children reported for each indicated in parentheses.
2 In March 2016, NDI launched an initiative known as #NotTheCost, Stopping Violence Against Women in Politics. See https://www.ndi.org/not-the-cost.

References

Bashevkin, Sylvia. 1998. *Women on the Defensive: Living through Conservative Times.* Toronto: University of Toronto Press.

–. 2009. *Women, Power, Politics: The Hidden Story of Canada's Unfinished Democracy.* Don Mills: Oxford University Press.

Campbell, Kim. 1996. *Time and Chance: The Political Memoirs of Canada's First Woman Prime Minister.* Toronto: Doubleday.

Childs, Sarah, and Mona Lena Krook. 2009. "Analysing Women's Substantive Representation: From Critical Mass to Critical Actors." *Government and Opposition* 44, 2: 125–45.

Dawson, Tyler. 2017. "Threats against Wynne Range from the Bizarre to the Serious, Documents Reveal." *Ottawa Sun*, 21 June. http://ottawasun.com/2017/06/21/threats-against-wynne-range-from-the-bizarre-to-the-serious-documents-reveal/wcm/3d7d50b1-db01-4810-ad48-8065c9ce67e3.

Ebner, David. 2018. "Ontario Takes Aim at Gender Wage Gap with Pay Transparency Bill." *Globe and Mail*, 7 March.

Giovannetti, Justin. 2018. "Wynne Shuffles Cabinet Heading into Election Run." *Globe and Mail*, 18 January.

Giovannetti, Justin, Caroline Alphonso, and Erin Anderssen. 2018. "Ontario Liberals Announce Child-Care Funding." *Globe and Mail*, 28 March.

Krook, Mona Lena, and Fiona Mackay, eds. 2011. *Gender, Politics and Institutions: Towards a Feminist Institutionalism.* Basingstoke: Palgrave Macmillan.

Mercier, Noémi. 2012. "Pauline Marois: L'étoffe d'un premier ministre?" *L'actualité*, 1 September: 29–44.

National Democratic Institute. 2018. #NotTheCost, Stopping Violence Against Women in Politics. https://www.ndi.org/not-the-cost.

O'Brien, Diana Z., Matthew Mendez, Jordan Carr Peterson, and Jihyun Shin. 2015. "Letting Down the Ladder or Shutting the Door: Female Prime Ministers, Party Leaders, and Cabinet Ministers." *Politics and Gender* 11, 4: 689–717.

O'Neill, Brenda, and David Stewart. 2009. "Gender and Political Party Leadership in Canada." *Party Politics* 15, 6 (November): 737–57.

Radwanski, Adam. 2018. "Can Wynne Convince Voters Government-Funded Daycare Is about Something Bigger?" *Globe and Mail*, 28 March.

Thomas, Melanee, and Lisa Lambert. 2017. "Private Mom versus Political Dad? Communications of Parental Status in the 41st Canadian Parliament." In *Mothers and Others: The Role of Parenthood in Politics*, ed. Melanee Thomas and Amanda Bittner, 135–54. Vancouver: UBC Press.

Wood, James. 2017. "Premier Rachel Notley Tied for Second as Canada's Least Popular Premier: Poll." *Calgary Sun*, 21 June. http://www.calgarysun.com/2017/06/21/premier-rachel-notley-tied-for-second-leas-popular-premier-in-canada-poll.

Acknowledgments

Like any volume whose title ends with a question mark, this collection is bound together by a sense of shared curiosity. I had the good fortune to share my fascination about women premiers with all the contributors as well as with talented graduate and undergraduate students at the University of Toronto. Many journalists, members of the general public, and political science colleagues also pressed for closer study of the core themes.

This book confirms a view that under optimal conditions the whole can exceed the sum of its parts. No individual researcher could have met, in a timely and contextually sensitive manner, the challenge that faced the contributors to this project as a group. Each chapter author was integral to the process of creating the study: we shared draft materials, commented on each other's work, and kept each other focused on the unifying themes. I am particularly grateful to Graham White for his assistance with the introduction and the section on the territories.

The study benefited from support from many sources, including the Insight Grants program of the Social Sciences and Humanities Research Council of Canada and the Department of Political Science at the University of Toronto. Graduate students at the University of Toronto – notably Jason VandenBeukel, Emma Gill-Alderson, and Erica Rayment – offered crucial research assistance.

Many scholars in Canada and beyond offered valuable guidance as the manuscript developed. I thank Sarah Childs and her UK colleagues, who participated in a gender and politics workshop held at Birkbeck, University of London in December 2017; Genevieve Johnson, David Laycock, and others, who attended a seminar in the Department of Political Science at Simon Fraser University in February 2018; and Louise Carbert and Mireille Lalancette, who served as discussants at a Canadian Political Science Association panel held at the University of Regina in May 2018.

Melissa Pitts, Randy Schmidt, Holly Keller, and their colleagues at UBC Press moved the project forward with skill and insight. The manuscript assessors secured by UBC Press wrote perceptive, detailed reports that improved each chapter.

I deeply appreciate these many votes of confidence. Each measurably advanced our collective goal of a more informed scholarly as well as public conversation about the consequences of women's arrival in the Office of the Premier.

Contributors

Clark Banack is an adjunct professor of political studies at the University of Alberta's Augustana Campus. He is the author of *God's Province: Evangelical Christianity, Political Thought, and Conservatism in Alberta* (McGill-Queen's University Press, 2016).

Sylvia Bashevkin is a professor of political science at the University of Toronto. Her most recent book is *Women as Foreign Policy Leaders: National Security and Gender Politics in Superpower America* (Oxford University Press, 2018).

Philippe Bernier Arcand is a part-time professor at Saint Paul University. His most recent book is *Le Parti Québécois: d'un nationalisme à l'autre* (Poètes de brousse, 2015).

Amanda Bittner is an associate professor of political science at Memorial University of Newfoundland. Her research focuses on elections and voting, including voter turnout, immigration, and women and politics in Canada and internationally.

Drew Brown is a writer living in St. John's. His work, much of which focuses on Newfoundland and Labrador politics, has appeared in *VICE, Newfoundland Quarterly, The Guardian*, and elsewhere.

Don Desserud is a professor of political science at the University of Prince Edward Island. His most recent publication is "The Senate Residency Requirement and the Constitution: 'He Shall Be Resident in the Province'" (2017).

Maura Forrest is an Ottawa-based political reporter with the *National Post*. She previously reported on territorial politics for the *Yukon News* and has published work in the *Globe and Mail*, the *Tyee*, *Arctic Deeply*, and elsewhere.

Elizabeth Goodyear-Grant is an associate professor of political science at Queen's University. She is the author of *Gendered News: Media Coverage and Electoral Politics in Canada* (UBC Press, 2013).

Sheena Kennedy Dalseg holds a PhD from Carleton University's School of Public Policy and Administration. She is the co-founder of *Northern Public Affairs*, the first public policy magazine for northern Canada.

Tracy Summerville is an associate professor of political science at the University of Northern British Columbia. She is co-editor with J. R. Lacharite of *The Campbell Revolution? Power, Politics, and Policy in British Columbia* (McGill-Queen's University Press, 2017).

Robin Sutherland holds a PhD in English literature. Her interest in contemporary women in politics stems from research on Lady Agnes Macdonald, who wrote about nationhood and nation building in her diary and in published travel and political sketches.

Melanee Thomas is an associate professor of political science at the University of Calgary. Her research examines gender and politics in Canada and other post-industrial democracies, with a particular focus on political attitudes, behaviour, and engagement.

Graham White, a professor emeritus at the University of Toronto, has studied northern politics since the 1980s. His latest book, co-authored with Jack Hicks, is *Made in Nunavut: An Experiment in Decentralized Government* (UBC Press, 2015).

Index

Page numbers with (f) refer to figures; pages with (t) refer to tables.